Homeopathic Practice

Homeopathic Practice

Edited by
Steven B Kayne

PhD, MBA, LLM, MSc, DAgVetPharm, FRPharmS, FCPP, FIPharmM, FFHom, MPS (NZ), FNZCP

Honorary Consultant Pharmacist, Glasgow Homeopathic Hospital, UK

Honorary Lecturer, University of Strathclyde School of Pharmacy, UK

With best wishes

Steven Kayne

London • Chicago **Pharmaceutical Press**

Published by the Pharmaceutical Press
An imprint of RPS Publishing

1 Lambeth High Street, London SE1 7JN, UK
100 South Atkinson Road, Suite 200, Grayslake, IL 60030-7820, USA

© Pharmaceutical Press 2008

(**PP**)is a trade mark of RPS Publishing

RPS Publishing is the publishing organisation of the
Royal Pharmaceutical Society of Great Britain

First published 2008

Typeset by Photoprint, Torquay, Devon
Printed in Great Britain by TJ International, Padstow, Cornwall

ISBN 978 0 85369 726 8

A catalogue record for this book is available from the British Library

For   Calum, Eilidh,
Tara, Alex
and Euan

Contents

Foreword

Homeopathy is one of several historically well-established, whole systems of complementary and alternative medicine that diverge from the orthodoxy of conventional western medical theory and clinical practice. Although proponents and sceptics may wish that the other side would come to their respective senses and embrace the 'right' position on homeopathy, the realities of the situation require a more measured approach. Homeopathy is neither an implausible nor a perfect form of healing. Rather, homeopathy is a richly varied and dynamic field of clinical care that has developed out of a core set of philosophical beliefs about the nature of life, health and disease. Well grounded in theory, homeopathy has grown and evolved through the actual clinical practice of its founder, Samuel Hahnemann, MD, and his successors, including present-day practitioners. In keeping with the tradition of homeopathy, this book reflects the real-world experiences of the people who endeavour daily to help relieve human suffering and cure disease through individualizing care, patient by patient.

One of several expressions of the long-standing disdain that conventional medicine holds for homeopathy is that academic allopaths have positioned themselves as the champions of evidence-based medicine.[1] By evidence, these mainstream providers typically mean the statistical group average outcomes from large studies of a single intervention targeting one manifestation of a specific disease in hundreds to thousands of patients. Critics then attack the extensive body of case evidence of individual, whole-person responses to homeopathic treatment as 'merely' anecdotal.

In reality, the data show that, for a host of reasons, allopathic practitioners in practice find it extremely difficult to apply the group statistical averages to a given individual in real-world practice.[2] Individual differences in the biology of the person with the disease, psychosocial circumstances, current and past health problems, drug–drug interactions and variations in adherence to recommended treatments all necessitate tailoring actual allopathic care, patient by patient. Even cutting-edge mainstream medical scientists in systems biology, a field that recognizes the indivisible and interactive complexity of living systems, are now feverishly working toward the goal of ... individualized medicine.[3, 4]

In short, homeopathy is at the leading edge of pragmatic health-care with its inherent grasp of patient-centred care and emphasis on the individual specifics of the whole case rather than group averages for the outcomes of body parts. The advantage of homeopathy is that the holism and the individualization are naturally woven into its basic theory of practice and exhibit themselves routinely in the unfolding evaluation, diagnosis, treatment process and patient response patterns. The potential contributions of homeopathy to the larger public health reside in its worldwide accessibility, low cost, long-standing safety record and adaptability to the ever-changing complexity of the manifes-tations of disease in living beings.

For homeopathy as a field, recognizing the right questions to ask about itself is paramount. The data that we need may not emerge from trying to answer the allopathically oriented question of sceptics: Does homeopathy work? Instead, homeopaths may need to ask homeopathic-ally oriented questions of their truly patient-centred system of care, i.e. For whom does homeopathy work? Under what conditions does home-opathy work or not work for a given person? What factors can help us improve our practices to help as many individuals as much as possible? and, ultimately, What are the best ways to modify, apply and integrate the elements of clinical practice – the homeopathic remedies, the poten-cies, the prescribing methods, the patient–provider relationship, con-comitant treatments, as well as the patient's personal history and current context – to facilitate healing and the emergence of outcomes greater than the sum of the parts? The chapters of this book offer valuable pearls of wisdom towards many practical and relevant answers.

Iris R. Bell MD MD(H) PhD
Professor of Family and Community Medicine
The University of Arizona College of Medicine
Tucson, AZ, USA

References

1.   Bell I R. All evidence is equal, but some evidence is more equal than others: can logic prevail over emotion in the homeopathy debate? *J Altern Complement Med* 2005; 11: 763–769.

2. Freeman A C, Sweeney K. Why general practitioners do not implement evidence: qualitative study. *BMJ* 2001; 323: 1100–1102.
3. Ahn A C, Tewari M, Poon C S, *et al.* The limits of reductionism in medicine: could systems biology offer an alternative? *PLos Medicine* 2006; 3: e208.
4. Noble D. The future: putting Humpty-Dumpty together again. *Biochem Soc Trans* 2003; 31: 156–158.

Acknowledgement

Supported in part by grants from the National Institutes of Health/ National Center for Complementary and Alternative Medicine (K24 AT000057, R21 AT000388, R21 AT0032).

Conflict of interest statement

Dr Bell serves as a consultant to Standard Homeopathic Company/ Hyland's Inc.

Preface

Putting together a 'dream team' of distinguished authors, such as those colleagues who have contributed to this book, is every editor's aim. It is a rare opportunity and one for which I am truly thankful. It also presents a problem – should I impose a standard style on the contributors, bearing in mind some are writing in a language other than their own, or should I let them express themselves in their own inimitable way? I chose the latter. To do otherwise would have missed the great opportunity of allowing the authors' well-respected characters to emerge. Inevitably with such a project there will be areas of overlapping subject matter but I believe this has been kept to a minimum. The multidisciplinary nature of the contributors reflects the developing team approach to patient care – both human and veterinary. I hope my colleagues who practise homeopathy with impressive success in dental surgery, podiatry and other similar disciplines will forgive their omission. I decided to exclude professions primarily involved with individual areas of the body.

There are many books on homeopathy so how is this one different? The aim was to produce a wide-ranging book that was both a source of inspiration and reflection in the style of modern continuing professional development, as well as a source of reference – a book that could be read rather than studied and that would appeal to knowledgeable amateur homeopaths and patients as well as to healthcare professionals interested in widening their scope of practice. It's mainly a pragmatic book – not evidence-based in the modern scientific meaning applied to these words – more about what happens in practice rather than about why or how it happens. That is not to imply that the paucity of robust scientific evidence for homeopathy can be overlooked; the need for more high-quality research is acute. However, I believe we should be getting on with the job of treating patients while we are waiting.

With this in mind I invited the contributors to adopt a practical patient-oriented perspective whenever possible. That seemed a logical approach in this modern age of patient-focused healthcare delivery. The chapter authors have provided a large number of case studies that vary in structure from the simple to the highly complex and from clinical to non-clinical, demonstrating the wide breadth of involvement in homeopathic practice.

The reader's journey through the book logically falls into three parts. Chapters 1–6 largely cover the basic concepts of homeopathy, Chapters 7–14 describe how homeopathy is practised in a variety of different environments and the final two chapters are personal accounts by physicians working in South Africa and Japan. I could have included a variety of different environments for this section, including India and South America, but I chose just the two countries with which I am more familiar.

My sincere thanks to my good friends around the world, all of whom readily agreed to support this project. It was a privilege working with you all. I owe you all a large dram of my country's finest malt!

Steven Kayne
steven.kayne@nhs.net
September 2007

Acknowledgements

The editor wishes to thank Dr Kim Jobst BA MA MB BS MRCP DM, Editor-in-Chief of the *Journal of Alternative and Complementary Medicine,* and John Saxton MRCVS VetFFHom, President of the UK Faculty of Homeopathy, for their helpful comments on the manuscript.

About the editor

Dr Steven Kayne practised as a community pharmacist in Glasgow for more than 30 years before retiring in 1999. He is currently Honorary Consultant Pharmacist at Glasgow Homeopathic Hospital and Honorary Lecturer in complementary and alternative medicine (CAM) at the University of Strathclyde. Steven currently serves on three UK Government Expert Advisory Bodies – the Advisory Board on the Registration of Homeopathic Products, the Herbal Medicines Advisory Committee and the Veterinary Products Committee.

Steven was involved in setting up the first homeopathic training courses for the UK Faculty of Homeopathy in the 1980s. He served as the first Faculty Pharmacy Dean from 1999 to 2003 and was a member of the Faculty and British Homeopathic Association Councils for many years, as well as chairing the European Committee on Homeopathy Pharmacy sub-committee. He was the first pharmacist to be awarded a fellowship of the Faculty of Homeopathy and was Pharmacy Dean of the Faculty 1999–2003.

He has contributed numerous papers and articles to journals and has presented as an invited speaker on a variety of topics associated with CAM in many countries worldwide. Steven has written, edited and contributed chapters to 12 books. He is the editor of *Simile*, the newsletter of the UK Faculty of Homeopathy, and a member of the editorial advisory boards of several peer-reviewed journals.

Contributors

John P Borneman, PhD, BS, MS, MBA

Dr John P Borneman is the chairman and chief executive officer of Standard Homeopathic Company and Hyland's Inc. He holds master's degrees in chemistry in business from St Joseph's University, Philadelphia, and a doctorate in health policy from University of Sciences in Philadelphia with a research interest in patient perceptions and patterns of use of complementary and alternative medicine (CAM). J P Borneman serves as emeritus director of the National Center for Homeopathy, director of the Consumer Healthcare Products Association (CHPA), as well as a director, editor and chairman of the Council on Pharmacy for the Homeopathic Pharmacopoeia of the United States. He is also chairman of the regulatory affairs committee for the American Association of Homeopathic Pharmacists, the industry trade association, and serves on the advisory board of the St Joseph's University College of Arts and Sciences and as an advisor to the board of the National Association of Chain Drug Stores.

Edzard Ernst, MD, PhD, FRCP, FRCPEd

Professor Ernst qualified as a physician in Germany where he also completed his MD and PhD theses. He was Professor in Physical Medicine and Rehabilitation (PMR) at Hanover Medical School and Head of the PMR Department at the University of Vienna. He came to the University of Exeter in 1993 to establish the first Chair in Complementary Medicine. He is founder/Editor-in-Chief of two medical journals (*Focus on Alternative and Complementary Therapies* (FACT) and *Perfusion*). His work has been awarded with 13 scientific prizes/awards and two visiting professorships. He served on the Medicines Commission of the British Medicines and Healthcare Products Regulatory Agency (1994–2005) and on the Scientific Committee on Herbal Medicinal Products of the Irish Medicines Board. In 1999 he took British nationality. Professor Ernst's publications include more than 1000 papers in the peer-reviewed literature, 39 books (translated into five languages) and dozens of chapters. He has given about 500 invited international lectures and has supervised 50 MD and PhD theses.

Peter Gregory, BVSc, Cert IAVH, VetFFHom, MRCVS

Peter Gregory qualified at Bristol in 1972 and worked in mixed practice in his native Sheffield for 5 years before emigrating to Australia where he became a partner in a mixed practice on the tropical coast of North Queensland. In 1984 he returned to the UK and discovered homeopathy. He qualified as a Veterinary Member of the Faculty of Homeopathy in 1991 and was awarded Veterinary Fellowship in 2004. In 1995 he set up a referral practice for alternative therapies on the edge of the Staffordshire Peak District and now works in the Holistic Veterinary Medicine Centre in Sussex.

He is managing partner of the Homeopathic Professionals Teaching Group (HPTG), based in Oxford, and has been responsible for developing the HPTG international courses in Australia, Ireland and South Africa. He lectures to veterinary surgeons and doctors in several countries and is a certified tutor with the International Association for Veterinary Homeopathy. He is ex-President of the British Association of Homeopathic Veterinary Surgeons.

Peter is co-author of *Textbook of Veterinary Homeopathy* and has contributed to other publications, including a chapter in *Passionate Medicine*, edited by Robin Shohet.

Elaine Hamilton, RGN, BSc, MFHom(nurse)

Elaine Hamilton was the first Nursing Dean of the UK Faculty of Homeopathy. She trained as a Registered General Nurse at North Lothian College of Nursing and Midwifery, Edinburgh, and then specialised in neurosurgical nursing, completing her Certified Clinical Nurse Specialist (CCNS) neuromedical/neurosurgical certificate in 1980. Elaine was employed as a practice nurse within primary care from 1990 until 2000. She obtained a Royal College of General Practitioners diploma in asthma in 1992.

Becoming increasingly interested in homeopathy, she then studied at Napier University, achieving BSc(Hons) Homeopathy and MFHom (nurse) and obtaining an extended/supplementary nurse prescribing certificate in 2002. Elaine is currently employed at Glasgow Homeopathic Hospital 2 days per week and is accountable for the homeopathic assessment, management and follow-up of patients in the first nurse-led NHS Homeopathic Clinic. She is involved in managing an organic beef farm in south-west Scotland where homeopathy is successfully integrated in the management of cattle for various acute and chronic illnesses.

Lee Kayne, PhD, MRPharmS, MFHom(Pharm)

Dr Lee Kayne graduated in pharmacy from the University of Aston, Birmingham, in 1993. Following pre-registration training at the Royal London Hospital and in industry, he undertook a PhD at the University of Nottingham and a postdoctoral fellowship at Harvard Medical School in the field of molecular biology. Returning to his native Glasgow in 1998, Lee now practises as a community pharmacist and has a special interest in complementary medicine. He was joint author of a book entitled *Homeopathic Prescribing Pocket Companion* and has contributed chapters and articles to many other publications.

Lee teaches at all levels of pharmacy and is involved in a number of projects with the University of Strathclyde, Glasgow, the Faculty of Homeopathy (as Pharmacy Dean) and the European Committee for Homeopathy (as Pharmacy Education Co-ordinator). In 2004, Lee became the first pharmacist to be awarded the qualification of MFHom(Pharm) by the UK Faculty of Homeopathy.

Bob Leckridge, BSc, MB, Ch, B, FFHom

Dr Bob Leckridge is a graduate of the University of Edinburgh and worked as a general practitioner in Ayrshire and Edinburgh until moving to his current position as Specialist in Homeopathic Medicine at Glasgow Homeopathic Hospital in 1995. He has developed postgraduate courses in homeopathy for healthcare professionals in Glasgow, Edinburgh (Napier University), Lisbon, Moscow and Tokyo and regularly teaches both in the UK and abroad. He also designed and delivers a very popular special study module in homeopathy for Glasgow University Medical School. He is the author of *Homeopathy in Primary Care* and is currently the Immediate Past President of the Faculty of Homeopathy.

Felicity Lee, MSc, MRPharmS, FSHom

Felicity Lee graduated in Pharmacy from Manchester University and has worked in hospital pharmacies in England, Wales, Canada and Australia. She moved to Cardiff for a year in 1973 to study for a masters degree in Applied Pharmacology and is still there, finding the lively Welsh capital city and its surrounding hills and mountains much to her liking.

Having established and run the Welsh Drug Information Service at the University Hospital of Wales for 9 years, she developed an interest in the philosophy behind complementary medicine. Eventually, she decided to retrain as a professional homeopath, first at the School of Homeopathy in Devon and later at the School for Advanced Homeopathic Studies in Malvern.

Felicity has been in full-time practice as a homeopath since 1985, and has also lectured at schools of homeopathy and to pharmacists, general practitioners and midwives. She has been chair of the Society of Homeopaths twice and has also been awarded the title of Fellow. She has been a member of the Medicines and Healthcare products Regulatory Agency (MHRA) Advisory Board on the Registration of Homeopathic Remedies since 1994.

David Lilley, MB, ChB, FFHom, LLCO

Dr David John Lilley FFHom was born in Leeds in 1940, the son of a homeopath. His family emigrated to South Africa in 1949. He studied medicine at the University of Pretoria and after qualifying spent 3 years at the Royal London Homeopathic Hospital and the London College of Osteopathy. He studied under Doctors Blackie, Twentyman, Raeside, Kennedy and Foubister.

After obtaining his MFHom David returned to South Africa and joined his father in a practice in 1966. He has been in an exclusively homeopathic and osteopathic practice for the past 40 years. In 1994 he commenced homeopathic courses for medical doctors in Johannesburg and Cape Town. The courses are accredited with the UK Faculty and the Allied Health Professions Council of South Africa. He presents regular postgraduate homeopathic seminars in London and Glasgow on behalf of the UK Faculty of Homeopathy. He is the present Dean of the South African Faculty.

David also presents lectures to the public, the purpose of which is to impart to the audience knowledge of homeopathy, which will permit them to play an informed and participatory role in the treatment of their families and themselves. Dr Lilley offers a way of looking at life and healing in a truly holistic manner.

Cleve McIntosh, MB, ChB, DMH, MCFP, DFHom, MFHom

Dr Cleve McIntosh grew up in Pretoria, South Africa, and initially studied theology for a year before qualifying as a medical doctor at the University of Cape Town. He worked in different parts of South Africa, eventually moving to a rural part of Limpopo Province to train clinical nurse practitioners serving in areas where there are too few doctors to provide primary care services. While training nurse practitioners, Cleve worked in the busy psychiatric ward at the local hospital.

This interest in psychiatry took him to Scotland, where he worked in psychiatry in Glasgow and Edinburgh, and on returning to South Africa he obtained a Diploma in Mental Health. He then began working full-time as a clinic doctor visiting isolated rural clinics and during this time he specialised in family medicine and obtained an MCFP(SA) as a family physician. Feeling frustrated at not being able to treat so many problems using only conventional medication, he started studying homeopathy. While studying toward a MFHom(UK), Cleve started integrating more and more homeopathy into his work as a clinic doctor.

Ton Nicolai, MD, FFHom(Hon)

Dr Ton Nicolai was born in 1947 and graduated in medicine at Leiden University in 1972.

He worked as a general practitioner in Rotterdam for 11 years. Confronted with the failure of conventional medicine to cure patients, he went searching for other therapeutic options, such as acupuncture, homeopathy, chiropractic, naturopathy and psychic healing. Eventually he chose homeopathy: he started a private practice in 1983 and has worked as a homeopathic doctor ever since. He has taken many seminars and training courses both at home and abroad in homeopathy as well as in personal development, awareness and mind–body health.

He was on the Board of the Netherlands Homeopathic Medical Association (VHAN) and the International Homeopathic Medical League (LMHI). He was one of the founders of the European Committee for Homeopathy (ECH) and has been one of its executives since its inception. Since 2000 he has been President of the ECH.

He is the author of several ECH publications on homeopathy, its professional practice and its position in European healthcare.

Dr Ryoichi Obitsu, MD, PhD, LFHom

Dr Ryoichi Obitsu graduated in medicine from the University of Tokyo. After working at the Third Department of Surgery in the University of Tokyo Hospital, he established the Obitsu Sankei Hospital and was its director from 1982 to 2000. During his 19 years of medical practice using holistic approaches, he has used homeopathic medicine for many cancer patients too. Ryouchi is President of the Japanese Physicians Society for Homeopathy (JPSH), Director of the Japanese Association for Alternative, Complementary and Traditional Medicine, Director of the Japanese Society for Integrative Medicine and Executive Director of the Obistu Sankei Hospital.

His many books include the titles *Medicine and Empathy in Life, Awareness of Self-Healing*, and *When a Close Relative has Cancer*.

David Reilly, FRCP, MRCGP, FFHom

Dr David Reilly is Consultant Physician at the Centre for Integrative Care, Glasgow Homoeopathic Hospital; Honorary Senior Lecturer at Glasgow University; Visiting Professor of Medicine in Maryland and faculty member at Harvard Medical School. Trained in orthodox medicine (as a physician and a general practitioner), complementary medicine (mainly homeopathy and acupuncture) and mind–body medicine, he looked for fresh ways of approaching medicine and human caring – emphasising the innate healing capacity in people, the factors that modify this, and their interaction with therapeutic process, especially in the therapeutic encounter. His ideas were recently used as core elements in the fifth Wave document on future public health development (www.scottish councilfoundation.org). Active in science, teaching and media, a musician and poet, he explores the synthesis of art and science (which he nicknamed 'artience') with compassion ('heartience'). He was Scotland's Dynamic Place Award Person of the Year in 2004 for achieving a new standard in healing environment created at Glasgow Homoeopathic Hospital (www.ghh.info).

David Riley, MD

Dr David Riley was born 30 July 1952 in Dallas, Texas. Dr Riley attended Georgetown University Medical School and graduated from the University of Utah Medical School in 1983. He has practised homeopathy half-time since 1989, exclusively classical, occasionally homotoxicology. As for other therapies, Dr Riley uses therapeutic yoga and herbal medicine.

Dr Riley teaches in the USA and Europe. He is the co-founder of the Integrative Medicine Institute and Southwest Health Options, an independent practice association (IPA) managing the delivery of complementary and alternative medicine for insured patients in Santa Fe, New Mexico. He is the medical editor of the journal *Alternative Therapies in Health and Medicine*.

David Spence, MB, BS, FFHom, MRCS, LRCP, DRCOG

Dr David Spence has worked full-time for the National Health Service (NHS) for 37 years since qualifying as a doctor from King's College, London and St George's Hospital Medical School, London.

David retired in 2006 from his post as Consultant Physician and Clinical Director of the Department of Homeopathic Medicine, part of the Division of Specialised Services at the United Bristol Healthcare NHS Trust – the major university teaching hospital in south-west England.

He is Director of the William Kadleigh Academic Department of Homeopathic Medicine in Bristol, running modular postgraduate courses for doctors, vets, dentists, pharmacists and nurses as well as providing undergraduate teaching modules for the University of Bristol Medical School.

David is Chairman of the British Homeopathic Association, the leading UK charity supporting research and education in homeopathic medicine and is also Vice-President of the European Committee for Homeopathy in Brussels. He is a Past President of the Faculty of Homeopathy.

Kathleen Tomlinson, RGN, RM, MFHom(nurse)

Kathleen Tomlinson qualified as a registered general nurse in 1987 having studied at Argyle and Clyde College of Nursing and Midwifery. She became a registered midwife in 1990 from Glasgow Western College of Midwifery and has worked at a consultant-led unit, the Southern General Hospital in Glasgow, ever since. At present, Kathleen is a team midwife working both in the labour ward and community, which covers a huge variety of clinical situations, e.g. antenatal clinics, classes, home births, postnatal home visits and support groups. She was integral in setting up antenatal classes for Asian women in the community and is a breast-feeding mentor to her colleagues, offering advice and support in more difficult cases. In October 2006, Kathleen became the first practising midwife to be admitted to membership of the Faculty of Homeopathy.

1

Homeopathy – an overview

Steven Kayne

Introduction

This chapter describes the reasons why people choose homeopathy to treat their ills. It also discusses the questions that they commonly ask their healthcare advisors to enable an informed decision to be made and in so doing provides readers with a general introduction to homeopathy. The basic principles outlined here are covered in greater detail and with different emphasis throughout the rest of the book.

Definition

Homeopathy is a holistic complementary and alternative therapy based on the concept of 'like to treat like'. It involves the administration of dilute and ultradilute medicines prepared according to methods specified in various homeopathic pharmacopoeias.

History

The founder of modern homeopathy, the German physician and apothecary Christian Friedrich Samuel Hahnemann, left a powerful legacy to successive generations and a history of the development of the discipline is included in almost every introduction to homeopathy. A brief outline follows; a more comprehensive account may be found in other texts.

Samuel Hahnemann was born just before midnight on 10 April 1755 in Meissen, Germany, an ancient town situated on the banks of the river Elbe 160 km (100 miles) south of Berlin and renowned for its porcelain factory where his father worked. He qualified as a physician at the Frederick Alexander University in Erlangen in 1779. In 1790 Hahnemann, an accomplished linguist, translated and annotated a materia medica written by the eminent Scottish physician William Cullen (1710–1790). Hahnemann disagreed with Cullen's suggestion in one of his publications that the mechanism of action of Cinchona bark in the treatment of marsh fever (malaria) was due to its astringent properties. As he knew of the existence of several astringents more powerful than Cinchona that were not effective in marsh fever, he decided to test the drug by taking relatively large doses himself. He found that the resulting toxic effects were very similar to the symptoms experienced by patients suffering from the disease. Hahnemann then tried a number of other active substances on himself, his family and volunteers to obtain evidence to substantiate his findings. In each case he found that the

Figure 1.1 Photograph of Samuel Hahnemann taken in 1841 (courtesy of Faculty of Homeopathy).

medicines could bring on the symptoms of the diseases for which they were being used as a treatment. Thus he systematically built up considerable circumstantial evidence for the existence of a law of cure based on the concept of 'like to treat like'. He called the systematic procedure of testing substances on healthy human beings in order to elucidate the symptoms reflecting the use of the medicine a 'proving' (see Chapter 4).

In 1810 Hahnemann published his most famous work, the *Organon of the Rational Art of Healing*[1] (commonly simply referred to as the '*Organon*'). A total of five editions appeared during Hahnemann's lifetime; the manuscipt for a sixth edition was not published for many years after his death. The subject matter in the sixth edition was set out in 291 numbered sections or aphorisms, usually denoted in the literature by the symbol § and the relevant section number.

Figure 1.1 shows a photograph of Hahnemann 2 years before his death, taken on 30 September 1841 by H Foucault of Paris. The photograph was originally the property of the Reverend T Everest, who recorded:

> It was a dark rainy day, with violent gusts of wind, all which circumstances by increasing the difficulty of taking the photograph, have given the countenance of Hahnemann an air of stiffness. Hahnemann was, moreover, rather unwell that day.

The principles of homeopathy

The main principles involved in the practice of homeopathy are presented briefly below. The theory underpinning these principles and its application to practice are discussed in depth in Chapter 3.

Like cures like

This principle first appeared in an article entitled 'Essay on a new principle for ascertaining the curative power of drugs'.[2] Hahnemann believed that in order to cure disease, one must seek medicines that can excite similar symptoms in the healthy human body. This idea is summarised in the phrase *similia similibus curentur*, often translated as 'let like be treated with like'. It was this method of prescribing according to the matching of symptoms and drug pictures that prompted Hahnemann in 1807 to coin the term 'homeopathy' from the Greek words *homoios* (similar) and *pathos* (disease or suffering). He termed the more orthodox treatment by the law of contraries 'allopathy' from *alloios*, meaning contrary. This principle is discussed in greater detail in Chapters 3 and 5.

Minimal dose

When Hahnemann carried out his original work he gave substantial doses of medicine to his patients, in keeping with contemporary practice. This often resulted in substantial toxic reactions; fatalities were not uncommon. He experimented to try and dilute out the unwanted toxicity while at the same time maintaining a therapeutic effect. There is much speculation as to how Hahnemann developed the method of serial diluting and agitating his remedies, which achieved his aim better than he could have hoped. To his surprise Hahnemann found that, as the remedies became more dilute, they became more potent therapeutically. To reflect this effect he called his new process 'potentisation'. The potentisation process is described in detail below. Hormesis is the term used to describe generally favourable biological responses to low exposures of toxins and other stressors. A pollutant or toxin showing hormesis thus has the opposite effect in small doses than in large doses.

Single medicine

Hahnemann initially believed that one should use a single remedy to treat a condition. Provings in all materia medicas relate to single remedies and there is no way of knowing whether or how individual remedy drug pictures are modified by combination with other ingredients. Classical homeopaths observe this rule carefully (see Chapter 3). In later life Hahnemann did use mixtures of two or three remedies. Modern day examples include Arsen iod, Gelsemium and Eupatorium (AGE, for colds and flu) and Aconite (or sometimes Arsen alb), Belladonna and Chamomilla (ABC, for teething).

Holistic approach

In addition to the three principles stated above, Hahnemann believed that homeopathy should be practised according to the holistic principles that are common to all complementary disciplines. Each patient should be treated as a complete individual. This means that remedies (or procedures) appropriate for one patient might be totally inappropriate for another even though the symptoms may be similar. Conversely, the same remedy may be used to treat very different conditions in different patients. It has been suggested that the term 'holism' has been eclipsed of late by the term 'integrative medicine'.[3] However the two terms are entirely different. Integration is used to describe the combined use of therapies whereas holism refers to the manner in which medicine is practised.

The demand for homeopathy

There are few people who are totally ambivalent about homeopathy.

- Some people have an almost religious belief in its perceived beneficial properties, believing it can heal in all circumstances regardless of cause or severity.
- Some believe that homeopathy is totally out of keeping with modern evidence-based medicine (EBM) and oppose its use in any circumstances.
- A third group believes that homeopathy may have a part to play but is uncertain exactly where it fits in.
- A fourth group is happy to consider homeopathy if its use offers the prospect of an effective solution to their health problems without worrying about whether it can be scientifically justified.

The reasons for the demand for homeopathy

Amongst those people who choose to use homeopathy a number of reasons for their decision may be identified.

The demand for homeopathy reflects that for complementary and alternative medicine (CAM) in general and is thought to be a search for a broader range of therapies, as well as a call for a different approach to care, with less emphasis on drugs, and a more whole-person approach.[4] Many people look to homeopathy and other CAM therapies when orthodoxy has failed. But homeopathy is also used as a first-line intervention for some, because of the worry about the side-effects of conventional treatments and a perception that orthodoxy has become dehumanised.

Vincent and Furnham[5] divided the reasons why people choose homeopathy into 'push' and 'pull' factors. *Push factors* relate to the perceived dangers of using conventional medicines, such as intrinsic toxicity associated with adverse drug reactions and poor invasive techniques which encourage patients to seek safer alternatives. *Pull factors* are those that encourage people to use complementary treatments (usually for particular complaints) while at the same time continuing to use orthodox treatments for other complaints.

Push factors

Perceptions of drug risks

Perceptions of drug risks have been found likely to influence patients' treatment choices.[6] The attitudes and perceptions of a representative sample of Swedish adults with respect to a number of common risks were studied by Slovic *et al.*[7] Respondents characterised themselves as persons who disliked taking risks and who resisted taking medicines unless forced to do so. Evidence for safety and efficacy appeared to make people much more tolerant of any risks. Prescription drugs (except for sleeping pills and antidepressants) were perceived to be high in benefit and low in risk. Homeopathic remedies were not included in the study, but the results for herbal medicines showed an extremely low perceived risk, only slightly higher than vitamin pills, and a perceived benefit approximately equal to vitamin pills, contraceptives and aspirin. Herbalism, homeopathy and the other related therapies that collectively make up complementary medicine are considered by many people to be attractive because they have acceptable risk–benefit ratios.

Disenchantment with orthodox medicine

Orthodox general practice and homeopathic consultations are traditionally organised around the key task of treating patients' health-related problems. Despite their different theories of healing, interactions between practitioners and patients in both environments share many features, though there are also clear differences in the ways in which the process of problem-solving proceeds.[8] For example, with homeopathy a diagnosis is not necessarily required as a prelude to a prescription. The intervention is based on symptomatology and the individual's characteristics and though the consultation takes longer it involves a higher degree of patient interaction and may therefore be perceived as more sympathetic. Lindfors and Raevaara[9] explored the variety of practices used by orthodox and homeopathic practitioners whilst discussing patients' eating and drinking habits in general practice and in homeopathic consultations. In these two fields of medicine the discussions on the patients' lifestyle have a different role in the healing process: in general practice, drinking is considered a possible health risk, but in homeopathy, information concerning patients' eating and drinking habits is needed for defining the patients' idiosyncratic characteristics. This difference is indicated in the ways in which questions about patients' lifestyles are posed and the ways in which patients design their responses. This in turn affects the nature of the ensuing discussion. Patients are less likely to feel threatened by the homeopathic approach.

It has been suggested that people who choose homeopathy and other complementary therapies may do so from disenchantment with, and bad experiences of, orthodox medical practitioners, rather than believing that traditional medicine is itself ineffective.[10] It is known that several factors affect the length and quality of a consultation in orthodox medicine, including the socioeconomic status of the patient, the gender of the practitioner and the gender of the patient.[11–13]

Bakx[14] has summarised some of the possible reasons for the development of widespread discontent with orthodox medicine amongst users of CAM.

- Orthodox medicine has culturally distanced itself from the consumers of its services.
- Orthodox medicine has failed to match its promises with real breakthroughs in combating disease created by modern lifestyles.
- Orthodox medicine has alienated patients through unsympathetic or ineffectual practitioner–patient interaction.

With the advent of healthcare consumerism and increasing pressure on the national healthcare budget the public are now encouraged to be more responsible for their own health. And that does not apply to self-treating trivial ailments alone. It means having a 'responsible' lifestyle too.

Balint[15] has reported a series of investigations based on the analysis of doctor–patient consultations to answer the question: why does it happen so often, that, in spite of earnest efforts on both sides, the relationship between patient and doctor is unsatisfactory and even unhappy? Balint pointed out that these situations can be truly unfortunate; the patient is desperately in need of help, and the doctor tries his or her hardest, but still, despite sincere efforts on both sides, things go wrong. One conclusion reached by the researchers was that the doctor should arrive at a diagnosis not on the basis of physical signs and symptoms alone, but also from a consideration of the so-called neurotic symptoms (see Chapter 3). It is likely that many doctors' beliefs, personality and behavioural standards affect the way in which patients are treated. This means that the management of a patient's disease may vary widely according to the practitioner consulted. Time is an important factor. In one large English survey 12% of patients complained about having insufficient time with their general practitioner (GP), but this figure rose to 30% when patients were seen for 5 minutes or less.[16]

Furnham *et al.*[17] asked three groups of CAM patients and an orthodox medicine group to compare the consultation styles of GPs and CAM practitioners. CAM practitioners were generally perceived as having more time to listen. Ernst *et al.*[18] tested the hypothesis that patients judge the manner of non-medically trained complementary practitioners more favourably than that of their GPs. Their data implied that the patient–therapist encounter is perceived to be more satisfying with CAM practitioners than it is with GPs. The authors suggest that the satisfaction with the consultation may go a long way towards explaining the current popularity with CAM.

There has been a threefold increase in the proportion of children among patients visiting homeopaths in Norway from 1985 to 1998.[19] In a qualitative study, parents who had taken their child to a homeopath for the first time during the last 3 months were interviewed in depth using a semistructured interview guide. It was concluded that parents took their child to a homeopath following unsatisfactory experiences with a medical encounter, due to recommendations from others or due to their own personal experience. Researchers from the University of Aberdeen, Scotland, analysed official prescribing data from 2003 to 2004, covering 1.9 million patients from 323 practices. Forty-nine per cent of practices prescribed a total of 193 different homeopathic remedies.[20] The researchers found particularly high levels of homeopathic prescribing to babies and children under 16.

Reduced efficacy of existing medication

Patients are thought to have turned to homeopathy as a result of dissatisfaction with the efficacy of allopathic medicine.[21] This has, rather unkindly, been called the 'Have you got something else (HYGSE)' syndrome to which the appropriate answer might be YIHGSE – 'Yes, I have got something else'.

Pull factors

Time to consider more than just symptoms

It has been suggested that homeopathy appeals to patients who like the feeling that attention is being paid to more aspects of themselves than just the symptoms.[22] Patients appreciate a sensitive recognition of themselves as unwell people, with feelings and emotions considered too, rather than accept treatment for a disease in isolation. An interesting Italian study[23] found that, in a population of 1223 individuals with a physical health status comparable to the reference national population, patients were seeking homeopathy to satisfy a desire for a treatment that was better suited to their emotional status.

In a survey of 161 CAM practitioners carried out by White *et al.*[24] it was found that the mean time spent with patients for a first consultation was 75 minutes (acupuncture), 90 minutes (homeopathy) and 40 minutes (chiropractic). Subsequent consultations were between a third and half shorter. There is substantial interpractice variation in consultation length of allopathic GPs in the UK, from a mean of 5.7 minutes to one of 8.5 minutes.[25] In some practices the longest average GP consultation time is about twice that of the shortest. However correlational analysis of patients from nine GP practices was used to test the hypothesis that patients' perceptions of consultation length are influenced not just by actual consultation length, but by other aspects of their experience of consultations.[26] Patient concerns about time may be as much about quality time as about actual time.

Cultural reasons

The mobility across national borders of people whose cultural backgrounds emphasise the use of holistic forms of medicine is another reason for increased demand for homeopathic medicines. Thus, migrants from the Indian subcontinent and from China bring their customs with them when they migrate. Either from an inherent mistrust of western medicine or from a misunderstanding of what it can achieve, such people prefer to continue using traditional methods that have proved successful over many centuries. Chao *et al.*[27] carried out in four languages a telephone survey of 3172 women aged over 18 years and older in the USA. Responders were asked about their use of medicines or other CAM treatments not typically prescribed by a medical doctor. Non-Hispanic white women were most likely to cite personal beliefs for CAM use. The authors concluded that racial/ethnic differences in reasons for CAM use highlighted cultural and social factors that are important to consider in public evaluation of the risks and benefits of CAM remedies and treatments.

Royal support

The UK royal family have always been keen proponents of homeopathy. In particular, the Prince of Wales' patronage of homeopathy is well documented and it is thought that this has encouraged many people to try the remedies. The Queen Mother was patron of the British Homeopathic Association for many years prior to her death in 2002. Other high-profile celebrities have also lent their support to homeopathy.

The green association

Complementary and alternative medicine is often portrayed as being 'natural' by the media appealing to the 'green' lobby. This has had the effect of making more people aware of the potential advantages of homeopathy and of stimulating demand.

Financial reasons

In the UK most homeopathic remedies retail at about half the cost of an average over-the-counter (OTC) sale, making them an attractive buy for customers.

There is also some advantage to the patient of having prescribed homeopathic remedies under the NHS, because in nearly all cases the cost of the remedy will be less than the UK prescription tax and pharmacists will generally invite patients who are subject to it to buy the remedies OTC at the lower retail price.

Encouragement by the media

There is no doubt that patients are being encouraged to question the suitability of existing treatments. For example, the celebrated English Rabbi Julia Neuberger has suggested that patients should ask their family doctor a series of questions, including the following[28]:

- What is the likely outcome if I do not have the treatment you are offering?
- What alternative treatments are available?
- What are the most common side-effects?
- Would you use this treatment?

Newspapers have been encouraging patients for many years to ask questions about their treatment and so make doctors accountable.[29] Viewing healthcare delivery as a customer-oriented service is an important development for patients and practitioners alike and helps to instil confidence in the consultation process.[30]

The profile of homeopathic consumers

A British study showed that it is generally the higher socioeconomic groups that buy OTC homeopathic medicines.[31] With frequently higher discretionary incomes these groups may also be less price-sensitive than other groups. This may mean that retailers can use more flexible pricing policies. It may also suggest that buyers of OTC homeopathic medicines are intelligent enough to become well informed about their purchases and be in a position to make a sensible assessment of the products. However, there is some evidence to suggest that the use of homeopathy and other CAM disciplines may now be wider than was found in this survey and is less confined to a well-circumscribed socioeconomic group.[32] A Norwegian study[33] found considerable differences in the homeopathic consumer profile over a 13-year period between 1985 and 1998. One in four of patients visiting homeopaths in 1998 were children between 0 and 9 years of age, compared to one in 10 in 1985. Almost half of the patients in 1998 had used prescription drugs provided by a medical doctor the previous month for the same complaints they presented to the homeopath. In 1998 patients sought homeopathy most often because of respiratory and skin complaints. In 1985 the most common reasons were musculoskeletal and digestive problems. The authors concluded that patients visiting homeopaths in 1998 differed in age and in diseases treated compared to previous users of homeopathy and general practice patients.

In the British study referred to above,[31] there was a predominance of polychrest homeopathic medicines (see Chapter 10) bought by respondents. This is understandable, as they are the type of remedy that is best suited to the OTC environment. With polychrests buyers can readily equate remedies with ailments and so buy the medicine most likely to be effective for their particular condition. Retailers also benefit by not having to offer what can be lengthy and complex advice to buyers. Point-of-sale materials such as charts and leaflets available in some outlets largely obviate the need for advice from staff, which can be very costly in terms of time. They may also reduce the need for extensive training for staff in homeopathy. However, the very large number of homeopathic medicines available and the complexity of matching remedies and ailments may still be confusing to some patients who will seek advice from the staff, particularly when there are several remedies for the same ailment. Some patients also like the comfort of a confirmatory word from a pharmacist or other member of staff when buying untried medicines.

Most of the buyers of homeopathic medicines in this study had bought them before, though they were not asked how many times or for how long they had been buying them. The authors suspected that many respondents had bought them for many years and that any advertising that does take place is not very effective in bringing new buyers into the market and generating sales.

Concern was expressed at the excessive length of time for which some respondents had taken their remedies, ranging from a few days to several years. Most homeopathic remedies offered for sale OTC are designed for short-term administration. Long-term chronic conditions are best treated under the guidance of a practitioner. Although taking homeopathic medicines for long periods should not do any harm, since the medicines are not in themselves harmful, patients may suffer because they may not be receiving appropriate treatment for their condition. On the other hand, there are many skilled and knowledgeable people who may be self-treating effectively over longer periods of time, so no firm conclusions can be drawn. Another factor that allows patients to continue to use the medicines longer than advised is the number of tablets in a typical container – 125. Taken at a rate of three per day, a single container will last well over a month, which could be too long for an acute condition.

For information on consumers and the demand for homeopathy in the US market, see Chapter 11.

Frequently asked questions

Experience in homeopathic practice reveals that the most frequently asked questions by patients are (Kayne SB, personal observations 1971–2006):

- Does it work?
- Is it safe?
- What can I treat?
- How does it work?
- Is it worth the money?

Practitioners ask similar questions but typically in a different order. In this instance the patients' view will prevail and the questions will be answered in their order.

Does homeopathy work?

Sources of evidence

A comprehensive review of homeopathic research will not be included in this chapter. The lead time in producing a book such as this means a review of current research is soon outdated. Libraries at Glasgow Homeopathic Hospital, the Royal London Homoeopathic Hospital and the Faculty of Homeopathy will be able to assist as well as online sources such as PubMed and Medline. The research section on the Faculty of Homeopathy website (www.trusthomeopathy.org/case/res_toc.html) is regularly updated by Dr Robert Mathie, the Faculty's Research Officer, and has references to reviews by Bell,[41] Jonas et al.,[35] and the University of York.[36] Dr Mathie has also published an excellent and balanced review himself.[37] The European Network of Homeopathic Research produced an overview of positive homeopathy research and surveys in 2005 (http://jhofaecker.de/html/enhr.html). A research review by Walach et al.[38] provides information on research in 2005. The reader is also referred to specialist texts and journals on this subject for such information.[39, 40] Lewith et al.[41] discussed the status and evidence base for homeopathy and a number of other complementary and alternative disciplines as well as the regulatory framework within which these therapies were provided. Although events have moved on since its publication, particularly with reference to the regulatory framework, the paper gives a good account of the circumstances prevailing in 2003. The Society of Homeopaths is also engaged in research (see Chapter 13). The US National Center for Homeopathy has a useful website with information at http://www.homeopathic.org/research.htm.

Availability of research funds

The availability of funds for research is relatively limited. Organisations such as the British Homeopathic Association and the Scottish Homeopathic Research and Education Trust (SHRET) have generously supported workers over many years but the sums available are modest. The relatively small value of the market means that manufacturers have little to invest in research outwith their own commercial requirements. In June 2006 the European parliament adopted an amendment to ensure the inclusion of CAM research in the Seventh Framework Programme for Research and Development. This represented a highly significant breakthrough and opportunity for extending research opportunities. In the USA research funding is available from the National Center for Complementary and Alternative Medicine (http://nccam.nih.gov/).

Quality of evidence

Assessing clinical effectiveness typically requires the application of evidence based medicine (EBM). This may be defined as being the conscientious, explicit and judicious use of current best evidence in making decisions about the care of individual patients. The practice of EBM means integrating individual clinical expertise with the best available clinical evidence from systematic research.[42]

Scientific evidence supporting the use of homeopathy is generally rather sparse and much of what is available suffers from poor methodology (see Chapter 2). Examples of the latter include dubious accuracy of test materials, inappropriate measurements and poor randomisation techniques.[43] Other material is inconclusive.[44] This is unfortunate because increasingly decisions on whether to use or purchase homeopathic services require evidence of positive outcomes and value for money. However there is much more circumstantial evidence that homeopathy is effective from case studies.

It has been suggested by David Colquhoun[45] that evidence on the effectiveness of CAM should be assessed by the National Institute of Clinical Excellence (NICE) in England. However Professor Colquhoun also stated that 'a strong argument can be made for NICE not having to spend time and money going through, yet again, evidence that we already know to be inadequate'. He continues: 'Since we already know there is little evidence for the effectiveness of complementary medicine, should more research be done?' In fact NICE already has a systematic review process that takes into account all available evidence, including observational studies, and failure to evaluate complementary therapies leads to health inequalities because of uneven access and missed opportunities.[46] For example, as complementary therapies are often relatively cheap, if shown to be effective they could save money currently spent on costly drugs. It is likely that NICE (and its equivalent body in Scotland – the Scottish Medicines Consortium) will evaluate at least some further aspects of CAM sooner or later, given the prevalence of CAM therapies in both the private and public sectors.[47] In this event NICE will require specific expertise on individual CAM therapies in order to maintain its standards of excellence in the appraisal process.

Areas of research

Broadly, homeopathic research to gather evidence of efficacy and effectiveness and improve its use falls into four main categories:

1. randomised controlled placebo studies designed to demonstrate that homeopathy is not merely a placebo response and satisfy criticism from sceptics
2. clinical trials to establish efficacy of specific treatments, meta-analyses and systematic reviews
3. audit and case study collection to establish effectiveness and improve the use of homeopathy.

Some examples of research in each category are given below.

Placebo studies

On 26 August 2005, several UK newspapers reported that the treatment effects of homeopathy are no better than placebo.[48–51] The newspaper articles were based on a systematic review by Shang *et al.*[52] of 110 trials each of homeopathy and conventional medicine compared with placebo for a range of medical conditions. The authors concluded that when the size and methodological quality of studies are taken into account, there is weak evidence that the specific treatment effects of homeopathy are better than placebo. Conversely, there is strong evidence that the specific treatment effects of conventional medicine are better than placebo. The newspaper reports of this well-conducted study were largely accurate. The authors of the research suggested that the context in which treatment is provided may influence the effects of an intervention and this should be the focus of further investigation. Ernst subsequently weighed into the debate, denouncing homeopathy as ineffective.[53] 'Homeopathic remedies don't work,' he told *The Observer* newspaper. 'Study after study has shown it is simply the purest form of placebo. You may as well take a glass of water than a homeopathic medicine.' Nor was Ernst's disdain confined to homeopathy. Chiropractic, which involves spine manipulation to treat illnesses, and the laying on of hands to 'cure' patients, are equally invalid, he said. Not surprisingly, his views and his studies provoked furious reactions amongst the CAM community and Shang *et al.*'s paper was widely criticised, not least by some of their Swiss medical colleagues.[54]

The first investigation of the placebo effect used the hypothesis that homeopathy was due to a placebo response rather than the converse. Following a pilot trial in 1983 with 35 patients,[55] the hypothesis was tested in a double-blind placebo-controlled trial, using a model based on the use of mixed grass pollens to treat 144 hayfever patients.[56] The authors concluded that homeopathy appeared to be effective in its own right, i.e. they disproved their original hypothesis. This result was reinforced by further work in this area.[57]

The evidence supporting the hypothesis that homeopathy may be solely a placebo response can be considered under a number of headings[58]:

- theoretical evidence – involving immunological-type responses to minute quantities of stimulant
- practical evidence – outcome measures based on patient-oriented methods demonstrate an improvement in both overall well-being and clinical symptoms
- laboratory research – difficult to replicate and apply to *in vivo* situations
- the self-healing response – in assembling the varying sources of evidence for the existence of a placebo response to homeopathy, the interesting idea is introduced of replacing the term 'placebo' with 'intention-modified self-healing response', which is affected by the circumstances of the healing encounter. Reilly suggests that the intention-modified self-healing response may exist alone or be combined with an intervention to give a therapeutic intention-modified self-healing response.[58]

A meta-analysis on 89 randomised clinical trials (RCTs) assessed whether or not the clinical effect reported in RCTs of homeopathic remedies was equivalent to that reported for placebo.[59] The results of the meta-analysis were not compatible with this hypothesis, but insufficient evidence was found from these studies that homeopathy was clearly efficacious for any single clinical condition.

Randomised clinical trials – systematic reviews and meta-analyses

Over the years various techniques have been developed for RCTs to facilitate their use in developing an evidence base for homeopathy, but most of these set out to test the therapy as an intervention versus placebo, rather than to test a specific remedy. Homeopathic RCTs are always scrutinised very carefully by the scientific community, so their quality needs to be extremely high for the outcomes to be accepted. The applicability of using RCT for homeopathy has been questioned by Milgrom[60] who concluded that alternatives to RCTs are urgently required that can take into account possible entangled specific and nonspecific effects during trials of homeopathy. That RCTs sometimes deliver positive results for the use of homeopathic remedies may be caused by residual entanglement arising from homeopathic remedy manufacture.

By the end of 2005 119 RCTs had been published, of which 57 were positive for homeopathy, 6 negative and 56 statistically inconclusive.[61] The objective of one of the most frequently cited papers on homeopathic clinical trials[62] was to establish whether or not there was any firm evidence of the effectiveness of homeopathy from all the many controlled trials that have been carried out in recent years. The methodological quality of 107 controlled trials published in 96 journals worldwide was assessed. The trials were scored using a list of predefined good criteria. A total of 81 positive trials were recorded. The five allergic trials included in the analysis were all positive: the next most successful therapeutic group, with 90% of its 20 trials positive, was trauma and pain. The authors acknowledge that the weight of presented evidence was probably not sufficient for most people to make a decision on whether homeopathy works or not, but that there would probably be enough evidence to support several common applications if it were an orthodox therapy.

A systematic review has been carried out of 32 trials (28 placebo-controlled, two comparing homeopathy and another treatment, two comparing both, i.e. comparing outcomes from trials comparing homeopathy with a placebo with outcomes from trials comparing homeopathy with another non-homeopathic treatment) involving a total of 1778 patients.[63] The methodological quality of the trials was highly variable. In the 19 placebo-controlled trials providing sufficient data for meta-analysis, individualised homeopathy was significantly more effective than the placebo effect but when the analysis was restricted to the methodologically best trials, no significant effect was seen. The results of the available randomised trials suggest that individualised homeopathy had a greater effect than placebo. The evidence was not convincing because of methodological shortcomings and inconsistencies.

Several individual trials have yielded negative results.[64–66] A high-quality randomised double-blind placebo-controlled trial was conducted involving 63 patients on the homeopathic prophylaxis of migraine using a technique approved by the International Headache Society under good clinical practice.[67] The authors concluded that homeopathy could not be recommended for migraine prophylaxis.

A German randomised double-blind placebo-controlled trial investigated the clinical efficacy and tolerance of Caulophyllum D4 using 40 pregnant women with premature amnion rupture.[68] The effect of the remedy in D4–D18 on smooth muscle was also investigated *in vitro*.

Patients between the 38th and 42nd gestational weeks with premature amnion rupture, no regular contractions and cervix dilation of less than 3 cm were randomised. Appropriate tests were used to measure outcomes. In the second experiment the effect of the homeopathic remedies was measured on the spontaneous contraction activity of smooth muscle obtained from the uterus and stomach of guinea pig and rats. It was concluded that the remedy was tolerated without adverse reactions, and had no myogene effects.

The influence of indicators of methodological quality on study outcome in a set of 89 placebo-controlled clinical trials of homeopathy has been investigated.[69] It was concluded that in the set studied there was clear evidence that studies with better methodological quality tended to yield less positive results.

Linde and Melchart[70] have published an overview of the methods and results of the available RCTs of individualised homeopathy. They included studies that used a variety of potencies. One study specified Rhus tox c6, another specified Sulphur c30 and also a serial application of c20, c200 and c1000. Controls included placebo, salicylate, chloroquine, Salazopyrin plus 5-aminosalicylic acid and dicyclomide hydroxide and faecal bulking agents. The homeopathy groups responded significantly better than controls in eight trials. The overall meta-analysis (19 trials) produced a rate ratio in favour of homeopathy.

Ernst has summarised the data from all trials of classic homeopathy versus allopathic medications.[71] Patients were adults and children with a variety of illnesses (rheumatoid arthritis, proctocolitis, irritable-bowel disease, malaria, otitis media or tonsillitis). The author did not describe his method for assessing validity, how decisions on the relevance of primary studies were made, how the papers were selected for the review or how many of the reviewers performed the selection. Two of the six studies (both non-randomised) suggested that homeopathic remedies were superior to conventional drug therapy. Two trials suggested the opposite. The remaining two studies suggested both interventions to be equally effective (or ineffective).

RCTs have yet to prove the efficacy or otherwise of homeopathic interventions. A great deal more work is necessary to establish a robust evidence base.

Audit and case study collection

In the current climate of audit collection it is not surprising that homeopathy has begun to get its act together with respect to gathering data on outcomes. Proposals have been presented for Europe-wide data collection.[40] Data-gathering schemes have also been suggested in Germany.[41] There is now an impressive amount of information about the effectiveness of many remedies.

Three examples of perception outcome studies have been carried out in homeopathic hospital departments in England. The first study at the Tunbridge Wells Homeopathic Hospital aimed to assess firstly, the range of diagnoses presented by patients and secondly, patients' own impressions of benefit.[72] A total of 1372 questionnaires were completed by patients, after their consultations, to record their impressions of the effects of homeopathic treatment. Patients were asked to score their responses on a –3 to +3 scale. The three main diagnostic groups were dermatology, musculoskeletal disorders and malignant disease, especially carcinoma of the breast. Overall, 74% of patients recorded positive benefits, with 55% recording scores of 3 or 2. The results of a 6-year study at Bristol Homeopathic Hospital (see Chapter 8) showed that over 70% of patients with chronic diseases reported positive health changes after homeopathic treatment.[73] The study, which was the largest consecutive homeopathic clinical series ever reported, echoed the findings from Tunbridge Wells Homeopathic Hospital and Liverpool Department of Homeopathic Medicine, where 76% of 1100 patients reported an improvement of their condition.[74]

The collection of case studies has always been an important aspect of homeopathic practice. Several publications accept these, including the journal *Homeopathy* and the Faculty of Homeopathy Newsletter *Simile*.

Attitude and awareness studies

These studies provide important information on topics such as why people turn to homeopathy and how they obtain the necessary guidance on which remedies to purchase.[75–76] The attitudes of providers of homeopathy are also important.[76, 77]

Attacks on homeopathy

The paucity of scientific evidence has prompted several adverse articles on homeopathy in both the medical and veterinary press, including a paper in recent years in the *Lancet* with its accompanying editorial entitled 'The end of homeopathy'.[79] In July 2006 BBC2's flagship current affairs programme Newsnight ran an item that focused on the supply of homeopathic 'antimalarial drugs'.[80] A researcher contacted several practitioners, pharmacies and clinics posing as a patient asking about homeopathy as an alternative to orthodox malaria prophylaxis. She then documented the responses received and the various remedies offered. The final report came across as rather damaging to homeopathy, adding more ammunition for the sceptics. Criticism of homeopathy was expressed by some members in the Upper House of the UK Parliament when the National Rules (see Chapter 10) were discussed in November 2006.[81] The general thrust of all this publicity was that homeopathy did not work and it should not be made more widely available to a naive public.

Over the past decade, several British universities have started offering bachelor of science (BSc) degrees in CAM, including six that offer BSc degrees in homeopathy. Some scientists have expressed concern over the availability of these qualifications, claiming that such courses give homeopathy and homeopaths undeserved scientific credibility.[82]

Ridicule has emerged in the USA[83] and from the British Veterinary Voodoo Society (http://vetpath.co.uk/voodoo/), drawing immediate response from the homeopathic community. Undoubtedly the debate will continue but it would seem that patients' right to choose the type of therapy with which they wish to be treated will be maintained, although the availability of certain isopathic medicines (see Chapter 10) could be subject to control in the future.

Is homeopathy safe?

Potential sources of concern on safety issues associated with homeopathy include the following.

Inappropriate treatment

Most ranges of homeopathic remedies available commercially for sale OTC are designed to be used for the treatment of simple self-limiting conditions. Some may also be used for ongoing conditions such as back pain or soft-tissue injuries. Clients who request unusual remedies or who return repeatedly to purchase the same remedy on several occasions should be gently reminded that advice from a physician or registered homeopath might be appropriate to confirm that their condition lends itself to self-treatment.

It is vital that all practitioners only offer advice and treatment according to their levels of competency. Patients whose problems fall outwith these boundaries should be referred to suitably qualified colleagues.

Side-effects

Adverse reactions have been investigated by Dantas and Rampes using electronic databases, hand searching, searching reference lists, reviewing the bibliography of trials and other relevant articles, contacting homeopathic pharmaceutical companies and drug regulatory agencies in the UK and USA, and by communicating with experts in homeopathy.[84] The authors reported that the mean incidence of adverse effects of homeopathic medicines was greater than placebo in controlled clinical trials (9.4 to 6.1) but effects were minor, transient and comparable. There was a large incidence of pathogenetic effects in healthy volunteers taking homeopathic medicines but the methodological quality of these studies was generally low. The researchers found that anecdotal reports of adverse effects in homeopathic publications were not well documented and mainly reported aggravation of current symptoms. Case reports in conventional medical journals pointed more to adverse effects of mislabelled 'homeopathic products' than to true homeopathic medicines. It was concluded that homeopathic medicines in high dilutions, prescribed by trained professionals, were probably safe and unlikely to provoke severe adverse reactions. Once again it was difficult to draw definite conclusions due to the low methodological quality of reports claiming possible adverse effects of homeopathic medicines. Some isolated cases in the literature have also been highlighted by Barnes.[63]

Despite attempts by the Pharmacy sub-Committee of the European Committee on Homeopathy to introduce a 'yellow card' reporting system tailored to the requirements of homeopathy,[85] no scheme yet exists to identify signals that may give cause for concern.

From time to time one sees a sensitivity to the lactose that forms the base of the tablet used to deliver the homeopathic remedy. This can be overcome by using a sucrose-based carrier or a liquid potency.

Aggravation

In about 10% of chronic cases the patient's condition may be exacerbated within 2–5 days of taking a remedy. Typically a skin condition may become worse after taking a low-potency remedy. Such a reaction usually only occurs on the first time the remedy is introduced to a treatment. This reaction, known as an aggravation, has been described as an adverse drug reaction and in the sense that it is unwanted by the patient it might be considered thus. When told of this possibility many patients will say that they expect to get worse before they get better. Far from being upset by the apparent adverse drug reaction, they consider an aggravation as a sign that the medicine is working (see Chapter 3).

If an aggravation appears the patient should be instructed to cease taking the remedy until the symptoms subside and then recommence, taking the remedy at a lower frequency. If the symptoms continue to get worse when the remedy has been temporarily suspended, then it is likely that the wrong remedy is being taken. Patients who are receiving prescribed medication should be advised to consult their practitioner, since ways of dealing with aggravations can differ.

Interactions

There is no evidence that homeopathic remedies interfere with any concurrent allopathic medicines and indeed they are particularly useful to treat trivial conditions in people who are taking a large number of orthodox medication. It is thought that steroids may inactivate homeopathic remedies to some extent and although this potential interaction is certainly not dangerous, it could reduce their expected effectiveness. Some homeopathic remedies are considered to antidote or inactivate other remedies in some circumstances. Examples include Camphor, Aconite and Nux vom.

Traditionally homeopaths usually advise patients to refrain from taking coffee, tea, chocolate and spicy food when taking homeopathic medication, but in fact there is little robust evidence that such abstinence is in fact necessary.

What can I treat?

This question and an associated question, What can I be treated for with homeopathy?, has implications for extrinsic safety – that is, the chance of a condition becoming worse through inappropriate medication. The simple answer to both these questions is 'a large number of conditions – but not all'. In particular conditions associated with deficiencies, hormonal imbalance or life-threatening infection respond better to orthodox medicine in many cases.

The limit between simple self-limiting conditions that lend themselves to self-treatment (see Chapter 10) and chronic or serious conditions that require professional guidance is not always easy to explain to the patient.

How does homeopathy work?

In many ways this is the easiest question to answer: 'We don't know'. Patients are seldom worried about – or in many cases are not even interested in – how a remedy works. There are many examples of similar uncertainty in allopathic medicine. Patients' main concern is safety and a positive outcome. The aspect of homeopathy that is implausible for many people is that its medicines are often diluted to the point where no molecules of the original substance can be detected with methods that are currently available. Where there are material doses of remedy present, generally below the 12c potency, it is easier to accept a pharmacological response, albeit not one that can necessarily be explained in standard pharmacological terms. Once the remedy has been diluted beyond Avogadro's number, theoretically there are no molecules of the drug present (see Chapter 10).

The emphasis on proving that homeopathy works has been overtaken by a wish to improve its use. However, there is no doubt that homeopathy would benefit from a plausible explanation of its mechanisms of action.

The leading current proposal for the mode of action of such 'ultramolecular' dilutions is that water is capable of storing information relating to substances with which it has previously been in contact and subsequently transmits this information to presensitised biosystems. The process is thought to be mediated by structural modifications of water, analogous to the storage of information by magnetic media. Such information is retained in physical rather than chemical form[86] (see Chapter 3).

Research on hydrogen bonds in water provides some support for this 'memory' theory. The Swiss chemist, Louis Rey, found that the structure of hydrogen bonds in homeopathic dilutions of salt solutions is very different from that in pure water.[87] He reached the conclusion that the phenomenon results from the vigorous shaking of solutions that takes place during homeopathic succussion.

The modification of the solvent could provide an important support to the validity of homeopathic medicine, that employs 'medicines without molecules'. Elia *et al.*[88] studied the physicochemical properties of extremely diluted aqueous solutions of homeopathic medicines and found increased conductivity in solutions in which material had been present compared with untreated solvent. The authors concluded that successive dilution and succussion can permanently alter the physico-chemical properties of the aqueous solvent.

An alternative mechanism is suggested by the results of research from South Korea. Studies on molecular clustering in water solutions showed that as a solution is made more and more dilute, very stable and larger aggregates develop in dilute solutions than in more concentrated solutions.[89] This means that residual molecular clusters of original substance might just be present in homeopathic dilutions. This work is notable since it was carried out by scientists who have no particular interest in homeopathy.

Whatever their mode of action, there is increasing evidence that homeopathic dilutions have a demonstrable effect on living organisms examined under laboratory conditions. Researchers in Germany have observed an inhibitory effect of ultradiluted dichlorophenol on the bacterium *Vibrio fischeri*.[90] There is also important work from a consortium of European laboratories showing that very high dilutions of histamine may exert a biologically significant effect on basophil cells.[91]

Despite the foregoing it has to be acknowledged that there has not been much progress since George Vithoulkas wrote in 1985: 'as far as is yet known, there is no conclusive explanation in modern physics or chemistry for the mechanism of action of homeopathy'.[92]

Is it worth the money?

The answer to this question leads on to a further question: Who pays for what? for the perception of whether homeopathy offers good value for money in terms of clinical effectiveness and economic value ultimately depends on who is providing the funds. This may be a public health system, an insurance company or an individual consumer.

Public health system

Homeopathic medicines have been fully reimbursed under the UK National Health Service since its inception in 1948. The net ingredient cost is, on average, substantially less than the cost of the newer orthodox medicines for a similar course of treatment, although this figure does not take into account the longer consultation times and does vary widely. In the case of older non-proprietary allopathic drugs the costs may be lower than homeopathic remedies. Overall cost-effectiveness has not been established conclusively. Apart from the work of Jeremy Swayne,[93] who carried out a study on the prescribing costs of 21 doctors, there has been relatively little economic evaluation work to examine the cost-effectiveness of homeopathy. Following a systematic search of the literature Swiss researchers concluded that robust data on the overall cost-effectiveness of homeopathy are unavailable at present.[94]

Swayne's results suggested that doctors practising homeopathic medicine issue fewer prescriptions and at a lower cost than their colleagues. Unfortunately, there were limitations to the study, not the least being that the sample was too small to allow generalisations to be made and no account was taken either of the extended consultation times involved. Similar cost advantages have been claimed by German dental surgeons.[95]

Jain[96] collected data for 4 years on 100 patients treated with homeopathy. Costs of homeopathic remedies and costs of conventional drugs that would otherwise be prescribed for these patients were calculated for the total duration of treatment. Average cost savings per patient were £60.40 (€89.94). As with Swayne's study, no allowance was made for the prescribers' consultation time and there is the possibility that patients were chosen according to the potential likelihood of savings being made rather then at random. It may be that the costs of the longer consultation time could be balanced by fewer follow-ups but there is no firm evidence to support this.

Slade *et al.*[97] claimed an annual saving of £2807.30 (€4175.67) in a study that evaluated the effect of a GP-led practice-based homeopathy service on symptoms, activity, well-being, general practice consultation-rate and the use of conventional medication. A limitation of this result was the absence of a control group.

Eighty general medical practices in Belgium where physicians were members of the Unio Homeopathica Belgica were surveyed.[98] All patients and their physicians visiting the practices on a specified day completed a questionnaire. A total of 782 patients presented with diseases of all major organ systems. Patients were very satisfied with their homeopathic treatment: both they and their physicians recorded significant improvement. Costs of homeopathic treatment were significantly lower than conventional treatment, and many previously prescribed drugs were discontinued. Trichard *et al.*[99] carried out a pharmacoeconomic comparison between homeopathic and antibiotic treatment strategies in recurrent acute rhinopharyngitis in children and concluded that the former could offer a cost-effective alternative.

Despite the fragmentary nature of the evidence, an investigation into the potential contribution of mainstream complementary therapies to healthcare in the UK in 2007 (the Smallwood report) concluded that there exist a number of treatments for specific ailments where the implementation of CAM therapies (including homeopathy) may offer significant cost savings to public health bodies and to the economy more widely, and others in which additional benefits to patients may be obtained cost-effectively.[100]

Insurance company

As far as a private health insurer is concerned, the acceptance of homeopathy for reimbursement depends on consumer demand, patient-oriented evidence of effectiveness and practitioner advocacy.

Individual consumer

Within reason, cost alone is not the overriding concern for consumers when assessing whether they are getting value for money. Reassurance of a positive benefit–risk ratio by the therapy provider as well as the whole healing experience will often be more important in the decision of whether to be treated with homeopathy or not. However, as already noted above, the relatively low price of OTC products certainly helps the demand for homeopathy.

References

1. Hahnemann C S. *Organon of the Rational Art of Healing*. Dresden: Arnold, 1810.
2. Hahnemann C S. Versuch uber ein neues Prinzip zur Auffindung der Heilkerafte der Arzneisubstanzen. *Hufland's J* 1796; 2: 2–3. Translated into English by Dudgeon R E. London: Lesser Writings, 1852: 295–352.
3. Fulder S. Remembering the holistic view. *J Altern Comp Med* 2005; 11: 775–776.
4. Reilly D. Comments on complemementary and alternative medicine in Europe. *J Altern Comp Med* 2001; 7 (Suppl. 1): S23–S31.
5. Vincent C A, Furnham A. Why do patients turn to complementary medicine? An empirical study. *Br J Clin Psychol* 1996; 35: 37–48.
6. Von Wartburg W P. Drugs and perception of risks. *Swiss Pharm* 1984; 6: 21–23.
7. Slovic P, Kraus N, Lappe H, *et al.* Risk perception of prescription drugs: report on a survey in Sweden. *Pharm Med* 1989; 4: 43–65.
8. Ruusuvuori J. Comparing homeopathic and general practice consultations: the case of problem presentation. *Commun Med* 2005; 2: 123–135.
9. Lindfors P, Raevaara L. Discussing patients' drinking and eating habits in medical and homeopathic consultations. *Commun Med* 2005; 2: 137–149.

10. Furnham A, Smith C. Choosing alternative medicine: a comparison of the beliefs of patients visiting a general practitioner and a homoeopath. *Soc Sci Med* 1988; 26: 685–689.

11. Saxena S, Majeed A, Jones M. Socioeconomic differences in childhood consultation rates in general practice in England and Wales: prospective cohort study. *Br Med J* 1995; 318: 642–646.

12. Howie J G R, Heaney D J, Maxwell M, *et al.* Quality at general practice consultations: cross sectional survey. *Br Med J* 1999; 319: 738–743.

13. Deveugele M, Derese A, van den Brink-Muinen A, *et al.* Consultation length in general practice: cross sectional study in six European countries. *Br Med J* 2002; 325: 472.

14. Bakx K. The 'eclipse' of folk medicine in western society. *Soc Health Illness* 1991; 13: 17–24.

15. Balint M. *The Doctor, his Patient and the Illness*, 2nd edn. London: Pitman Paperbacks, 1971.

16. Department of Health. The national survey of NHS patients: general practice: 1998. http://www.dh.gov.uk/PublicationsAndStatistics/PressReleases/Press ReleasesNotices/fs/en?CONTENT_ID=4080484&chk=F61f5g (accessed December 2006).

17. Furnham A, Vincent C, Wood R. The health beliefs and behaviours of three groups of complementary medicine and a general practice group of patients. *J Altern Comp Med* 1995; 1: 347–359.

18. Ernst E, Resch K L, Hill S. Do complementary medicine practitioners have a better bedside manner (letter)? *J R Soc Med* 1997; 80: 118–119.

19. Steinsbekk A, Bentzen N, Brien S. Why do parents take their children to homeopaths? An exploratory qualitative study. *Forsch Komplementarmed* 2006; 13: 88–93.

20. Ross S, Simpson C R, McLay J S. Homeopathic and herbal prescribing in general practice in Scotland. *Br J Clin Pharmacol* 2006; 62: 647–652.

21. Alvina R L, Schneiderman L J. Why patients choose homeopathy. *West J Med* 1978; 128: 366–369.

22. English J M. Homeopathy. *Practitioner* 1986; 230: 1067–1071.

23. Pomposelli R, Andreoni C, Costini G, *et al.* Opinions and self-reported health status of Italians seeking homeopathic treatment. *Homeopathy* 2006; 95: 81–87.

24. White A R, Resch K R, Ernst E. A survey of complementary practitioners' fees, practice, and attitudes to working within the national health service. *Complement Ther Med* 1997; 5: 210–214.

25. Carr-Hill R, Jenkins-Clarke S, Dixon P, *et al.* Do minutes count? Consultation lengths in general practice. *J Health Serv Res Policy* 1998; 3: 207–213.

26. Cape J. Consultation length, patient-estimated consultation length, and satisfaction with the consultation. *Br J Gen Pract* 2002; 52: 1004–1006.

27. Chao M T, Wade C, Kronenberg F, *et al.* Women's reasons for complementary and alternative medicine use: racial/ethnic differences. *J Altern Comp Med* 2006; 12: 719–722.

28. Neuberger J. Availability of information in an open society. In: Marinker M, ed. *Controversies in Healthcare Policies: Challenges to Practice*. London: BMJ Publishing Group, 1994.

29. Anonymous. Patient power makes doctors think. *Glasgow Herald* 1994; 9 December.

30. Harrison J, Innes R, van Zwanenberg T. *Rebuilding Trust in Healthcare.* Oxford: Radcliffe Medical Press, 2004.

31. Kayne S B, Beattie N, Reeves A. Buyer characteristics in the homeopathic OTC Market. *Pharm J* 1999; 263: 210–212.

32. Wolsko P, Ware L, Kutner J, *et al.* Alternative/complementary medicine wider usage than generally appreciated. *J Altern Comp Med* 2000; 4: 321–326.

33. Steinbekk A, Fønnebø V. Users of homeopaths in Norway in 1998 compared to previous users and GP patients. *Homeopathy* 2003; 92: 3–10.

34. Bell I R. Evidence-based homeopathy: empirical questions and methodological considerations for homeopathic clinical research. *Am J Hom Med* 2003; 96: 17–31.

35. Jonas W B, Kaptchuk T J, Linde K. A critical overview of homeopathy. *Ann Intern Med* 2003; 138: 393–399.

36. NHS Centre for Reviews and Dissemination. Homeopathy. *Effect Healthcare Bull* 2002; 7: 1–12.

37. Mathie R T. Clinical outcomes research: contributions to the evidence base for homeopathy. *Homeopathy* 2003; 92: 56–57.

38. Walach H, Jomnas W B, Ives J, *et al.* Research on homeopathy – state of the art. *J Altern Comp Med* 2005; 11: 813–829.

39. Bellavite P, Signorini A. Is homeopathy effective? In: *Homeopathy. A Frontier in Medical Science.* Berkeley, CA: North Atlantic Books, 1995: 37–55.

40. Ernst E, Hahn E G (eds) *Homeopathy. A Critical Approach.* Oxford: Butterworth Heinemann, 1998.

41. Lewith G T, Breen A, Filshie J, *et al.* Complementary medicine: evidence base, competence to practise. *Clin Med* 2003; 5: 235–240.

42. Sackett D L, Rosenberg W M C, Muir Gray J A, *et al.* Evidence based medicine: what it is and what it isn't. *BMJ* 1996; 312: 71–72.

43. Kayne S B. *Homeopathic Pharmacy – An Introduction and Handbook.* Edinburgh: Churchill Livingstone, 1997: 164–167.

44. Ernst E. Classical homoeopathy versus conventional treatments: a systematic review. *Perfusion* 1999; 12: 13–15.

45. Colquhoun D. Should NICE evaluate complementary and alternative medicines? *Br Med J* 2007; 334: 507.

46. Franck L, Chantler C, Dixon M. Should NICE evaluate complementary and alternative medicine? *Br Med J* 2007; 334: 506.

47. Mackinnon J. The expertise to evaluate. Letter: Rapid response to David Colquhoun. Should NICE evaluate complementary and alternative medicines? www.bmj.com/cgi/eletters/334/7592/507#163064 (accessed 10 September 2007).

48. Natural cure rap. *The Sun* 2005; 26 August: 20.

49. Homeopathy: are remedies from nature all in the mind? *Daily Mail* 2005; 26 August: 4.

50. Effects of homeopathy 'are all in the mind'. *The Independent* 2005; 26 August: 23.

51. As a fourth study says it's no better than a placebo, is this the end for homeopathy? *The Guardian* 2005; 26 August: 3.

52. Shang A S, Huwiler-Müntener K, Nartey L, *et al*. Are the clinical effects of homeopathy placebo effects? Comparative study of placebo-controlled trials of homeopathy and allopathy. *Lancet* 2005; 336: 726–732.

53. McKie R. Professor savages homeopathy. *The Observer* 2005; December 18.

54. SAHOP Swiss Association of Homeopathic Physicians – open letter to editor of the Lancet. *Forsch Komplementarmed Klass Naturheilkunde* 2005; 12: 252–253.

55. Reilly D T, Taylor M A. Potent placebo or potency? A proposed study model with initial findings using homeopathically prepared pollens in hayfever. *Br Homeopath J* 1985; 74: 65–75.

56. Reilly D T, Taylor M A, McSharry C, Aitchison T C. Is homeopathy a placebo response? Controlled trial of homeopathic potency with pollen in hayfever as model. *Lancet* 1986; ii: 881–888.

57. Taylor M A, Reilly D, Llewellyn-Jones R H *et al*. Randomised controlled trial of homoeopathy versus placebo in perennial allergic rhinitis with overview of four trial series. *Br Med J* 2000; 321: 471–476.

58. Reilly D. Is homeopathy a placebo response? What if it is? What if it is not? In: Ernst E, Hahn E G, eds. *Homeopathy – A Critical Approach*. Oxford: Butterworth-Heinemann, 1988: chapter 8.

59. Linde K, Clausius N, Ramirez G *et al*. Are the clinical effects of homoeopathy placebo effects? A meta-analysis of placebo-controlled trials. *Lancet* 1997; 350: 834–843.

60. Milgrom L R. Are randomized controlled trials (RCTs) redundant for testing the efficacy of homeopathy? A critique of RCT. *J Altern Comp. Med* 2005; 11: 831–838.

61. Faculty of Homeopathy e-Newsletter April 2007 http://tinyurl.com/346g4g (accessed April 2007).

62. Kleijnen J, Knipschild P, ter Riet G. Clinical trials of homoeopathy. *Br Med J* 1991; 302: 316–323.

63. Barnes J. Complementary Medicine: Homeopathy. *Pharm J* 1998; 260: 492–497.

64. Walach H, Haeusler W, Lowes T *et al*. Classical homeopathic treatment of chronic headaches. *Cephalalgia* 1997; 17: 119–126.

65. Hart O, Mullee M A, Lewith G, Miller J. Double blind placebo-controlled randomised clinical trial of homeopathic arnica C30 for pain and infection after total abdominal hysterectomy. *J R Soc Med* 1997; 90: 73–78.

66. Ernst E, Barnes J. Are homeopathic remedies effective for delayed-onset muscle soreness? A systematic review of placebo-controlled trials. *Perfusion* 1998; 1: 4–8.

67. Whitmarsh T, Coleston-Shields D M, Steiner T J. Double blind randomised placebo-controlled trial of homeopathic prophylaxis of migraine. *Cephalalgia* 1997; 17: 600–604.

68. Beer A-M, Heiliger F, Lukanov J. Caulophyllum D4 to introduction of labour in premature rupture of membranes – a double blind study confirmed by an investigation into the contraction activity of smooth muscles. *FACT* 2000; 5: 84–85.

69. Linde K, Scholz M, Ramirez G *et al*. Impact of study quality on outcome in placebo-controlled trials of homeopathy. *J Clin Epidemiol* 1999; 52: 631–636.

70. Linde K, Melchart D. Randomized controlled trials of individualized home-opathy: a state-of-the-art review. *J Altern Comp Med* 1998; 4: 371–388.

71. Ernst E. Classical homoeopathy versus conventional treatments: a systematic review. *Perfusion* 1999; 12: 13–15.

72. Clover A. Patient benefit survey: Tunbridge Wells Homoeopathic Hospital. *Br Homeopath J* 2000; 89: 68–72.

73. Spence D S, Thompson E A, Barron SJ. Homeopathic treatment for chronic disease: a 6-year, university-hospital outpatient observational study. *J Altern Comp Med* 2005; 11: 793–798.

74. Richardson WR. Patient benefit survey: Liverpool Regional Department of Homoeopathic Medicine. *Br Homeopath J* 2001; 90: 158–162.

75. van Haselen R A, Reiber U, Nickel I, *et al.* Providing complementary and alternative medicine in primary care: the primary care workers' perspective. *Comp Ther Med* 2004; 12: 6–16.

76. Attitudes of medical, nursing, and pharmacy faculty and students toward complementary and alternative medicine (CAM). University of Minnesota Center for Sprituality and Learning Research Topic. www.csh.umn.edu/csh/research/topics/attit/home.html (accessed March 2007).

77. Reid S. A survey of the use of over-the-counter next term homeopathic medicines purchased in health stores in Central Manchester. *Homeopathy* 2002; 91: 225–229.

78. Davies M, Kayne S B. Homeopathy – a pilot study of the attitudes and aware-ness of pharmacy staff in the Stoke-on-Trent area. *Br Homeopath J* 1992; 81: 194–198.

79. Editorial: The end of homeopathy. *Lancet* 2005; 336: 690.

80. http://news.bbc.co.uk/1/hi/programmes/newsnight/5178122.stm (accessed December 2006).

81. O'Dowd A. New rules for homoeopathic remedies anger UK peers. *Br Med J* 2006; 333: 935.

82. Giles J. Degrees in homeopathy stated as unscientific. *Nature* 2007; 446: 352–353.

83. Weissmann G. Homeopathy: Holmes, Hogwarts, and the Prince of Wales. *FASEB J* 2006; 20: 1755–1758.

84. Dantas F, Rampes H. Do homeopathic medicines provoke adverse effects? A systematic review. *Br Homeopath J* 2000; 89 (Suppl. 1):S35–S38.

85. Kayne S B. *Homeopathic Pharmacy: Theory and Practice*, 2nd edn. Edinburgh: Elsevier Churchill Livingstone, 2006: 202–203.

86. Bellavite P, Signorini A. *The Emerging Science of Homeopathy*, 2nd edn. Berkeley, CA: North Atlantic, 2002.

87. Rey L. Thermoluminescence of ultra-high dilutions of lithium chloride and sodium chloride. *Physica A* 2003; 323: 67–74.

88. Elia V, Baiano S, Duro I, *et al.* Permanent physico-chemical properties of extremely diluted aqueous solutions of homeopathic medicines. *Homeopathy* 2004; 93: 144–150.

89. Samal S, Geckeler K E. Unexpected solute aggregation in water on dilution. *Chem Commun* 2001; 21: 2224–2225.

90. Brack A, Strube J, Stolz P, *et al.* Effects of ultrahigh dilutions of 3,5-dichlorophenol on the luminescence of the bacterium *Vibrio fischeri*. *Biochim Biophys Acta* 2003; 1621: 253–260.

91. Belon P, Cumps J, Ennis M, *et al.* Histamine dilutions modulate basophil activation. *Inflamm Res* 2004; 53: 181–188.
92. Vithoulkas G. *The Science of Homeopathy.* New York: Grove Press, 1985: 103.
93. Swayne J. The cost and effectiveness of homeopathy. *Br Homeopathic J* 1992; 81: 148–150.
94. Bornhoft G, Wolf U, Ammon K, *et al.* Effectiveness, safety and cost-effectiveness of homeopathy in general practice – summarized health technology assessment. *Forsch Komplementarmed* 2006; 13 (Suppl. 2): 19–29.
95. Feldhaus H-W. Cost-effectiveness of homeopathic treatment in a dental practice. *Br Homeopathic J* 1993; 82: 22–28.
96. Jain A. Does homeopathy reduce the cost of conventional drug prescribing? A study of comparative prescribing costs in general practice. *Homeopathy* 2003; 92: 71–76.
97. Slade K, Chohan B P S, Barker P J. Evaluation of a GP practice based homeopathy service. *Homeopathy* 2004; 93: 67–70.
98. Unio Homeopathica Belgica Survey 2001. www.homeopathy.be/f-docs/659%20Unio%20Homeopathica%20Belgica%20survey%202001%20report.pdf (accessed December 2006).
99. Trichard M, Chaufferin G, Nicoloyannis N. Pharmacoeconomic comparison between homeopathic and antibiotic treatment strategies in recurrent acute rhinopharyngitis in children. *Homeopathy* 2005; 94: 3–9.
100. Smallwood C. The role of complementary and alternative medicine in the NHS. www.freshminds.co.uk/PDF/THE%20REPORT.pdf (accessed 11 September 2007).

Further reading

Kayne S B (2002) *Complementary Therapies for Pharmacists.* London: Pharmaceutical Press.
Kayne S B (2005) *Homeopathic Pharmacy*, 2nd edn. Edinburgh: Elsevier Churchill Livingstone.
Kayne S B, Kayne L R (2007) *Homeopathic Prescribing.* London: Pharmaceutical Press.

Research topics

Bellavite P, Signorini A (1995) *Homeopathy. A Frontier in Medical Science.* Berkeley, CA: North Atlantic Books.
Dean M E (2004) *The Trials of Homeopathy.* Stuttgart: KVC Verlag, 245–246.
Lewith G T, Aldridge D (eds) (1983) *Clinical Research Methodology for Complementary Therapies.* London: Hodder & Stoughton.

General reading

Blackie M (1976) *The Patient, Not the Cure.* London: Macdonald and Jane's.

Handley R (1997) *In Search of the Later Hahnemann.* Beaconsfield, UK: Beaconsfield Publishers.

Wood M (1992) *The Magical Staff. The Vitalist Tradition in Western Medicine.* Berkeley, CA: North Atlantic Books.

Wright-Hubbard E (1990) *Homeopathy as Art and Science.* Beaconsfield, UK: Beaconsfield Publishers.

2

The importance of having a robust evidence base – a personal view

Edzard Ernst

This chapter explores the necessity of obtaining high-quality evidence to support the use of homeopathy.

At first glance, the title seems entirely obvious (perhaps I should mention that it was not my choice but was given to me). However, when reflecting more deeply, things become more complex.

- Evidence of what?
- What is evidence anyway?
- What is robust?
- And what is important?

In turn, I will try to deal with these issues separately. Subsequently I will contribute a few thoughts on what all this might mean in the context of homeopathy. In doing so, I will mainly draw on my experience – this does not seem to be a subject where hard data are all that helpful (an intriguing apparent contradiction to some of my statements below).

Evidence of what?

Over the years, I seem to have acquired a reputation as an advocate of randomised clinical trials (RCTs) who disrespects all other types of data, examples of which are provided in Chapter 1. It is, of course, nice to have a reputation but I don't think I really deserve this one. I have stated numerous times that one of the most crucial things in research is to find the optimal match between the research question and the research design. To put it bluntly, if I want to find out whether my wife still loves me (research question), I would be ill advised to conduct an RCT (research design)!

So, evidence of what? There are far too many topics to mention them all:

- Who tries homeopathy?
- Of those who try it, who continues to use it?
- Why do people use homeopathy?
- What type of patients employ homeopathy?
- Are users of homeopathy in any way different from non-users?
- What different types of homeopathy are practised by whom?
- Are homeopaths different from non-homeopathic clinicians?
- What remedies are prescribed in which situations?
- What are the risks of homeopathy?

For none of these research questions do we need RCTs. But if we want to find out whether homeopathy (or any other medical intervention) is efficacious (i.e. works under ideal conditions) or effective (i.e. works under real-life conditions) in alleviating a given health problem, the RCT is a well-tested and adequate tool. For that specific set of research questions it is better (meaning it provides more definitive and less biased answers) than any other methodology we currently know.[1] It so happens that this is one set of research questions in which I am interested (hence my reputation perhaps) and which is generally deemed important (see below). Therefore most of the discussion that follows is on this theme.

What is evidence anyway?

Complementary medicine in general and homeopathy in particular are deeply rooted in a tradition where experience comes first and science second. The arguments usually claim that hundreds of years of experience on thousands of patients are innumerably stronger than scientific studies which normally only include a few patients and are far removed from 'real life' anyway. Others simply note that 'business is booming' (Arkopharma's homeopathic products business increased by 7.7% last year[2]) and say: 'what more do you want?' Thus there often is a gap as wide as a canyon between homeopaths' and non-homeopaths' views of what constitutes evidence.

Few people – certainly not I – would deny that hundreds of years of experience do constitute important information. For the scientist, this type of information is valuable foremost for formulating hypotheses. If, however, we want to test hypotheses regarding the effectiveness of a medical intervention, it is not normally all that useful. The reason is simple: there is not one but a multitude of possible explanations for any clinical outcome (Figures 2.1 and 2.2). In other words, there are certainly many types of evidence but uncontrolled data are wide open to

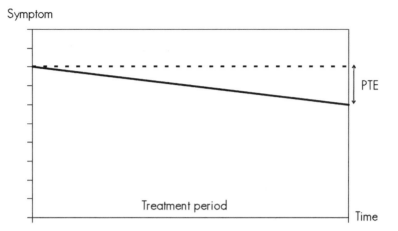

Figure 2.1 Schematic analysis of a case report, case series, observational study or other types of uncontrolled data. When patients are treated, symptoms are likely to decrease over time. Without a control group, this decrease equals the perceived therapeutic effect (PTE).

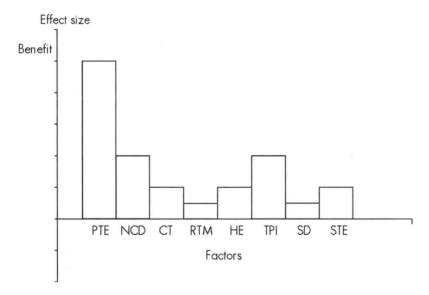

Figure 2.2 Schematic differentiation of factors contributing to the perceived therapeutic effect (PTE). Effect sizes are arbitrary. NCD, natural course of the disease; CT, concomitant treatments (e.g. self-administered over-the-counter drugs patients forget to tell their doctors about); RTM, regression towards the mean; HE, Hawthorne effect; TPI, therapist–patient interaction; SD, social desirability (i.e. patients say they are improved to please their doctor); STE, specific therapeutic effect.

bias. Evidence pertaining to the efficacy/effectiveness of a treatment must be unbiased, otherwise it is not conclusive (i.e. there is more than one explanation for the observed effects). This precondition is met by some types of clinical studies and not by others (see below).

A recent response from the UK Royal College of General Practitioners regarding their attitude towards homeopathy confirms this view: 'to advocate the use of a therapy, we have to have robust scientific evidence for its use. Generally this means RCTs which is the standard for clinical effectiveness studies of controversial drugs'.[3] To put it in the words of Manheimer and Berman: 'high-quality data from RCTs and systematic reviews trump expert opinion, pathophysiological rationale, clinical observation, or tradition'.[4]

Evidence-based medicine (EBM) does, of course, have few homeopathic friends. Perhaps the reason for this is that EBM is often misunderstood by homeopaths. It follows a simple five-step model.[1]

1. asking answerable clinical questions
2. searching for the evidence
3. critically appraising the evidence
4. making decisions by integrating the evidence with the practitioner's expertise and the patient's values
5. evaluating performance.

This seems common sense to me, and I find it difficult to understand why anyone could object to EBM – the widespread prejudice that it amounts to 'cookbook medicine' or to a political instrument for healthcare rationing is ill conceived.

What is robust?

My dictionary defines robust as 'having or exhibiting strength'. Robust evidence therefore has to withstand criticism and misinterpretation. Robust evidence is the stuff that convinces sceptics while anecdotes usually only convince the convinced. In scientific terms robustness means that bias is minimised and transparency as well as reproducibility is maximised. So let's consider the different types of evidence in the context of therapeutic effectiveness in this light:

- Hundreds of years of experience, case reports and observational studies could be (and often are) confounded by a host of factors[5] (Figures 2.1 and 2.2).
- Controlled clinical trials can be burdened with selection and other biases (Table 2.1).

- If not placebo-controlled, RCTs could also be biased, for instance through the effects of expectation[6] (Table 2.1).

Table 2.1 Potential contributors to an observed therapeutic effect in various situations

Contributing factor	Situation			
	Uncontrolled observations	CCT experimental versus no treatment	RCT experimental versus no treatment	RCT double-blind placebo-controlled
Regression towards the mean	✓	NAC	NAC	NAC
Therapeutic relationship	✓	✓	✓	NAC
Placebo effect	✓	✓	✓	NAC
Concomitant treatments	✓	NAC	NAC	NAC
Social desirability	✓	✓	✓	NAC
Nocebo effect of non-treatment	NAC	✓	✓	NAC
Hawthorne effect	NAC	✓	✓	NAC
Patient preference	NAC	✓	NAC	NAC
Specific therapeutic effect	✓	✓	✓	✓

✓, factor is likely to contribute to the observed therapeutic response; CCT, (non-randomised) controlled clinical trial; RCT, randomised clinical trial; NAC, not a contributor to the outcome.

This leaves us with the placebo-controlled, double-blind RCT. I am aware of the fact that homeopaths do not like the RCT – or do they? I sometimes fear that they do subscribe to RCTs as long as 'the results are positive'[7] and they don't when they are 'negative'.[8]

But homeopathy is different from conventional medicine, many homeopaths would counter: more subtle, more individualised and, if required, homeopaths respond to changes in the clinical picture of an individual during the treatment. Therefore, many homeopaths argue, the RCT is not ideal for testing homeopathy: the beauty of a rose cannot be measured with a ruler!

After discussing such arguments for over a decade, I have formed a strong suspicion that they are, in the majority of instances, based on a series of misunderstandings and sometimes even on a deliberate attempt to mislead the public. Pragmatic trials can capture the real-life situation of clinical practice.[9] There are numerous adaptations to the RCT to accommodate the special requirements of homeopathy.[10] Even if one agrees with Thompson and Weiss that the specific effects of homeopathy also include phenomena like the remedy-matching process,[11] RCTs could still be designed and conducted to test this concept. For instance, patients could be randomised into a group receiving homeopathy with consultation and their results compared with those from a group receiving conventional treatment or a homeopathic remedy without consultation.

It would be wrong, however, to claim that the RCT is perfect.[12] Like all human endeavours, the RCT does clearly have its limitations. The crucial point, however, is that there is no design for testing therapeutic efficacy/effectiveness which is more robust. Some important questions to ask when evaluating the robustness of an RCT[1] are listed in Table 2.2.

Table 2.2 Questions to ask when evaluating the robustness of randomised clinical trials or systematic reviews

Randomised clinical trials	*Systematic reviews*
• Is the research question well defined?	• Are the primary data of high quality?
• Are patients allocated at random?	• Are the procedures described such that one could reproduce them?
• Was randomisation successful?	
• Are all patients accounted for?	• Are the included studies consistent?
• Were the researchers 'blind'?	• Are the results applicable and important?

The results of RCTs are rarely totally uniform, a fact that can create considerable confusion (in any type of medicine) about which data set to trust. The solution to this particular problem is, I think, quite simple: selection of RCTs, for instance, according to the direction of their results, can be seriously misleading. What is needed is a transparent and reproducible assessment of the *totality* of the evidence of a certain type (e.g. design or methodological quality), independent of personal preferences. This approach is realised in systematic reviews, i.e. research projects that minimise selection and random biases by critically and transparently summarising and assessing the totality of the available data.[13] The best (most transparent and independent) systematic reviews are often those of the Cochrane Collaboration (www.cochrane.org/). Our most recent systematic review of homeopathy focused on the paediatric population which, according to homeopathic conviction, should respond optimally to the homeopathic approach. Yet, even in this situation, the 'evidence from rigorous clinical trials ... is not convincing enough for recommendations in any condition'.[14]

Again systematic reviews are not infallible,[15] but until we have a research tool which is demonstrably superior, we are, I think, well advised to consider its strengths.

And what is important?

Obviously you get different answers to this question depending on who you ask. Psychologists might want to investigate why people use homeopathy (a research question that might be addressed with indepth interviews, i.e. qualitative research) and sociologists could insist that we need to know who uses it (a research question that might best be answered with survey methodology). At the risk of sounding hopelessly old-fashioned and narrow-minded, I have always strongly felt that the most important research questions related to *any* medical treatment are: is it safe, and is it effective? I believe that, in the interest of patients, these are the most important things to know. I would even go one step further: to offer or promote a treatment without robust evidence on those two questions can be considered unethical.[16] It is some comfort to me that, after months of deliberation, sifting through tonnes of data and listening to dozens of interested parties, the House of Lords inquiry into complementary medicine came to a very similar conclusion:[17]

> To conduct research into the CAM [complementary and alternative medicine] disciplines will require much work and resources, and will therefore be time-consuming. Hence, we recommend that three questions should be prioritised and addressed in the following order:
>
> • To provide a starting point for possible improvements in CAM treatment, to show whether further inquiry would be useful, and to highlight any areas where its application could inform conventional medicine – does the treatment offer therapeutic benefits greater than placebo?
> • To protect patients from hazardous practices – is the treatment safe?
> • To help patients, doctors and healthcare administrators choose whether or not to adopt the treatment – how does it compare, in

medical outcome and cost-effectiveness, with other forms of treatment?

Where do placebo effect and plausibility come in?

EBM ranks biological plausibility of treatments not highly. The main question in EBM is not how does it work, but does it work? Therefore, it is not prohibitive for EBM that a therapy is implausible (as most scientists insist homeopathy is), i.e. we do not yet understand its mechanisms of action. Incidentally, the 'bone of contention' in relation to homeopathy is not the current lack of understanding of its mechanism of action; the much more serious issue is that scientists insist that there cannot be a plausible explanation of homeopathy which could possibly be in line with what we know about physiology, physics, chemistry and pharmacology. This clearly represents a huge obstacle for the acceptance of homeopathy. But I stress again: it is no hindrance for EBM to assess its clinical value.

The placebo effect is important for all areas of clinical medicine. Intuitively, one suspects that homeopathy is associated with powerful non-specific effects: its consultations are lengthy, the clinicians are empathetic and expectations are often high. One might argue that non-specific effects alone would justify the use of homeopathy in routine healthcare – after all, the main thing is to help patients regardless of how this is achieved. The arguments against this notion are that firstly, placebo effects are notoriously unreliable and secondly, all treatments (even those that are effective beyond placebo) generate placebo effects. We should therefore make best use of both specific and non-specific effects by administering evidence-based treatments in an empathetic fashion. In other words, any treatment that is devoid of specific effects is short-changing patients.

Implications for homeopathy

To put it provocatively in a nutshell, what I have suggested so far essentially means that rigorously defining the safety and effectiveness of homeopathy is an ethical imperative – especially for homeopaths. Without it there will be little progress and our efforts in obtaining (research) funding will continue to be frustrated.[18]

Reviewing what the most robust evidence about homeopathy's effectiveness currently tells us is sobering even for non-homeopaths.[12] This is not the place (nor is it my allocated task) to discuss this evidence in detail, but it is difficult to deny that this evidence fails to show convincingly that homeopathy is effective beyond a placebo response. A recent statement by the UK Royal College of General Practitioners[3] confirms this view:

> when it comes to homeopathy the College is not convinced that there is sufficiently robust evidence to support its general use. Indeed the national Electronic Library for CAM seems to suggest that there is little evidence for its efficacy. Thus currently the College would not generally support its use. If the evidence-base changes we would, of course, be happy to reconsider.[3]

If one accepts this conclusion (and I doubt that many homeopaths will), the implications for homeopathy are obvious: until convincing data to the contrary emerge, homeopathy cannot be considered a therapeutic approach that is demonstrably better than placebo. The formidable challenge to homeopathy lies in generating convincing data.

Homeopaths, I fear, may go into denial and insist that RCTs are not applicable but that observational studies are.[19] The General Secretary of the European Council of Classical Homeopathy recently argued that 'patients have their own system of evidence-based medicine – seeing someone else who has benefited from treatment'.[20] This creation of double standards is, in my view, short-sighted, arrogant and counterproductive – it will only convince those who don't really need convincing, i.e. homeopaths. And it will almost inevitably lead to accusations that homeopaths fail to behave responsibly and endanger their patients' health.[21] Consequently, I predict that this will contribute to the closure of the UK homeopathic hospitals. In order to convince those who presently doubt, robust evidence along the lines described above is not just important but essential.

Acknowledgement

I thank the person who reviewed a draft of this manuscript. This criticism enabled me to formulate my arguments more powerfully.

References

1. Heneghan C, Badenoch D. *Evidence-based Medicine Toolkit*. Oxford: Blackwell, 2006.
2. Anonymous. French Arkopharma posts 137.4 million Euro revenue. *French Business Digest* 2006; 12 July.

3. Correspondence between Les Rose and Dr Graham Archard, RCGP, Vice Chair and Chair of the RCGP CAM Group. 2006; 27 May.
4. Manheimer E, Berman B. Exploring, evaluating, and applying the results of systematic reviews of CAM therapies. *Explore (NY)* 2005; 1: 210–214.
5. Grimes D A, Schulz K F. Bias and causal associations in observational research. *Lancet* 2002; 359: 248–252.
6. Sackett D L. Bias in analytic research. *J Chronic Dis* 1979; 32: 51–63.
7. Weatherley-Jones E, Nicholl J P, Thomas K J, *et al*. A randomised, controlled, triple-blind trial of the efficacy of homeopathic treatment for chronic fatigue syndrome. *J Psychosom Res* 2004; 56: 189–197.
8. White A, Slade P, Hunt C, *et al*. Individualised homeopathy as an adjunct in the treatment of childhood asthma: a randomised placebo controlled trial. *Thorax* 2003; 58: 317–321.
9. Roland M, Torgerson D J. Understanding controlled trials: what are pragmatic trials? *Br Med J* 1998; 316: 285.
10. Ernst E. Randomised clinical trials: unusual designs. *Perfusion* 2004; 17: 416–421.
11. Thompson T D B, Weiss M. Homeopathy – what are the active ingredients? An exploratory study using the UK Medical Research Council's framework for the evaluation of complex interventions. *BMC Comp Altern Med* 2006; 6.
12. Celermajer D S. Evidence-based medicine: how good is the evidence? *Med J Aust* 2001; 174: 293–295.
13. Bigby M, Williams H. Appraising systematic reviews and meta-analyses. *Arch Dermatol* 2003; 139: 795–798.
14. Altunic U, Pittler M H, Ernst E. Homeopathy for childhood and adolescence ailments: systematic review of randomized clinical trials. *Mayo Clin Proc* 2007; 82: 69–75.
15. Hopayian K. The need for caution in interpreting high quality systematic reviews. *Br Med J* 2001; 323: 681–684.
16. Miller F G, Emanuel E J, Rosenstein D L, *et al*. Ethical issues concerning research in complementary and alternative medicine. *JAMA* 2004; 291: 599–604.
17. House of Lords Select Committee on Science and Technology. *Complementary and Alternative Medicine*, 6th report. Session 1999–2000. (HL123). London: Stationery Office, 2000.
18. Buchanan D R, White J D, O'Mara A M, *et al*. Research-design issues in cancer-symptom-management trials using complementary and alternative medicine: lessons from the National Cancer Institute Community Clinical Oncology Program experience. *J Clin Oncol* 2005; 23: 6682–6689.
19. Spence D S, Thompson E A, Barron S J. Homeopathic treatment for chronic disease: a 6-year, university-hospital outpatient observational study. *J Altern Comp Med* 2005; 11: 793–798.
20. Gordon S. Homeopathy's real results. *The Guardian* 2005; 29 August: 17.
21. Henderson M. Malaria risk for tourists who trust alternative practitioners. *The Times* 2006; 14 July: 34.

3

Important concepts and the approach to prescribing

Ton Nicolai

Introduction

This chapter describes the most important concepts in homeopathy and the most widely accepted modern approach to prescribing. It should be noted that there are different emphases in different countries or different schools of homeopathy. Homeopathic history is filled with innovators whose ideas, though sometimes criticised, have influenced homeopathy. On the other hand there are more traditional homeopaths who are averse to any kind of development of the method after Hahnemann's original ideas. Expectations are, however, that when there is a balance between creation and maintenance and all parties are willing to keep a dialogue between them, the discipline will remain effective and vibrant.

Health and illness/disease from a homeopathic perspective

Systemic versus local focus

Homeopathy is based on a systemic approach to organisms. The modern concepts of systems biology, complex science and psychoneuro-immunology are surprisingly consistent with the concepts of homeopathy, in which the individual patient is considered as an integrated whole, including the physical, mental, emotional, spiritual, social and other aspects of the total person. Individuals are seen as living systems that are self-healing, self-renewing, homeostatic and adaptive. Health is not merely the absence of disease/illness, but the ability of a system, e.g. cell, organism, family, society, to respond adaptively to a wide range of environmental challenges. Psychological stressors, infectious agents and injury are viewed as destabilising, energy-draining factors, whereupon internal system agents act or are ready to act to maintain constancy or homeostasis. Illness/disease is defined as a disruption of one or more parts of a biological system, a breakdown, a failure of adaptive response, which impairs the normal operation of the organism.

The definition of health and disease in homeopathy differs greatly from that in conventional western biomedicine. In biomedicine disease is considered to be a defect of biological and chemical processes of the body that need to be 'repaired' and restored to the biomedically defined norms (by drugs or surgery). Health is what is 'left over' when a person is free of all disease symptoms and the disturbed pathophysiological processes have been 'repaired'. In homeopathy the concept of disease has a far wider meaning: it also includes the person's experience of dysfunction and everything that contributed to the person's inability to resist disease. Many people may even be in a continuing state of moderate ('subclinical') disease, even though they may not have symptoms of any particular disease detectable by physical examination or routine laboratory investigations. Since the recent discovery of biomarkers, i.e. endogenous substances or parameters indicative of a disease, the subclinical stage of disease has been increasingly recognised by biomedicine.

While the terms 'illness' and 'disease' are often used interchangeably, there is some difference between them. Illness, although often used to mean disease, mostly refers to a person's experience of dysfunction, an impaired sense of well-being. Disease in biomedical terms implies the presence of objectively identifiable abnormalities in physiological or biochemical pathology of body function or structure. In this context, disease can be independent of the subjective experience of the person. In this section the word 'disease' will be used as a general term referring to both its subjective and objective aspect.

In contrast to biomedicine, which is primarily focused on defeating disease by offensive intervention, destroying infectious agents or cancer cells or blocking specific pathophysiological pathways, homeopathy is aimed at mobilising and reinforcing the healing resources, in other words restoring patients' own natural systems for fighting disease. Homeopathy has a long-term focus on creating and maintaining health and well-being and embraces a philosophy of health based on all aspects of a human being – physical, mental, emotional and spiritual – which is fully in line with the World Health Organization definition of health: 'Health is a state of complete physical, mental, and social well-being and not merely the absence of disease or infirmity' (Preamble to the

Constitution of the World Health Organization as adopted by the International Health Conference, New York, 1946).

Vital force

The vital force, also called vital energy or life principle, is considered as a causal agent permeating all living organisms and directing the life processes – the one thing that distinguishes a living organism from inanimate matter and keeps all parts of the organism in admirable, harmonious vital operations. The vitalist tradition of medicine traces its roots to Hippocrates. While according to the mechanistic world view all biological phenomena will eventually be explained in terms of the laws of physics and chemistry, proponents of vitalism postulate the existence of a non-physical entity, which Hahnemann called the vital force. Interestingly, the gap between the mechanistic and vitalist view is currently being bridged by the emerging theory of living or 'self-organising' systems, because the construct of vital force can now be understood as the organisational structure governing the mutual interplay of all parts within a living organism.[1]

This vital force, responsible for maintaining the body's state of health and balance, is constantly assaulted by destabilising factors, such as poor nutrition, toxins, vaccines, allopathic medications, pollution, radiation, emotion upheaval or constant stress. All these factors challenge us, make an impact on us, drain our energy, force us to adapt to changed circumstances and can thus have a negative impact on our health. If the organism fails to adapt, the disturbed vital force can impart to the organism the adverse sensations and induce in the organism the irregular functions that we call disease. In other words disease is primarily a dynamic/energetic disturbance, a 'mistunement' of the life principle, leading to physical abnormalities. The equation is simple: if the life force goes down, the pathology goes up. The signs of this disturbance are the signs and symptoms of the disease, which can be expressed at many different levels. It may only be a skin rash or it may go deeper and present as arthritis or chronic intestinal problems. The vital force may be weakened as time goes on and the disease moves to a deeper level, i.e. to more important organs. Since disease is primarily a dynamic/energetic disturbance, healing is also intended to take place at the very same dynamic/energetic level. It is on this energetic level that homeopathic medicines are meant to catalyse or trigger a response by the organism by administering a more powerful but similar 'disease' (= the homeopathic medicine), and the two then cancel each other out.

When after starting the homeopathic treatment patients say that they feel much better, in other words their energetic state has improved, the homeopath is certain that the patient's health will be improving as well.

Symptoms and signs, totality and holism

In English a difference is made between the terms 'signs' and 'symptoms'. A symptom is a sensation or change in health function experienced by a patient, a more subjective indication of disease, e.g. fatigue/tiredness, pain, or nausea which is conveyed to the physician during case-taking. The term 'sign' is mostly used to refer to any objective evidence or manifestation of disease or disorder, e.g. warts, a bloodshot eye, hoarseness – in other words, perceived by those around the patient and observed by the physician. It is not necessarily the nature of the sign or symptom that defines it, but who observes it.

The diverging concepts of health and disease in conventional medicine and homeopathy also lead to contrasting approaches to the appreciation of signs and symptoms. In the biomedical model only those signs and symptoms that are viewed as contributing directly to pathology or that most patients of a particular disease have in common (pathognomonic symptoms) are thought to yield more 'objective' data and are assigned value. This model emphasises the similarities among persons and situations and advocates diagnosing medical problems in a standardised way. Clearly visible symptoms lead to the choice of drugs and all other symptoms, the 'subjective' ones are ignored. By contrast, the homeopath focuses on the patient's uniqueness and differentiating qualities, e.g. how this one eczema patient differs from all other eczema patients. In fact, pathognomonic symptoms have little value in differentiating between each individual patient. In homeopathy the relevant signs and symptoms are much more numerous and include behaviour (i.e. attitudes, positions and performances indicating the mental and emotional state), indications of condition (i.e. abnormalities in feelings, functions and sensations), and appearance (i.e. objective signs, both those that are readily observable and those that involve tests or the use of diagnostic instruments). All these signs and symptoms are considered as the external manifestation of the internal (invisible) disease state of the individual patient.

The outwardly reflected picture (or 'gestalt') of a disease is more than just an exhaustive list of all symptoms, because the symptoms are only an approximation of the actual internal (invisible) state and can never be equivalent to the state of being itself. In this context, homeopaths also use the word 'totality' of signs and symptoms, which means the sum of the aggregate of the symptoms, their organic whole as an individuality. The totality needs to reflect the inner essence of the disease of the person, with the detail necessary to distinguish this individual case of disease from others of similar nature.

You as a reader could feel the state of being of Ignatia amara (*Strychnos ignatii*) if you imagine that you have invested all hopes in a love relationship with someone and suddenly the relationship is broken and your whole world collapses. You cannot talk, you find it hard to cry, but feel like crying most of the time. You frequently sigh and may have a nervous constriction of your throat, headaches, trembling and palpitations. The painful situation remains very vivid in your mind, as if it had happened yesterday.

The state of being of Stramonium (*Datura stramonium*) is completely different. It's the feeling of being alone in a dark, dangerous environment where unknown creatures are ready to pounce. The reader can easily imagine and even feel what kind of physical sensations will accompany this inner state. It is this very inner state of being that counts rather than the range of symptoms.

Similarity principle

The similarity principle introduced briefly in Chapter 1 states that a substance capable of causing a specific state of being on any level in healthy subjects (in a proving) can be used as a medicine to treat a similar state of being that is experienced by people when they are ill. Skilled homeopathic prescribing requires that the state of being that can be elicited by the chosen medicine (in a proving) should be as similar as possible to the disease state of the patient. This closest match is called the most similar or (in Latin) *simillimum*. The more detailed the understanding of the state of the patient, the more accurate the prescription. If the case is well taken, a clear pattern will emerge that can be easily recognised so that the corresponding simillimum can be identified. Other remedies may be of limited benefit, but one will be uniquely helpful.

Recognising a picture, a pattern in the totality of the patient's signs and symptoms, an image 'gestalt' that is greater than a mere collection of its symptomatic expressions, is key to prescribing the indicated medicine. The patient's mental and emotional state will often tip the scale on the selection of the homeopathic medicine. It is obvious that the most striking, unusual and characteristic symptoms will facilitate this process of pattern recognition and thus the finding of a matching medicine. Leading characteristics or predominating symptoms or modalities of a specific homeopathic medicine (called keynotes), are highly indicative of it. However, keynotes alone are not sufficient for prescribing a certain medicine; the remaining symptoms should always confirm it.

Generally, the medicine should cover the patient's pathology. This means that the pathognomonic signs of the medicine correspond to the essential pathognomonic signs of the patient. But to differentiate between the eligible medicines, the characteristic signs of the medicines need to be matched to the characteristic signs of the individual. If there are no outstanding pathognomonic signs which allow a primary selection of a medicine group, then we have to turn at once to the characteristic symptoms of the individual, i.e. the most characteristic of the individual constitution should match those of the medicine, even when there are no confirmed cures of such an ailment, and even when no other signs of this pathology ever appear in the provings or were only rarely observed.

Clinical application of theory

Trauma

In trauma an external impact is causing disturbance and the focus is usually on the external cause. In these cases, the homeopathic medicine Arnica montana is often used as the medicine of choice. Still, the best medicine will always be the one that fits the patient's particular reaction to the trauma. Arnica is indicated in cases where people have been physically traumatised, feel sore and bruised all over their body, are usually sensitive to being touched and do not want people to get too close to them because of that. If they have been affected mentally by the trauma, they often express the feeling that they are quite well even though they clearly are not. Several other medicines may be indicated in the case of trauma, including Bellis perennis, Conium maculatum, Hypericum perforatum, Symphytum officinale, Ledum palustre, among others, each with its own specific characteristics. Homeopathy is always best prescribed through an individualisation of each prescription.

Acute disease

Two cases of acute otitis media may show how patients can be different and therefore need a different homeopathic medicine.

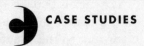

CASE STUDIES

Case 3.1   Otitis media

The first case is a child who develops an earache after being out in a cold wind. The external ear may be red, hot and swollen and the ear pain is worse at night and in a warm room. There is a yellow to green thick discharge from the nose. The child is worse in general from warmth, wants fresh air and has little or no thirst. The child is weepy and wants to sit quietly on his mother's lap, lunging towards the mother and burrowing into her bosom.

 The child needs Pulsatilla pratensis.

Case 3.2   Otitis media

The second case is a child with a severe ear pain. There is a clear nasal discharge, usually of watery consistency. The child is extremely irritable, screams and cries angrily, doesn't want to be touched or comforted, may strike out and only calms down when carried about and petted constantly. Symptoms are worse when stooping or bending over and improved by warmth or being wrapped in warm covers.

 The child requires Chamomilla (*Matricaria recutita*)

It is the whole picture that counts, a pattern in the totality of the patient's physical and emotional/behavioural signs and symptoms. The difference between a Pulsatilla and a Chamomilla picture may be quite obvious; in other cases the pictures may be subtler and harder to differentiate and require much more expertise on the part of the homeopath.

 Acute diseases are quick in onset and vanish within a comparatively short time if the defence mechanism is capable of handling the disturbance on its own, or lead to the death of the patient. The homeopathic medicine is intended to accelerate the natural processes which were set in motion by the defence mechanism. The homeopath prescribes only on the symptoms of the acute ailment and ignores the underlying symptoms belonging to the chronic state. The symptoms of the acute disease include a complete picture of the complaints, including the history of the onset, the course and evolution of the symptoms, the frequency, duration, intensity, sensation, location, extension, modalities (modifying factors that change the symptom) and concomitants of each symptom (symptoms associated in time with the main affliction) and the exact sensations experienced. In acute diseases the principal symptoms present themselves spontaneously, which means that the necessary prescribing indications may be yielded in a matter of minutes. The main question is how the patient feels compared to the situation before the acute disease.

Migraine or asthma attacks can present themselves acutely, but these acute events are in fact repeating expressions of a chronic disease (see below). Many acute diseases are actually acute exacerbations of the chronic states latent within the constitution that have been brought forth by exciting factors. In case of the latter, a more deep-seated approach is required to prevent future acute flare-ups.

Epidemic

In the case of an epidemic no one patient will show the full array of symptoms characteristic of that particular epidemic. By combining the signs and symptoms of all sufferers and analysing them together as a group, it is possible to find one or two medicines that are specific to the individual occurrence of the epidemic and that will be helpful for all the patients affected. This group of symptoms describes the 'genus epidemicus'.

Chronic disease, constitution and miasms

Chronic diseases are diseases that do not usually resolve spontaneously. They are slow and insidious in onset and gradual in progression over a number of years. The origins of chronic disease lie in genetically acquired weakness or susceptibility to pathogenic influences as well as in the various shocks the organism may receive during a lifetime (which can be accidents, viral infections, drugs or mental/emotional stresses). Chronic disease must be distinguished from diseases that are maintained by continual exposure to avoidable noxious factors (including drug toxicity and stress). These are not considered as true chronic diseases, because in these cases health returns spontaneously when the noxious factors are removed.

Constitutional prescribing

The majority of chronic diseases are related to susceptibility – whether inherited or acquired – as the predisposing and most fundamental and determining factor for disease. However, very few chronic diseases will develop without obvious factors to trigger the disease. The equation is simple: susceptibility plus precipitating factors (or disposition and exposition) equal disease. Some of the exceptions would include diseases that are purely genetically determined and apparently do not require any precipitating factors for their development. Susceptibility, or the degree to which a person is vulnerable to an outside influence, is strongly related to another term that is much used in this context – constitution. Basically, an individual's constitution is the inherent tendency to respond automatically along qualitatively predetermined characteristic individual patterns when the individual comes under stress. Constitutional differences are the differences of response patterns (coping mechanisms) to identical situations. The term 'constitution' is mostly used when referring to 'constitutional prescribing' to indicate the consideration of a wider, deeper totality than that called for by an acute episode. Constitutional prescribing is treating the patient's susceptibility by addressing the inner disturbance which gives rise to outward disease symptoms.

Miasms

Hahnemann, who found that, despite quick cures of patients' ailments, their underlying state of health often remained unaffected or even continued to worsen, called the underlying predisposition to disease a 'miasm'. In his view it could be contracted by a parasitic (microbial) agent, become internalised by suppressive treatments and then passed on to future generations. He described three miasms – psora, sycosis and syphilis – and related them to scabies, gonorrhoea and syphilis respectively. The miasm theory has evolved over time, the number of miasms has further expanded and nowadays miasms are considered as a broad classification of constitutions and their associated predisposition to disease.

Taking the case – the larger picture

Especially in the case of patients with chronic diseases, it is important for the homeopath to have insight not only into the health history and any incidental symptoms and general body functions, but also sensitivities to different temperature and weather, peculiarities about energy, sleep, appetite, digestion, perspiration, sensitivities to noise, light, odour, anxieties and fears, misconceptions of reality, sensitivities, temperament, disposition, exciting cause or trigger for the disease state, evolution of the illness over time and modifications of the constitution arising from previous diseases, accidents, vaccinations, effects of life-style, their own and their family health history. All these latter elements relate to the underlying predisposition (susceptibility) to disease or they actually are the disease in the wider homeopathic sense. Since the mental and emotional symptoms are highly relevant, a fair amount of psychological insight is required on the part of the homeopath. The history of homeopathy shows large numbers of examples of diseases which had been treated in vain with all sorts of medicines, but which only disappeared after exploring all the constitutional symptoms, choosing among these the most essential and most characteristic to find a matching medicine.

Complex chronic diseases are often made up of many inter-dependent components rather than one single constitutional factor. Although many cases have been ameliorated by just one constitutional prescription, in a more complex long-standing chronic disease it may not be so easy to pigeonhole the entire case into one single medicine. The total symptom picture is composed of symptoms contributed by each of the layers and there is not necessarily one medicine that can match the complete symptom picture. A complete cure will take a relatively long time, while the homeopath systematically peels off layer upon layer of predisposing weaknesses by carefully prescribing each remedy based on the totality of symptoms in the moment. This is why it is necessary to know in what order the layers of the case formed along the timeline so that they may be unravelled in the reverse order to which they developed.

Direction of cure

Homeopaths have developed quite detailed means of assessing progress towards health. The very beginning of improvement is usually indicated by a 'sense of greater ease, composure, mental freedom, higher spirits, and returning naturalness'. Experience has shown that there are certain rules of cure. Whereas chronic disease has the tendency to evolve from outside to inside, gradually affecting more vital organs, especially if symptoms are suppressed, e.g. by allopathic drugs, the healing process, in contrast, should go in the opposite direction. The renowned American homeopathic physician Constantine Hering formulated the rules of the direction of cure, which state that the healing process should progress as follows:

- the presenting symptoms disappear in the reverse order of their appear-ance, i.e. from the most recent condition to the oldest (Case 3.3)

 **CASE STUDY**

Case 3.3 A common story of a child developing eczema

After treatment with a topical hydrocortisone cream the eczema quickly disappears. But a few months later the child gets a nasty attack of hayfever. At first the antihistamines work, but each summer the symptoms get worse and the doses higher. After a course of desensitising injections there is no sign of the hayfever, but she seems generally low in energy and gets a few attacks of wheezing bronchitis that develops into chronic asthma for which a salbutamol inhaler is prescribed. The common interpretation is that the eczema and hayfever are apparently 'cured', but now there is a new problem, namely asthma. From the homeopathic perspective the disease expression is not cured but has only been shifted and pushed to a deeper level, from the superficial skin to the lungs. The disease has in fact progressed. The correct homeopathic treatment will relieve the asthma, but the previously suppressed eczema may recur in a mild form again. This too will be cured in time, as the patient continues her homeopathic treatment.

- improvement occurs from centre to circumference with the more vital organs and systems first, then the less vital ones, from within outwards, and from the upper body parts downward to the lower body parts.

These rules guide homeopaths to whether the homeopathic treatment course is correct and is following the right direction towards cure. This means that the disease symptoms that have appeared last should be the first to respond to a correctly chosen homeopathic medicine, whereas symptoms that have been present for a longer time and are in more superficial organs will respond later. Only once the more recent disease symptoms have been cured can the older and more chronic problems be resolved. Homeopaths may reconsider their prescription if the healing process does not follow this direction.

Environmental factors such as a workload that cannot be changed, an unhealthy diet or toxic environment or people around the patient with negative behaviour that the patient cannot change can pose serious obstacles to a cure. A significant emphasis should therefore be made on paying attention to the patient's lifestyle, diet, environment, general hygiene, good diet and a sensible balance between work, exercise and rest.

The homeopathic consultation

Interview and diagnosis (see also Chapter 6)

A conventional medical diagnosis is based on manifest signs and symptoms plus the underlying proximate physical pathology and classifies diseases as actual entities (the so-called nosological way of categorising) whereby only those symptoms viewed as contributing directly to pathology are assigned value and the other symptoms are ignored. The disease is considered to be explained when this pathology has been diagnosed. Homeopathic physicians also make a conventional diagnosis to determine the location and the pathological changes involved, to judge the seriousness of the disease and the prognosis for the future. However, medical diagnosis alone will not provide the full nature of disease with its multifaceted, holistic dimensions. Homeopaths consider the conventional diagnosis, which is basically only a name for a perceived pathologic phenomenon, as just a sign of the disease, because in homeopathy the disease has a far wider meaning. In fact, the conventional medical

 **CASE STUDY**

Case 3.4   Pain
A 49-year-old woman has had terrible pains in the nape of the neck, left thorax and arm for several years. The thorax has highly tender spots. Her right knee is often swollen, hot and painful so that she can hardly walk. She is totally worn out, oversensitive, irritated at trifles, restless, sleepless and sensitive to bright light. She was treated at a rehabilitation centre and some cervical nerves were burnt, but with hardly any improvement. She has been working as a geriatric helper for more than 30 years and was declared unfit to work 3 years ago. She has been helping people all her life, working her fingers to the bone. The conventional diagnosis, i.e. brachialgia (pain in the arm), overwork, fibromyalgia, Tietze's syndrome, recurrent arthritis, is totally inadequate to describe the state the patient is in. The patient's life theme 'going on to the bitter end without complaining' belongs to the plant family of the Rutaceae. Her craving for coffee confirmed the choice of *Angostura vera*, a species of the Rutaceae family. This medicine in 30K and later on 200K has reduced her pains to a large extent: she regained her energy, became much more relaxed and she slept like a log as she used to do. (For an explanation of Korsakovian (K) potencies, see Chapter 10.)

Case 3.5 Premenstrual syndrome
A 33-year-old slender woman has been suffering from premenstrual syndrome for 3 years, since her pregnancy. A whole week prior to her menses she is aggressive and even smashes things on the floor. She is very open, highly sensitive, easily offended and loves meeting people and reading. She feels responsible for her parents, brothers, husband and children; in fact, since her childhood she has always thought it was her duty to make everyone happy. She has a strong aversion to fish. The whole image has strong phosphor-like elements, but because of her sense of duty (which is suggestive of a Kali compound) eventually the medicine Kali phosphoricum was prescribed. After a few months her premenstrual anger completely disappeared and for the first time in her adult life she even gained 3 kg without having changed her food habits or activities.

diagnosis may be of minor importance in prescribing the homeopathic medicine. Cases 3.4 and 3.5 provide examples from practice.

These examples show that homeopathic diagnosis includes information not only about the patient's actual complaint and conventional diagnosis, but, especially in chronic disease, also about the patient's constitution, emotional and mental make-up and the way the patient responds to physical, emotional and mental influences and stress in his/her life. A homeopathic diagnosis (and treatment) is even possible if there is no conventional diagnosis, as in the case of functional somatic symptoms or subclinical disorders, where there is an abnormality in the physical functioning of the body, although it is not detectable by physical examination or routine laboratory investigations.

It is of the essence – and Hahnemann emphasised this again and again – that homeopaths need to be open-minded, unbiased observers who are sincerely interested in their patients. A good interview needs great sensitivity and receptivity to the patient, and careful and respectful observation, not interpretation, not only because judgements narrow the homeopath's perception of the patient but also because only an unprejudiced, non-judgemental and understanding attitude will open up the patient. It is a matter of perceiving the patient's experience in his/her own context. It is not about acquiring as much data as possible but rather eliciting a living image of the patient's state of being. This looks easier than it is, but it requires the homeopath to have a good insight into his/her own possible bias and prejudices. The feelings elicited in the homeopath by the patient can also be helpful in uncovering the deeper emotional issues involved and thus improve prescribing.

Information on homeopathic medicines

Information on the homeopathic medicines can be found in the materia medica, which is a compilation of proving symptoms, toxicological data and clinical experience of the homeopathic medicines used (see Chapters 4 and 5). It also deals with the origin, composition and properties of the medicines and the special techniques associated with their preparation (see Chapter 10).

The quantity of information available for homeopathic medicines varies widely. Usually a distinction is made between polychrests and 'small remedies' but in reality there is more of a continuum of information without sharp discontinuities between well-known and lesser-known remedies: polychrests are homeopathic medicines of which a wide range of symptoms is known whereas small remedies are just lesser-known medicines. The latter are often poorly described, because they had had an inadequate proving or are only known from limited toxicological symptoms.

One of the more recent developments in homeopathy has been the transition from considering remedies as stand-alone entities to seeing them as members of medicine families that share common characteristics (see Chapter 13). Computer software has for the first time made it possible to study remedies in a more systematic way. Nowadays homeopaths think of medicines as members of a group of similar substances, such as the Kali and Natrum salts, the halogens, the venom of snakes, the spiders, the plant families of the Apiaceae, Lamiaceae or Ranunculaceae. The medicines in each family have many similarities, yet each retains its unique characteristic symptoms that set it apart within the family. The homeopath's accuracy in prescribing plant medicines can be highly refined by understanding plants in taxonomic groups (families – genera – species). In the case of minerals, the use of the periodic table of elements as an organising principle has been invaluable. Single elements on the periodic table, that are either unproved or barely proved, have been used successfully, based on careful extrapolation of the known characteristics of similar substances. Classification makes differential diagnoses clearer and simpler and makes the growing number of medicines easier to handle, understand and remember. It can help the homeopath organise his/her thinking and understand the patient and the materia medica better and frequently can point the homeopath to a better-fitting prescription. This development also means that the study of mineralogy, botany and zoology becomes a more intrinsic part of homeopathic training.

Posology

The principle of the minimum dose states that the smallest amount of medicine should be given to the patient which still has the desired effect.

This logic is certainly not unique to homeopathy, because it is only prudent to use the smallest dose necessary to have the desired result. It is assumed that the choice of the dose depends on several factors, such as the susceptibility of the patient, the seat of the disease, the nature and intensity of the disease, the stage and duration of the disease as well as the previous treatment of the disease.

Homeopaths have the experience that the more similar the medicine, the more clearly the totality of symptoms of the patient take on the peculiar and characteristic form of the medicine, the greater the susceptibility to that remedy, and the smaller the dose that is needed to alter health. It is widely believed that disease states characterised by diminished vital action or structural pathology require lower potencies, whereas disease states characterised by increased vital action or functional pathology usually respond better to high potencies. Hypersensitive people are mostly given low potencies. For a full explanation of how medicines are potentised, see Chapter 10.

From homeopathy's inception, the single-medicine prescription has been the ideal to pursue. Hahnemann never dropped his official proscription against the use of more than one medicine at a time. Still, the use of more than one medicine at a time has always been the subject of much debate in homeopathic circles. Some homeopaths prescribe two or more medicines simultaneously, either in alternation with each other or as a combined formula (polypharmacy or pluralism). Also proponents of polypharmacy refer to Hahnemann, whose own case records show that he did experiment with giving two medicines at a time.

Proponents of administering one single medicine at a time argue that if a cure is possible with one single medicine, why should you settle for two or more medicines given simultaneously? In addition, since any individual can only be in one single state at any given time, can there be more than one corresponding most similar medicine totality? Judging the effects of a single medicine requires great awareness: the interactions of two or more would make the task extremely complex. Obviously, if more than one therapeutic agent (medicinal or otherwise) at one time is prescribed there are too many variables, and the homeopath cannot learn in a precise and systematic way. Many homeopaths early on in their practice have been in the situation of feeling that two or more medicines seem equally indicated for a particular case, whereas later on they realised that this resulted from not having grasped the true nature of the core problem underlying the patient's illness, or the true nature of the medicine in the materia medica which would be curative. Hahnemann could very well have had the very same experience. Most probably the ideal of one medicine at one time could not always be attained because the range of medicines was rather limited compared to the present day.

Also the question of a single unique dose or repeated doses has been subject to much discussion. Hahnemann's understanding of the concept of the single dose changed over time, and he moved from advocating long intervals (allowing the dose to exhaust itself) to more frequent doses. There were five editions of the *Organon* between 1810 and 1833. An unfinished sixth edition was discovered after Hahnemann's death in 1843 but it was not published until 1921.[2] In this edition he suggested that cure can be hastened if one repeats the dose in medicinal solution with modification of potency each time by succussion (see Chapter 10). In addition, he suggested that the degree of potency should deviate somewhat from the previous and subsequent ones, in order to avoid the development of accessory symptoms. Nevertheless many homeopaths still advocate long intervals following the advice of influential teachers such as the American homeopath James Tyler Kent (1848–1916) who, due to the delay in publication of the sixth edition of the *Organon*, was unaware of Hahnemann's more recent insights.[3]

Much about the different dosage methods is still unclear and needs further investigation, especially if homeopathy is to develop as a science. Hahnemann himself was a great experimenter, changing his ideas as he developed new insights. Had he lived longer, the *Organon* may have gone through even more editions as Hahnemann continued to refine his methodology until the end of his life.

Influence of allopathic medicine

The systemic approach of homeopathy undoubtedly requires considerable time and investment in case-taking as well as a fair amount of homeopathic and psychological understanding. That is why large numbers of doctors are dissuaded from using homeopathy in their practices. They see the systemic approach as being so difficult and requiring such an enormous investment of time. For this reason and because they are trained in conventional (allopathic) medicine, which involves prescribing standard medicines to a given pathological condition, they have always sought for ways to simplify homeopathy. This has led to the current situation where a continuum exists between homeopathy in its most individualised form and prescribing homeopathic medicines based on a conventional diagnosis *per se*. Most differences between the various approaches can be explained by the extent to which individual patient characteristics are taken into account.

Abridged method of prescribing

In formula homeopathy – also called 'clinical homeopathy' or 'abridged method' – the choice of the medicine is based on the conventional diagnosis (e.g. vertigo, otitis, tonsillitis) or a prominent and easily recognisable symptom. A few possible homeopathic medicines are considered, each with some characteristic modalities or general symptoms. It implies ready knowledge of a simplified materia medica and direct applicability in a busy day-to-day practice for a defined and limited number of targeted, mainly acute conditions. There are a relatively small number of medicines to choose from (the polychrests) so that most practitioners do not need a repertory. They might have a working knowledge of 100 or so medicines and use a unified posology (e.g. giving a dose of Belladonna 5c 3 times a day for 5 days) and low potencies. This approach naturally appeals to newcomers to homeopathy (see also Chapter 10).

Polypharmacy

Polypharmacy or pluralism allows the prescription of two or more medicines concurrently, either in alternation or in sequence related to different aspects or levels of the clinical picture. Also, from this perspective different concurrent diseases (nosological categories) may need different medicines or different medicines are believed to have an additional effect. An additional medicine can be chosen because it is directed at the specific diathesis or is expected to have a specific immunomodulating or 'drainage' effect. Drainage is believed to be involved in helping to eliminate toxic accumulation and to stimulate the proper function of organs in order to improve the patient's overall health. These toxins in the body may be considered to be the cause of many different symptoms and diseases. Polypharmacy may be individualised, whereby several remedies are given concurrently or alternately according to indications in each individual case. According to this approach practitioners may prescribe 2–3 (or more) medicines daily in 7–9c to drain toxins and a 15–30c 'constitutional' medicine once a week for long periods of time. This approach undoubtedly helps to simplify the complex business of choosing homeopathic medicines in chronic disease.

Complex homeopathy

Even closer to western allopathic medicine is complex homeopathy, in which multi-ingredient preparations – fixed combinations of homeopathic remedies – are prescribed according to a conventional diagnosis. These preparations are composed of medicines whose materia medica indicates that they should be of some benefit for a specific clinical problem and are based on the clinical experiences of homeopathic practitioners. Each combination is composed so as to induce the individual active agents to target the corresponding illness with cumulative and/or synergistic force. While the medicines chosen by a particular company may be correlated to a certain extent with a particular condition, the correlation will usually be an arbitrary one.

From the perspective of experienced homeopathic doctors these medicines are less precisely targeted than individualised (systemic) homeopathy. Still, many practitioners have used complexes and several controlled trials have shown the efficacy of homeopathic complexes for a number of acute conditions. Many people use complexes to self-treat common conditions and may become familiar with homeopathy in the first instance through such products (see also Chapter 10).

Isopathy and tautopathy

Isopathy usually refers to the prescription of medicines made from the supposed causative agents or products of a disease to a patient suffering that same disease (see Chapter 10). It is a concept different from homeopathy: the substances used in isopathy – isodes – were never proven on healthy human subjects and are given based on the identical (rather than the similar) nature of disease and isode. Isodes may be used to treat residual problems following an illness. This method has been expanded to include prescribing potencies of substances to which a patient is hypersensitive or allergic, such as wheat, nuts, milk, animal dander or pollen. A variety of isopathy is tautopathy. If patients report that they have 'never been well since' taking a certain drug, receiving a vaccination or swallowing a poisonous chemical, the prescription of the substance in a potentised form can easily solve the problem. Isopathy and tautopathy are usefully employed as an adjunct to carefully selected homeopathic medicines covering the patient's presenting symptomatology.

Further reading

Rottler G. Constitution and chronic diseases – the value of constitutional symptoms as seen by G.H.G. Jahr. http://www.curantur.de/English/Articles/Constitution/constitution.html (accessed 25 September 2006).

Sananes R (1999) *Unicisme, Pluralisme, Complexisme; Les Trois Dimensions de l'Homéopathie*. Sainte Barbe, France: Editions Lehning.

Swayne J (1998) *Homeopathic Method – Implications for Clinical Practice and Medical Science*. Edinburgh: Churchill Livingstone.

Vithoulkas G (1980) *The Science of Homeopathy*. New York: Grove Press.

Watson I (1991) *A Guide to the Methodologies of Homoeopathy*. Kendal, Cumbria: Cutting Edge Publications.

Whitmont EC (1980) *Psyche and Substance: Essays on Homeopathy in the Light of Jungian Psychology*. Berkeley, CA: North Atlantic Books.

References

1. Kurz C. *Imagine Homeopathy – A Book of Experiments, Images, and Metaphors*. Stuttgart, Germany: Georg Thieme Verlag, 2005.
2. Hahnemann S. *Organon of the Medical Art*. Edited and annotated by W Brewster O'Reilly. Redmond, WA: Birdcage Books, 1996.
3. Kent J T. *Lectures on Homeopathic Philosophy*, 4th edn. Philadelphia, PA: Boericke and Tafel, 1932.

4

Homeopathic drug provings

David Riley

Introduction

Homeopathic medicines are prescribed for patients by integrating the symptoms patients experience with the symptom picture of the medications available in a materia medica (see Chapter 5). This chapter concentrates on the proving, the main method of obtaining the symptom picture.

The historical bases of the prescribing information available for homeopathic medications are threefold:

1. homeopathic drug provings
2. toxicological profile (when a substance such as Arsenic is toxic in mother tincture but used therapeutically when diluted and prepared homeopathically)
3. clinical usage (Arsenic, for example, has a known toxicological profile and a homeopathic drug proving. As it has been used therapeutically for the past 200 years other symptoms have emerged clinically that are associated with the successful use of this homeopathic medication.).

A homeopathic drug proving is a clinical trial designed to clarify the symptom picture associated with a homeopathic medication. In a homeopathic drug proving a homeopathic medication is given to subjects who note their reactions to the homeopathic medication in personal diaries or journals for a defined period of time. The symptom picture that emerges from a homeopathic drug proving is the compilation of the symptoms recorded by individual subjects. This in turn provides useful clinical information for the treatment of individuals experiencing a pattern of symptoms similar to those generated during the homeopathic drug proving.

Homeopathic drug provings are similar to a phase I trial as outlined in the US Code of Federal Regulations (CFR) and by the European Community (EC). Unlike a phase I trial, the emphasis is on potentially useful symptoms experienced by the subjects rather than potential toxicity. Homeopathic drug provings, in conjunction with clinical practice and relevant toxicological data, provide the necessary information for physicians to treat patients successfully. In 1992 we began to explore the history of homeopathic research in general and homeopathic drug provings in particular with the goal of conducting homeopathic drug provings using contemporary scientific methodology. Data collection was carried out using a diary/journal format, consistent with the historical methodology, yet we also used a double-blind, placebo-controlled format with a placebo run-in phase.

Provings and the *Organon*

The *Organon* of Hahnemann[1] outlines the research methods followed by Samuel Hahnemann in the early 1800s with many specific and useful suggestions noted under the following numbered sections (known as 'aphorisms' and signified by the symbol §):

§ 106

The whole pathogenetic effects of medicines must be known; that is, all the morbid symptoms and alterations in health that each of them is specially capable of developing in the healthy individual must first have been observed as far as possible before we can hope to be able to find among them, and to select, suitable homeopathic remedies for most natural diseases.

§ 107

If, in order to ascertain this, medicines be given to *sick* persons, only, even though they be administered singly and alone, then little or nothing precise is seen of their true effects, as those peculiar alterations of the health to be expected from the medicine are mixed up with the symptoms of the disease and can seldom be distinctly observed.

§ 108

There is, therefore, no other possible way in which the peculiar effects of medicines on the health of individuals can be accurately ascertained – there is no sure, no more natural way of accomplishing this object, than to administer the several medicines experimentally, in moderate doses, to *healthy* persons, in order to ascertain what changes, symptoms and signs of their influence each individually produces on the health of the body and of the mind; that is to say, what disease elements they are able and tend to produce, since, as has been demonstrated (§§ 24–27), all the curative power of medicines lies in this power they possess of changing the state of man's health, and is revealed by observation of the latter.

§ 110

I saw, moreover, that the morbid lesions which previous authors had observed to result from medicinal substances when taken into the stomach of healthy persons, either in large doses by mistake or in order to produce death in themselves or others, or under other circumstances, accorded very much with my own observations when experimenting with the same substances on myself and other healthy individuals ... None of these observers ever dreamed that the symptoms they recorded merely as proofs of the noxious and poisonous character of these substances were sure revelations of the power of these drugs to extinguish curatively similar symptoms occurring in natural diseases, that their pathogenetic phenomena were intimations of their homeopathic curative action, and that the only possible way to ascertain their medicinal powers is to observe those changes of health medicines are capable of producing in the healthy organism; for the pure, peculiar powers of medicines available for the cure of disease are to be learned neither by any ingenious *a priori* speculations, nor by the smell, taste or appearance of the drugs, nor by their chemical analysis, nor yet by the employment of several of them at one time in a mixture in diseases; it was never suspected that the history of medicinal diseases would one day furnish the first rudiments of the true, pure Materia medica.

Protocols for provings

Conventional medications are customarily prescribed on general symptoms associated with a person's response to an illness. The central and often unstated thesis of conventional medicine and conventional medical research is that group characteristics are more important than an individual patient's reaction. In homeopathy, the symptoms of the individual are of the utmost importance. Can conventional research methodology be applied to homeopathic drug provings? A research model with potential relevance for clinical trials in homeopathy is that of single case studies outlined by Kiene and Von Schön-Angerer.[2] In essence, homeopathic research into the symptoms picture of an individual medication as experienced in an individual subject is a collection of individual responses fitting into a pattern. Recognizing the individual symptoms of a patient and matching them with the symptom pattern associated with the homeopathic medication is the key to the successful practice of homeopathy.

In the more than 70 homeopathic drug provings I have conducted (many of which have been published[3–6]) at the Integrative Medicine Institute with Aimee Zagon we have chosen to follow conventional clinical research guidelines for human subjects according to the Helsinki Accord as well as CFR and EC guidelines for good clinical practice (GCP). We have used a dilution of a single homeopathic medication in our homeopathic drug provings that have ranged from 12c to 30c where there is little or no toxicological risk due to the extremely low concentration of the homeopathic medication. The concentration of a 12c remedy, for example, is 1×10^{-24}, so low that it is unmeasurable with analytic methods available today.

We have gained experience in this research method using a consistent but flexible research protocol, attempting to increase the scientific rigor and maintaining the usefulness to the homeopathic practitioner. We have introduced a placebo run-in phase and symptom selection criteria for symptom extraction from the prover journals in a homeopathic drug proving and have developed a general methodological outline for what we think constitutes a high-quality drug proving in conjunction with others interested in this area of clinical research. At this point we advocate using a cross-over design where all subjects receive verum at some point during the homeopathic drug proving and all subjects receive placebo at some point during the homeopathic drug proving.

Recording symptoms

The process by which the symptoms experienced by subjects in a homeopathic drug proving are included in the symptom picture from a homeopathic drug proving has not previously been systematically tested before we began doing this, either prospectively or retrospectively. Further complicating the process is that there is no one standard for symptom selection. Symptom selection remains one of the most challenging parts of a homeopathic drug proving and as this becomes standardised and validated it will increase the reproducibility of this qualitative research methodology. It is dependent on a careful review of the symptoms each subject experienced during a proving based on an understanding of that specific person. Some homeopaths conducting homeopathic drug provings have approached the symptom selection process by proposing general criteria for including symptoms experienced during a homeopathic drug proving with an admonition of 'when in doubt, leave it out'. The task of symptom selection in a homeopathic drug proving is further complicated by the observation that some symptoms from provings in the 1800s initially appeared unimportant but were later clinically verified and are now medication keynotes. Other symptoms experienced by many subjects are general in nature and do not assist in the individualisation process of a homeopathic prescription.

Each symptom in our provings is entered as a record in a customised computer database as well as being available in the journal that each subject keeps while participating in the homeopathic drug proving. The 'symptom selection criteria' field is one of 19 fields in the database record we have created. Any field in the record can be sorted, from demographic information, the date and timing of an individual symptom, medication potency, to the symptom selection criteria. (For a full explanation of potency, see Chapter 10.) This allows for a comprehensive evaluation of the data within a proving, and for a comparison of data across provings. We have integrated the following symptom selection criteria into our database and the final report from a homeopathic drug proving:

1. modalities (something that makes a symptom better or worse)
2. concomitants (something occurring in conjunction with a symptom)
3. timing of the symptom (periodicity, specificity of timing)
4. localisation (sides, extension)
5. unique descriptions of a symptom (descriptive adjectives)
6. intensity of the symptom
7. a symptom is new or has not been experienced in the past 12 months
8. a symptom occurred after taking the medication on at least two occasions during the homeopathic drug proving
9. a symptom experienced when the proving started which disappeared or is significantly ameliorated after the administration of the proving medication is classified as a cured symptom
10. a symptom was experienced in more than one prover.

The symptom selection criteria outlined above evolved to extract the symptoms entered by the subjects in their journals during a homeopathic drug proving in a systematic fashion and be able to evaluate their usefulness retrospectively. It is based on practical experience and subject to modification and further testing as dictated by experience. Consistent methodology in the research protocol used in conducting a homeopathic drug proving is important in assuring a systematic commitment to reliable results. The following protocol guidelines outline a general framework for a protocol for conducting a homeopathic drug proving and cover most of the categories of information which should be included or considered before beginning a homeopathic drug proving.

The names and addresses of all persons who are responsible for carrying out the homeopathic drug proving should be identified. We further suggest that the proving director should have at least 5 years' experience in homeopathy and 2 years' experience in homeopathic drug provings and that proving supervisors be experienced homeopaths. Experience in clinical trials and clinical research is also highly desirable.

Objectives of proving

Each proving protocol should define the objective of the homeopathic drug proving. The homeopathic drug proving should contain information concerning the duration of the homeopathic drug proving, the location and time of year of the provings and information regarding the duration of the proving for an individual prover. The design section should consider using the following descriptive terms about the proving protocol: monocentre/multicentre, prospective/ retrospective, randomised/non-randomised/stratified, open/single-blind/double-blind, controlled (placebo, active medication)/non-controlled, parallel/cross-over, run-in phase/preobservation period, and total number of subjects.

Number of subjects

The number of subjects for the homeopathic drug proving should be stated. In multicentre homeopathic drug provings the total number of subjects, the planned number of participating centres and the intended number of subjects per centre should be stated. It is important to define the inclusion/exclusion criteria for subjects who are to be included (or excluded) in the homeopathic drug proving. They should be as specific as possible and contain information that would allow others to conduct a similar proving with similar criteria.

Study medication

The study medication should be clearly defined. This is of critical importance given the contemporary difficulties we have regarding clear understanding of even something as basic as the starting material in many of the provings from the 19th century. This section should also include information concerning the name (and trade name) of the medication, starting material and method of preparation, the manufacturer of study medication, lot numbers, potency, manner of administration and dosage, and stability where applicable of starting material and study medication. Any special storage conditions or instructions should also be mentioned.

Observations

All phases of the homeopathic drug proving (preobservation phase or run-in phase, beginning of the drug proving or placebo phase) and the planned examinations (check-ups, final examination, follow-up) should be described in the protocol. A sample timeline might look like that shown in Figure 4.1.

Drop-outs

Any reason requiring the withdrawal of an individual subject from a homeopathic drug proving (e.g. if the subject drops out) or the premature termination of the homeopathic drug proving at any time for medical and/or organisational reasons should be clearly described. Any adverse events should also be documented and reported to the proving director.

Symptom selection

The symptom selection criteria (an example is mentioned earlier in this chapter) should be stated in advance and documented in the final report from the homeopathic drug proving. The procedures used for data extraction and analysis of the symptoms, e.g. qualitative or quantitative methods, and preparation of the final report should be described.[7]

Legal issues

All legal provisions, requirements and regulations that might affect the homeopathic drug proving should be discussed before the beginning of the proving. Each subject or potential subject should be informed by the investigator about homeopathic drug provings in a comprehensible and clear manner in advance; this includes the fact that subjects may

Proving timeline and events	Week 1	Week 2	Week 3	Week 4	Week 5	Week 6	Week 7–9
Initial interview	✖						
Inclusion/exclusion criteria reviewed	✖	✖	✖	✖	✖	✖	
Subject training	✖						
I: Pre-proving observation	✖	✖					
Daily subject journal entries	✖	✖	✖	✖	✖	✖	
Ongoing weekly evaluations	✖	✖	✖	✖	✖	✖	✖
II: Medical/placebo (cross-over design)			✖		✖		
III: Medication/placebo (cross-over design)			✖		✖		
Post-proving observation							✖
Data evaluation and final report							✖

Figure 4.1 Sample proving timeline.

experience symptoms while participating in a homeopathic drug proving. Before participating in a homeopathic drug proving each subject must provide written informed consent. Prior to initiation of the homeopathic drug proving, the protocol, a blank copy of a subject's diary and the informed consent form should be submitted to the appropriate committee for approval if applicable.

Recording of data

All data recorded should be treated in strict confidence according to GCP guidelines for clinical research. During documentation and analysis of the homeopathic drug proving the subjects should only be identified by their identification number. A homeopathic drug proving sponsored as a research trial with US Institutional Review Board or ethics commission approval should have insurance for the subjects. If there is no sponsor, the proving director bears the responsibility for any adverse events that require medical evaluation and treatment.

Proving procedure

In the provings we have conducted each prospective subject was required to maintain a journal for 1–2 weeks prior to taking the homeopathic medication, recording the rhythm of his/her daily life. After this period of time, the journal was reviewed to assess the quality and completeness of the journal prior to taking the homeopathic medication or placebo. Failure to complete the intake documents or to maintain an adequate journal were possible reasons for exclusion from the drug proving. Once the baseline data collection phase was completed the homeopathic medication was given to the subject.

Beginning with the first dose of the first medication and continuing for 4–5 weeks, subjects were required to note any symptoms that they were experiencing. Journal entries were made daily, noting the occurrence or absence of symptoms. Each subject was contacted daily and extended weekly visits were done to enter data from the subject's journal into the database. At the conclusion journals were reviewed during an extensive exit interview for clarification of specific details and modalities associated with the recorded symptoms in the journals.

All of the subjects for the homeopathic drug provings we have conducted were recruited by advertisement. Prior to attending a homeopathic drug proving orientation session, each prospective subject was evaluated according to the inclusion and exclusion criteria for that specific homeopathic drug proving. Each subject had to be in a general state of good health for that person and both the proving director and the potential subject had to concur that the subject was in a state of good health. A brief history and physical examination were done to corroborate this. The subject agreed in advance to comply fully with instructions for keeping the journal and agreed not to engage in any elective medical treatments or undergo any major life changes (moving, getting married or divorced) during the homeopathic drug proving. Subjects were excluded if they had current or ongoing medical treatment or were pregnant or nursing. They were required to complete the journal during the preproving observation period.

The medication in our homeopathic drug provings was produced by a well-known homeopathic manufacturing facility in order to ensure compliance with the *Homeopathic Pharmacopoeia of the United States* (HPUS)[8] production guidelines prior to use in a homeopathic drug proving. A certificate of analysis and batch number were on file with the manufacturer. Each vial of homeopathic medication was coded with letters and numbers created by the manufacturer. All of the subjects were educated on the nature of homeopathy and informed that they might experience symptoms following the administration of the homeopathic medication. They were told that the symptoms could be experienced on a mental, emotional or physical level and that these symptoms might adversely affect their daily life. During the proving each subject was monitored for evidence of adverse effects associated with taking the homeopathic medication. In more than 70 homeopathic drug provings we have yet to have a subject withdraw because of adverse events.

When the provings were finished all of the symptoms experienced by each patient were reviewed again individually with the patients at an exit interview. Symptoms were then sorted and a final report was created organising the data according to the format found in a homeopathic repertory, by symptoms and by subjects. In addition a materia medica for each homeopathic drug proving was also created. The information from some of the provings has been published in medical journals; all of the information from most of these homeopathic drug provings has been included in two computer-based repertory programs, MacRepertory and Radar. Ideally the symptom picture developed in these homeopathic drug provings and the symptom selection criteria used to extract symptoms will link the proving with the clinical practice, providing verification of the proving and the symptom selection criteria used in the proving. The final arbiter on the validity of any symptom experienced in any proving remains the clinical responses of patients treated with the medication.

Conclusion

Clinical usage of homeopathic medications remains the cornerstone of clinical verification. This has historically been done over time in the individual practices of homeopathic practitioners and has informally worked its way into the materia medicas and repertories used by almost all practicing homeopaths. Homeopaths have used the homeopathic symptom picture that emerges from homeopathic drug provings, toxicology information (when available) and the clinical practice of other homeopaths to identify specific symptoms or therapeutic applications for each homeopathic medication. In addition to the informal methods that have been used in the past, clinical trials from case series to outcome studies to practice-based data collection networks have been used for specific remedies. And of course randomised controlled trials have been conducted to evaluate specific claims but are generally limited to specific indications rather than the homeopathic symptom picture, which is often much more complex. It is challenging to establish a formal process linking the homeopathic drug provings to the clinical practice of homeopathy.

References

1. Hahnemann C S. *Organon of the Rational Art of Healing*. Dresden: Arnold, 1810.
2. Kiene H, Von Schön-Angerer T. Single-case causality assessment as a basis for clinical judgement. *Altern Ther Health Med* 1998; 4: 41–47.
3. Riley D S. A proving of *Fumaria officinalis*. *Homoeopathic Links* 1994; 7: 18–20.
4. Riley D S. Proving report – *Veronica officinalis*. *Br Homoeopath J* 1995; 84: 144–148
5. Riley D S. Nicotinamide adenine dinucleotide (NAD): a proving. *J Am Inst Homeopathy* 1994; 87: 74–78.
6. Riley D, Zagon A. Clinical homeopathic use of RNA: evidence from two provings. *Homeopathy* 2005; 94: 33–36.
7. Riley D S. Extracting symptoms from homoeopathic drug provings. *Br Homoeopath J* 1997; 86: 225–228.
8. *Homeopathic Pharmacopoeia of the United States*. Accessed online at: www.hpus.com.

5

The homeopathic materia medica

David Lilley

Introduction

This chapter discusses the importance of the homoeopathic materia medica of which provings (see Chapter 4) provide the essential framework. The materia medica is an unparalleled treasure trove of accumulated and systematically documented facts regarding homeopathic remedies, their nature and their interaction with the human constitution. It is a unique body of therapeutic knowledge that constitutes the very heart of homeopathic theory and practice.

As well as being an indispensable bank of information, giving the therapeutic repertoire of remedies, the materia medica also provides a rich and profound source of insight into the development of the structures of the ego personality with its distorted perspective of objective reality, its dysfunctional thinking and feeling, and pictures the associated and resulting psychosomatic and pathological states. Its study is an endless, lifetime's occupation, which never palls, and is infinitely rewarding and empowering. Its contemplation provides a medical education far broader and deeper than any provided by conventional academies. It is majestic, boundless and cosmic in its scope, yet embraces every nuance of human thought and behaviour, and the finest detail of functional and physical change. Students of the materia medica not only enlarge and expand their knowledge of human nature and disease, but also gain invaluable insight into their own inner state. A process of self-revelation is embarked upon, which, through the deepest immersion in the subject, facilitates a process of self-healing and individuation.

History

In 1790, Samuel Hahnemann performed a now famous experiment, which was to prove of critical significance to medical science and the first step towards his later elaboration of the fundamental principle on which homeopathy is based: the law of similars. He was translating into German a book entitled *A Treatise on Materia Medica* written by the highly respected Scottish physician, William Cullen, and published in 1789.[1] Cullen was considered an authority on the pharmacology of medicinal substances. In his annotations to the translation, Hahnemann expressed his scepticism of the author's conclusions regarding the mode of action of Cinchona, or Peruvian bark, in the cure of intermittent fever (malaria). The distinguished physician's conclusion was that the therapeutic success of the remedy rested upon its gastric tonic powers. Doubting this, Hahnemann decided that the only scientific way to determine the drug's action was to test it on himself.[2, 3] 'I took for several days, by way of experiment, twice a day, four drachms of good China [cinchona]'. He describes the nature of the symptoms: 'these were all the symptoms usually associated with intermittent fever; all made their appearance' and noted 'the symptoms lasted from two to three hours every time and recurred when I repeated the dose and not otherwise. I discontinued the medicine and I was once more in good health.' In a subsequent annotation, he momentously writes: 'Peruvian (cinchona) bark, which is used as a remedy for intermittent fever, acts because it can produce symptoms similar to those of inter-mittent fever in healthy people'. In these few words he postulated an eternal wisdom.

This was the first *proving* (homeopathic pathogenetic trial) of a medicine on a healthy person, and the first step towards the compilation of the materia medica. Modern proving procedures are described in Chapter 4.

At first, Hahnemann collected herbs from the hedgerows, fields, and surrounding hills and mountains. From these he prepared alcoholic tinctures, and with characteristic thoroughness and meticulous attention to detail he tested them on himself, carefully noting all the symptoms produced. Finally, he gathered together an enthusiastic band of medical colleagues, family and friends to collaborate with him in the proving of new remedies. Under his strict supervision, this group of healthy volun-teers subjected themselves to the effects of various substances drawn from the botanical, zoological and mineral kingdoms. The proving procedures that he laid down were exacting and rigorous, ensuring the accuracy of the observed phenomena. Even the diet and habits of the participant had to conform to Hahnemann's stringent requirements, lest any extraneous factor should falsify the outcome. Each *prover* was required to submit a detailed account of the doses taken, symptoms experienced and any modifying influences (*modalities*) discerned, e.g. time, temperature, weather, menstrual cycle, movement, mental exertion. Hahnemann would finally go through the account with them: 'asking questions so as to complete from their recollections that which requires to be more explicit'. All mental and physical symptoms and signs, which could confidently be attributed to drug effect, were carefully noted and systematically assembled to form a specific drug picture.

In those early years, tinctures and low potencies (see Chapter 10) were frequently used and certain intrepid provers knowingly exposed themselves to the dangers of drug toxicity in their selfless determination to reveal the medicinal potential of poisonous substances. Their efforts and sacrifice can only be described as heroic. Over time, with the Hahnemannian method as the basis, the procedures and protocols of proving medicines became refined to an exact, scientific methodology.

The compiled results of this Herculean work were published in Hahnemann's *Materia Medica Pura,* published in six volumes between 1811 and 1821.[4] The English translation is contained in two volumes. The term *pura* indicated that the information contained in the work was derived solely from provings and not from clinical cases or drug toxicology. The symptoms of 66 individual remedies were recorded. Those symptoms, which through their frequent occurrence or intensity of expression showed themselves to be most characteristic of a remedy, were noted in bold type. In his preface, Hahnemann comments: 'I have arranged the symptoms of the more perfectly observed medicines in a certain order, whereby the search for the desired medicinal symptom will now be facilitated'. His chosen format commenced with vertigo, confusion, deficient mental power and loss of memory and then extended from the head downwards to the extremities, covering all the systems of the body, and finishing with 'disturbances of the disposition, affections of the mind'. In addition he included instructions for the homeopathic preparation of the medicines, their historical use and their major clinical indications. In a footnote, he urges the homeopathic physician to acquire a thorough knowledge of materia medica, greater than that of the simple carpenter for his tools:

> What conscientious physician would consent to work away at hap-hazard on a sick person ... no carpenter would work upon his wood with tools whose uses he was ignorant of. He knows every one of them perfectly, and hence he knows when to use the one and when the other, in order to effect *with certainty* what he intends to do; and it is only wood he works upon, and he is but a carpenter.

Although modernising changes and improvements have been made to Hahnemann's original symptom layout, notably the advancement of the mental and emotional symptoms to the pre-eminent position they deserve, usually following immediately after an introductory section, the Hahnemannian order of arrangement has remained a template for all subsequent materia medica and most repertories. Furthermore, it is a tribute to the thoroughness and accuracy of Hahnemann's research methods that modern reprovings have simply confirmed the findings of the original pathogenetic trials. To this day the *Materia Medica Pura* remains a work of scientific importance, and the tabulated symptoms it contains have been incorporated into all major materia medica. These newer works also contain symptoms and clinical conditions derived from toxicological data and from clinical experience.

Materia medica appear in different forms. The oldest and most comprehensive works, like Allen's *Encyclopaedia*,[5] Hering's *Guiding Symptoms*,[6] and Clarke's *Dictionary*,[7] are truly encyclopaedic, presenting exhaustive compilations of all the symptoms and signs gleaned from the provings. These were followed by good digests, like Kent's,[8] Tyler's[9] and Nash's,[10] which are useful for study purposes, and desk-top reference books, like Boericke's,[11] Phatak's,[12] Clarke's *Prescriber*[13] and, more recently, Morrison's[14] and Vermeulen's,[15] which are indispensable for clinical work. Some materia medica are confined to a particular clinical condition or body system, and others concentrate exclusively on the psychological sphere, e.g. those of Coulter[16] and Bailey.[17] Under the impetus of modern teachers, researchers and proving schools, the established remedy pictures are being further developed and more deeply understood, and new remedies are constantly being added to the materia medica.

The materia medica and the repertory

The wealth of material contained in the materia medica soon necessitated the development of an index to facilitate access to the symptoms and disorders associated with remedies. From this need, the homeopathic *repertory* was born, at first in book form, now additionally available in various electronic versions.

In homeopathic practice, there can be no substitute for the frequent, day-to-day use of the materia medica. After taking the case history, noting constitutional characteristics, listing and grading all the important emotional, mental and physical symptoms, with their modalities and causative influences, an analysis of the case is achieved through *repertorisation* followed by confirmatory study of the materia medica. In this way, as close a match as possible is sought between the symptom picture presented by the patient and that of the most similar remedy in the materia medica. Although materia medica and repertory work hand in hand, it is the materia medica that is the final arbiter in remedy selection.

In the words of Kent in his *Lectures on Homoeopathic Philosophy*:

> Disease must be brought out in symptoms, with the end of its becoming a likeness of some remedy in the Materia Medica. All the diseases known to man have their likeness in the Materia Medica, and the physician must become so conversant with this art that he may perceive this likeness.[18]

Clarke states in *The Prescriber*:[13]

> There is no road to the practice of homeopathy – whether it is the clinical road or the symptomatic road – which does not entail close and constant study of the Materia Medica.

Expanding the materia medica

Homeopathy is an art and science of healing, but it does not stand-alone, either as an art or as a science. It is not an island – it is part of an artistic and scientific field, which is both cosmic and multidimensional in scope. The materia medica and the study of homeopathy need to be developed in this context, judiciously incorporating knowledge and wisdom from other sciences and philosophies, from other therapies, both ancient and modern, and from the intuitive and received wisdom of all peoples. These additions enrich and deepen not only our understanding of our sublime subject, but also of the creation. Such investigation and exploration bring the excitement and joy of revelation, the unravelling of mysteries, insight into the hidden genius of remedies and an unassailable conviction of the oneness of all. Some important sources from which a more universal picture of our remedies, their uses and correspondences can be built are miasmatic theory, cosmology, evolutionary science, geology, natural science, mythology, folklore, symbolism, the doctrine of signatures, chakra theory, colour theory, numerology, analytical psychology, psychoanalysis and spiritual philosophy.

A modern materia medica that collates remedy material from a wider source than just the provings is *Prisma* by Frans Vermeulen,[19] which is subtitled, *Similars and Parallels Between Substance and*

Remedy. In his foreword, the author, when comparing the days of Hahnemann and Hering to our own, observes: 'We have much more information at our disposal today and it seems foolish not to use all available resources to build a better Materia Medica', and 'Based on law and common sense, natural science constitutes the modern version of the ancient doctrine of signatures and here much information can be found about the peculiar features of substances'.

Although it is not possible in this chapter to encompass all the different sources from which extra information may be gleaned, some of the most important will be discussed. Not least among these is the concept of the *archetype*.

Archetypal images within the materia medica

A materia medica remedy picture confined to the symptoms derived from provings of a remedy provides a framework or armature upon which the fully fleshed likeness of the similar patient still needs to be built. Even the addition of toxicological material only adds to and strengthens this framework. Nonetheless, from the outset, provings revealed more than just the symptom picture characteristic of the remedy. It was soon noted that amongst any group of provers there would be those who produced either no symptoms at all, or few of any value; those who showed a definite sensitivity and experienced significant symptoms; and a small number, often a single person, who evidenced exceptional susceptibility to the remedy's influence, yielding an entire spectrum of symptoms, many of them 'strange, rare and peculiar'. Likewise, in treating cases with a particular remedy, it became apparent that, as with provers, a certain type of patient or constitution proved to be particularly vulnerable to the healing power of the remedy. The exceptional prover and the successfully treated patient often showed common shared characteristics of build, colouring, features, demeanour, character, mannerisms and behaviour, which added together produced a remedy/patient profile that became recognisable – a homeopathic archetype.

To the profile of many of the major remedies must be added the characteristics and attributes of two other archetypal forms connected with them: the *atavistic* archetype and the *mythical* archetype. The essence of both resides in the deep collective unconscious: a field of interactive images, forms and patterns of behaviour innate within all life, and symbolically reflected in all aspects and structures of the manifest universe. When activated these archetypal energies emerge and exert a powerful influence upon the physical constitution, the ego personality and the personal unconscious of the individual. Considered homeopathically, their effects are central to the psychological and physical symptoms and signs of the patient.

The atavistic archetype

The atavistic archetype may be defined and recognised as a resemblance to a remote ancestor or more primitive form, either animate or inanimate. The ancestral lineage of humanity extends back 15 billion years to the creation of the first atom, *hydrogen*, amid the expanding sea of energy of the young universe. The first atavistic archetype of the materia medica is therefore hydrogen, which, as can be surmised, represents a flighty, ungrounded, vacuous individual, insubstantial, impractical, and out of touch with reality and the demands of material existence. In the mind, fantasy rather than reality holds sway. Next follows *helium*, an archetype that hovers reluctantly on the fringes of incarnation, alive and yet not fully alive, in the world and yet not of the world, without projection, interaction or unfolding: an autistic recluse. From the fusion of helium atoms, the process of cosmic alchemy then produces the first substantial atom, *carbon*, destined to become the pillar of all biological life forms. Thus, in a significant, ordered sequence, the elements of the universe come into existence, but it requires an awesome stellar-death, the titanic, supernova explosion, to fabricate the heaviest elements – gold, lead and uranium. All elements, their salts and their compounds, are our inorganic forebears, lying latent within us. From the prebiotic, inorganic world arose the biological world and the first organisms which, once established, rapidly diversified into a myriad of evolving life forms, our organic forebears: a continuum of life, culminating in the emergence of the paragon of animals, *Homo sapiens*.

Standing at the peak of sentient life, we possess, therefore, within the matrix of our being a mosaic or unique mix of atavistic or ancestral archetypes: a rich field of dynamic images, which in health are maintained in homeostatic balance by the integrating action of the *vital force*. This balance is represented by an ordered and harmonious frequency. In illness, a dissonance develops, disrupting the harmony of homeostasis. In compensation, the vital force causes an atavistic archetype, which resonates most closely with this disordered frequency, to rise into relief out of the mosaic of ancestral forms. In the illness of *Aurum*, responding to the call of its specific frequency, the metallic element, gold, emerges as a powerful metaphor, or symbol, capable of profoundly influencing the entire constitution, moulding or warping the form, features, faculties, functions and feelings of the patient. We may say that the patient then sees life through the eyes or filters of gold, moves with the body of gold and reacts to life with the passions, fears and prejudices of gold. To all intents and purposes, the patient is gold, the illness is gold and the remedy is gold.

The mythical archetype

Archetypes are also inherited, deep-seated universal patterns of perception, values, belief, behaviour, drives and identity, derived from the collective unconscious of the human race and innate in the personal unconscious of the individual. From time immemorial, the mythological archetypes have been continuously conceived within the fantasy world of the human imagination and laid down as great, primordial fantasy images within the structure of the collective unconscious. Here they form complexes of integrated and associated ideas bound together by shared emotional charge and capable of dynamically influencing conscious awareness, judgement, response, behaviour and experience. They are given expression and life in the ever-repeated themes and stories of the fabulous heroes and heroines, villains and rogues that people the myths, legends and folklore of all traditions, regardless of race, religion, culture, country or historical period. Hence, we have, amongst many others, the archetype of the king, warrior, thief, maid, mother and crone; their Greek mythical counterparts – Zeus, Ares, Hermes, Persephone, Demeter and Hecate; and their common equivalents in the materia medica – Stannum, Ferrum, Mercurius, Pulsatilla, Magnesium carbonate, and Sepia. The archetype of the divine child is particularly dear to the heart and soul of all cultures, and the theme recurrently appears in stories old and new, e.g. in sacred texts – the lives of Zoroaster, Moses, Jesus, Buddha, Krishna; and in modern literature – the quest of Frodo Baggins in Tolkien's *Lord of the Rings*, and the adventures of J K Rowling's Harry Potter. No matter how often retold, or in what guise or setting, the theme of the divine child captures the imagination and touches the quick of our deepest aspiration; for are we not all ring-bearers on a mystic quest, and are we not all divine children?

The archetype gives rise to the folklore and mythologies of the people, and its influence is revealed in the fantasy and dream life of the individual. A myth may be considered a universal dream, and a dream a personal myth. Both enrich the content of the materia medica, and both can assist in achieving a deeper understanding of the dynamics of a patient's case. Throughout our lives and the lives of our patients, the directional push and sometimes subtle, sometimes startling promptings of synchronistic happenings and the seemingly bizarre and distorted content of our dreams offer invaluable cues to correct decision-making and right action. These significant coincidences and cryptic messages from our unconscious are often missed or pass unheeded. Since the situation, circumstances, experiences and life events of a patient are never fortuitous, they must be regarded as being of great significance, and of vital importance in the evaluation of the case history, especially when they suggest the action of synchronicity, and appear archetypal. It is these incidents and occurrences that stimulate the instinctive inner world of the individual, and energise and evoke the archetype within. Our inner reality determines our outer reality. The arising of the archetype so energised reproduces in the individual's life history the same images, patterns and associations as are revealed and enacted in the ancient lore and legends of the people: an eternal replay of unresolved issues in the collective experience of humanity and in the personal experience of the individual, which must be lived out, overcome and transcended. The veiled wisdom of myth needs to be received into homeopathic lore.

With profound insight, Ralph Twentyman draws our attention to the importance of archetypal wisdom in his essay on *Argentum* (*The Science and Art of Healing*)[20]:

> The human soul responds to the processes and substances of our world through myth, legend and poetic imagery, and these may be considered the revelation of a higher reality lying latent like a sleeping princess, within the natural phenomena. They constitute, one might also say, a homeopathic proving in a very clear and heightened form. In contemplating these images and symbols we may be led deeper into the hidden genius of the substance and its remedial actions than by confining our attention strictly to the realm of material effects and the statutory rubrics of official provings.

The marriage of archetypes

Remedies of mineral origin, whose molecules are compounded from more than one element, are, in consequence, a combination of more than one atavistic archetype, e.g. calcium and carbon in Calcarea carbonica; potassium, calcium and sulphur in Causticum. Nevertheless, the essence of such combinations, as in that deriving from the more complex structure of plants and animals, always represents the qualities and characteristics of a single, unique atavistic archetype, even though the presence and influence of the constituent archetypes remain recognisable. Knowledge of the archetypal patterns combined in a mineral, such as Calcium phosphate (calcium and phosphorus), enables the researcher of materia medica to recognise, interpret, surmise and even predict the consequences of the dynamic interaction of the two elements and foresee the remedy picture that will evolve. In this instance, the marriage of incompatible partners, the grounded, dour, passive and insular calcium, preoccupied with security and safety, and the flighty, imaginative, passionate and expansive phosphorus, ever in pursuit of excitement and thrills, produces an archetype constantly tormented by inner conflict and dilemma. In recent years, Jan Scholten has opened up our understanding of the marriage of elements.

The fruit of Scholten's pioneer work in mapping the clinical pictures of the elements according to their relative position in the periodic table is contained in two important contributions to the homeopathic materia medica: *Homeopathy and Minerals* [21] and *Homeopathy and the Elements*.[22] By superimposing on the periodic table a grid divided into seven series, represented horizontally, and 18 stages, represented vertically, he has been able to anticipate and deduce personality characteristics, behavioural traits and emotions, even in elements and minerals, which have not yet been tested by means of pathogenetic trials. All elements within a specific series share common themes regarding the stage or arena upon which individuals requiring these elements act out their lives, and the problems that arise and challenge them as a result of these activities. Scholten's theory proposes a progressive unfolding and line of development that evolve from one series to the next. The series are further divided into stages, which correspond to the inevitable, universal and personal cycles of creation, preservation and destruction found in all aspects of the natural world: the rising and developing, achieving and maintaining, declining and deteriorating sequence, which the order of elements within each of the seven series parallels. In accordance with the stages, the elements of each series are charted over a convex curve uniting 18 points of continuity. Each element lies on the ascending, aspiring limb, the achieving, sustaining crest, or the descending, degrading limb of the curve. The coordinates of series and stage provide remarkable insights into the likely situations, delusions and reactions of the specific elemental archetype. This knowledge can be applied to the analysis of minerals, to the analysis of patients and to the matching of the two, thus assisting in the search for the *simillimum*.

The presence of more than one mythical archetype may be discerned in a remedy picture. In the Calc. carb archetype the characteristics of the goddesses Hestia, Demeter, Hera or Aphrodite are frequently apparent, each matching a particular facet or expression of the Calc. carb nature. However, when a number of divinities or legendary archetypes are potential within the psychological picture of a remedy, one will invariably prove dominant. While the identification of an atavistic archetype lies within the scope of common, homeopathic knowledge and repertorising skill, the recognition of the mythical archetype depends upon familiarity with mythology. Although the never-ending tales of mythical beings, their exploits, their sufferings and their triumphs are common to all cultures, it is the eternal wisdom contained within the Greek myths that can most profitably be used to deepen and augment our understanding of our remedies and the psyche of our patients. Many traditions, other than the Hellenic, have been assimilated into the richness of the mythological legacy left to us by the Greeks. This legacy has been rendered accessible to the homeopath by the work of Carl Gustav Jung and the insights of analytical psychologists who have followed him. This invaluable body of knowledge can be confidently added to the corresponding pictures of the atavistic archetypes when the association is clearly identified, e.g. the mythology of the sun god, Apollo, with Aurum metallicum, and that of the god of war, Ares, with Ferrum metallicum.

The doctrine of signatures

Nature is the great creator of symbols through which she reveals her otherwise hidden wisdom. Einstein stated: 'what is impenetrable to us really exists, manifesting in the highest wisdom and the most radiant beauty, which our dull senses can comprehend only in their most primitive (symbolic) form. This sensation, this knowledge, is at the centre of all true religiousness' – and, we might add, all true science.

The doctrine of signatures is a postulate coming down to us from the distant past, first formulated in the Middle Ages and firmly espoused by Paracelsus. This doctrine states that the external appearance and characteristics of a substance, be it plant, animal or mineral, are indicative of its healing properties. Clarke alludes to this phenomenon when he writes in his introduction to Magnesia carbonica: 'It is often found that the physical characteristics of substances correspond with their dynamic influences'.[7] His observation related to the softening effect on water of magnesia, which he compared to the soothing effect of Magnesia carbonica on the emotions and the nervous system.

This postulate, which even Hahnemann disparaged as being 'the folly of the ancients', has been a source of contention amongst homeopaths ever since, and a target for the derision of our adversaries. The ancients, however, were aware of being children of nature, nurtured at her bosom, sheltered and supported by the surrounding world. Their cosmos was filled with purpose and intelligence, created for the benefit of humanity. They were conscious of other dimensions and of unseen powers, which they vested with divinity, creating a pantheon of gods and goddesses, and a multitude of nature spirits. All life forms were sacred to some divinity and imbued with mystical properties. Plants too had their mythology: Pulsatilla, the meadow anemone, sprang from the blood of the dying Adonis, and the tears of his lover, Aphrodite; Aconite, monkshood, took life from the saliva of the savage, three-headed hound of Hades, Cerberus. Every transient form was a metaphor for something timeless and eternal.

The shamans and medicine men of ancient societies (and of the few remaining primitive tribes still uncorrupted by civilisation) had reverence for the healing wisdom and power implicit within nature's symbols and sought to decipher their meaning. They worked from the premise that the beneficent creator must have provided a cure for all the ailments that beset humanity, and furthermore must have made it possible for even the unsophisticated mind to identify the cure for a particular malady by certain outward signs that the remedy would bear. These constituted the therapeutic signature of the remedy, by which its resemblance to the disease or organ it could cure, and its healing properties, would be recognised. The shaman also knew that the greatest poisons proved to be the greatest remedies. The signature lay in the external appearance of the symbol – its colour, scent, taste, growth-pattern, behaviour, habitat, geology, chemical properties and natural history. Today, this knowledge has been broadened by the advance of science, adding new levels of information to our understanding of remedy signatures. Sometimes these are bold and easily interpreted; sometimes they are subtle or cryptic, open only to intuitive or scientific analysis.

In contrast, the bleak perspective of Newtonian science banished God from the heavens and replaced the Almighty with a merciless, purposeless, clockwork universe. With the loss of God came the loss of nature, now no longer experienced as a nurturing and loving mother, mindful of our needs, imparting her wisdom and instruction through her wondrous images. The modern, analytical mind spurns her embrace, and indifferent to the beauty of her wholeness, tears her apart, seeking to understand, control and overwhelm her, using her for its own ends, heedless of the consequences – an example of the enslavement of the feminine by the masculine. In pursuit of knowledge, wisdom is ignored; in analysis of matter, spirit is lost. More than all others, the homeopathic mind must not fall into this arrogant trap.

The very art of homeopathy is the art of deciphering metaphors – the metaphor of the substance and the metaphor of the patient, and matching the one to the other. The process of acquiring an understanding of the characteristics of a substance and of a patient is the same. In Vermeulen's words, both need to be 'consulted' or 'interviewed'.[19] In the case of a substance, the consultation involves the gathering of information about that substance from every possible source and viewpoint, gleaning the essence and totality of its signature. The picture compiled from this accumulated evidence provides a profile equivalent to that achieved in the case history of a patient. Remarkable parallels and similarities between the essence of substance and subject are revealed. Such clear correspondences should convince even the most sceptical of the validity of the doctrine of signatures. The 'consultation with the substance' provides a wealth of valuable detail to supplement the remedy information contained in the materia medica.

Signature examples

Latrodectus

Who can fail to marvel at the significant, scarlet hourglass, symbolic of the two-chambered, primitive heart, depicted upon the ventral aspect of the abdomen of the black widow spider, *Latrodectus mactans*, a creature whose poison provides such a specific remedy for the agony of cardiac angina?

Anacardium

Who can fail to be intrigued by the correspondence that exists between the black, heart-shaped nut of *Anacardium orientale* shown in Figure 5.1 and the nature of the patient needing its help? Within the hard shell lies a sweet-tasting, shiny-white kernel surrounded by the mesocarp that contains an acrid, bitter, resinous juice, which is a pale milky colour when fresh, but soon turns black and hardens on exposure to air. This juice, when mixed with chalk, produces ink used for marking, or imprinting, cotton fabrics – hence its common name, marking nut. The signature is powerful. The 'Anacardium subject' has an awareness of a duality of nature, of two selves, one destructive, cruel and evil (acrid, hard and black) and the other wholesome, gentle and good (bland, sweet and milky). The sweetness and meekness of the inner kernel is masked by the corrosive, black juice of vindictiveness and malice. There is a conflict between two wills, expressed by provers as the awareness of a devil sitting on one shoulder, prompting evil, and an angel sitting on the other, forbidding it. The change of colour and the hardening of the resin on exposure, and its use for marking material, are analogous to the disastrous effects of traumatic life experiences upon the Anacardium personality: the blackening and hardening of a previously sensitive, sweet nature due to terrible imprinting, often producing an antisocial personality. The name Anacardium derives from the heart-shaped nut. This shape also gives us a signature, for the remedy is beneficial for those who lack heart, who lack courage and are faint-hearted. It is often the remedy for examination nerves and school phobia. The hardness and blackness of the nut show a correspondence to those who are hard-hearted, black-hearted or heartless. It also restores heart to those who have lost confidence or experience cardiac anxiety after suffering a heart

Figure 5.1 Anacardium.

attack or undergoing heart surgery. I would draw the attention of cynics, who turn their backs on the doctrine of signatures, to the pleasure and ease with which remedy pictures can be learned and retained in this way. Even if their lack of trust and loss of nature take them no further, let them bear this in mind.

Silica

Silica, rock crystal, or quartz, has always been known to possess healing energy. Often it is worn as a protective talisman. It is the cosmic architect, shaping the crags and ravines of our planet's crust, furnishing us with a stage upon which we can play out the drama of our lives. The world of quartz is a world of forms, magnificent shapes and wonderful colours. The crystal possesses an infinite capacity to grow and expand

Figure 5.2 Venus sponge.

through ever-repeated prismatic faces, built up of itself and from itself, yet always constrained by an inner, formative force, which imposes strict geometrical restraints upon the creative process, ensuring that the design always achieves the final crowning, closing pyramid. In the sea, silica is utilised by sea creatures to construct their homes and their skeletons. These structures are intricate art forms of exquisite beauty, which reach their ultimate expression in the Venus flower basket or deep-sea glass sponge, *Euplectella,* shown in Figure 5.2, a veritable cathedral of pure, silica spicules, elaborately executed in six axes or planes. Viewing its perfection, we are looking into the very heart and soul of the remedy, witnessing its grace, refinement and gentility but possibly also gaining an impression of overattention to detail, and a baroque-like fussiness and flamboyance. This excess of embellishment, in human terms, would suggest a need for approbation and approval, an artistic nature troubled by self-doubt, and obsessed with image and appearance. Such is the consultation with the substance (see Case study 5.1).

 **CASE STUDY**

Case study 5.1
A young, unmarried woman of 25 years presented with complaints of persistent acne since puberty, and debilitating menstrual pain that would immobilise her entirely and required strong analgesics for relief. Her menstrual cycle was often delayed, averaging as few as nine a year, and she had always been terribly constipated. Laparoscopy revealed moderate signs of endometriosis; this had been cauterised and cleaned up during the procedure. Temporary relief had resulted, but now the symptoms were as bad as ever. The contraceptive pill brought little improvement and caused her to gain weight, which she found intolerable, although it had improved her acne. A 6-month course of Roaccutane cleared her skin, but dried it out terribly. After discontinuing it, her skin once again steadily deteriorated. Disenchanted, she now refused antibiotic and hormone therapy, and wished to try homeopathy.

She was of medium height and athletic build, slim and lithe, with a perfect posture. Her features were refined and very attractive, set off to perfection by large, luminous blue eyes and a glorious head of long, lustrous, reddish-blonde hair, which, I later learned, took her an inordinate amount of time to

→

⊃ CASE STUDY (continued)

groom each day. She made great play of its luxurious beauty by often permitting it to fall forward over her face and then throwing it back with a graceful and studied toss of the head. Her trim body resulted from training assiduously, both on the road and in the gym, and following a very strict, though healthy, diet regime; always imagining that she was putting on weight. Her breasts had been tastefully augmented in her early 20s. Although her skin was noticeably pitted and raised by old and current acne lesions on her cheeks and along the line of her jaw, this was always meticulously camouflaged. In addition, her daily make-up was a work of art, cleverly enhancing her aristocratic features and compelling eyes.

Investigation revealed that she was a perfectionist in every aspect of her life. She was always fastidiously and fashionably dressed; she was extremely particular about cleanliness, neatness and order, and was unable to relax until everything was put away and shipshape. It was her partner, an equally immaculate person, who offered the information that she took infinite care and time when tidying up and restoring clean laundry to cupboards and drawers, because anything which had to be placed in a pile had to be carefully and exactly sized up so that a pyramid was formed, with the largest object below and the smallest on top. This applied to clothes, linen, magazines, books and any stacked articles. He was exasperated by her lack of belief in herself, her lack of confidence in her intellectual ability, despite holding a responsible position, and her hypercritical attitude to her appearance, despite her natural beauty of face and form. Of a very sensitive and fragile disposition, she was remarkably sensitive to criticism or censure, and empathetic to the point of suffering for others. She loved children, but could not contemplate having any of her own because of the body changes this would necessitate. Such was the consultation with the subject.

Each consultation, of substance and of subject, provided a template for the other, and the remedy Silicea given in ascending potencies over a period of 18 months brought about a very satisfactory result. Her periods and bowels were regular, her dysmenorrhoea had gone and her skin was almost clear. Ongoing treatment was required for the facial scarring, and this was well within the scope of Silicea to achieve. She will always be a fussy perfectionist, but even in this regard she had become more relaxed and no longer obsessive. The treatment of the case was assisted by Magnesium phosphate 200, given for short-term relief of the dysmenorrhoea in the early stages of treatment, and later Tuberculinum residuum 200, given at 1–2-weekly intervals to facilitate the improvement of scarring. Many of the symptoms, especially the panperfectionism and anxiety, might have indicated a need for Arsenicum album, but her deeply compassionate nature was at odds with the generally callous and often cruel nature of Arsenicum.

Aurum as archetype, signature and remedy

To the alchemists, Aurum metallicum, gold, was the metal of the sun and hence, the monarch of the world of metals, unsurpassed in excellence, perfection and eminence. Forged in the cataclysmic explosion of a supernova, gold's cosmic nature and nobility remain unsullied by the normal, earthly processes of weathering, oxidation, corrosion, rust and calcification – gold remains incorruptible. Like a resplendent, shining stranger from a higher dimension, gold sheds glory and light upon the earth, but is not of the earth. Yet despite its radiance, its magnificent, glowing lustre and serene splendour, it is also immensely dense, ponderously heavy, cold and hard. Gold possesses a duality more extreme than any other archetype. The paradox of the ethereal and the gross, the honourable and the corrupt, exists in gold. Aurum is indicated equally for the devotional nature aspiring to spiritual perfection and the utter materialist whose entire focus is on worldly success and affluence. Its radiance speaks for the illumined being, the 'old soul', who brings the message of wisdom and love to humanity; its heaviness portrays a solemnity and seriousness of nature, or a tendency to become oppressed

Figure 5.3 Mask of Agamemnon.

and weighed down by negative emotions, even to the point of suicidal depression. The ambivalence of Aurum is mythologically revealed in the dynamics of the ancient and hallowed, Delphic shrine of Apollo. For 9 months of the year Apollo was the resident divinity, but in his absence, during the 3 months of winter, his half-brother Dionysos enjoyed sole rule and worship at Delphi. Apollo, the sun god, embodied all that is aesthetic, harmonious and moderate in art, music, literature and poetry, and he represented all that is sane, rational, splendid, measured and balanced in life. He was possessed of a lofty nobleness of spirit, aloof yet caring. Dionysos was his antithesis, god of ecstasy and rapture. He represented spontaneity, passion, intensity and freedom, but also wildness, sensuality, excess, frenzy, madness, destruction and dismemberment. He was exquisitely androgynous. He is the feminine and shadow side of both Apollo and Aurum. The monarch of metals embodies both mythological archetypes.

The illustration of the so-called 'mask of Agamemnon' (Figure 5.3), the High King of Mycenae at the time of the Trojan war, wrought in pure gold, admirably depicts the venerable dignity and regal power that the metal symbolises (see Case study 5.2).

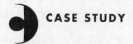

CASE STUDY

Case study 5.2

A highly successful married man of 50 attended the practice, suffering from intense anxiety and depression. By his ambition, drive and intense commitment to achieving his goals, as well as his organisational, leadership and entrepreneurial skills, he had amassed a fortune, and found himself at the pinnacle of his profession, respected and admired, yet unfulfilled and restless, with the feeling that all his endeavours to that point had only benefited himself, his family and his colleagues. He became intoxicated by an altruistic ideal, and a determination to devote himself to professional philanthropy. He forthwith naively threw himself, emotionally and financially, into unfamiliar waters and trusted himself and his money to those who professed similar objectives, only to find himself the victim of duplicity and villainy. He lost a considerable sum of money, yet was unable to bring the offenders to justice. The 'dream', with which he had become so infatuated that he had even neglected his family, collapsed and he was left suffering from frustrated anger,

(continued overleaf)

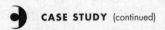 **CASE STUDY** (continued)

indignation, humiliation and resentment. These emotions, with nowhere to go, distilled into deepening depression, coloured by anxiety, pessimism, loss of confidence, fear of failure and a fear of never being able to add value to life.

Previously a good sleeper, he was now plagued by persistent insomnia. He was a dark-complexioned man with strong features, wiry, grey-black hair, well dressed, with a dignified bearing and appeared serious, solemn and lacking in humour. He was known for his competitiveness, integrity, honesty and loyalty. He had always been a perfectionist and a workaholic, and stated that he was always at his best when under pressure and when facing a formidable workload. For him work was essential, providing his identity and his inspiration.

This incorruptible, noble, austere man found in Aurum the remedy that enabled him to throw aside his anger, his anxiety and his depression. It restored his drive, his optimism and his capacity to sleep. He subsequently made good his losses, and found great fulfilment in financing the education of underprivileged children. Aurum also released the repressed Dionysian energy within this too rigid, aloof and serious man. The more feminine influence of the god softened and warmed him, permitting him licence to play. He is no longer the admired but absent husband and father. His wife has even persuaded him to join her in ballroom dancing.

Other sources of materia medica knowledge

Some of the many sources of knowledge, which can add to an understanding of homeopathic remedies and enrich the standard materia medica, have been highlighted. As mentioned above, there are a number of others, some of which will be briefly mentioned here.

A miasmatic analysis needs to be incorporated into the materia medica of each remedy, indicating its predominant miasmatic relationship, and, where relevant, evidence of the combined effect of more than one miasm on its picture (miasmic theory is discussed in full in Chapter 3). Similar analysis of the patient's predominant miasmatic presentation is essential, especially when dealing with complex cases where well-selected remedies fail to act, bring about only a temporary response or are followed by the emergence of a different picture. Miasmatic knowledge of both remedy and patient are often of great value in selecting appropriate therapy and monitoring progress.

Colour is one of the most important elements in nature's cosmic code, expressing relationship to organs, systems, functions, emotions and levels of consciousness, which in turn correspond to the energy centres of the body – the chakras. Sulphur is an intensely yellow element. Yellow is the colour of the third chakra. This chakra is located in the solar plexus and is known as the power chakra. It is a multidimensional, spinning concentration of energy within the vital force field, which controls the metabolism and the digestive organs – stomach, liver, gallbladder, pancreas and duodenum. Psychologically it relates to personal power and will – our drive, our motivation, our ambition, our confidence and our vitality; its element is fire, and its miasm is syphilis. When flowers of Sulphur are heated, they melt and change in colour from yellow to a deep, sullen red. Red is the colour of the first chakra, which is located in the perineum and has to do with the instinctual life, survival, flight and fight responses, the adrenal medulla, animal sexuality and aggression; its element is earth, and its miasm is psora. As it burns, Sulphur produces a blue flame. Blue is the colour of the fifth chakra, which is located in the throat and is related to creativity and communication; the thyroid gland, the parathyroids and the thymus; its element is ether or sound, and its miasm is cancer. From the above brief example, even without going into the emotional pictures associated with each of these three colours, we gain some insight into how valuable such knowledge can be in our analysis and deeper understanding of remedies.

In considering *Atropa belladonna*, we see that the berry, which is as big as a small cherry, is an intense, shining-black colour. Black is primordial; all other colours emerge from it. The potential of black is infinite; it contains the universal light. It is synonymous with the void, with cosmic darkness before the first stars brought light to the creation, with the Dark Goddess, she who is the life force in matter, the sacred energy of creation, and with the shadow aspect of the psyche; black is a cornucopia of plenty. Black is the starting point of the individuation path of the soul. Even in the acute Belladonna state, with its high fever, violently aggressive and destructive delirium, a more subtle process is at work – the release of repressed energy from the shadow realm, expediting individuation.

Nature also expresses her 'silent knowledge' through numbers. The pendant, bell-shaped flowers of Belladonna possess five lobes, or petals. Five is associated with fire and the colour red, both of which signify fever and inflammation. Five is analogous with the five faculties and the sense pleasures, and through its relationship to fire, it is symbolic of initiation, cleansing and regeneration. The shadow aspect of five portrays insatiable desire for sense gratification, luxury, promiscuity, substance abuse and the destructive emotions – jealousy, hatred, pride, aggression, viciousness and malice. When studying the drug pictures of Belladonna and its related remedies of the Solanaceae, especially Stramonium and Hyoscyamus, their correspondence with the number five is apparent.

The Jungian concept of the structure of the psyche – the ego, the collective and personal unconscious, the complexes, the persona, the shadow, the anima and the animus – provides a template by which an intelligent analysis and understanding of the diverse mental and emotional symptoms of any remedy can be achieved. Similarly, Freud's theories of the psychosexual developmental phases and the topological structure of the psyche give us insight into the dynamics of ego personality development.

The importance of dreams in case analysis and as a monitor of therapeutic progress is extremely important. We all view objective reality through the subjective filters of our ego personality, hence we are all, to a greater or lesser degree, living in a state of delusion, which in turn gives rise to our fears and our pathology. The unravelling and understanding of the personal delusion of the patient, often in the light of his or her fears, and helped by dream analysis, frequently yield the successful prescription.

Conclusion

The study of the materia medica leads us along many paths, providing us with a lifetime of adventure and exploration. It widens and deepens our knowledge of the natural world, and awakens our consciousness to the presence of an all-pervading, caring intelligence, which is manifest in all aspects of the creation and constitutes the oneness of all things. This awareness brings us trust in the face of an often intimidating and awesome task – finding, within the vast annals of the materia medica, a remedy for the patient before us. When homeopathy becomes an intrinsic and essential part of our lives, when delving into the riches of the materia medica becomes a constant source of delight, the remedies are installed deep in our fibre, our memory and our unconscious, and we can be confident that our diligence will be rewarded by some clue, some prompt, some inspiration, which will open the case for us. Not least of all, since it is a manifestation of the universal oneness, is the phenomenon of synchronicity. For it is not by chance or fortuity that the ways of physician and patient cross, it is ordained by destiny. When the homeopath is ready, the patient appears; when the remedy is learnt, the case appears.

References

1.   Cullen W P. *A Treatise on Materia Medica*. Edinburgh: Cruckshank and Campbell, 1789.
2.   Haehl R. *Samuel Hahnemann: His Life and Work*. London: Homoeopathic Publishing Company, 1992.
3.   Cook T M. *Samuel Hahnemann: The Founder of Homoeopathic Medicine*. Northamptonshire: Nene Litho, 1981.
4.   Hahnemann S. *Materia Medica Pura*. Liverpool: Hahnemann Publishing Society, 1880. Also available online at http://www.hpathy.com/materiamedica/hahnemann-materia-pura/index.asp (accessed March 2007).
5.   Allen T F. *Encyclopaedia of Pure Materia Medica*. New Delhi: B. Jain, 2003.
6.   Hering C. *The Guiding Symptoms of the Materia Medica*. New Delhi: B. Jain, 2003.
7.   Clarke J H. *The Dictionary of Practical Homoeopathic Materia Medica*. Saffron Walden: CW Daniel, 1991.
8.   Kent J T. *Materia Medica of Homoeopathic Remedies*. Sittingbourne: Homeopathic Book Service, 1989.
9.   Tyler M L. *Homoeopathic Drug Pictures*. Sittingbourne: Homeopathic Book Service, 2002.
10. Nash E B. *Leaders in Homeopathic Therapeutics*. New Delhi: B. Jain, 1999.
11. Boericke W. *Homoeopathic Drug Pictures*. Sittingbourne: Homeopathic Book Service, 1999.
12. Phatak S R. *Materia Medica of Homoeopathic Medicines*. London: Foxlee Vaughan, 1988.
13. Clarke J H. *The Prescriber*. Sittingbourne: Homeopathic Book Service, 2002.
14. Morrison R. *Desktop Guide to Keynotes and Confirmatory Symptoms*. Grass Valley, CA: Hahnemann Clinic Publishing, 1993.
15. Vermeulen F. *Concordant Materia Medica*. Haarlem: Emryss bv, 2000.
16. Coulter C R. *Portraits of Homoeopathic Medicines*, vols I–III. St Louis: Quality Medical Publishing, 1998.
17. Bailey P M. *Homeopathic Psychology*. Berkeley, CA: North Atlantic Books, 1996.
18. Kent J T. *Lectures on Homeopathic Philosophy*. Berkeley, CA: North Atlantic Books, 1979. Also available online at: http://www.homeoint.org/books3/kentlect/index.htm (accessed March 2007).
19. Vermeulen F. *Prisma: The Arcana of Materia Medica Illuminated*. Haarlem: Emryss bv Publishers, 2002.
20. Twentyman R. *The Science and Art of Healing*. Worcester: Billing, 1989.
21. Scholten J. *Homeopathy and Minerals*. Utrecht: Stichting Alonnissos, 1993.
22. Scholten J. *Homoeopathy and the Elements*. Utrecht: Stichting Alonnissos, 1996.

6

The therapeutic encounter – a personal view

David Reilly

Introduction

Having looked at the building blocks of homeopathic practice in the opening chapters of the book the elements of the therapeutic encounter will be considered in this chapter.

In 2002 a study showed that when antidepressants help people, changes in their prefrontal cortex can be mapped using quantitative electroencephalography – an elegant demonstration of how our science of the last 50 years can work brilliantly.[1] But, in the same study, the researchers were surprised to discover that the significant number of patients whose depression was being helped by placebo also showed objective changes in the same area. At the end of this study, when the people who got better while taking placebo were told what they had been taking, almost all relapsed and had to be placed on 'real' medicine.

If you look deeply enough into this story you can discover for yourself what you can use this chapter to explore: your reflections on improving your care, and our systems of care. Towards that end, in the introduction to this chapter we will:

- prepare ourselves for the later clinical exploration with some theoretical and scientific background
- look at human healing responses
- consider some of their potential and limits and examine factors currently known to modify them.

To avoid this becoming dry or detached, it may help if you ask of each of the scientific studies we look at – How might this impact on my daily practice?

In the second part of this chapter, we will wonder how we might better provoke healing responses in ourselves and others, how to improve our meetings, consultations and encounters.

To assist with this, in the final section there will be some more specific comments about these universal factors in the context of a given therapy, using homeopathy as a model. Hopefully this will help to stimulate you afresh, and help you wonder how you are doing in this realm in your own work, and how you might develop yourself further.

The healing response

The consultation begins long before the consultation, and ends long after it finishes. A potential for change is inherent – and a creative meeting may be the potent agent of its release – with or without prescriptions. In our meetings, the worlds of our interventions meet those of the patient, the practitioner and the contexts: to speak of one in isolation is to deny that each world will have its impact, for better or worse, each changing the outcome – each interacting with the others. So it is of critical value to study the impact of encounters in their own right. Without this knowledge we may reduce the effectiveness of an intervention, or wrongly attribute a powerful impact of meetings solely to our interventions. This is confusing, it misses key creative opportunities to help people better to help themselves, and it leads to wrong information entering our practice, teaching and textbooks.

The core purpose of our meetings is to help the relief of suffering, through creative change – or we could say, to support healing, or healing responses. And healing responses are deeper than any particular living organism's patterns, they are deeper than our own biography or personal self. On the foundations of life's drive for wholeness sits our biological healing responses. On that is layered our individual biography and our inner and outer cultures. Our individual and collective minds are connected from above down into our biology, and they meet and interact with the tides rising from that biology. While our inherited self sets the drives and limits of our healing, as conscious and cultural beings we can modify this for better or worse. Medicine is catching on to this, through areas like psychoneuroimmunology and anthropology, but it is we as individuals and communities who have to learn how to engage creatively with this complexity.

I studied a range of whole-person approaches in an attempt to improve at my work as a doctor. This included hypnoanalysis in my clinical work, and the literature about placebo in my academic work. Along the road I came across homeopathy and observed powerful changes being produced in people. I suspected this was due to the discipline's advanced approach to history-taking, and I was sceptical about the dilutions. So I spent 15 years of my academic work conducting four rigorous randomised double-blinded placebo studies to test this. I could not ethically or scientifically justify to myself prescribing something without adequate evidence for its effectiveness. The outcome? The homeopathy worked. It was better than the excellent placebo responses it also produced. This caused much scientific heat and some light.[2-4]

So it seems both factors were active – the medicines and the method – and that is a powerful mix. Having made that journey I then returned to my original enquiry that had caused me look at homeopathy in the first place – the human potential for change, self-healing and transformative process. I remember the day when I took the plunge and asked someone who was seeking homeopathy from me for a chronic problem: 'Given that this has been an important meeting together just now, do you still want a prescription?' The person said: 'No'! In the months that followed around 40% answered that way and I was able to learn with them that sometimes quite amazing changes and improvements would happen, showing the same patterns of initial aggravations and patterns of change that traditional natural therapists including homeopaths have described. Importantly, I was forced to reflect that if a remedy had been used, we would have attributed these changes to it – an attribution that I now see can generate confusion, medicalisation and missed opportunity for empowerment. When appropriate, it is now my first instinct to start this way, adding an intervention later if need be, once the foundations of self-change are in place. I think if we do not study these self-healing patterns in their own right, we are restricted in our capacity to use our interventions at their best, and to judge their effect.

The first part of the journey begins with a brief look at one key source of knowledge in western medicine about healing – the placebo response.

The puzzle: predict – pill or placebo?

Here's a challenge. A drug, a homeopathic medicine, a herb, is prescribed and a strong response occurs. How do you know if it was a 'real' response, resulting from the specific intervention, or if it was triggered by the 'non-specific/context/placebo effects' (as it's variously called in academic debates)? Is there a difference, and how can we tell? Averaging between groups is one way. Figure 6.1 shows a group of 35 patients in a randomised double-blinded trial in a university hospital asthma clinic, where a homeopathic allergen desensitising technique is

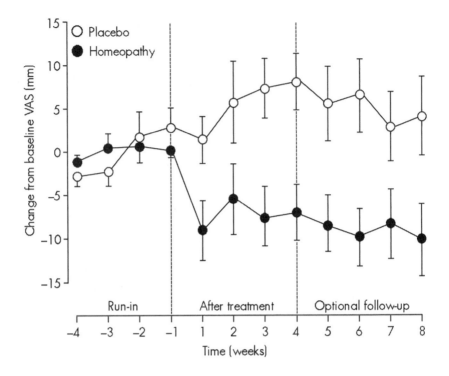

Figure 6.1 The averaged results of a comparison of homeopathy and placebo in patients with asthma.[5] VAS, visual analogue scale.

added to ongoing conventional asthma treatments. On average, it proved superior to placebo.[5]

But what about in single individuals? Can you tell if the response they show is due to placebo? Figure 6.2 shows 4 patients with asthma who all had placebo at the initial stage in their treatment, then one or more had a real drug at the second prescription point.[6]

Under the averaged results of the group a fascinating individual complexity was buried. The consent form had explained that you 'will have a 50:50 chance of getting only placebo' and there was 'a chance of symptoms getting a bit worse before they would improve'. Note carefully that the first prescription is a placebo in every case – the researchers knew this but the patients did not (single-blinded), whereas the second prescription is randomised and double-blinded. The placebo and active medicine were exactly matched for taste, colour and form, and were given in the same way by the same people at each visit. Here's the puzzle: who got 'real medicine' and how do you know?

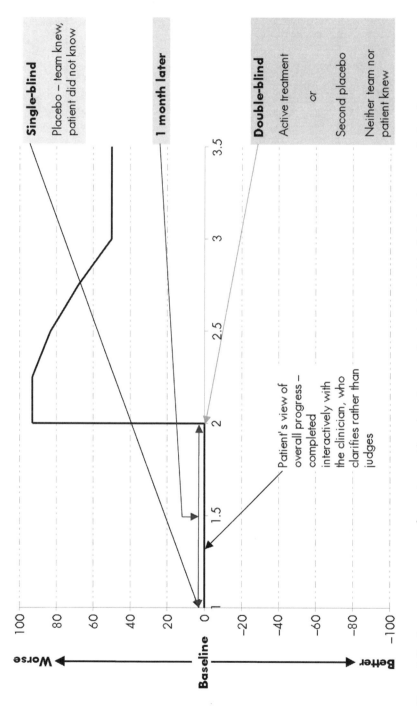

Single-blind

Placebo – team knew, patient did not know

1 month later

Double-blind

Active treatment

or

Second placebo

Neither team nor patient knew

Patient's view of overall progress – completed interactively with the clinician, who clarifies rather than judges

Worse

Baseline

Better

Figure 6.2   An outcome measure for patients with asthma in a randomised double-blinded placebo-controlled trial.

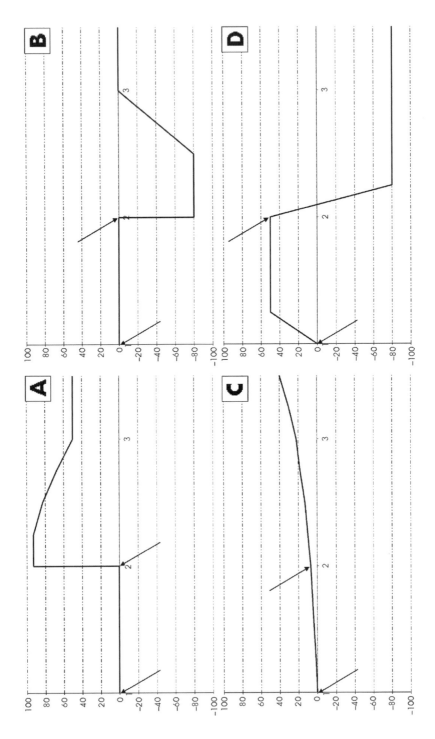

Figure 6.3   Scans from charts completed interactively by four different patients and their doctor at three visits, a month apart, during a randomised double-blinded study of a treatment for asthma.

In the graphs shown in Figure 6.3 the vertical scale is ± 100%, a rise is an improvement in symptoms and the line descends in a deterioration. Point 1 on the horizontal axis marks the first visit when each patient had a single-blind placebo. Four weeks on, at point 2, the patient has been given, randomised and double-blind, either a second placebo or active medication. At point 3 a repeat third prescription of the same type as the second prescription is given only if required. The challenge is to determine who got an active medication at the second visit versus who received a second placebo. The answer is given later in the article.

A. No response to the first single-blind placebo. Dramatic improvement within hours to the double-blind randomised prescription – ran a marathon! Waned to 50% within about a month.
B. No response to the first single-blind placebo. Dramatic aggravation within hours to the double-blind randomised prescription. 'Worst ever', plus return of old symptoms (rhinitis) and a new symptom of mid-thoracic nausea and back pain. Settled.
C. No response to the first single-blind placebo. A smooth and sustained improvement to the double-blind randomised prescription.
D. Marked improvement with the first single-blind placebo. Dramatic aggravation within hours to the double-blind randomised prescription.

Transmitted expectations

Two key questions: (1) Can a placebo trigger improvements and deteriorations like these? (2) Can people respond differently to two sequential placebos given in an identical manner by the same people? The answer to both questions: yes. Only patient C got the real medicine; patients A, B and D had different, even opposite, reactions to two placebos given by the same carers in the same context.

So what might have happened? Look again at the graphs and recall that at point 2 on the horizontal axis the prescription changes from single-blinded to double-blinded. The *expectations* of the carers change. They knew there was now a *chance* of an active medicine (with its initial risk of adverse effects), and somehow this seems to have 'activated' the placebo's impact on healing, for good or bad, even 'cancelling' previous healing responses, and even overriding the patient's ongoing back-ground pharmacology. This neural alchemy is likely triggered by 'the transmitted clinician's expectation of outcome'.[7] This matters for study design and treatment comparisons[8] but even more so for individual patient care and safety. Alter the expectation of carers and you may activate different outcomes, for harm as well as good. Patients pick up these signals as 'active ingredients'. Perhaps pause a moment to think through some implications of this for your practice.

Nocebo: 'I hurt'

A placebo response can sometimes give a positive outcome – but the negative impact seen in the graphs may appear surprising. A nocebo response (originally meaning 'I hurt'), it is the induced harmful effects of negative beliefs.[9] Like placebo, the triggers vary as widely as the contexts, but the end results may have final common pathways. Some apparent placebo effects are artefacts, or coincidental,[10] but, as in a blush, feelings may affect our body.

In laboratory experiments, inhaled saline produced increases or decreases in airways resistance according to what people were told to expect. Also, when given a true bronchodilator, its effects were twice as great if patients were told it would produce this effect.[11, 12]

The primary purpose of this chapter is not to discuss placebo or nocebo, but to give some indications through examples of placebo action about self-healing and self-destructive potential, and to highlight how important it is when we prescribe to lay a path in our encounters towards establishing a therapeutic bond, addressing patients' fear and ensuring a trust in a prescription issued with integrity, and being conscious of the expectations that have been produced. I do not use placebo – it would undermine trust.

These built-in pathways can produce pain in normal subjects. Headaches were reported by 70% of medical students told that a (non-existent) electric current was passing through their heads.[13] The overall incidence of adverse events in healthy volunteers during placebo administration is 19% (from a review of 109 double-blind trials[14]). Negatively impacting consultations can, and do, harm.[15]

To get a sense of the power of these negative pathways, consider life shocks. George Engel (father of the 'biopsychosocial' model) analysed 107 sudden deaths related to emotional shocks.[16] They were mostly linked to personal danger (whether real or symbolic), the collapse or death of a close person and during acute grief – that is, situations which can't be ignored and where you believe you have no control. In our work we are commonly dealing with people whose welfare is threatened, or, just as potent to the inner world, when we are in the grip of a belief that this threat exists.

The most dramatic extreme of nocebo is voodoo death.[9] Anthropologists believe that we are born and die twice: biologically and socially. In voodoo death you die socially first. Reviewing nocebo, Herbert Spiegel describes a 'medical voodoo' when a hospitalised man who was wrongly and unnecessarily given the last rites by a priest died within 15 minutes.[17] The west brings many forms of social death – imprisonment, old-age home, psychiatric long-stay ward, retirement, stigmatised diagnoses – with their resultant impact on health. We can help neutralise negative messages of such predicaments (including medical ones) by developing psychological defences. For example, learning to deal with hopelessness was an outstanding feature noted in a group of the women with breast cancer whose longevity was apparently extended on average by 18 months by joining support group meetings.[18] A key aim of our meetings is the reframing of experiences and beliefs.

We know that a human recovery reaction is a built-in potential, and we have just seen that it can be modified for good and bad by human interaction. A study of the positive and negative impacts of placebo helps us understand what triggers self-healing, and self-destruction.

The horizons of self-learning

Placebo then can induce and provoke change indirectly. But can we learn to do so more directly? The pathways for placebo action are between our consciousness and our biology, and that's where we need to look. The practical application of this has been missing in academic debate about placebo,[19–21] but the discovery, like the one mentioned in the opening reflection, that people responding to placebo show objective brain scan changes (for example, in depression, Parkinson's disease[22] and pain[23]), is now bringing to light the issue of training our brain, our biology, through our own practice. Skilled meditators have demonstrated in functional magnetic resonance imaging scanners the ability to activate directly their positive mood centres, such as the left prefrontal cortex changes seen in the antidepressant studies.[24] Where the mind leads the body follows. And this capacity to train our minds is largely uncharted by science or medicine, which has mostly ignored traditional contemplative and meditation contributions to understanding and health. Cognitive psychology is now touching on this territory, and we see through cognitive-behavioural therapy the first steps away from the emphasis on drugs as the only or primary way to deal with wayward mind and biology.

Before leaving the discoveries about placebo there a few other areas from the research that are worth reviewing, as stimulants to fresh thinking about self-healing and self-destructive tendencies.

Who responds?

Normal people respond. Everyone has self-healing potential. There is probably no simple predictive measures. People who respond to placebo have normal personalities, and those who don't have more rigid personalities, are suspicious and sometimes don't respond to 'ordinary' medicine.[25]

To what message?

In a study of 300 medical students looking at the effects of psychotropics, 50% had psychic changes and 60% had physical effects. The students identified the pink pills as stimulatory and the blue as sedatives. All the pills were placebos.[26]

Along with colour, the form of the intervention has an impact. Larger capsules tend to be viewed as stronger, and two placebo capsules are stronger than one – unless the small size of a pill signals the message that it is very strong. Injections produced larger effects than pills. Red or yellow capsules tend to be viewed as stimulants or antidepressants, blue as sedative and white capsules tend to be perceived as analgesics or narcotics.[27, 28]

How we prescribe – powders, tablets, single doses, daily drops – can be received by the patient's mind in differing ways. Symbolism has a powerful impact. This is highlighted in the 'ritual' of surgery.[29] In 1959, surgeons made skin incisions in patients expecting to have their internal mammary artery tied to help blood flow to their heart and so help their angina. However, a random selection never had the operation and were just sewn back up. All 18 non-treated patients had less angina 6 weeks afterwards, some had improved exercise electrocardiograms and in some the effect lasted for years.[30]

In which culture?

The adverts, the packaging, the hypnotic names,[31] the cultural labels of 'new,' 'traditional,' 'alternative' and 'scientific' carry messages to our inner worlds as well as our rational minds, often bypassing the latter. The brand name on that free plastic pen the drug rep gives to us has an effect. In one study, branded tablets were significantly more effective than unbranded tablets for the treatment of headaches.[32] A powerful message in one culture may be meaningless in another.

Expecting what?

These pathways in us modify our distress: saline was as effective as morphine in 40% of people after surgery, and the same happened for emotional pain – about 70% of patients respond to placebo for depression.[33] But the outcomes tend to be what might be expected. For example, aspirin placebo causes aspirin-like effects, morphine placebo causes morphine life effects – and side-effects. This system has puzzling specificity. And it interacts with the drug's action synergistically or disruptively. Bronchoconstriction of atropine and other anticholinergics can be reversed by suggestion (with saline inhalation) and bronchoconstriction of suggestion can be blocked by ipratropium.[34] Previous experience and learning all have an effect, like Pavlov's dogs salivating to the sound of the feeding bell. Rats given repeated scopolamine injections show the same depressed behaviours when given later placebo injections.[35] If a prescription helped (for example, in reducing anxiety), a patient might repeat what he or she had 'learned' to a later placebo version of the same treatment. So it is better to 'anchor' patients on their own self-coping rather than on the prescriber or the prescriber's treatments, so they have a template referencing their self-capacity on which they can call, and build, in the future.

Drugs are modelled in the laboratory and tested in animals. But it is naive to expect only predictable 'hard' pharmacological outcomes. They become an ingredient in a complex reactive system. This means it is also naive to believe that the 'real' effect is that part left after subtracting placebo. Because 1 + 1 might come out as 4. And you might be one of the active ingredients.

From which carer?

Push the square peg of medicine into the round hole of healing and you end up with ugly words like 'iatroplacebogenics'[36] to explain that results are influenced by who does the caring, and how. The carer's personality and attitude, warmth and empathy or hostility towards the patient, and attitude towards the treatment ('active-enthusiastic or passive-nihilistic') all have an impact on outcome. A review of controlled trials found that physicians who adopted a warm, friendly and reassuring manner were more effective than those whose consultations were formal and did not offer reassurance.[37]

Good caring + a weak medicine can give a better outcome than poor caring + a strong medicine.[38] This means that the placebo arm of one study can sometimes have better results than the active arm of another study. This causes endless confusion and complicates the search for evidence-based practice. Single-blinded design is even more shaky, which brings us back to expectations.

In a study of people having teeth removed, patients were told that they might get one of three injections for pain control that would make their pain 'better, worse, or have no effect': namely, fentanyl (a strong painkiller), naloxone (an opiate antagonist that would make pain worse) or placebo. The patient was 'blind'[39] but the dentist knew which group each patient was in. Figure 6.4 shows the response *to placebo* in the two groups of patients.[40] When the dentists knew the patient had a chance of a 'real' painkiller (PNF group), the placebo was 'activated' and was as distinct from the other placebo response as a 'real' medicine from an inert medicine. The carer knew there was a *chance* of receiving

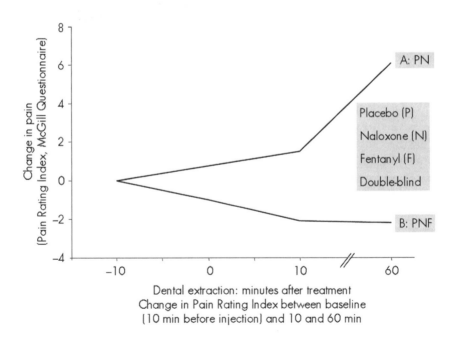

Figure 6.4   The transmitted clinicians' expectation of outcome influencing placebo response to pain of dental extraction.[40]

a 'real' medicine and somehow transmitted this to the patient, who then activated his or her own healing systems.

We can just as readily destroy such a reaction. Patients receiving 8 weeks of placebo or antidepressants were improving equally until those taking placebo were told so.[41] Most deteriorated and ended up on medications.

So the treatment, its presentation and expected effects interact with patient factors blended with the carer and the context to affect healing systems. It seems that the best results are achieved when a patient has confidence in the carer, the institution or the system of care and when these are congruent with the patient's attitudes, beliefs and expectations. The West has often ignored or marginalized direct engagement with self-healing (hypnotherapy has been one important approach), but, as Box 6.1 shows, anthropologists have seen that every human culture must engage these same dimensions, whether consciously or not.[42]

Box 6.1   Some universal cultural features in healing rituals (adapted from Helman[42])

1. Healer must have a coherent frame of reference or explanation – origin and nature of the problem and how it can be helped – germs, curse, chi
2. Symbolic bridge is made – a way of integrating relationships and situation in terms of the culture, and the healer's frame of reference
3. Healer aims to activate the bridge (often subliminal), persuade the client that the problem can be explained in their frames of reference: 'I can see you have ... cancer, curses, suppressed anger, irritable bowel'
4. Once cognitive consensus, now need emotionally involved, attached to the symbols, the frame of reference, e.g. convince the client he/she is possessed by a spirit, or depression, or has food allergies, and it will kill/damage him/her if not treated
5. Techniques and guided symbols of reference employed, e.g. prescription, exercise, diet, exorcism. Now over time the patient can reframe the situation in the light of the healer's reference, e.g. talk about the medicine's effect or the chakras balancing
6. Healed patient has acquired new narrative and way of functioning. We need a story to explain what happened: the tablets worked, the spirit is gone

---

Some of the mechanisms that link these external and internal modifiers to the body and its healing pathways are being discovered, for example, the science of psychoneuroimmunology.[43]

Inside the encounter

We now move from analytical reflection to life in action in the encounter.

The encounter is human. There will always be a relationship, even if only fleeting. The key ingredient you can influence is you.

Activating yourself – coming to presence

Recall for a moment the difference between music on in the background and listening to that music. The transition is clear between the two states, even though to an onlooker there is nothing to see. As an exercise, try repeatedly taking yourself 'into' and 'out of' music. How do you make that transition – how does it feel when you do it? Study and think about this internal change, because whatever this natural ability is it may be crucial for good human contact and so good consulting. It can even be the difference between a good outcome, no outcome and a bad outcome. It can be the difference between a healing relationship and a complaint. Or maybe you can think of this transition in relation to a meeting, or a movie, or a poem, or a wonderful conversation, or drawing, or singing, or playing an instrument, or making love or sports. Try finding examples from your own life of the movement between these two states and study it carefully. How do you achieve this 'listening', what blocks it, what helps it? How could you access it consciously? Attention, presence, awareness, mindfulness – a range of terms exists around this, but the reality is uncomplicated: we are either there or we are not. With practice focusing on this, encounters will improve, without any other change to current actions. Much of what follows is an expansion of this key point.

Active sensing

These ordinary abilities are so natural that we can fail to notice them. When you begin to talk to someone, at a professional function or a party, how long is it before you know if they are really interested? It is extremely quick – the blink of an eye. Behind those head nods, smiles and well-contacted eyes you know they are not really interested – there will be no lunch. Gut-feeling, subliminal facial gestures, their energy field – whatever our explanatory model – we sense this. And that's without communication skills training or that course in psychology – you have this skill already. And the more present we are, the more these sensing abilities can get through to us.

Active context – countering complacency

These innate abilities are heightened when a person's welfare or life is at stake – or they fear it is. For us that next patient is potentially just another case, for that 'case' it is their meeting – and their bullshit detectors are fully tuned on you. Charm won't fool their alarm system – their 'gut feelings'. We are often in a complacent and familiar state, it's our daily work after all, so consciously reminding ourselves of how important the situation is to our patient can help wake us up.

Preactivation: begin before the beginning

The consultation begins before the consultation begins. Have you ever been a patient or been involved in a loved one's medical encounter? These experiences are among the best teachers. Was it good? 'Why was I referred, what will they find, will I appear stupid, will the wait for the appointment allow things to get worse?' You check and double-check the appointment card on the mantelpiece, the transport to get there, who will come with you, if anyone. Then it's the night before – what will I wear? what will I say? will it be a doctor I've never met?

The context is powerful and preloaded, the stakes are up – and the opening seconds can make it or break it. Get this right and build the opening well and there can be such forgiving leeway in what then occurs that you will be surprised. Even if you are not in a heightened state it is best to assume the patient is – they usually are.

Beauty and the healing space

Consider the physical environment and make it as right for yourself and your patient as you can. We are wired for beauty. Calmness and harmony on the outside create conditions for creating this within ourselves. Research shows that contact with nature or views of nature are healing.[44] A few comments and illustrative examples on 'creating healing space' may be found on the website linked from www.ghh.info. It may not be your space, of course, and you may have little or no control over it, but perhaps you could at least have a few shells or stones you place on your desk.

The transition

Your preparation is critical. If you can, do something to support your move from the previous experience to the one you are about to have. This could be some sort of signal to yourself – perhaps just holding the case sheet of the next patient and reading the previous notes. But we are often rushed, so at a minimum grant yourself one good deep breath and a moment of calmness. It may help you to go and get the patient. Just the few seconds walking towards the waiting area can be used to focus yourself, and then seeing the patient for a second before, and as he or she reacts to you can be very helpful.

Motivation

We have spoken about reminding yourself of the importance to the next patient of what you are about to do, but you may need to help yourself find the motivation at this point, to find a reason to do your job. This is a subject in itself, but as I'll mention later, moving ourselves towards our core motivation, our compassion, is actually the most effective way to work, and the best for our own health.

Beginning or ending?

So here we are barely beyond the opening seconds, the beginning of the therapeutic alliance or the beginning of its end. And sometimes not a word has yet been spoken. If we could only change one thing that might help, it would be helping ourselves get out of the 'background music mode'. Truly be present and much else follows naturally.

Looking ahead – to creating join up

The natural flow that we want to follow next is towards connection. Imagine a dance, the type where you will move together. Your partner is already in a rhythm as you approach, and it may take time, and it could be awkward and 'sticky' at first as you come towards matching and moving with him/her. Once you have reached some connection, or 'join-up', there is a chance you can interact, influence, and even lead you both if appropriate to a different pace. This is the place from which good creative work will emerge. After join-up, ideas that are rejected before this state will be considered; information that would otherwise be forgotten may become meaning that changes us. What was the doctor being 'unkind' before join-up will become, after we are connected, the healthy confrontation that we needed. This is a way to build what the medical concept calls 'concordance' – good mutual connection helps lead to agreement between the practitioner and patient.

The key point is relationship. We are in the first stages of establishing trust and safety and respect. Time is not the issue here; time stands still in these moments. Some research even suggests that when we are near to someone, our heart tracing (electrocardiogram) can be read in his/her brain wave (electroencephalogram).[45] We affect one another.

When you really come into someone's presence, the feelings *you* begin to feel are important – sometimes that awkwardness or sadness or stilted conversation is letting you know how the other person is inside. Monitor these in yourself as the meeting begins and unfolds. Scan yourself and be aware of what is appearing. Keep some of your consciousness in your own body; this helps you stay present, and also feeds you information. In time we can learn to discern the difference from what we are sensing to what we are generating internally.

You

So they have had their preparation, and you have had (or failed to have) yours. A long night on call, a long decade in general practice, a way-too-short personal phone call spinning in your mind, as you approach the room, trolley, bed, counter. What are you going to have to do to access that music, resist it being background noise? You know how annoying and tiring that noise can be – 'get it off' or 'give me a break'. The only hope is to begin to listen, to become absorbed.

Your intention, motivation and attitude are underlying forces here. We need to keep these under review.

Your map

Your inner models of what the job is will determine what happens. I strive to see the person's strength, maybe buried under concrete for sure, maybe forgotten, and I wonder how it might be contacted, activated, released. This view will of course then automatically shape what follows in my meetings. Different maps give different journeys, like 'What can I do to take away your pain?' or 'What is your medicine?' Can you consider what are your current core maps that guide your work – and where do they lead you?

Approach in positive-neutral

As best you can, approach your patient in neutral, sensing, watching, listening carefully. It's best not to impose a standard consulting style on yourself and your patients, giving you flexibility to read and respond to what is appropriate. Incongruence can be there right away if you are, say, 'Dr Happy' for everyone.

The way the person walks in will speak volumes. For creative process, 'Who am I meeting?' can be more critical than 'What is the diagnosis?' This is one way I introduce myself: 'Hello. As I mentioned in the waiting area, I am David Reilly – call me David, Dr David or Dr Reilly – whatever is comfortable for you – how should I address you?' In an important situation, if someone calls you by the wrong or unfamiliar name – how does it feel?

When the room disappears

As things develop, you know you are moving there 'when the room disappears' – that state of 'being there' – you know it when watching a movie and you become engrossed and unaware of the room you are sitting in (as opposed to 'this is a coded pattern of light projected on a screen of illusion' sort of mental state). You know 'when the room disappears' in a great conversation, in a bad argument, in moments of creativity, in moments of change. It's natural, you have it already. It is one of the hallmarks of a consultation as opposed to a chance or haphazard crossing of paths. Will you bring this ability to create and enter that state to your work? Or will the patient remain as another diagnosis X, another heart sink or another old person?

Art

Although it can help our study to label and reference things, this can take what is human and turn it into technique. Imagine that we are talking about aspects of art. Music needs the technical things to be sound and working right – the scientific bits – but then something more is needed – an artistic self – and that applies as much to participating by listening as by making. Maybe this is what used to be called the 'art of medicine'. In our medical art we have to strive to become familiar with our tools (say drugs, surgery, remedies, acupuncture needles, communication techniques), but equally important is the creative processes that they serve. And both are transformed by underlying intention.

Create the conditions to create – and use more than one brain

The artist Jane Kelly says: 'first create the conditions to create, then create'. Knowing how to help access at conscious will a 'present' state (listening to the 'music' that is your patient) will in turn help make a creative state in yourself. This will help generate a creative state in the patient and so your interaction. Studying and practising other ways of getting into this mode can be of definite help – such as learning to draw, sing, dance, play music – whatever moves and inspires you – then use it to cross-fertilize your work. But none of these is essential however – every meeting with a patient will bring you an opportunity to develop this ability.

A useful scientific analogy for 'when the room disappears' comes from the Nobel prize-winning work of Sperry[46] which first described how the right and left cerebral hemispheres tend towards different ways of perceiving, processing and experiencing things. 'Right hemispheric mode' (best called R mode as it's not actually just in the right hemisphere) is characterised by whole-pattern, non-verbal, analogic, non-temporal, intuitive processing ('artistic') – likely the creative-listening state we have discussed here. In contrast, 'left hemispheric' (L mode) is analytical, verbal, reductionist, temporal, logical ('scientific') modes of thought. Our practical L mode contributions are more effective when we are also accessing and using active 'R mode'. Why consult with one hemisphere's hand tied behind your back? Betty Edwards' book *Drawing on the Right Side of the Brain*[47] can help you practise entering R mode at will. Learning a meditative practice is also deeply helpful.

Unmind

Creating a steady background field for all this to operate in is so important, and meditation and other 'non-doing', 'being' states, are important training practices to help us develop connection with the silence, the stillness in us between our thoughts, the witnessing consciousness that observes our thoughts and the thinker of these thoughts. Perhaps the study of what some call 'mindfulness' would be helpful (such as the writings of Thich Nhat Hanh[48]).

OK, I'm listening: what now?

Of course, access of the state we have been exploring is just a beginning: what are you going to do in and with it? Often we do not know what to do! Don't panic. Fortunately, the situation and your patient are creative in their own right (an old saying is 'listen to your patients, they are trying to tell you what is wrong with them'), and your effective listening and engagement will facilitate their efforts, sometimes with no other role required from you. You can definitely lean on this in the early part of your career, trusting that your active listening means you will be more sensitive to normal cues and signals and natural instinctive responses, while getting on with the usual technical jobs you have to do.

The heart of the matter

Your struggle to access this real connection with your patients will bring you to understand them and their predicament better, and so will naturally help bring out your empathy, compassion and other aspects of healing care. It is not sympathy we are seeking – a man experiencing sympathetic labour pains is not much use to his partner at that moment. Empathy is the capacity to imagine yourself in the other's shoes, with the focus on him/her. Your endeavour to achieve this is sensed and valued by the other. Patients rarely feel empowered if they do not experience the doctor as empathic. In one study of 200 consultations at the Glasgow Homoeopathic Hospital high levels of enablement/empowerment were found and this correlated to three main factors: expectations, the doctor's feeling that a therapeutic relationship was established, but much stronger than either of these was the patients' rating of their experience of the doctor's empathy. There was not one case of a patient scoring high enablement when the empathy score was low.[49]

As we build empathy, our compassion is brought to life, an emergent quality – the aspect of deep caring, of mercy, of wishing that someone might be released from suffering. This is a transformative medicine.

Change – zones of conditions

Let us move on now towards the subject of change. There are zones of conditions that allow change to occur, where trauma can be processed and ideas can change. This is influenced by all we have spoken about so far and includes the altered, focused states of presence that these meetings encourage in the patient and that we must encourage in ourselves. From this web of factors emerges the alliance – standing together with shared aims – and on this we can build a relationship: founded on safety and trust, real two-way flow between us can begin. Then we can build consensus, and fresh perspectives.

Projections

On this route will inevitably come the projections, transferences and countertransferences that are the stuff of deeper relationships. As humans have a tendency to project the light of our own ideas on to the other, so we end up matching our pre-existing inner maps. The world is not as it is, but as we see it. As we become more aware of that process, we can sometimes turn down the intensity of that projected light, and allow ourselves to begin to see the light emerging from the situation, and the person, rather than simply a projection of our inner movies on to it. Understanding this can help us not take personally patients' projections on to us – their anger, fear, accusation or excessive praise. And help us not dump our stuff on to them (in countertransference). This is a whole deep subject in itself, and here we can only flag up its critical importance.

Changing maps and stories

So much of our suffering is generated by the thoughts we believe – I'll call that a map – and the resultant stories we generate in our minds. A map, followed in time, becomes a story or a journey. Emotions follow from thoughts, as we generate and deepen our internal movies. Body follows mind as we become engrossed in the movie. We tell ourselves stories of what we call 'the past' and this usually generates sadness, bitterness, regret and guilt. We tell ourselves stories of 'the future' and this will cause anxiety and fear, or we go and live in an imaginary future and from there look back and make sadness in ourselves about imaginary pasts. But all this happens only in the *now*. It is now we construct virtual worlds of imaginary times past or to come. This holds the key to change. Change occurs in the present, and therapeutic conditions can seed new, more successful ideas in ourselves, picking from the seed bank inside, and those offered by the practitioner, or system of care. An intervention is first and foremost a symbol – the carrier of a new idea and a different story. It says 'change is possible, follow me'.

This can be done automatically, without conscious process or increased awareness. 'Oh, that's better, doctor, thank you, it's fixed, that medicine (remedy, technique whatever) was great. I'll certainly come back to see you if things go wrong again.'

Or, more powerfully, change can also happen in a way that increases our awareness and understanding of these mechanisms of mind, learning as a result to enter a self-discovery cycle and releasing ourselves in stages from the impact of these mechanisms. 'You know, I have come to see things differently. I had no idea I was so uptight, and still afraid of that.'

Be it automatically or consciously, we first journey with the healer (at times we can take that role for ourselves) through the stages of feeling when our story is heard without judgement, with respect, with compassion. This in itself catalyses change. Then the next stage involves a negotiated change in our original story. Here often the practitioner directly or indirectly offers fresh and different stories. The language may be directly symbolic, metaphoric, poetic, that of the inner world – or this is carried indirectly by the symbols of our care – our tablets, our procedures each carry a story layered with meaning. 'I think you would benefit from a remedy' (already hope is being seeded, a fresh story with potential in it). 'It is called Staphysagria, a plant' (more symbolism). 'It is about helping to free the impact of suppressed anger and past hurt. It may facilitate an initial release of old material at first' (powerful delivery of a restructuring story of how I got here, the fact that I can change and what it may involve). 'This may take some time, and we will check in together at intervals along the way' (signalling the healing journey and its stages).

A more automatic change can of course still be engendered by a silent style, or authoritarianism, not even naming the remedy or saying what it is about, and silence carries messages. Meaning is context-bound as much as it is in the specific elements of our action and inaction.

A consciousness about this process is central to the development of our practice beyond that of our technical skill. It is a lifetime work, but the issue is: we *are* having an impact even if we are not aware, and help or harm is potentially only a word away. As we are already impacting, it is better to make it a more conscious process.

If we know that at this time, in our career, our life right now, in this meeting today, we cannot tackle a more creative engagement with the specific aspects of a particular encounter, that is critically helpful self-knowledge that will prevent harm. If we do not know what to say, say nothing, and keep seeking the patient's guidance, hold the situation. Fortunately the general factors we have discussed are so often the critical ones, and the more 'crafted' elements used by experienced practitioners should not be equated with the encounter. A seed knows how to grow; our job is to set the conditions.

Evidence-based poetry

Can this stuff be studied? Yes, if what is sought is the experience of the people involved. We know if a poem moved us, and no 'objective' view by someone else will do. In one of the qualitative studies at Glasgow Homoeopathic Hospital, Stewart Mercer's interviews with patients helped summarise some key ingredients they saw in their successful encounters – and they were all possible without advanced 'therapy' skills[50]:

- Patients valued the time available, the whole-person approach and being treated as an individual.
- They felt their story was listened to (often for the first time) and all their symptoms were taken seriously.
- They felt that doctors at Glasgow Homoeopathic Hospital were trustworthy, compassionate and positive, often engendering hope.
- Equality of membership was a major theme with a strong sense of mutual respect.

Self-care

This would be a good time to reflect on your self-care:

- How can you remain in balance as you develop the ability to be present in this way with people, and continue to do so repeatedly patient after patient?
- How can you open up to greater compassion and peace inside yourself?
- How will you discharge your responsibility to keep alive your passion and enjoyment?
- What are you doing about your burnout, your own self-neglect, work addiction – your whatever?

To experience your own stress fully, breakdown and path to recovery is our best teacher here. You give help to others, now will you bring it to yourself? Help from others, self-support and self-healing practices are critical for you as a practitioner.

Building a wall between you and your job and clients will only isolate you and cut you off. Remember I mentioned that skilled meditator in the brain scanner? The form of meditation that most woke up his positive mood centre was the meditation on compassion – which is practised firstly with a focus on ourself, and then towards others. Worked this way, our amazing job of connecting with people in a healing way can also help us to help ourselves.

Dealing with particular techniques

This chapter has been about the common ingredients in all creative therapeutic encounter, in seeking change, whatever the toolbox of the given practitioner. Box 6.2 reflects on these shared foundations of healing change.

Box 6.2 The shared foundations of healing change

Seeking change
In a context of inherent change
In a safe relationship
Anchored to the present
We share and experience our stories
Together, we build
Compassionate acceptance
New understanding of the mind and story
Assisting fresh review
Catalysing
Supported by symbol and ritual if need be
New viewpoints and meaning
Emergent change

Now let us consider how it is framed on particular occasions.

Maybe the ritual on this occasion is a prescription, or eye movement desensitization and reprocessing, or neurolinguistic programming or narrative-based exploring, or a spinal manipulation, or the recommendation of a book, a poem, writing, drawing, crying, a dreaming journal, exercise. The variations of what we build on the shared foundations discussed here are endless, with a spectrum from authoritarian external 'fix-it' to no intervention apart from the sparking of the person's own motivation for change.

So let's look now at these aspects applied in the context of a particular technique: homeopathy.

Homeopathy

In homeopathic practice, there is usually acknowledgement that two great elements combine: the homeopathic remedy and the homeopathic method. As already suggested, if we do not study the latter, and the linked issues of the potential of healing responses and relationships without remedies, then our assessments of the responses to remedies will be naive.

Synergy

In this chapter we have not concerned ourselves with the medicine's biological mechanisms, more its power as a symbolic catalyst of inherent self-healing mechanisms. Yet, if the view is correct that homeopathic medicines act through the body's own self-healing mechanisms, then I may be right in the hypothesis that it acts at times on the same biological pathways as spontaneous healing. The placebo and nocebo studies seem to be underlining how critical it is to line up these two forces of intervention and inherent responses in harmony together. By achieving concordance between the patient's beliefs, expectations and enthusiasms, and those of the practitioner and the system of care, we will improve the result.

Science and the double-positive paradox

This dynamic impacts on the debate about the scientific efficacy of homeopathy. In controlled trials if the 'non-specific/placebo' impact is strong, the competing active medication has less chance of demonstrating any additional impact (the statistical power of the trial is reduced). As a result either very large studies are needed, or a context that reduces the placebo effect – but that in turn would risk also compromising the remedy action. I have explored this elsewhere under the term 'the double-positive paradox' because some 'negative trials' actually show excellent clinical results in both groups.[51]

The healing response and the medicine response

As homeopathy acts by stimulating natural healing, all the phenomena seen after a remedy acts can be seen when healing has been catalysed by other means. I have seen, when no remedy has been given, whole-person response patterns, aggravations, direction of cure, return of old trouble, generation of well-being before local change, generation of dreams, development of insight, change in functional and organic illness.

So we need to question not the part of our consultation that determines *if* healing is occurring, only the *why*. It is wise to keep a certain uncertainty around this. But the concepts of stages of recovery and obstacles to cure apply equally if viewing things homeopathically or generally.

Not prescribing

If the context allows, best to check if the person still wants a prescription at all. I have spoken of the power in the situation when the patient says no, then you both have a chance to see what happens – later to add a medicine if need be. It's rare for any medical intervention to be a necessity at any given moment – threats to life and function are relatively rare. However contexts and cultures often determine that a prescription will be needed, or it will be the last time you see that patient.

Choosing the prescribing

If you are going to prescribe, check what aspect of the situation the patient feels is the most important to tackle, bringing you both into agreement as best you can. What are the patient's ideas of what needs to be done? Does the patient think a remedy is needed now? Aimed at what (If we could help one thing …? What is the main obstacle to your progress?)? Which remedy had the patient thought of? When you are swaying between choices of remedy (not exactly a rare situation), the answers to these questions can usefully guide you.

The medicine's story

You have seen the power of homeopathy to encode common human patterns of distress and response. Their strength is drawn from not being theoretical but directly describing our shared human experiences. The medicine or remedy 'picture' is well named. These beautiful portraits encode powerful stories – we see ourselves in them, mirrored back in fresh light. It raises us from our isolated and stuck states and seeds new thoughts of change, new possibilities. Sharing a little of the story of what you are about to prescribe *is* to prescribe. The change may begin in that moment.

The dosage regime

You can go further in this lining up together of you, your patient, the patient's story, your story, the remedy and the story of the intervention.

Many people will have a clear reaction when you say: 'Remedies can be given as either ongoing daily doses in tablets or drops, or more like a vaccine with occasional booster doses'. You may not even have finished when you are interrupted: 'Drops'. So you continue: 'I would like you to take 3 or 4 drops each day, and perhaps as you do you can remember the main points of our conversation and those commitments you have just made to yourself'. This can retrigger work you did together in the consultation (see Chapters 3 and 10).

Of course some people will let you know that in their eyes all these decisions are your call, which is an interesting story in itself to bring out.

The relationship

So we creatively line up the elements, tuning the many parts involved. All the while it is the quality of our connection that is allowing us to read how things are going. 'What do you make of that?' becomes a common question, and history-taking evolves from that of events toward the impact of the events. It is in the end not what happens to us sometimes, but the received meaning of this which makes the impact. Here the specific homeopathic method can enhance the general processes, but we need to be aware that it can also be used mechanistically in an even crazier version of tickbox medicine than our conventional practices have created.

It is the quality of our human caring, an authentic compassion, that raises the awareness of these technical realities of mind and therapy to a level above that of technique, to let them simply serve as supports for the real work of our human caring.

Acknowledgement

Earlier versions of some sections of this article appeared in my seven-part student *Br Med J* article on creative consulting in 2002, and from that I wish to thank Zeldi di Blasi, who co-wrote the section on placebo research.

Further reading

Further references, ideas and information on David Reilly's teaching can be reached on www.adhom.com and www.davidreilly.net.

Kaplan B (2001) *The Homeopathic Conversation*. London: Natural Medicine Press.

Owen D (2007) *Principles and Practice of Homeopathy*. Edinburgh: Churchill Livingstone Elsevier.

Swayne J (1997) *Homeopathic Method*. Edinburgh: Churchill Livingstone.

References

1. Leuchter A F, Cook I A, Witte E A, *et al*. Changes in brain function of depressed subjects during treatment with placebo. *Am J Psychiatry* 2002; 159: 122–129.
2. Reilly D T, Taylor M A. Potent placebo or potency? A proposed study model with initial findings using homoeopathically prepared pollens in hay fever. *Br Homoeopathic J* 1985; 74: 65–75.
3. Reilly D T, Taylor M A, McSharry C, *et al*. Is homoeopathy a placebo response? Controlled trial of homoeopathic potency, with pollen in hay fever as model. *Lancet* 1986; ii: 881–886.
4. Taylor M A, Reilly D, Llewellyn-Jones R H, *et al*. Randomised controlled trial of homoeopathy versus placebo in perennial allergic rhinitis with overview of four trial series. *Br Med J* 2000; 321: 471–476.
5. Reilly D T, Taylor M A, Beattie N G M, *et al*. Is evidence for homoeopathy reproducible? *Lancet* 1994; 344: 1601–1606.
6. Reilly D T, Taylor M A. Individual patients and their responses – OPICS. *Comp Ther Med* 1993; 1 (Suppl. 1): 26–28.
7. Gracely R H, Dubner R, Deeter W R, *et al*. Clinicians' expectations influence placebo analgesia. *Lancet* 1985; i: 43.
8. Reilly D. The unblind leading the blind: the Achilles heel of too many trials. *J Altern Comp Med* 2000; 6: 479–480.
9. Benson H. The nocebo effect: history and physiology. *Prevent Med* 1997; 26: 612–615.
10. Kienle G S, Kiene H. The powerful placebo effect: fact or fiction? *J Clin Epidemiol* 1997; 50: 1311–1318.
11. Luparello T, Leist N, Lourrie C H, *et al*. The interaction of psychological stimuli and pharmacologic agents on airway reactivity in asthmatic subjects. *Psychosom Med* 1970; 32: 509–513.
12. Isenberg S A, Lehrer P M, Hochron S. The effects of suggestion and emotional arousal on pulmonary function in asthma. A review and a hypothesis regarding vagal meditation. *Psychosom Med* 1992; 54: 192–216.
13. Schweiger A, Parducci A, Pav J. Nocebo: the psychologic induction of pain. *Biol Sci* 1981; 16: 140–143.
14. Rosenweig P, Brohier S, Zipfel A. The placebo effect in healthy volunteers: influence of the experimental conditions on the adverse events profile during phase I studies. *Clin Pharmacol Ther* 1993; 54: 578–583.
15. Thomas K B. Is there any point in being positive? *Br Med J* 1987; 294: 1200–1202.
16. Engel G L. Sudden and rapid death during psychological stress: folklore or folk wisdom? *Ann Intern Med* 1971; 74: 1325–1335.
17. Spiegel H. Nocebo: the power of suggestibility. *Prevent Med* 1997; 26: 616–621.

18.   Spiegel D, Bloom J R, Kraemer H C, *et al*. Effects of psychosocial treatment on survival of patients with metastatic breast cancer. *Lancet* 1989; ii: 886–891.

19.   Kienle G S, Kiene H. The powerful placebo effect: fact or fiction? *J Clin Epidemiol* 1997; 50: 1311–1318.

20.   Kienle G S, Kiene H. The placebo effect: a scientific critique. *Comp Ther Med* 1998; 6: 14–24.

21.   Hrobjartsson A, Gotzsche P C. Is the placebo powerless? An analysis of clinical trials comparing placebo with no treatment. *N Engl J Med* 2001; 344: 1594–1602.

22.   de la Fuente-Fernández R, Ruth T J, Sossi V, *et al*. Expectation and dopamine release: mechanism of the placebo effect in Parkinson's disease. *Science* 2001, 293: 1164–1166.

23.   Petrovic P, Kalso E, Petersson K M, *et al*. Placebo and opioid analgesia – imaging a shared neuronal network. *Science* 2002; 295: 1737–1740.

24.   Goldman D. *Destructive Emotions – A Scientific Dialogue with the Dalai Lama*. New York: Random House, 2003.

25.   Lasagna L, Mosteller F, von Felsinger J M, *et al*. A study of the placebo response. *Am J Med* 1954; 16: 770–779.

26.   Lasagna L, Mosteller F, von Felsinger J M, *et al*. A study of the placebo response. *Am J Med* 1954; 16: 770–779.

27.   Buckalew L W, Coffield K E. An investigation of drug expectancy as a function of capsule colour and size and preparation form. *J Clin Psychopharmacol* 1982; 2: 245–248.

28.   de Craen A J M, Roos P J, de Vries A L, *et al*. Effect of colour of drugs: systematic review of perceived effect of drugs and of their effectiveness. *Br Med J* 1996; 313: 1624–1626.

29.   Beecher H K. Surgery as placebo. *JAMA* 1961; 176: 1102–1107.

30.   Cobb L, Thomas G I, Dillard D H, *et al*. An evaluation of internal-mammary-artery ligation by a double-blind technique. *N Engl J Med* 1959; 260: 1115–1118.

31.   Holm S, Evans M. Product names, proper claims? More ethical issues in the marketing of drugs. *Br Med J* 1996; 313: 1627–1629.

32.   Branthwaite A, Cooper P. Analgesic effects of branding in treatment of headaches. *Br Med J Clin Res Ed* 1981; 282: 1576–1578.

33.   Kirsch I, Sapirstein G. Listening to Prozac but hearing placebo: a meta-analysis of antidepressant medication. In: Kirsch I, ed. *Expectancy, Experience and Behaviour*. Washington, DC: American Psychological Association, 1999: 303–320.

34.   Butler C, Steptoe A. Placebo responses: an experimental study of psycho-physiological processes in asthmatic volunteers. *Br J Clin Psychol* 1986; 25: 173–183.

35.   Herrnstein R J. Placebo effect in the rat. *Science* 1962; 138: 677–678.

36.   Shapiro A K. Iatroplacebogenics. *Int J Pharmacopsychiatry* 1969; 2: 215.

37.   Di Blasi Z, Harkness E, Ernst E, *et al*. Influence of context effects on health outcomes: a systematic review. *Lancet* 2001; 357: 757–762.

38.   Walach H. The efficacy paradox in randomised controlled trials of CAM and elsewhere: beware of the placebo trap. *J Altern Comp Med* 2001; 7: 213–218.

39. Gracely R H, Dubner R, Deeter W R, *et al*. Clinicians' expectations influence placebo analgesia (letter). *Lancet* 1985; i: 4.

40. Mercer S W, Reilly D. A qualitative study of patients' views on the consultation at the Glasgow Homoeopathic Hospital, an NHS integrative complementary and orthodox medical care unit. *Patient Educ Couns* 2004; 53: 13–18.

41. Fox M. Brain scan study shows how placebo aids depression. 01.01 2002 Reuters. http://www.forbes.com/newswire/2002/01/01/rtr467478.html.

42. Helman H. Placebo and nocebos: the cultural construction of belief. conference: the placebo response: biology and belief. In: Peters D, ed. *Understanding the Placebo Effect in Complementary Medicine*. London: Churchill Livingstone, 2001: 3–16.

43. http://www.studentBr Med J.com/issues/02/04/education/97.php.

44. Ulrich R. Views through a window may influence recovery from surgery. *Science* 1984; 224: 420–421.

45. McCraty R, Atkinson M, Tiller W. The role of physiological coherence in the detection and measurement of cardiac energy exchange between people. In: Proceedings of the Tenth International Montreux Congress on Stress. Montreux, Switzerland: 1999.

46. Sperry R W. Hemisphere disconnection and unity in conscious awareness. *Am Psychol* 1968; 23: 723–733.

47. Edwards B. *Drawing on the Right Side of the Brain*. London: Souvenir Press, 2000.

48. Nhat Hanh T. *The Miracle of Mindfulness*. London: Rider, 1991.

49. Mercer S W, Watt G C M, Reilly D. Empathy is important for enablement. *Br Med J* 2001; 322: 865.

50. Mercer S W, Reilly D. A qualitative study of patients' views on the consultation at the Glasgow Homoeopathic Hospital, an NHS integrative complementary and orthodox medical care unit. *Patient Educ Couns* 2004; 53: 13–18.

51. Reilly D. When is useful improvement a waste of time? Double positive paradox of negative trials (letter). *Br Med J* 2002; 325: 41.

7

The diverse nature of homeopathic practice

Bob Leckridge

Introduction

This chapter looks at the global diversity of homeopathic practice, showing how it may be applied in different communities.

Homeopathy as a therapy has been argued over constantly from the time of Hahnemann right up to the present day. There have always been quite different and sometimes apparently contradictory schools of homeopathic practice. Within one single community you will find a diversity of styles of approach and of practice. Between different communities in different countries the amount of variation increases. How can there be a multitude of differences in homeopathic practice? Is there one true pure homeopathy and everything apart from that is some kind of heresy? Such questions are extremely common in the world of homeopathic practice.

The reasons for this are not hard to understand. Homeopathy, like happiness, or love, or even health, is not an entity. It cannot be succinctly defined and codified. However, there are certain themes or characteristics that are common to all homeopathic practice, even though they are expressed quite differently. A good analogy can be found in biology where an organism has a certain genotype which it shares in common with other members of its species but also has a particular phenotype fashioned and formed by interaction between the genetic themes and the contexts of the environments in which the organism lives.

To understand the variety of 'phenotypes' of homeopathy, it is necessary to clarify the 'genotype' which they all share. This can be done by looking at homeopathic practice as it arose from the original observations of Samuel Hahnemann. His first observation remains the essential characteristic of all homeopathic practice. It was that 'like cures like'. In all the diversity of practice, this principle is applicable.

Whoever the practitioner is, whatever the culture in which he or she is working, the approach to treatment will be founded on this observation. Hahnemann's second observation arose from his method of preparation of the drugs he chose to use. Starting from the intention to tip the balance of benefit versus harm towards benefit and away from harm, he set out to discover what the minimum effective dose would be. In other words, how little of the drug could produce the maximum benefit with the least possible harm. His preparation method involved two procedures – dilution and succussion (see Chapter 10). At each stage of preparation the drug would be subjected to further dilution and further succussion. Somewhat to his surprise he discovered that the drugs seemed to increase their therapeutic potential the *more* they were diluted and succussed. This led to what remains the most controversial element of homeopathic practice – the use of preparations which not only do not contain any molecules of the original starting material *and* the belief that the more dilute and succussed doses are clinically *more* powerful. Scientific discoveries since Hahnemann's day have failed to explain this observation and some scientists believe that both such phenomena are so implausible that the entire homeopathic method must be at best a placebo or sham method and at worst delusion or deceit. The arguments about this can be had elsewhere. Suffice it to say that this method of drug preparation is unique. No other therapeutic regimen prepares its medicines in this manner (there is an overlap in method with the preparation of some anthroposophical medicines but it is not identical). There are several different ways to prepare homeopathic medicines according to these principles. This leads to different potency scales – decimal, centessimal and LM scales. Hahnemann experimented with all three of these scales in his clinical practice (see Chapter 10).

These two distinct characteristics of the homeopathic method devised by Hahnemann are applied to greater and lesser extents by contemporary practitioners. The fact that they are applied variably is the basis of much of the diversity of homeopathic practice. However, there is a third element which contributes much to the variation. Hahnemann's approach was holistic. He was interested in the entire experience of the patient, not just in any symptoms that would be indicative of a particular lesion or disease. He considered that everything of the patient's experience was relevant and that *all* the changes the patient was experiencing constituted the picture of the disease. This observation and principle was used therapeutically by being applied to both the patient and to the medicine. In order to apply his 'like cures like' method, Hahnemann had to understand the potential of medicinal substances in the same holistic way as he understood the patient. He did this by carrying out observational studies of groups of healthy individuals who volunteered to take the substances and experience their effects. These studies were called 'provings' and when published formed the starting information for the materia medica of homeopathic medicines (see Chapters 4 and 5).

Categorisation of symptoms

Hahnemann's holistic approach led to the categorisation of symptoms as local, general or mental. *Local* symptoms are symptoms attributed to a distinct part of the body. They are largely physical sensations which form the patient's presenting complaint and they mainly arise from what doctors would term the 'disease', i.e. from the pathology of the patient's illness. *General* symptoms are best understood as the whole-body disturbances of a person's illness. They are general because they are not related to single parts of the body. Typically a general symptom is a kind of environmental symptom – chilliness, heat intolerance, perspiration, weather influences, sleep patterns and the effects of different foodstuffs on the person, for example. *Mental* symptoms encompass both cognitive symptoms such as concentration, memory and speech, and emotions such as anger, sadness and fear. The mental symptoms constitute not just the personality characteristics of the patients but both their beliefs about the world and their coping strategies when challenged.

At its most holistic, homeopathic practice is based on what Hahnemann called the 'totality' of symptoms. This is really an impossible ideal! Can a prescriber really take into consideration absolutely every local, general and mental symptom the patient mentions and match them *all* against the remedy which has been shown to have every single one of those symptoms in its materia medica picture? Rarely, if ever, but it is still a useful principle because it means that the greater the extent of the match between the patient's symptoms and the symptoms of the homeopathic medicine, the greater the response is likely to be. However, the situation is just a little bit more complicated than that because the presentation of a patient's symptoms spread evenly over 'locals', 'generals' and 'mentals' is more two-dimensional than it should be. Whilst it is true that from a homeopathic perspective illness is always about the whole person, in reality some illnesses involve a lot more disturbance of particular parts of the human being than others. This has been referred to as 'centre of gravity' of a case. What this means is that, rather than being evenly spread, symptoms in any individual circumstance may well be clustered primarily around just one or two of these three category areas.

To summarise: there are three threads or themes of homeopathic practice (the homeopathic genotype) which interact in widely variant ways to produce a rich diversity of clinical practice (the homeopathic phenotype). These three threads are: (1) the principle of 'like cures like'; (2) the technique of homeopathic drug preparation; and (3) the holistic understanding of symptoms clustered around 'locals', 'generals' and 'mentals'. Let us now consider a number of different examples to show just how diverse homeopathic practice can be.

A focus on the 'mentals'

At the turn of the 20th century, the American homeopath Kent and his colleagues promoted the concept of a 'hierarchy of symptoms'. They argued that not all symptoms were equally important or useful in helping the homeopath to find the homeopathic medicine which was most likely to help a particular patient. In fact, they argued that mental symptoms were more important than general ones which were, in turn, more important than local ones. This hierarchy therefore emphasised the patient's illness (individual mental and general features) over the disease (the pathognomonic features of the disease expressed in the local features). This had two consequences. Firstly, it emphasised a holistic and individualised approach. Secondly, it promoted the mental symptoms as being the most important in understanding illness. Both of these effects have been extrapolated forwards to the current day. Many people would argue that the holistic emphasis which downplays the significance of the pathognomonic local symptoms is entirely consistent with Hahnemann's orginal description of his own approach. Adherents have claimed the label of 'classical' to describe this style of practice (classical homeopaths also adhere to certain other principles, as will be considered later). However, others have moved away from Kent's holism towards something almost psychoanalytic. The work of Vithoulkas and his followers from the 1970s onwards tended increasingly to emphasise the mental symptoms to the extent that in every circumstance they would seek an understanding of the patient's personality, emotional and mental wounds from the past, and behavioural coping strategies. Probably one of the best-known schools of practice which emphasised the mental symptoms is that of the Indian homeopath, Rajan Sankaran, whose earlier books described his method of focusing on the 'central delusion' of the patient. By this, simply, he meant uncovering the main mental symptom. Over the last 30 years or so, this became the dominant model of homeopathic practice amongst classical homeopaths. It has partly contributed to experimentation with models of homeopathy which emphasise the non-specific effects of the method. This has led to both good training in consultation techniques and to a side-stepping of the issues of the mechanism of action of the homeopathic drugs.

The focus on the 'mentals' can take a patient by surprise. Imagine someone who is experiencing weakness and loss of sensation due to nerve damage with the disease multiple sclerosis. The symptoms might be only footdrop and numb patches on one leg, but the homeopath starts to ask about mood, about anger and grief, about the need for company, about the patient's weepiness, and so on. The patient can begin to think 'What's all this got to do with my left foot?' or even to worry that the homeopath just does not believe the patient has a physical disease, preferring a psychological explanation for the symptoms instead. Of course, this is a misunderstanding which can be avoided by clear communication and explanation about the reasons for the questioning in the first place, but in more controversial illnesses, e.g. chronic fatigue syndrome, such misunderstandings can cause unnecessary suffering.

One of the major problems with the more extreme focus on the mental symptoms is that not everyone likes to talk about their emotions. If the homeopath understands the patient's illness, almost exclusively, in psychological terms, then it can be difficult to 'find the remedy' and help the patient.

From a first-principles basis, it may be that the 'centre of gravity' of the case is not in the mental sphere. If this is the case then seeking the solution in that area will be doomed to failure. Perhaps it is for these reasons that even the schools that emphasised the focus on the 'mentals' have developed more recently to broaden their teaching to include a better understanding of the 'generals'. This is more consistent with the original method of Hahnemann.

A focus on the 'generals'

Towards the end of the 19th century, another homeopath, Boeninghausen, taught the homeopathic method which gave great emphasis on the patient's 'general' symptoms. These symptoms could primarily be understood by uncovering the whole-person experiences of the patient (the symptoms which were expressed with 'I' rather than 'my', e.g. 'I feel worse in the cold' versus 'My foot pain is worse in the cold'). This method was different from that proposed by Kent because it paid less attention to the mental symptoms. Historically, in much of the world, this particular approach has not found much favour until very recently. It is currently undergoing something of a resurrection. Perhaps this is in part a kickback from the overly psychological methods of those who have emphasised the patient's mental symptoms.

With this method, the homeopath is particularly interested to understand the contexts of the patient's experience – what exactly does the patient feel and in which circumstances? ('Circumstances' include time of day, body position or activity, relationship to food, etc.) This is an interesting method because it is focused on the whole patient and is particularly revealing about the patient's non-psychological adaptive strategies, which is quite an unusual approach in medicine. However, this method suffers from the same type of problem as the one focused on the mentals. The homeopath really does need to explain to the patient why he or she is interested in the patient's relationship to the weather, patterns of change over time and relationship to foodstuffs or the patient will be quite unsure why these things are being asked about. Again, according to first principles, if the 'centre of gravity' is not in this area, then the exploration of the 'generals' will be unrevealing and unhelpful.

A focus on the 'locals'

The symptoms which the homeopath classifies as 'local' tend to be the ones most closely related to the actual pathology in the patient. For this reason, this approach is sometimes referred to as the 'pathological' approach, or a 'disease-focused' one. At the end of the 19th century, when Kent was championing the method based around the 'mentals' and Boeninghausen was championing the one based around the 'generals', Boger was the champion of the method that gave precedence to understanding the patient's disease. Indeed it is this model which is potentially the most easily understood by both doctors and their patients. Doctors understand it because they are trained to make diagnoses and assume a direct relationship between symptoms and pathologies. Patients understand it because the local symptoms are typically their presenting complaints. This method is, however, criticised for two reasons. Firstly, it is less holistic, giving more attention to the disease which the patient has than to the patient who has the disease. Secondly, it is less individualised and therefore tends to lead to prescribing on the basis of certain drugs for certain diseases (whereas the other two methods emphasise the likelihood of any two patients with the same disease actually receiving entirely different homeopathic drugs).

The method focusing on the mentals is considered to be almost diametrically opposed to the method that focuses on the locals. However, the 'centre of gravity' question can solve the conflict by leading the homeopath to use the method most appropriate to the individual patient's main problem.

Different cultures, different emphases

In certain countries cultural and historical factors have produced a predominance of one style of practice over the others. The following simplification is based mainly on personal observations and meetings with homeopathic colleagues internationally.

The American approach typically emphasises the mental symptoms. Hence, Kent's Repertory[1] (and its more modern configurations) is a common tool used by American homeopaths. American patients expect a homeopathic consultation to be lengthy and will feel comfortable with much of that time being spent on allowing them to talk about their thoughts and their feelings. In fact, American people are often more comfortable talking about such things than people of other nationalities so this mentals-focus approach works well in the USA. In India, it is much less likely that patients will express themselves using mental symptoms. They are much more likely to understand and express their bodily symptoms than their psychological ones. For this reason, consultations in India tend to focus on the patient's local and general symptoms and the Indian homeopathic doctor often seems adept at moving between the three approaches according to the 'centre of gravity' of the case.

A good example of this was the collection of books I saw on the desk of an Indian doctor's consulting room. He had three repertories (these are the books homeopaths use to prompt them to think about a particular remedy for a patient) as opposed to the more usual one. In the UK and the USA I have only seen Kent's Repertory on homeopaths' desks (or one of the modern Kentian versions), but in India this particular doctor had Kent's Repertory (used when the focus was on the mentals), Boeninghausen's Repertory (used when the focus was on the generals) and Boger's Repertory (used when the focus was on the disease – the locals). Physical pathologies are also often presented at more extreme states of development in India than they are in the USA, so the Indian homeopathic doctor often has to deal with more severe and obvious physical disease than the American one.

For other cultural and historical reasons, a pathological approach is very common in France, where typically a patient's disease is the leading focus of the consultation and the prescription is often less individualised than in India or the USA.

In Chapters 15 and 16 there are personal accounts of homeopathic practice in South Africa and Japan.

In every country then, the dominant style of practice will be influenced by the cultural and historical factors that fashion the way in which people express their suffering in addition to the traditions of teaching in a particular society. It can also be argued that each society finds its own way to adopt Hahnemann's findings and create a style of homeopathic practice which is most appropriate for their own circumstances.

Styles based on prescription

The classical approach involves more than just a particular focus or approach to the patient's symptoms. As it emphasises a holistic approach which highly individualises every analysis, so the prescription tends to one of the single most appropriate homeopathic drug – the one that represents the closest simillimum. In this approach the patient will most likely receive a prescription for only homeopathic medicine, and the patient may be prescribed only a single dose. For these reasons, the French refer to this method as the 'uniciste' approach. The prescription is made on the basis of totality and the one single remedy is expected to stimulate a deep and holistic cure. The French call a method which involves the prescription of several remedies at once a 'pluraciste' approach. A Chef de Service at Hôpital St Jacques in Paris (a homeopathic hospital where this method was used and taught) once explained to me that when patients presented their symptoms to him he saw them like a diamond with a number of facets. Certain facets would shine towards him and his prescription would then be on the basis of one remedy for each facet (every remedy being chosen to be the best simillimum for that facet). This was a poetic way to explain his approach but one that I have remembered forever. By facets, he meant clusters of symptoms, and his prescription would include one remedy for certain local symptoms, another for others, maybe a third for the general symptoms and yet another for the mental ones. This approach has been dismissed by some classical homeopaths as polypharmacy but it is a widely used method which has been developed in several different countries. With different homeopaths the facets they choose to consider may be different. In the example above the facets related to clusters of symptoms around the traditional locals, generals and mentals. In others, facets may relate to what are referred to as 'levels of disturbance' with specific medicines being chosen to treat each disturbed level – from superficial to deep, from acute to chronic, from totality to miasmatic. The complexities of the large number of variations of this method need not be considered in this particular chapter but the basic point is to see that in addition to a 'uniciste' (single best remedy) method, there is a 'pluraciste' one (several remedies, each selected for particular aspects of the patient's illness). Another feature that is held in common amongst the variety of different 'pluraciste' approaches is that, whilst a prescription may contain a number of homeopathic medicines, there will be a schedule of prescribing. Remedy A may be prescribed to be taken daily, remedy B weekly, and remedy C only taken on the first day of the regime, for example.

A third approach prescribes several homeopathic medicines all at the same time. The French refer to this as the 'complexiste' approach. The medicines prescribed are known as complexes and contain several different homeopathic remedies in one tablet. The method of composition of these complexes tends to be on the basis of a pathological approach. Each complex contains a number of medicines all prepared homeopathically, each of which is considered to be commonly indicated in the treatment of a specific disease. So, for example, there may be one combination for travel sickness, one for insomnia and so on. This has the advantage for pharmaceutical companies that the particular complex can be branded and marketed on a simple over-the-counter basis. The disadvantage is that, although the drugs are prepared homeopathically, the prescribing is neither holistic nor individualised. It's easy to see that such wide diversity of approach can be confusing for patients and causes enormous controversy between the adherents to the different methods.

The use of complexes varies enormously between countries. In the UK their use is currently limited whereas in France there are many complexes on the market and the strong homeopathic pharmaceutical manufacturers even run their own short training courses to teach doctors how to prescribe their products.

Different styles for different clinical contexts

The wide variety of styles described above can be found to varying degrees in any country where homeopathy is practised. The extent to which any particular style of practice is available in any particular country is influenced by historical and cultural factors that particularly influence the teaching of new practitioners in one country and by the market features of the homeopathic drug production and distribution of that country. However, within these variations there is also a tendency for some methodologies to predominate in an entirely appropriate way in certain clinical contexts. For example, in the clinical context of acute medicine, the main method may well be the pathological approach. This is due to a number of factors. Firstly, there is a time pressure to acute work. Patients are presenting with a high degree of clinical urgency and there is simply not enough time to take a full homeopathic history to reveal the totality of the case. Secondly, in all illnesses the picture is a mixture of the features generated by the pathology and the features of the particular person as he or she expresses disturbance and tries to cope with it. In chronic illnesses patients typically show a wide variety of symptoms and patterns. This is because over time the features from the pathology become smaller and smaller parts of the overall picture as everyone copes in their own individual way. In acute illnesses, however, the pathological processes tend to be more dominant. The symptoms experienced when someone breaks a leg, for example, are much less diverse than the symptoms (from a holistic homeopathic viewpoint) experienced by someone who has had eczema for 10 years. This means that a good understanding of the typical acute symptoms of common homeopathic remedies for different diseases can enable a practitioner to select the appropriate treatments for their acutely ill patients using a pathological approach to prescribing. Therefore, a nurse, doctor or pharmacist working in a predominantly acute clinical sector will find that the pathological approach works well. Physiotherapists or other sports medicine specialists will find that their requirement for treatments of common injuries and sprains will also lead them to use the pathological approach. Similarly, certain professions specialise in diseases of only part of the body. Think, for example, of dentists or podiatrists. In such a clinical context it is again highly relevant and useful to take a focus on the 'locals'.

On the other hand, general practice is a very holistic form of medicine which requires doctors to deal with a wide range of both acute and chronic illnesses. The time demands on a general practitioner may lead to a predominant use of the pathological approach but with experience good homeopathic general practitioners will be able to spot and use an increasingly wide range of 'general' and 'mental' symptoms of their patients. They will then be able to vary their practice, sometimes using a pathological approach, sometimes a predominantly general or mental one, and sometimes a typically classical approach encompassing all three areas.

Different styles for different patient contexts

An interesting consequence of the holistic understanding of both illness and medicines (the latter as demonstrated in the materia medica of homeopathy) is that the cultural and social determinants of behaviour and of expression of illness result in certain homeopathic medicines being more commonly prescribed in some communities than they are in others. There is a growing trend in homeopathy to understand groups of remedies that share many common features as 'families' or remedies (see Chapter 5). For example, all the remedies prepared from spiders share certain characteristics such as chilliness and restlessness, whereas all the remedies prepared from potassium salts (the Kalis) share characteristics of a desire for order and need for predictability in life. These examples are gross oversimplifications but the basic idea is that there are certain striking features shared by each group (or 'family') of remedies. Reviews of practitioners' work show distinct differences in their most commonly prescribed groups of remedies. Whilst some of this may be due to their own education, a significant and interesting factor is the way people experience and express illness in different communities. The typical Italian way of understanding and communicating suffering is very different from the typical Japanese way. The consequence of this is that a doctor practising in Italy is likely to make frequent use of certain remedies which a doctor practising in Japan hardly ever uses. Does this make a significant difference to their style of practice? Yes, it does. Some patients love to talk about their feelings and their thoughts. They express those parts of their experience very easily. Others seem to hate talking about themselves. They are either much more reserved or private, or they experience most of their disturbances physically rather than emotionally. If these characteristics are strongly culturally determined then there will be a significantly higher proportion of patients with certain ways of presenting in one community than with another. This not only leads to a preponderance of certain remedies being prescribed but it also appropriately determines such things as consultation duration and even therapeutic style. If a patient focuses on mental symptoms then the practitioner is more likely to use a method which also focuses on the mentals, whereas if a patient focuses on the disease then the practitioner is more likely to be led to focus on the locals. In this way, an external observer will quickly see quite marked diversity of practice which is highly appropriate for the context created by the patient.

'Unorthodox diversity'

The diversity described above covers most homeopathic practice in the world but one of the basic principles of homeopathy has led to the development of some practice which is well outwith this range. The principle here is the one of potentisation (see Chapter 10). This is one of the most controversial elements of homeopathic practice and is the one feature most likely to lead to the whole homeopathic method being dismissed as bogus or placebo by those scientists who subscribe to a strictly biophysical view of reality. Some people find this one of the most appealing features of homeopathy because it fits with their view of the world as being spiritual. They are attracted to what is mystical and un-explainable. This has led to a kind of esoteric tradition within homeo-pathy which can involve such practices as dowsing, meditation, the prescribing of a remedy by just thinking about it, or even in one group the prescribing of remedies by writing their names on pieces of paper on which the homeopath stands a glass a water, and the patient is then instructed to 'take' the remedy by drinking the water. Practices such as dowsing have a long tradition of their own but they are certainly well outwith the mainstream of homeopathic practice. There has been a case of a doctor being reprimanded by the General Medical Council in the UK for using a pendulum over a book of materia medica to 'find the remedy'. Technological developments have built upon the bio-energetic model of dowsing, resulting in the invention of machines (these days frequently computer-based) which claim to diagnose the patient, find the remedy and even manufacture the remedy in the con-sulting room by 'imprinting the energy of the remedy' electronically.

Even Hahnemann's original instructions for conducting provings has been abandoned by such groups who prefer instead to place samples of a remedy under their pillows and record their dreams, which are then shared as useful information about the remedy (these are called 'dream provings').

Such practices are almost exclusively found in 'alternative' cultures and communities (frequently described as being founded on New Age beliefs). This particular trend places homeopathic practice well outwith the mainstream of society and medical practice. The adherents of such beliefs tend to relish this antiestablishment potential of homeopathy.

Future trends

The biomedical model is increasingly being judged to be inadequate. Holistic models based on the more recent insights from complexity science are becoming more common and this is leading to some convergence between homeopathic practice and the rest of medical practice. If this trend continues, homeopathic practice as described here could be integrated without losing its diversity. On the other hand there are, within developed countries, clear trends of subcultural development towards esoteric and antiestablishment beliefs and attitudes which may well see further development of what may be termed 'unorthodox diversity'. It is quite possible that both trends will continue and diversity of homeopathic practice will increase as a result.

A potentially exciting development is that the information about homeopathic medicines acquired from provings has until now been obtained almost exclusively from western European/North American cultures. As homeopathy becomes known and developed in Africa and Asia, then provings conducted in those countries may well potentially reveal quite different information about each remedy as expressed in these radically different cultures. This may potentially lead to even greater diversity of practice.

Reference

1.   Kent J T. *Repertory of the Materia Medica*, 3rd edn. Sittingbourne: Homoeopathic Book Service, 1993.

8

Homeopathy in the UK National Health Service healthcare environments

David Spence

Introduction

This chapter outlines the integration of homeopathy into the primary and secondary levels of healthcare in the UK National Health Service (NHS). From the inception of the UK NHS in 1948, homeopathy was included in the NHS Act of Parliament and has remained available as an integral part of the NHS ever since.

Availability of homeopathy in the UK NHS

Primary care

Patients can access homeopathy within the primary care sector of the UK NHS from a number of appropriately trained professionals within the multidisciplinary healthcare team. The point of access may be their local pharmacist, their general dental practitioner, their general medical practitioner (GP) or a member of the primary medical team, e.g. midwife, practice nurse or health visitor.

Secondary care

In parallel with all specialist secondary care provision in the NHS, homeopathy can only be accessed by referral, either from a primary care healthcare professional or from another secondary care physician in a different specialty. There are five specialist homeopathic hospital units in the UK, situated in Bristol (Figure 8.1), Glasgow (Figure 8.2), Liverpool, London (Figure 8.3) and Tunbridge Wells. All these centres provide outpatient care but inpatient care is only provided in Glasgow and London. Referring practitioners may request treatment for patients with a very wide spectrum of disease. At each centre the referral letters

Figure 8.1 Specialist homeopathic hospital in Bristol.

are screened by one of the senior medical staff and any that are thought to be inappropriate for any reason are usually discussed with the referring clinician in order to obtain a clearer picture and assess the role for homeopathy in that particular case.

Over the past 20 years, the numbers of referrals from primary care to the specialist homeopathic hospital units have grown exponentially and, in the past 5–10 years, there has been a steadily increasing incidence of referrals for homeopathic treatment from other specialist physicians within the secondary care sector of the NHS. This clearly reflects the very considerable public demand for homeopathic treatment that exists within the UK population.

Figure 8.2 Specialist homeopathic hospital in Glasgow.

Figure 8.3 Specialist homeopathic hospital in London.

Training and qualifications for NHS healthcare professionals

Postgraduate training and qualifications are essential for the various members of the healthcare team in order to allow them to use homeopathy appropriately and effectively in their particular area of clinical practice. The postgraduate qualifications also enable other healthcare professionals who are seeking homeopathic treatment for their patients to know that the practitioner to whom they are referring has the necessary training.

Faculty of Homeopathy

The Faculty of Homeopathy was first founded in 1844 as the British Homeopathic Society and changed its title to the Faculty of Homeopathy in 1943. Following the creation of the NHS in 1948, all postgraduate specialist medical education and qualifications were reviewed and the Faculty was incorporated by Act of Parliament (Faculty of Homeopathy Act 1950). This Act of Parliament empowers the Faculty to train, conduct examinations and issue postgraduate qualifications to healthcare professionals.

The Faculty coordinates its training programme through five academic centres located in Bristol, Glasgow, London, Oxford and Tunbridge Wells. These centres are subject to rigorous accreditation by the Faculty, and this accreditation is conducted by an external team of Faculty inspectors and is renewable at regular intervals. This is in line with the accreditation procedures and practice of all postgraduate medical Royal Colleges and Faculties in the UK.

The Faculty awards several categories of postgraduate qualifications. The first stage is a licentiate certificate, which recognises that the successful healthcare professional possesses a basic level of knowledge of homeopathy and an understanding of its role in everyday clinical practice and is able to use it safely in a restricted number of targeted clinical situations. This level of qualification is available to all statutorily registered healthcare professionals in the UK. Successful candidates are permitted to use the letters LFHom after their names with their appropriate discipline in parentheses, e.g. LFHom(Pharm). The next stage is the membership diploma, which denotes a much wider and more specialised knowledge of homeopathy with the ability to use it appropriately in many clinical situations, including chronic disease, whilst still remaining under supervision of a more experienced Faculty mentor. Successful professionals use the letters MFHom with their discipline in parentheses, e.g. MFHom(Pharm). The highest level of Faculty qualification is the Specialist Register (SR), which is achieved after some years of specialist supervision, the presentation of a dissertation and an oral examination.

The Faculty also awards fellowship diplomas to healthcare professionals who have already achieved all the previous levels of qualification and have also gained further expertise through many years of specialist homeopathic practice. These professionals are designated by the letters FFHom.

All Faculty-qualified healthcare professionals are required to participate in continuing professional development and to provide certified evidence of this to the Faculty's academic office in order to maintain the validity of their postgraduate qualifications in homeopathy.

Clinical practice in the UK NHS

An overview

Demand from the public has escalated enormously over the past two decades and, at the same time, healthcare professionals have become more open-minded in their view of complementary medicine. This altered mind set has been stimulated in large part by the experience of the majority of healthcare professionals of the limitations of conventional medical treatments not only in terms of effectiveness but also their potential for producing adverse reactions. This has led to healthcare professionals asking themselves what else they might use in order to help their patients. Homeopathy is often then considered and, for all of us in healthcare practice, a number of questions then arise: What is its relevance in the NHS today? What types of conditions might it help? What sorts of individuals might benefit? Is there any evidence to support its use? Can it be taken safely alongside conventional medicine? What about cost? These and other questions we will now consider.

Relevance in clinical practice today

As healthcare professionals treating patients with conventional medicine, we are often faced with a quandary when they fail to respond, experience inadequate benefit or are unable to tolerate the treatment on account of adverse drug effects. In the process of arriving at this point, they may have been referred to one or more specialists without any positive health gain. Do we then adopt a position that it is not possible to help these patients? Do we then tell such patients: 'There is nothing more that can be done for you' or 'You will have to learn to live with it'? These are phrases that are all too commonly used in healthcare today. These patients are then thrown out on to what I often call the 'medical scrapheap'. Here, immediately, is a relevant role for homeopathy in clinical care.

Many patients today are very concerned about adverse drug effects and are thus reluctant to accept conventional drugs, preferring to receive safer, non-toxic treatment. There are also a number of patients who would rather not have conventional drugs at all for a variety of reasons. All these fall under the category of 'patient choice', which has become a popular 'buzz phrase' in the UK NHS today.

The main relevant areas for the use of homeopathy in the UK NHS today are listed below:

- failure to respond to conventional medical care
- inadequate response to conventional medical care
- adverse drug effects
- no conventional treatment exists for the patient's condition
- conventional treatment is contraindicated
- potential additional benefit from adding in homeopathy
- homeopathy is the better treatment option
- patient choice.

What conditions might homeopathy help (clinical scope)?

This is a very important question, as indeed is the 'flip-side-question': For what conditions is homeopathy inappropriate? Both questions need to be constantly in our minds in everyday clinical practice so that we are giving the best clinical advice to each patient. The clinical scope of homeopathy is best considered in the light of its perceived method of action. As it employs the potential ability of toxic substances, albeit in controversially tiny doses, to stimulate the body's defence mechanisms and autoregulatory responses, it follows that homeopathy can be appropriate in any condition where our medical knowledge indicates to us that the body would have the ability to self-correct. It follows that it can help or even cure any clinical condition where the body's healing mechanisms have the potential to reverse the change that has occurred. Conversely, irreversible breakdown of function and deficiency disorders are not appropriate areas for the use of homeopathy.

In everyday practice, therefore, the generalist clinician, especially in the primary care setting, is faced with a wide variety of diseases. Some of these will be better treated with conventional medicine; others, for which there may be no conventional treatment, might only be treatable with homeopathy, but there will be a large number of patients – in what be called the middle ground – for whom either approach would be appropriate. Many NHS clinicians today find that, as their homeopathic training and experience increase, they are more frequently suggesting homeopathic treatment in the middle ground and the principal reasons are, firstly the opportunity of using a non-toxic therapy rather than a potentially toxic one and, secondly, because homeopathy is significantly less expensive. In the cash-starved state health systems of the 21st century, this last point is of particular relevance.

What sorts of individuals might benefit?

It is often stated that patients have to 'believe in homeopathy' in order to experience any benefit from it. This is an important factor in any form of medicine, conventional and complementary alike, and there is no tangible evidence to suggest that it is any way a greater factor in homeopathy. In fact, positive clinical trial results using homeopathy in veterinary medicine, especially in large-animal practice, would tend to endorse this.[1, 2]

There is evidence that children respond better to homeopathy than adults.[3] This is not surprising as we know that children's autoregulatory responses react more quickly than those of adults. Children also have 'cleaner' systems than adults, as they have been bombarded with fewer noxious substances, and children have greater ability to self-correct than patients in middle to later life. It has been factually noted that more adult females seek homeopathic treatment than adult males but the same pattern is seen in conventional general medical practice.

What evidence is there to support its use (see also Chapters 1 and 2)?

Evidence-based medicine is very much the 'buzz phrase' of NHS 21st-century treatment and decision-making, for healthcare policy-makers and practitioners alike. But there is no doubt that the type of evidence that is rated as important has undergone a sea change in recent years. Sackett et al.,[4] in a book entitled *Evidence-Based Medicine*, define it as 'the integration of best research evidence with clinical experience and patient values'. Clinical effectiveness studies and patient choice thus become a very important part of the spectrum of evidence. The slavish adherence to the randomised controlled trial (RCT) as the only worthwhile arbiter for evidence is now becoming outdated and a wider spectrum of clinical evidence is being examined. This mirrors the experience of many clinicians who have found that the results of RCTs are often not reflected in their everyday clinical practice in the real world. This is especially true in the primary care environment. Therefore, clinicians are now attaching just as much importance to evidence derived from clinical experience from colleagues and from patients as they do to evidence from trials. The trials that are of importance also now include practical clinical outcome studies and qualitative research studies as well as the traditional RCT. Pragmatic clinicians really want evidence that will help them decide what treatment is likely to provide positive health gain for their patients in the real-world circumstances that they face on a daily basis.

Although much more research needs to be done, especially by dentists, pharmacists, nurses and midwives, there is now a significant evidence base from doctors for the integration of homeopathy within the UK NHS in both the primary and secondary care sectors. In primary care, different studies have prospectively tracked homeopathic prescriptions whilst others have retrospectively evaluated outcome.[5, 6]

Within the specialist hospital sector, studies of several thousand sequential outpatients have reported positive health gain in the UK homeopathic hospital outpatient departments. There has been remarkable similarity in the response levels seen in these studies, with 65–70% of patients reporting positive health gain.[3, 7, 8] Two separate studies of 100 sequential patients treated in the inpatient unit at the Glasgow Homoeopathic Hospital also revealed that 70% of patients reported positive health gain.[9] Recent qualitative studies also endorse these findings.[10] For the practical clinician, such a body of evidence clearly shows the value of the integration of homeopathy into the spectrum of practical therapeutic options available for patients.

Other issues – safety and cost (see also Chapter 1)

The intrinsic safety of the homeopathic medicines themselves is well established, there being no potential for life-threatening adverse drug effects. This view is upheld by both critics and supporters. The safety of integrating homeopathy alongside conventional medical approaches is also well established with extensive clinical experience within the UK

NHS across the whole spectrum of both primary and secondary care for almost 60 years. Thus homeopathy can be used safely and effectively alongside other medications providing enhanced healthcare for the patient. Furthermore, it is important that this is provided within the envelope of their medical care to avoid fragmentation of care and the creation of an either/or mind set.

However, risk can occur when homeopathy is misapplied – a risk that is shared with other areas of medical care and not unique to homeopathy. This potential risk throws into stark perspective the absolute need for the statutory regulation of the practice of healthcare and the need for clinicians to adhere strictly to the bounds of their professional competence and discipline.

Cost-effectiveness is another important consideration in integrating homeopathy into UK NHS healthcare and this is becoming ever more the case in a cash-strapped health service. Homeopathic medicines are very inexpensive, thus making them an attractive alternative to more expensive conventional drugs. Some data from primary care suggest that homeopathic prescription items cost on average about a quarter of the conventional prescription item[11] and average cost savings per patient have also been shown.[12] Hospital pharmacy data show that homeopathic drug costs for hospital outpatients are also very advantageous.[5]

Case reports

Within the limited space available, it is only possible to give a few clinical examples of the integration of homeopathy into UK NHS healthcare in different areas of practice.

Primary dental care

Two simple cases recounted by a dental surgeon colleague working in the university hospital department of dentistry are given below.

Primary pharmacy care

Applications of homeopathy in pharmacy practice are detailed in Chapter 10. An example is given in Case 8.3.

Another example of the use of homeopathy in pharmacy practice is given in Chapter 10.

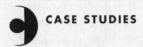

CASE STUDIES

Case 8.1   Application of homeopathy in dental surgery

A young man of 21, who was extremely nervous of dental treatment (even though his mother was a dental nurse), had a history of repeated syncope when he attended a dental surgery. He presented with pain from a carious tooth which needed a large restoration. He was as white as a sheet and visibly trembling. He was given Aconite 30c while he was waiting for his appointment, with a repeated dose as soon as he came into the surgery. He tolerated the local anaesthetic really well and the treatment was completed without any problems. Needless to say, he asked if he could have the Aconite again next time!

Case 8.2   Application of homeopathy in dental surgery

A female dental student aged 20 who was very fit and well consulted at 10 a.m. on a Monday morning saying that she was developing a cold sore on her upper lip. She suffered from recurrent herpetic lesions so she knew the signs very well. She was given Rhus tox 30c and told to repeat the dose every 30 minutes. Three hours later the lesion had completely disappeared and there was no further development thereafter.

CASE STUDY

Case 8.3   Application of homeopathy in pharmacy

A female customer in her 30s presented with classical heat bumps during the hot weather and a history of these having become a recurrent problem whenever she was exposed to heat or sun. She was given Apis mellifica 30c to be taken four times a day and then repeated on hot sunny days thereafter. She returned to the pharmacy 2 weeks later to report that, after 3 doses of the Apis, the heat bumps had completely disappeared. She had used the medication on three hot sunny days subsequently and had not developed any heat bumps at all. This is a condition for which we have no adequate conventional over-the-counter pharmaceutical and illustrates the everyday practical usefulness of homeopathy in primary care pharmacy practice.

Primary nursing care

Applications of homeopathy in nursing practice are described in Chapter 12. Practice nurses working in the treatment room in UK NHS primary care centres now deal with considerable numbers of patients as the first point of practitioner contact (see Case 8.4). Other examples of the use of homeopathy in nursing practice are given in Chapter 12.

 **CASE STUDY**

Case 8.4   Application of homeopathy in nursing practice
One practice nurse reports the increasing use of homeopathy for many straightforward first-aid conditions and also its usefulness where there is no other conventional treatment. She reported a difficult case of trauma where a 42-year-old male had acquired a splinter 1 cm in length driven in under the nail of his left index finger. On examination, the finger was becoming swollen and there was no visible part of the splinter available to attempt instrumental extraction. The patient was in considerable discomfort. The option of a ring-block and splitting the nail was considered but she decided to give Silica 30c every 2 hours. The patient returned 24 hours later, bringing the offending splinter with him, and the finger had returned to a normal size. The practice nurse took a digital photo showing the healed finger and the length of the splinter.

Primary midwifery care

Applications of homeopathy in midwifery practice are covered in Chapter 12. The primary care midwifery team find the integration of homeopathy extremely helpful, especially in postpartum care. The use of Arnica to reduce swelling and bruising of the perineum is well known and many mothers who have experienced childbirth both with and without the help of Arnica postpartum are absolutely definitive in their reporting of the positive benefit that they experienced with the use of Arnica.

The use of Calendula lotion to promote healing and reduce discomfort postepisiotomy is found to be very effective by both mothers and the primary care midwives. A solution is made up by diluting 5 ml of Calendula lotion in 200 ml of cooled boiled water and it is applied by dabbing on with cotton wool several times per day for as many days as required.

Following caesarean section or instrumental delivery, many mothers experience difficulty passing water and require catheterisation. Following this a number of mothers develop a urethra syndrome with dysuria. Midstream urine specimen is usually negative with no sign of any overt infection. Prescription of Staphisagria given four times a day is very effective in these cases, with resolution of symptoms occurring very quickly, usually within 48 hours. The doses are discontinued when the symptoms have resolved.

Other examples of the use of homeopathy in midwifery practice are given in Chapter 12.

Primary health visitor care

Homeopathic medicines can easily be administered to infants and very young children by giving two or three drops of solution into the infant's mouth (see Case 8.5). The solution is prepared by crushing two tablets of the appropriate medicine (e.g. Colocynth 30c) between two clean teaspoons and dissolving the resultant powder in about 50 ml of cooled boiled water in a clean tumbler. This solution is then stirred prior to each dose and kept covered between doses. A fresh solution is made up each morning.

 CASE STUDY

Case 8.5 Applications of homeopathy in primary health visitor care
A 10-week-old breast-fed infant with chronic and persistent colic which was causing a good deal of stress and anxiety to both his parents was brought to the mother and baby clinic. He was gaining weight satisfactorily and was not overtly constipated. There were no other symptoms or signs indicative of other possible problems and infantile colic was diagnosed. Colocynth 30c was suggested, to be given just before each feed. The following week, the mother returned to report that the colic now hardly ever occurred and was really no longer a problem. She was instructed to reduce the frequency of the doses over the next 2 days and then stop. She was told that she could restart the medication if the colic recurred.

Primary medical care

The asset of integrating homeopathy into UK NHS primary care cannot be overemphasised and, from those who have experienced it, phrases such as 'I don't know how I ever did general practice without homeopathy' are often heard. The addition of homeopathic drugs into the medical armamentarium expands the clinical ability of the primary care physician to a considerable degree. Not only are there new options for patients with whom the doctor has 'become stuck', having exhausted all the conventional options, but there is the option to treat many situations, especially in children, with non-toxic drugs, thus removing the potential for side-effects and also reducing the practice drugs bill at the same time. Many primary care doctors are concerned about what their patients will say if they start using homeopathy in their practice. They have this image of patients thinking: 'Oh dear, he/she has finally gone off with the birdies and started using homeopathy'. Those who have taken the step of integrating homeopathy report that nothing could be further from the truth. Patients are actually very positive and pleased to be given homeopathic medication and it would be true to say that the vast majority of the public would, where appropriate, prefer to receive non-toxic medicine that works via the body's own natural mechanisms than to ingest potentially toxic drugs with the possibility of side-effects.

Primary care physicians could fill an entire book with the types of cases for which they find homeopathy particularly effective; a few examples are given here. The treatment of an acute condition is shown in Case 8.6.

Children with prolonged coughs who have already had a course of antibiotics without benefit will often respond very quickly to homeopathy. The medication needed will depend on the nature of the cough, e.g. Ipecacuanha for the child with a wheezy cough with nausea or vomiting, especially when coughing is maximal at night, or Drosera for the child with paroxysmal bursts of cough, which often end in retching or even vomiting.

Premenstrual syndrome often responds well to homeopathy and several medicines, including Sepia and Pulsatilla, can be very effective. Irritable-bowel syndrome, a frequent presenting problem in primary care, can also be treated effectively and medicines such as Lycopodium can bring great relief to the sufferer. Menopausal flushing and night sweats in women where hormone replacement therapy might be medically contraindicated will often respond to homeopathy and medicines –

CASE STUDY

Case 8.6 Acute treatment

I well remember a teacher in her 50s coming to see me in NHS primary care many years ago on the evening of 23 December. She had all the classical signs and symptoms of a florid flu-like viral infection and she informed me that all her extended family was coming to her to be entertained on Christmas Day. She stated categorically that she wanted 'some proper medicine' and did not want homeopathy as she did not believe in it. I gently pointed out to her that there was no conventional treatment available for her condition and the only chance she had of being well enough to cope with Christmas was to have some homeopathic treatment. Extremely reluctantly, she accepted a prescription for some Gelsemium sempervirens, which she was told to take frequently. Very graciously, she contacted me about a week after Christmas and reported that the response had been dramatic, 'almost miraculous', that she had been able to cope with all the entertaining perfectly well, and that there was no doubt at all that the homeopathy had worked despite her lack of belief.

for example, Lachesis – can prove very effective in reducing or removing symptoms and restoring sleep patterns.

Secondary medical care

The spectrum of morbidity that is seen in patients who are referred to the homeopathic hospital outpatient departments in the UK NHS is enormous. In response to the question: 'What sort of patients are referred to the homeopathic hospital?' I have usually responded: 'Everyone else's failures'. This nicely sums it up in a few words. These are the patients who have long-standing chronic problems, which are being inadequately managed by conventional means, whether due to lack of response or intolerable side-effects. Other conditions that are referred are those for which there is no known conventional treatment. It would be fair to say that it is not a very promising caseload with which to start. Therefore, the fact that large-scale outcome assessment studies show that circa 70% of such patients report positive health gain following homeopathic intervention is noteworthy and suggests that serious consideration should be given for increased availability, especially given the low cost of medication. Space only permits me to give a couple of case histories to illustrate the health and cost benefits that can be achieved.

Case 8.7 illustrates the use of homeopathy where conventional treatment had failed to control and where no further conventional drugs were needed. Case 8.8 illustrates the integration of homeopathic medicines alongside conventional drugs to achieve additional clinical improvement.

CASE STUDY

Case 8.7 Use of homeopathy where orthodox medicine has not controlled a condition

A 30-year-old female NHS hospital manager was referred to the homeopathic hospital outpatient department with increasingly debilitating migraine headaches. Her migraines had started 9 years previously but had been becoming more frequent and intense for the past couple of years despite all the conventional attempts to control them. She was currently using sumatriptan but without adequate benefit and had tried two other triptans. She reported having had 31 migraines in the 10 months leading up to her appointment, each lasting 2–3 days, and the consequent loss of time from work and productivity were becoming serious problems to both her and the NHS, as her employer. A full medical history and individual homeopathic profile were taken. Previous clinicians had explored the areas of lifestyle, stress and diet with her but alterations in these areas had failed to produce significant change. She was given Natrum arsenicosum 30c on a single day and given a review appointment.

Review at 8 weeks: she reported that she had not had any migraines at all. She was not given any further medication.

Review after a further 3 months: she remained completely free of migraines. No medication.

Review 2 months later: Her grandfather and her father had died within a week of each other. She had not had any migraines but was feeling very tense and felt that she was losing control and that she might have a migraine. Her medication was repeated as at the initial consultation. She had gone 7 months free from migraines.

Review after a further 6 months: Still no migraines even though she is under great stress at work. No medication.

Review after a further 6 months: She had to give evidence in court 2 weeks previously in an unpleasant NHS complaint case. She had a migraine just

(continued overleaf)

prior to the hearing. This was the first migraine since starting homeopathic treatment 19 months previously. Her medication was repeated and she was told to take it again if she had any further migraines.

Review after a further 12 months: She had experienced a break-up of her relationship during the year and had one migraine, following which she repeated her medication. She was advised to continue the regime of repeated doses if migraines occur.

In summary, the incidence of her migraines was reduced from almost once a month prior to treatment to only two in 2½ years, both of which occurred under extreme stress of bereavement. As she was a member of the NHS staff, she remained in contact and was still free of migraines a further 2 years later.

The total homeopathic drug cost of this patient's treatment has amounted to £5 over a 5-year period. Given the significant cost of such drugs as sumatriptan, this represents a huge drug saving to the NHS. She has also been able to work without loss of days from sickness with far greater productivity. Far more importantly, however, we now have a fit and healthy young woman enjoying a normal life.

CASE STUDY

Case 8.8 Use of homeopathy in place of surgical intervention

A 45-year-old male microbiologist was referred by a consultant colleague from the gastroenterology department at a neighbouring hospital because of failure to achieve adequate control of his ulcerative colitis. He had recently been referred to a surgical colleague who had advised a panproctocolectomy and ileostomy. The patient was anxious to avoid this, if possible, and hence the referral to homeopathic outpatients. He had had ulcerative colitis for 7 years with frequent attendances at the gastroenterology department and use of all available conventional medical interventions. The frequency and urgency of his bowel actions often made it difficult for him to do a full day's work, necessitating absence from the microbiology department for parts of days on a regular basis. Once again, this was a very significant issue for him and the NHS, as his employer.

At presentation, he reported 10–12 bowel actions per day and he was also being disturbed 2–3 times in the night to use his bowels.

→

> **CASE STUDY** (continued)
>
> After a full medical history, examination and a homeopathic profile, he was prescribed Lycopodium 30c to be taken alongside his conventional medication, which was not altered. At his first outpatient review, he reported a marked improvement with fewer bowel actions and a reduction in the nighttime activity. This patient was followed up regularly in hospital outpatients over the next 5 years with alteration of both his conventional and homeopathic medication as and when needed. To date, surgical intervention has been avoided and his quality of life has been improved. The patient is delighted to have avoided surgery.
>
> The additional drug cost of introducing homeopathy alongside his conventional medication has been minimal – estimated at £20 per annum. Considering the fact that surgical intervention has been avoided as well as the very considerable continuing cost of stoma care, the savings to the NHS are in the region of £8000.

Conclusion

It can readily be seen from all the above clinical cases that conventional healthcare clinicians who acquire the additional postgraduate training and skill to be able to integrate homeopathy in the UK NHS find that it is of great value in the extension of their clinical effectiveness. Not only does this bring great benefit to their patients but it also significantly enhances the clinician's job satisfaction.

References

1. Searcy R, Reyes O, Guajardo G. Control of subclinical bovine mastitis. Utilization of a homoeopathic combination. *Br Hom J* 1995; 84: 67–70.
2. Albrecht H, Schütte A. Homeopathy versus antibiotics in metaphylaxis of infectious diseases: a clinical study in pig fattening and its significance to consumers. *Altern Ther Health Med* 1999; 5: 64–68.
3. Spence D, Thompson E, Barron S. Homeopathic treatment for chronic disease: a 6-year university hospital outpatient observational study. *J Altern Comp Med* 2005; 11: 793–798.
4. Sackett D L, Richardson W S, Rosenberg W M C, *et al. Evidence-Based Medicine: How to Practice and Teach EBM*, 2nd edn. London: Churchill Livingstone, 2000.
5. Reilly D, Duncan R, Leckridge B. International data collection centres for

integrative medicine. University of Exeter 2nd Annual Symposium on Complementary Health Care December 1995.

6. Robinson T. Responses to homeopathic treatment in National Health Service general practice. *Homeopathy* 2006; 95: 9–14.

7. Clover A. Patient benefit survey: Tunbridge Wells Homeopathic Hospital. *Br Hom J* 2000; 89: 68–72.

8. Richardson W. Patient benefit survey: Liverpool Regional Department of Homeopathic Medicine. *Br Hom J* 2001; 90: 158–162.

9. Mercer S, Thompson T, Duncan R. Evaluation of integrated complementary and orthodox care at Glasgow Homeopathic Hospital. *FACT* 1998; 3: 190.

10. Thompson T. Can the caged bird sing? Reflections on the application of qualitative research methods to case study design in homeopathic medicine. www.biomedcentral.com/content/pdf/1471-2288-4-4.pdf (accessed March 2007).

11. Chaufferin G. Improving the evaluation of homeopathy: economic consideration and impact on health. *Br Hom J* 2000; 89 (Suppl. 1): S27–S30.

12. Jain A. Does homeopathy reduce the cost of conventional drug prescribing? A study of comparative prescribing costs in general practice. *Homeopathy* 2003; 92: 71–76.

13. Spence D. Cost effective treatment of chronic disease. 60th International Congress of Homeopathic Physicians, Berlin 2005.

9

Practising homeopathy in continental Europe

Ton Nicolai

In this chapter the context within which homeopathy is practised in European countries other than the UK is examined.

Demand for homeopathy

Over the past few decades homeopathy has benefited from growing demand from the public in most European countries and a trend is starting to integrate it together with other complementary and alternative medicine (CAM) therapies into healthcare systems. According to a European Commission report order in 1997, three Europeans out of four know about homeopathy and about 29% of these use it for their healthcare,[1] making it the most popular CAM therapy in Europe.

Interest in homeopathy and other CAM therapies has increased considerably among physicians too. In Germany the number of physicians practising homeopathy doubled over the last decade and currently there are approximately 5500 active physicians with an additional qualification (Zusatzbezeichnung) in homeopathy.[2] That is, 2% of the number of active doctors or one homeopathic doctor for 15 000 inhabitants – more than 10 times greater density than in the UK. France has approximately 6000 general practitioners (GPs: 6% of the total number of 100 000) whose particular type of practice or *mode d'exercice particulier* is designated as *orientation homéopathie*,[3] although there is no formal requirement for this qualification. When looking at the European Union (EU) as a whole, approximately 30 000 doctors, mainly in the ambulatory sector/general practice, have taken a training course in homeopathy. About 6–8 times more GPs prescribe homeopathic medicines on a regular basis without specific training, and even more do so occasionally – 40% of all French GPs and as many as 75% of all German GPs. There are several thousands of homeopathic practitioners without a full medical education in Europe. In Germany alone approximately 3000 out of the 15 000 Heilpraktikers (state-registered CAM practitioners) practise homeopathy[4] (see Chapter 13).

Government regulation

Homeopathy has a form of legal recognition in a number of European countries. Yet there are wide variations among countries in the degree of legal recognition and the ways in which it is practised.[5-8] In most European countries on the continent, mainly in middle and southern Europe, only doctors, veterinary surgeons and dentists can legally perform treatment-related activity.

This all-regulated or monopolistic system, as it is termed, exists in Austria, Belgium, Bulgaria, Cyprus, the Czech Republic, Estonia, France, Greece, Hungary (where Natural Medicine Professionals are also licensed, but only doctors are allowed to practise homeopathy), Italy, Latvia, Lithuania, Luxembourg, Poland, Portugal, Romania, Slovakia, Spain and Switzerland (in some Swiss cantons homeopathic practitioners without a full medical education are also regulated).

In several of these countries homeopathy has been officially recognised by the government as a system of medicine, medical specialty or additional qualification, notably in Belgium (1999), Bulgaria (2005), Hungary (1997), Lithuania (1999), Portugal (2003) and Romania (1981). In some countries (e.g. Austria, France, Italy, Slovenia and Spain), the authorities have delegated the regulation, registration and supervising authority to the medical federations, which means that these federations have the authority of defining which CAM treatments can be made available to the public. The practice of homeopathy outside of regulated healthcare is illegal in these countries and violations are considered an offence. Homeopathic practice by non-regulated practitioners without a full medical qualification, however, is widespread and is even legal as long as the CAM providers define themselves as 'consultants' or counsellors of 'healthy lifestyle', and do not present themselves as health personnel. They are mostly not prosecuted unless there is clear evidence of harm to patients.

Since 1939 Germany has had a specific regulation for CAM practitioners without a full medical education. These practitioners, or Heilpraktikers, have to qualify for a licence. Health authorities subject the candidates to an examination in order to assess that they have sufficient public health knowledge as well as some basic medical knowledge to prevent them from constituting a public health risk. There is no commonly agreed required training level and the German Länder (states) may apply specific rules relating to the content of the examination, which means that the length and quality of the education vary widely. From an international perspective this profession has quite a unique position: rather than registering providers with accredited professional bodies for single CAM therapies, as in the UK, anyone wanting to practise the 'healing art' in Germany outside the publicly funded healthcare sector has to obtain the same state licence for Heilpraktikers, as outlined by federal law. The generic qualification of Heilpraktiker lends itself more to multitherapeutic practice, but there is a clear development towards specialisation, with individuals having to demonstrate their ability, skill and knowledge in a single therapeutic area, through registration with a professional body. Heilpraktikers only practise in the ambulatory sector and are not allowed to work in the same surgery as a physician. There are approximately 15 000 Heilpraktikers or state-registered CAM practitioners in Germany, which is about half the number of physicians offering CAM services. About 3000 Heilpraktikers practise mainly homeopathy, about 700 of them up to the level of the European Council for Classical Homeopathy (ECCH) educational guidelines (see below).

Other countries, mainly in northern Europe, i.e. Denmark, Finland, Iceland, Ireland, the Netherlands, Norway and Sweden, as well as Liechtenstein, Malta and Switzerland (some cantons) have a semi-regulated system like the UK. Both regulated and non-regulated individuals may treat, the latter being only limited by certain restrictions with regard to which conditions can be treated, and the procedures to be utilised. Only specific 'risky' medical procedures (performing surgery, administering anaesthetics, prescribing prescription-only drugs, giving injections, using X-ray) or the treatment of serious diseases are restricted to medical practitioners with a university degree, although the range of these medical acts may differ from country to country. In these countries the practice of homeopathy by practitioners without a full medical education is tolerated, although mostly not regulated. As a matter of fact, they constitute the core homeopathy providers.

Over the last few years statutory regulation for CAM practitioners without a full medical education has been established in some of the Nordic countries, where traditionally CAM practice among medical doctors has been almost non-existent. In Denmark (2003), Norway (2004), and Iceland (2005) official registers have been established and expectations are that Sweden and Finland will follow suit in the foreseeable future. The registers include practitioners who 'have well defined criteria for education and are members of an organisation for practitioners that will take on the necessary tasks for registration and maintaining the register'.[9] The register is voluntary and practitioners are self-regulated through their member associations. The purpose of the registration is to safeguard and ensure the rights of consumers who seek registered CAM providers. A registered CAM provider must have a membership in a government-approved providers' federation. For a federation to be approved, educational qualifications, certain ethical rules, rules for responsible professional conduct, rules for confidentiality as well as procedures for documentation are most often required. Typically the federations must have membership requirements concerning educational qualifications, ethical rules, claim of responsible professional conduct, of confidentiality and documentation routines. The health authorities do not undertake supervision of the practice of registered CAM providers. If CAM providers are registered, violation of the rules of the federation may exclude the person from membership of the federation. The CAM provider will thereby lose his/her registration.

In Belgium and Portugal a basic law regulating CAM was approved by parliament in 1999 and 2003 respectively but still awaits implementation. Both the Belgian and the Portuguese law recognises homeopathy – as well as chiropractic, osteopathy and acupuncture – and provides for the recognition of other CAM techniques to come. Individuals who comply with the law's conditions and its implementing orders will be able to obtain a licence for a recognised technique (individual registration). In both countries the law itself does not forbid practitioners without a full medical education from practising homeopathy but the implementation regulations are still to be decided.

Position of the national medical associations

Several national medical associations, similar to the British Medical Council and British Medical Association in the UK (in several countries there is one single body instead of two), have recognised homeopathy as a therapeutic medical method. In Germany doctors can obtain, after passing an examination, an additional qualification, Homöopathischer Arzt, which is recognised by the national medical association, the Bundesärztekammer. A similar situation exists in Austria where the additional qualification Homöopathie is recognised by the Öster-reichische Ärztekammer. The Latvian medical association Latvijas Arstu Biedriba, which regulates and supervises all medical specialties, conferred homeopathy the official status of a clinical specialty in 1995. A subspecialty under the term of 'certificate of capacity in homeopathy' has been in place in Switzerland since 1998 in collaboration with the Swiss medical association Foederatio Medicorum Helveticorum (FMH), for doctors holding a title of a current specialty such as general medicine, internal medicine or paediatrics.

In other countries a similar development can be seen. In 1997 the French medical association Ordre National des Médecins recognised homeopathy as an existing therapeutic medical method and stated that homeopathic education should be installed at universities, leading to a diploma authorised by the Ordre, and that systematic information on homeopathy should be given within the undergraduate medical curriculum. In 2002 the Italian medical association Federazione Nazionali degli Ordini dei Medici Chirughi e degli Odontoiatri (FNOMCeO) recognised homeopathy, among other CAM modalities, as a medical method and insisted on legislation in this field. Other national medical associations, notably in Spain, the Organización Médica Colegial, and in Greece, the Panellinios Iatrikos Syllogos, are also more and more open to CAM.

In a few other countries the medical establishment, including the national medical association, are less favourably disposed towards homeopathy. In Sweden and Slovenia the medical associations even take a very negative attitude towards homeopathy (and other CAM modalities), leading to doctors who practise homeopathy being struck off the register.

Homeopathy at universities and hospitals

In all European countries homeopathy is taught at private training institutes. In some countries postgraduate homeopathic training courses are provided at universities, in France at eight universities (Aix-Marseille, Besançon, Bordeaux II, Lille, Limoges, Lyon, Paris-Bobigny and Poitiers), in Germany at five (Berlin, Düsseldorf, Freiburg, Hanover and Heidelberg), in Poland at seven (Gdansk, Katowice, Krakow, Lublin, Poznan, Warsaw and Wroclaw), and in Spain at four (Barcelona, Murcia, Seville and Valladolid).

Professorial chairs in homeopathy do not exist in continental Europe as yet. There are, however, chairs in CAM at some universities, e.g. in Switzerland (universities of Bern and Zürich), in Germany (universities of Berlin, Duisburg/Essen and Witten/Herdecke) and there is a Centre for Complementary Medicine Research (ZNF) at the Technical University of Munich and at the University of Tromsø (Norway). Joint research projects with other clinical departments of the universities are conducted here and lectures about specific complementary medical topics for students and doctors are provided as well as familiarisation courses in the undergraduate medical curriculum to introduce students to the potential uses of CAM, the procedures involved, their potential benefits and their main strengths and weaknesses.

At many more universities familiarisation courses in homeopathy and other CAM methods have been introduced or are about to be introduced into the undergraduate medical curriculum. These courses are compulsory in Germany and optional at many universities all over Europe. A recent review by the University of Debrecen (Hungary)[10] revealed that 42% of the medical faculties at universities in the former 15-member EU provide teaching courses involving CAM; in 31% of the faculties the course is evaluated by an exam, and in 13% of the faculties the courses are compulsory, although there is a wide variation between medical schools in students' level of exposure to these therapies. Branches of CAM regularly mentioned as being part of the curriculum include acupuncture, homeopathy, herbal medicine and massage. In the 10 member states that accessed the EU in 2004, 20% of the medical faculties provide such courses. To allow use of CAM methods in conventional medical practice, additional courses are required by 10% of the faculties in the 15-member EU and 20% of them in the 10 'new' EU member states.

Not only in the UK but also in mainland Europe – for example, Austria, France, Germany, Italy, Spain and Switzerland – some hospitals currently provide homeopathic treatment by medical doctors in their outpatient departments.

Coverage by the health insurance systems

The coverage of homeopathy and other CAM therapies varies from country to country. In some European countries homeopathic treatment is reimbursed by the public health insurance system, in other countries by private insurance companies, in most countries by neither of them. An initiative by the German homeopathic doctors' association has led to the situation that more than 70 health insurance companies are now reimbursing homeopathic treatment performed by contracted homeopathic physicians. According to the contract homeopathic medical care is offered to the insured free of extra charge, if provided by homeopathic doctors with a specific homeopathic qualification who have joined the agreement. The contract guarantees homeopathic physicians a definitive and reasonable remuneration for their care, including specific facilities for individualised homeopathy, which requires more time-consuming consultations. This latter item in particular is unique in Europe: in other European countries a standard tariff for a 10-minute GP consultation is charged, which is totally insufficient in the treatment of patients with chronic disease.

Veterinary practice (see also Chapter 14)

There are about 2000 veterinary surgeons in continental Europe who provide homeopathic treatment to pets, food-producing and other animals (slightly more than 1% of the total number of vets). As in medical homeopathy there are wide variations among countries in the degree of legal recognition and the ways in which veterinary home-opathy is practised. Whereas in Sweden vets are not allowed to use homeopathy in their treatment, a few hundreds of vets in Austria, Ireland and Switzerland have a qualification in veterinary homeopathy that is recognised as a specialty (comparable to the situation in the UK). In most countries there are special homeopathic training pro-grammes for veterinarians, usually taking 120–400 hours over 3 years. In Hungary and Norway programmes are given at universities, in some other countries by the veterinary organisations and in most countries at private training institutes. The International Association for Veterinary Homeopathy (IAVH) has established minimum training standards and the requirements for teaching programmes, examinations and continuing education. The examinations lead to the qualification CertIAVH.

Although the American Veterinary Medical Association (AVMA) recognises the interest in and use of complementary and alternative vet-erinary medicine (CAVM) and is open to its consideration, the organisa-tions of veterinary surgeons in Europe are less favourably disposed towards homeopathy and other CAM modalities. The Federation of Veterinarians in Europe (FVE) urged its members 'to work only on the basis of scientifically proven and evidence-based methods and to stay away from non-evidence-based methods',[11] whereas the European Board of Veterinary Specialisation (EBVS), an organisation that over-sees veterinary specialisation, is now officially moving against CAM. It seems that conventional vets are fighting a rearguard action, because the use of homeopathy in animals is increasing. In addition, in all EU member states in organic husbandry animals, when they become sick or injured, should be treated immediately by giving preference to homeo-pathic or herbal medicinal products and by limiting to a strict minimum the use of chemically synthesised allopathic medicinal products in order to guarantee the integrity of organic production for consumers.

European regulatory authorities and the practice of CAM

Both the European parliament and the Council of Europe advocate the official recognition of CAM. The parliament, in its resolution of 29 May 1997,[12] called on the European Commission:

a. to launch a process of recognizing non-conventional medicine and, to this end, to take the necessary steps to encourage the establishment of appropriate committees;
b. to carry out a thorough study into the safety, effectiveness, area of application and the complementary or alternative nature of all non-conventional medicines and to draw up a comparative study of the various national legal models to which non-conventional medical practitioners are subject;
c. to make, in formulating European legislation on non-conventional forms of medicine, a clear distinction between non-conventional medicines which are 'complementary' in nature and those which are 'alternative' medicines in the sense that they replace conventional medicine;

and further calls on the Council of Ministers after completion of the preliminary work referred to above (at b.) to encourage the development of research programmes in the field of non-conventional medicines covering the individual and holistic approach, the preventive role and the specific characteristics of the non-conventional medical disciplines; Parliament undertakes to do likewise.

To date, the European Commission has not taken any action in this field, referring to the EU treaty stipulating that healthcare systems are a national responsibility.

The parliament resolution was welcomed by the Council of Europe, the continent's oldest political organisation, which groups together 46 countries and is distinct from the 27-nation EU. The Council of Europe adopted a resolution (1206) on CAM in 1999,[13] in which it called on 'member states to promote official recognition of these forms of medicine in medical faculties and to encourage hospitals to use them'. In addition, 'appropriate courses should be offered in universities to train allopathic doctors in alternative and complementary forms of treatment'. The Council of Europe clearly stated that 'the best guarantee for patients lies in a properly trained profession, which is aware of its limitations, has a system of ethics and self-regulation and is also subject to outside control'. Although neither a resolution of the European parliament nor a resolution of the Council of Europe is a binding act but rather is a declaration of policy, these resolutions have made several countries consider revising legislation in the field of CAM.

Europe and the regulatory position of homeopathic medicines

The legal and terminological framework for homeopathic medicinal products in the EU is clearly laid down by the European Pharmacopoeia and the European Council directives. Two European directives on homeopathy came into force on 1 January 1994[14] – as with all EU directives, they require member states to transpose their provisions into national law – one applicable for homeopathic products for humans and one applicable for homeopathic veterinary products. It was the EU's intention:

> to create a legal frame that would allow patients access to the medicinal products of their choice provided all precautions were taken to ensure the quality and safety of the said products; to provide users of these medicinal products with a very clear indication of their homeopathic character and with sufficient guarantees of their quality and safety and to harmonise the rules relating to the manufacture, control and inspection of homeopathic medicinal products to permit the circulation throughout the Community of medicinal products which are safe and of good quality.

By these directives, all 27 EU member states were obliged to register homeopathic medicinal products.

Later on, the provisions for homeopathic medicinal products were integrated into the EU pharmaceutical legislation, in directive 2001/82/EC (veterinary use) and 2001/83/EC (human use) – recently amended by directive 2004/28/EC and directive 2004/27/EC respectively – on the Community Code relating to medicinal products. These directives regulate manufacturing, inspection, marketing and labelling. Directive 2001/83/EC provides two procedures for introducing homeopathic medicinal products into the market: either by a simplified registration (article 14) without indication or by a marketing authorisation (article 16.2) allowing medicinal claims. The simplified registration procedure applies to medicines containing less than one part per 10 000 of the undiluted tincture or less than 1/100th of the smallest dose used in conventional medicine and is restricted in ways of administration (oral/external). The most recent changes provide for a mutual recognition procedure of existing simplified registrations, which means that a homeopathic medicine can be registered in a certain EU member state by referring to an existing registration in another member state. One common dossier template for applications for the registration (article 14 of CD 2001/83/EC) of homeopathic medicinal products in the EU will specify the requirements for registration in detail so that dossiers in different countries can be compared more easily. As for homeopathic medicinal products that require a market authorisation (article 16.2), i.e. low potencies and complex preparations, member states may introduce or retain in their territory specific rules for the toxicological and pharmacological tests and clinical trials (proof of effectiveness) in accordance with the principles and characteristics of homeopathy as practised in that member state. Some EU member states have provided for such rules; most of them, however, have not. The adaptation process is ongoing and more important steps towards harmonisation are still necessary.

The directives stipulate that homeopathic medicinal products be prepared in accordance with a homeopathic manufacturing procedure described by the European Pharmacopoeia or, in absence thereof, by the pharmacopoeias currently used officially in the member states. That means that the European Pharmacopoeia, which belongs to the jurisdiction of the Council of Europe and is managed by the European Directorate for the Quality of Medicines (EDQM) in Strasbourg (France), will be playing an increasingly more important role. To date, it has included some general and several substance-specific monographs on homeopathic starting materials and this process will proceed over the next years. The European Pharmacopoeia overrides any official national pharmacopoeias in the EU member states and it is intended that all regulations in national homeopathic pharmacopoeias will eventually merge into the European Pharmacopoeia.

In order to facilitate the resolution of procedural, regulatory and scientific issues arising from variation procedures, the Homeopathic Medicinal Products Working Group (HMPWG) was established and mandated by the Heads of Medicines Agencies (HMA), the body joining the medicines regulatory authorities in the EU and Iceland, Liechtenstein and Norway. In fact, the HMPWG is a forum for exchange of regulatory and scientific expertise regarding the assessment of the quality and safety of homeopathic medicinal products in the member states and provides guidance on the assessment of homeopathic medicinal products.

The stringent requirements for registration involve high dossier costs, i.e. the costs of manpower for the manufacturer to make a complete dossier with all necessary requirements for submission to the registration authorities. Manufacturers affirm that the costs of a simplified article 14 registration may vary from €2500 to €10 000 per dossier. The result is that only a few hundreds of 'best sellers' out of a total range of 3000 homeopathic medicinal products will be on the market and a large group of less frequently prescribed medicines will not be registered because the dossier costs are too high compared to their low turnover. In countries where 'old' registrations (i.e. from before 31 December 1993) are still valid, this is not an issue so far, but the recently introduced mutual recognition procedure will require a common dossier template for applications, in other words harmonised registration requirements. This could lead to a situation where manufacturers will bring their own *Pulsatilla pratensis* (a common homeopathic medicine) on the market but less frequently prescribed medicines will not be available. This means that some patients seeking homeopathic treatment will not be able to receive adequate treatment, unless magistral or officinal preparation of the less frequently prescribed medicines are sufficiently available. In addition, since homeopathy is a developing therapeutic method in which new homeopathic medicines are continuously being tested, leading to an ever-increasing homeopathic armamentarium, the unavailability of new medicines may hamper the development of homeopathy.

The arbitrary 1:10 000 limit for the simplified registration procedure is illogical for harmless substances, inadequate in a small number of highly toxic starting materials, and, therefore, needs improvement. A safe potency list for all homeopathic medicinal products would be a good alternative, reflect the spirit of the 1:10 000 limit rule and permit a greater availability of homeopathic medicinal products. A new procedure mentioned in the latest version of the directive will provide the possibility of registering more concentrated homeopathic medical products according to the simplified procedure. The so-called simplified procedure, article 14, for single homeopathic medicines is, in practice, not as simple as could be expected according to the original EU regulation. The objective of the original directive 92/73/EC that 'patients should be allowed access to the medicinal products of their choice' is not yet in sight.

In addition, stricter regulations and increasing requirements as to viral (and prion) safety at a European and national level have already resulted in a reduction of medicines derived from animal and human source material in a number of countries. Oddly enough, middle and high potencies of some homeopathic medicines that are totally harmless are no longer available because the starting material of these medicines (which are never used as such) may imply safety issues. Pharmacists and practitioners from the European homeopathic community are sharing their expertise to find Europe-wide solutions that meet both the governmental virus safety requirements and the homeopathic quality standards. These solutions include other manufacturing procedures/techniques that may provide the same level of viral safety as sterilisation but still guarantee the maintenance of the original structure of this material.

A non-EU country, Switzerland, has its own registration system for homeopathic medicines. The procedure for products with an indication is similar to the EU market authorisation procedure, but there are two simplified procedures for products without indication (single homeopathic medicines) depending on their potential risk.[15] The simplest level is an electronic notification procedure for the large majority of homeopathic medicines (currently about 2000) that are on a list of homeopathic medicines (to be extended upon request), each with its safe dilution limit. The manufacturers have to keep dossiers specifying the procedures to guarantee the quality, which need not be submitted for registration but only be available with the manufacturer. This procedure includes, for example, Belladonna in potencies above 4D/X, but also nosodes above 12C. The next level is a simplified registration procedure that requires a limited dossier to be submitted in case of homeopathic medicines in low potencies, medicines of human/animal origin below 12c or 24D/X as well as injectables. This system, which resulted from mutual agreement between regulatory authorities, industry and practitioners, seems to be a much more feasible and less bureaucratic system than the current EU system.

It is incumbent on the European Pharmacopoeia Commission (EPC) to standardise and harmonise homeopathic medicinal products in Europe, especially in view of the free circulation of products in Europe and future registration through the mutual recognition procedure. State-of-the-art, harmonised and standardised European monographs and a consistent nomenclature system that links up with the current nomenclature in botany, zoology and chemistry have to be developed. To reach this aim, the EPC needs the steady input and commitment of the homeopathic community, i.e. homeopathic pharmacists and practitioners.

As far as the position of homeopathic medicines in Europe is concerned, an important stakeholder is the European Coalition of Homeopathic and Anthroposophic Medicinal Products (ECHAMP), established by the large majority of European companies active in the production and distribution of homeopathic and anthroposophic medicinal products. This European Economic Interest Grouping (EEIG) currently represents 51 European companies and strives for Europe-wide availability of these medicines by health professionals and the general public. They also work to further the integration of home-opathic and anthroposophic medicine into the national health systems and the integration of homeopathic and anthroposophic medicinal products and its pharmaceutical procedures into official pharma-copoeias. The organisation seeks and co-ordinates common positions amongst its members in order to provide European and member state institutions with unified and representative positions.

Homeopathic practitioners joining forces

In the early 1990s, when the European Commission prepared the first directive in the field of homeopathy to harmonise the rules relating to the manufacture, control and inspection of homeopathic medicines, homeopathic doctors realised it was high time to establish a European platform to reach consensus about homeopathic matters. This platform was the European Committee for Homeopathy (ECH). In 1991 the organisation started to work on a common standard for a basic train-ing course and gradually extended its activities to other areas, such as documentation, research and politics. The general aim of the ECH is the promotion of homeopathy as a specific clinical method used by statut-orily recognised health professionals, i.e. medical doctors, veterinary surgeons, dentists and pharmacists, all within their own bounds of com-petence. To date 39 homeopathic doctors' associations in 24 European countries are affiliated to the ECH, and also many homeopathic veter-inarians, dentists and pharmacists in Europe have joined the ECH. In a similar vein, the ECCH, the European association of homeopathic practitioners without a full medical education, has been working on professional standards for this group of practitioners. These practi-tioners have been trained solely in homeopathy as a discrete clinical discipline. The ECCH is aimed at establishing registers of trained and regulated homeopaths and maintains a code of ethics and practice to which their members are accountable. It unites 24 associations in 20 countries.

The systemic approach in homeopathy (the systemic approach includes information not only about the patient's actual complaint and conventional diagnosis, but also about the patient's constitution, emotional and mental make-up) requires much time and investment in case-taking as well as a considerable amount of homeopathic and psychological understanding. Doctors, being trained in conventional (allopathic) medicine, which involves prescribing standard medicines to a given pathological condition, have always sought for ways to simplify homeopathy and may prescribe on isolated symptoms or give more than one medicine at a time. This has led to the situation where in actual practice there is a continuum between homeopathy in its most individualised form and prescribing homeopathic medicines based on a conventional diagnosis *per se*. The simplified, abridged or 'clinical' approach has been widely practised among European doctors for a long time but for a few decades now there has been a revival of the systemic approach in homeopathy. This systemic approach is being taught as the current standard at most European homeopathic schools.

Up to the present day, homeopathy in France has been somewhat different from homeopathy in other European countries. A lot of the specific French approach is due to the fact that none of the writings of James Tyler Kent was translated into French until the 1950s and the complete Kent's Repertory was not translated until 1991 (the first partial translation was published in 1966). The systemic approach in homeopathy was, therefore, hardly existent in France for a very long time. French homeopathic doctors such as Léon Vannier developed a system in which they classified human beings according to their physical and psychological characteristics, the conditions and problems to which they are prone, and then described homeopathic remedies to which the individual types respond best – usually a group of six to eight related remedies dominated by a major polychrest. This practice of polypharmacy or pluralist homeopathy uses a kind of unified posology, i.e. a dose of Belladonna 5c 3 times a day for 5 days or two to three (or more) remedies daily in the 7–9c as 'drainage' remedies for organs (to clear the pathways from accumulated toxins) and a 15–30c 'constitutional' remedy once a week for long periods of time. With the rise of biomedicine in the second half of the 20th century the clinical approach made inroads in the French homeopathic community and blended with existing pluralism. Through some schools established by homeopathic manufacturers the French approach was exported to Italy, Portugal and Spain, but in these countries the systemic approach of homeopathy became more and more prevalent (see also Chapter 7).

Obviously, high-quality practice implies a common agreement on the state-of-the-art method and the required educational standards, the establishment of professional profiles, requirements as to quality and competence, as well as rules for quality assurance. Consumers are best served by ensuring that all practitioners are able to practise the skills of their particular therapy in a safe and competent matter. Therefore, the harmonisation of homeopathic education was one of the first objectives of the ECH. The ECH Medical Homeopathic Education standard was based on the existing standards in the majority of countries involved in the ECH from the beginning. In Austria, Germany and Switzerland the national training standard was recognised by the national medical associations, and this was another good reason for adopting this standard. The standard describes the qualification requirements – knowledge, understanding, skills and attitudes – for a safe and effective practice of homeopathy, and outlines the syllabus for examinations leading to a qualification in homeopathy and has now gained acceptance as the standard for medical homeopathic education across Europe. To date, approximately 10 000 doctors have taken homeopathic education at this level, which means a number that is comparable to the number of doctors in certain medical specialties. In several countries a system of registration of qualified homeopathic doctors has been established so that all doctors who use the title of homeopathic doctor have received appropriate education and training, and have demonstrated an ability to apply their therapeutic skills in practice. Recently the ECH has started a programme of accreditation of those teaching centres whose basic educational and examination standards meet the ECH requirements. The ECH takes the position that the combination of high-quality training and qualification in homeopathy and a full medical qualification is a considerable asset if homeopathy is to be integrated into the existing European healthcare system as a fully fledged branch of medicine.

As for veterinary homeopathy, the requirements for the teaching programme, the examination and the continuing education of veterinarians have been laid down by the IAVH, an organisation that cooperates closely with the ECH.

In the absence of a European association of homeopathic pharmacists, the pharmacy subcommittee of the ECH has been working on a basic framework for a harmonised intermediate-level European qualification in homeopathic pharmacy tailored to the specific professional requirements of pharmacists. It builds on the introductory knowledge provided by a basic-level course. The diploma syllabus is intended to offer guidance to those member states wishing to operate a course over a period of 24 months, with at least 6 full-day teaching sessions and a minimum of 60 hours of self-study.

The ECCH has also been working on a training standard. Currently there are about 4500 homeopathic practitioners without a full medical education in Europe who have taken a training course at the level of ECCH European Guidelines for Homeopathic Education (40% of them in the UK).

Other European projects for the professionalisation of homeopathy

Apart from education, the ECH has been working on several other projects, such as the accessibility of information. One of the projects in this area was the *Homeopathic Thesaurus*,[16] a list of key terms to be used by indexers of the homeopathic literature, and to help people searching the literature. It has hierarchical lists for English, French, German and Italian terms and is meant to be an addition to other thesauri of medical terms such as MeSH (Medical Subject Headings) and AMED (Allied and Complementary Medicine). Other projects in this area were an online journals database, the International Guide on Homeopathic Documentation Resources (IGHDR) containing a list of 40 homeopathic libraries and a joint list of theses and dissertations.

Some other projects were related to the enhancement of homeopathy's scientific basis, such as standards on data collection and provings (homeopathic pathogenetic trials). Practice-based research such as prospective data collection is needed to evaluate the effectiveness of homeopathy in 'real-life' circumstances and there is a huge need for cooperation between various data collection projects in order to create synergies and gain a valid database in a harmonised format that allows exchange and/or comparison of data. An international standard for data collection in homeopathic practice, 'Data Collection in Homeopathic Practice – A Proposal for an International Standard' was published in December 1999.[17] The *Homeopathic Drug Provings Guidelines*[18] were based on the structure and contents of the *Guidelines for Good Clinical Practice* of the International Conference on Harmonisation (ICH), and reprocessed and amended for the requirements of homeopathic medicine provings. They also outline the minimum criteria for a good homeopathic proving protocol. Currently, the ECH is seeking to establish a provings database to be accessible on a website.

Objectives for the near future

There is a continuous need for developing standards for the professional practice of homeopathy. The final aim is the full integration of homeopathy within the European healthcare system, which will meet the growing demand among European citizens for homeopathic care within a professional context. To reach this aim there is a need for working relationships between the homeopathic community and institutions at the European level, such as the European parliament, the European Commission, the EPC, the European Drug Regulatory Authorities, the EDQM concerning the European Pharmacopoeia, the HMPWG of the HMA, the European Medicines Agency (EMEA) and the European doctors' organisations (Comité Permanent des Médecins Européens (CPME)). The ECH has become a member of the Health Policy Forum that advises the European Commission about European public health affairs.

Concerted action of the homeopathic practitioners, the joint European homeopathic industry (ECHAMP) and the European homeo-pathic patients' organisations (European Federation of Homeopathic Patients' Associations: EFHPA) are needed. European associations of homeopathic practitioners and patients are members of the European Public Health Alliance (EPHA), an influential non-govermental organ-isation representing over 100 non-governmental and other not-for-profit organisations working on public health in Europe. Building alliances with other European organisations with the aim of integration of homeopathy into European healthcare; networking with key stake-holders in the European health policy arena, including EU policy-makers, member state governments, patient groups, healthcare professionals, health finance organisations; and raising homeopathy's profile by informing political and medical bodies, scientific press about the benefits of and scientific progress in homeopathy remain the principal aims for the years to come.

References

1. European Commission. *Commission Report to the European Parliament and Council on the Application of Directives 92/73 and 92/74.* COM(97)362 final. Brussels, Belgium: EC, 1997.
2. Marstedt G, Moebus S. *Gesundheitsberichterstattung des Bundes: Inanspruchnahme alternativer Methoden in der Medizin.* Berlin, Germany: Verlag Robert Koch-Institut, 2002.
3. Commission des Comptes de la Sécurité Sociale. *Document de Travail: Les médecins, Estimations au 1er janvier 2002.* Paris, France: Direction de la Recherche, des Études de l'Évaluation et des Statistiques (DREES), 2002. (4256 GPs homeopathy, 1741 homeopathy and acupuncture.)
4. Dixon A, Riesberg A, Weinbrenner S, *et al. Complementary and Alternative Medicine in the UK and Germany – Research and Evidence on Supply and*

Demand. London, UK: Anglo-German Foundation for the Study of Industrial Society, 2003.

5. Ersdal G, Ramstad S on behalf of the CAM-CANCER Consortium. *How are European Patients Safeguarded when Using Complementary and Alternative Medicine (CAM)? Jurisdiction, Supervision and Reimbursement Status in the EEA area (EU and EFTA) and Switzerland.* Tromsø, Norway: NAFKAM University, 2005.

6. Maddalena S. *Alternative Medicines: On the Way Towards Integration? A Comparative Legal Analysis in Western Countries.* Bern, Switzerland: Peter Lang, 2005.

7. World Health Organization. *Legal Status of Traditional Medicine and Complementary/Alternative Medicine: A Worldwide Review.* Geneva, Switzerland: World Health Organization, 2001.

8. World Health Organization. *WHO Global Atlas of Traditional, Complementary and Alternative Medicine.* Kobe, Japan: World Health Organization, the WHO Centre of Health Development, 2005.

9. European Council for Classical Homeopathy. *Recognition and Regulation of Homeopathy in Europe.* Brussels, Belgium: European Council for Classical Homeopathy, 2005.

10. Varga O, Márton S, Molnár P. Status of complementary and alternative medicine in European medical schools. *Forsch Komplementärmed* 2006; 13: 41–45.

11. *New Scientist.* Homeopathic vets come under fire. Accessible online at: http://press.newscientist.com/data/pdf/press/2529/252908.pdf.

12. European Parliament (1997). *Resolution on the Status of Non-conventional Medicine.* A4-0075/1997. Accessible online at: http://www.europarl.europa.eu/sides/getDoc.do?pubRef=-//EP//TEXT+REPORT+A4-1997-0075+0+DOC+XML+V0//EN&language=EN.

13. Council of Europe. A European approach to non-conventional medicines. Resolution 1206. Accessible online at: http://assembly.coe.int/main.asp?Link=/documents/adoptedtext/ta99/eres1206.htm.

14. Council Directive 92/73/EC and Council Directive 92/74/EC on homeopathic medicinal products. *Official J Eur Commun* 1992; L 297/8, L 297/12.

15. Ordinance of the Swiss Agency for Therapeutic Products on the simplified authorisation of complementary and herbal medicines products (ordinance on complementary and herbal medicinal products, KPAV /OAMédcophy) of 22 June 2006. Accessible online at: www.swissmedic.ch (document KPAV_englische_Uebersetzung.pdf).

16. European Committee for Homeopathy. *Homeopathic Thesaurus – Keyterms to be Used in Homeopathy – Tree Structure and Alphabetical List. English, German, French, Italian,* 3rd edn. Brussels, Belgium: European Committee for Homeopathy, 2007.

17. European Committee for Homeopathy. *Data Collection in Homeopathic Practice – A Proposal for an International Standard.* Brussels, Belgium: European Committee for Homeopathy, 1999.

18. European Committee for Homeopathy. *Homeopathic Drug Provings Guidelines.* Brussels, Belgium: European Committee for Homeopathy, 2004.

10

Roles of the UK homeopathic pharmacist

Lee Kayne

Introduction

The role of the UK pharmacist

This chapter will examine the varied roles of the homeopathic pharmacist in the UK and consider how these impact on the quality, efficacy and administration of homeopathic medicines. These roles are:

- the preparation of homeopathic medicines
- the provision of advice and assistance in the promotion and maintenance of good health to patients and fellow health professionals and the choice of medicines to self-treat
- the supply of homeopathic medicines by dispensing prescriptions and over-the-counter (OTC) sale
- the clinical role – prescribing medicines under the National Health Service.

The major drivers for change in healthcare delivery in the UK are the government (new legislation), the professions (new models of care, encouraging specialism), the industry (new products) but, most importantly, the *patient*. To adapt to the demands of the modern patient, the role of the pharmacist has changed beyond recognition even in the last decade, and with it the requirement for new educational initiatives. In the emerging environment of multidisciplinary healthcare, the pharmacist is an integral part of the delivery team. Always considered to be experts in medicines, pharmacists are increasingly being asked to extend this expertise to include *all* medicines, not simply allopathic ones, both by the public and by healthcare colleagues.

In order to deliver this role effectively and ethically, a pharmacist should undertake some formal training over and above any undergraduate exposure to homeopathy. Although all UK Schools of Pharmacy offer some homeopathic content, this may be in the form of only a lecture or two and is unlikely to be sufficient alone for practical use when qualified.

The preparation of medicines

Homeopathy is a system of medicine that typically employs over 3000 medicines, in over 8000 different potencies in a wide range of dosage forms. In addition, dosing schedules are sometimes rather complicated, as are the storage and administration instructions. Therefore, it really should come as no surprise that, as the link between practitioner and patient, the pharmacist is integral to homeopathic practice.

Only a relatively small number of pharmacists will have a direct role in the preparation of homeopathic medicines, but it is important for all to have some knowledge of the quality controls and methods involved in order to fulfil their important advisory role to patients and professional colleagues.

Sources of homeopathic medicines

Homeopathy and herbalism are often confused or considered to be the same therapy, as plants are used to prepare medicines in both systems. Indeed, in many cases, the *same* plant is used to prepare both a homeopathic medicine and a herbal remedy, albeit with very different constituents, methods of manufacture and clinical indications. Although it is certainly true that many plants are used to prepare homeopathic medicines, only about 65–70% of the available medicines is actually derived from plant material. The majority of the remainder utilise a wide range of source materials, including animals, insects and a few 'energetics' or 'imponderables' such as electricity, X-ray and sol (potentised sunlight).

There is also a group of medicines prepared from potentised allergens (*allergodes*), biological material from healthy sources such as bodily secretions or synthetic sources such as bacterial cultures (*sarcodes*), biological material from disease sources (*nosodes*) or potentised conventional drugs and vaccines (*tautodes*). As mentioned in Chapter 3 these medicines are said to be *iso*pathic and are used clinically on the principle of 'same to treat same' rather than the traditional homeopathic principle of 'like to treat like'. They are usually considered to be homeopathic in nature. This raises an interesting issue: if a medicine is not used according to homeopathic principles, how can it be called homeopathic? Indeed, what makes any medicine homeopathic? It is not clinical use and it is not its appearance in a homeopathic materia medica. Interestingly, to be considered a homeopathic medicine, it need only conform to the rather generic definition given in UK Statutory Instrument 1994 number 105, which in turn is quoted from the European Parliament Directive 92/73/EEC.[1]

> A 'homoeopathic medicinal product' means a medicinal product (which may contain a number of principles) prepared from products, substances or compositions called homoeopathic stocks in accordance with a homoeopathic manufacturing procedure described by the European Pharmacopoeia or, in the absence thereof, by any pharmacopoeia used officially in a[n EU] member State.[2]

Therefore, the definition of a medicine as homeopathic refers to the method by which it was manufactured rather than the purpose for which it is used. These methods are found, together with monographs detailing the sources and analytical criteria for medicines, in a reference source known as a pharmacopoeia, of which there are several that pertain to homeopathy.

The homeopathic pharmacopoeias

Although an increasing number of homeopathic medicine sources are now beginning to appear in the *European Pharmacopoeia* (EuPh),[3] it is still predominantly the two largest 'member state' pharmacopoeiae that are used in Europe – the *French Homeopathic Pharmacopoeia*[4] (also known as the FHomP, FP or FHP) and the *German Homeopathic Pharmacopoeia*[5] (also known as the GerHomP, GHP or most often the HAB for *Homöopathisches Arzneibuch*). In the USA, the *Homeopathic Pharmacopoeia of the United States*[6] (HPUS) performs a similar role (see Chapter 11). There is also a *British Homeopathic Pharmacopoeia*[7] (BHomP) which is designed to be used in conjunction with the HAB.

It is likely that the FHP and HAB will remain the primary references in Europe until further progress is made on the long-awaited unified *European Homeopathic Pharmacopoeia* (EuHomP) which, it is hoped, will become the single standard throughout Europe. However, despite many years of hard work by a great many contributors, the EuHomP contains only a handful of monographs. It seems that a complete version is still many years away.

Variation in standards

Applying the standards of the pharmacopoeias to homeopathic manu-facturing ensures the highest standards of quality and reproducibility are obtained as the monographs for individual medicines are very precise. For plants, the cultivation, collection, processing and preparation of mother tincture and potentisation are all explicitly described but there are some differences. For example, the FHP states that *Calendula officianalis* mother tincture should be prepared from fresh leaf tips, whereas the HAB specifies the whole aerial flowering parts and the HPUS the flower tips. Similarly, a mother tincture may be diluted one part to 99 parts of 60–70% alcohol according to the FHP to prepare the first centesimal potency (1c), or two parts to 98 parts of 43% ethanol according to the HAB. The HPUS method differs again, directing a one in 10 dilution of a 10% mother tincture in 88% ethanol. As all subsequent centesimal potencies are prepared from the 1c, homeopathic medicines available in different countries may not be precisely the same in terms of their manufacturing process. As the pharmacopoeial reference used in the manufacture of a medicine is not always clear from the label of the finished item, it is not always possible to know precisely the methods by which it was prepared. Whether this has any effect on the clinical efficacy of the medicines is a subject of great discussion amongst pharmacists, homeopathic practitioners and patients.

Variation in source materials

In some cases a completely different species of the plant may be specified as the source material by the different reference sources and we would expect this to have considerable clinical implications. For example, the widely used homeopathic medicine Pulsatilla is considered in most references sources to be Pulsatilla nigricans, sometimes known by an official alternative botanical name – *Pulsatilla pratensis*. The FHP has a monograph for a different species, *Pulsatilla vulgaris*, and the HPUS has a further monograph for *Pulsatilla nuttalliana*. Interestingly, the HPUS also has a 'generic' Pulsatilla monograph that gives *both Pulsatilla pratensis* and *Pulsatilla vulgaris* as 'contemporary names' and *Pulsatilla nigricans* among the Latin names. The HAB contains a monograph for *Pulsatilla pratensis* (*nigricans*), but just to confuse matters further, it also has a slightly different monograph for *Pulsatilla vulgaris*! Bharatan and colleagues, in their extensive botanical research at the London Museum of Natural History, confirm that *Pulsatilla nigricans* and *Pulsatilla pratensis* may be considered the same plant under the International Code of Botanical Nomenclature, but the use of *Pulsatilla vulgaris* as a synonym is in fact incorrect.[8]

Another hotly debated topic is whether we are using exactly the same medicines today as Hahnemann was using in his day. The realistic answer to this is 'probably not', but it is not necessarily the fault of modern manufacturers. Hahnemann's records of the sources used for his medicines were often incomplete at best, and, with no pharmacopoeia available to him, were unlikely to be standardised from one preparation to the next. With the well-publicised environmental changes taking place over the last 250 years, it is almost certain that the plants and minerals used as sources for homeopathic medicines have changed. Although we therefore cannot say for certain that the medicines we use today are the same as they were in Hahnemann's time, we can, because of the standardisation of materials and methods prescribed by the pharmacopoeias, be certain that a medicine prepared by one manufacturer to, for example, the HAB standard, will be exactly the same as that prepared by a different manufacturer using the same reference source.

Abbreviated names

When dispensing prescriptions or otherwise supplying medicines to patients at the request of a prescriber, pharmacists must also be aware that there is no standard system of homeopathic abbreviations, leading to some confusion for practitioners and patients. This is one very important issue regarding homeopathic medicine prescriptions that is not addressed by the pharmacopoeias. Although detailed information is given in each monograph regarding the primary and alternative

Table 10.1 Confusing homeopathic abbreviations

Prescription	Possible medicines
A. Sulph.	Acid Sulph, Aluminium Sulph, Ammonium Sulph, Antimonium Sulph, Argent Sulph, Aurum Sulph
Arg-m.	Argent Metallicum, Argent Muriaticum
Arum.	Arum Mac, Arum Trip, possibly Aurum or its salts (especially on hand-written prescriptions!)
Ferr-p.	Ferrum Phosphoricum, Ferrum Picricum
Merc.	Any one of 20+ Mercurius types, e.g. Merc Sol
Nat-m.	Natrum Marinus, Natrum Muriaticum
Nux.	Nux Moschata, Nux Vomica
Sang.	Sanguinaria, Sanguisuga
Urtica	Urtica Dioica, Urtica Urens
Zinc	As for most metals, many different salts are available, e.g. Zinc Carb, Zinc Phos, Zinc Sulph

nomenclature of the medicine, no definitive guidance is given on standard abbreviations. Some examples of confusing abbreviations are illustrated in Table 10.1 and represent real prescriptions received at a homeopathic pharmacy. In most cases, the practitioner, when contacted for clarification, was unaware that the abbreviation might be misinterpreted and that the patient could have received the wrong medicine.

Many major reference sources give what are purported to be the standard abbreviations for homeopathic medicines but these are not always as 'standardised' as the author might have you believe. In the *Concordant Materia Medica*, for example,[9] Argent Met is abbreviated Arg-m, whereas in the *Complete Repertory*,[10] the same abbreviation is used to denote Argent Mur, with Argent Met being abbreviated to simply Arg.

New homeopathic medicines

New homeopathic medicines are continually being proposed, proved and prepared. It is not unusual for a specialist homeopathic pharmacy to stock several thousand medicines and add 100 or more each year. In recent times, work by leading homeopaths around the world has given us new medicines prepared from birds, animal milk, snake and spider venoms, as well as many plants and mineral compounds. Of course these new medicines do yet not have pharmacopoeial monographs and so the preparation of such medicines is usually conducted following the methods detailed in the original proving. In the absence of a formal proving, medicines will be prepared by 'generic' methods described by the pharmacopoeia being used.

Manufacture of homeopathic medicines

Before considering the methods used to prepare homeopathic medicines in detail, it is important to discuss the potency scales used in homeopathy (see Table 10.2).

Although it cannot strictly be considered a potency, mother tincture has been included in this table as often the tincture extracted from plant material will be the medicine itself without further preparation. This may be applied topically, e.g. Arnica, Symphytum, Calendula, or taken internally, e.g. Crataegus, Spartium, Valerian.

Early work in homeopathy by Hahnemann and his contemporaries concentrated on the use of centesimal potencies which are prepared by a dilution factor of 1 in 100 and are designated 'c', e.g. 6c, 12c, 200c.

Table 10.2 Potencies of homeopathic medicines

Potency scale	Designation	Dilution factor
Mother tincture	Ø	None
Centesimal	c, cH, cK, K	100
Decimal	x, D	10
Quinquagimillesimal	LM, Q	50 000

In the UK it is fairly common to refer to the potency by number only, the 'c' being inferred, although this practice is discouraged, particularly as the decimal potencies have become more popular with practitioners in recent years and confusion could lead to the patient receiving an incorrect potency. Those prepared by traditional Hahnemannian methods are sometimes also designated 'cH' to differentiate from those prepared by Korsakovian methods, which are termed 'cK' or simply 'K' (see below). In addition, roman numerals are used to designate higher potencies, e.g. M (1000), CM (10 000), MM (1 000 000). Decimal potencies prepared by a dilution factor of 1 in 10 are designated with the suffix 'x' or the prefix 'D', e.g. 6x or D6.

In later life, Hahnemann began to move away from his previous work utilising centesimal potencies and began to experiment with potencies he termed quinquagimillesimal, also known as LM or Q potencies, which are, as the name suggests, prepared by process of 50 000 dilutions. A recent review of Hahnemann's casebooks found evidence of over 1500 cases using LM potencies between 1837 and his death in 1843, leading many commentators to suggest that he was using LM potencies almost exclusively in his latter years.[11] The preparation of all potency scales will be discussed in greater detail below.

Depending on source and the potencies being prepared, a homeopathic medicine is prepared from the raw material according to the methods described in the homeopathic pharmacopoeiae. The procedures used to prepare source materials for centesimal and decimal potencies are summarised in Figure 10.1.

Stage 1

Plant materials are collected as described in the appropriate pharmacopoeial monograph and first subjected to maceration to break up the material, followed by processes of incubation (also termed percolation) and extraction (filtration) to obtain the mother tincture. The equipment

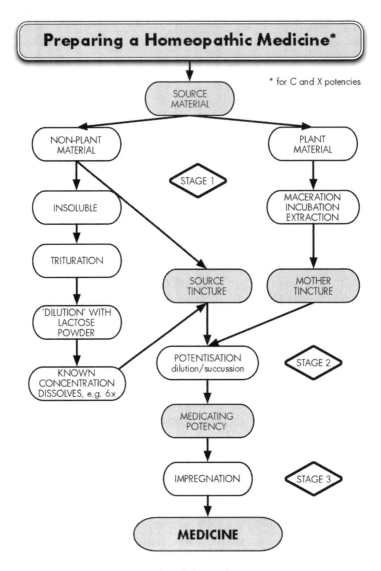

Figure 10.1 Preparing centesimal and decimal potencies.

utilised in each stage is shown in Figures 10.2–10.4. It should be noted that the term 'mother tincture' can only be applied to the raw extract of a plant-based source material obtained after the procedures documented above. Despite mention in a number of homeopathic texts, no true mother tinctures of Arsenicum Alb, Sulphur, Merc Sol, Carbo Veg, Natrum Mur, Phosphorus and other non-plant material actually exist.

Figure 10.2   Processing of plant materials: maceration.

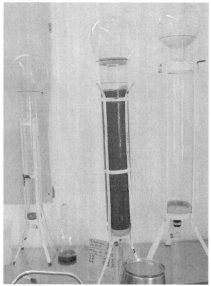

Figure 10.3 Processing of plant materials: incubation.

Figure 10.4 Processing of plant materials: extraction.

Soluble non-plant materials may be dissolved in ethanol or distilled water at a known concentration to produce a 'source tincture', the equivalent homeopathic potency of which will vary with each material. Similarly, non-soluble materials are triturated (ground) and diluted with known quantities of lactose until such time as the mixture dissolves to produce the source tincture of known concentration. In many pharmacies this is still performed by hand using that most quintessential of pharmaceutical equipment, the mortar and pestle, but large-scale manu-facturers will often use a mechanised version. Once again, the exact homeopathic potency attributed to this source tincture will vary accord-ing to the source material but is typically in the ranges of 2–6c (10^{-4} to 10^{-12} mg/ml) and/or 4–9x (10^{-4} to 10^{-9} mg/ml) depending on the potency scale being prepared. Occasionally, when an insoluble sub-stance is required at a lower potency such as 3x, the mixture of source

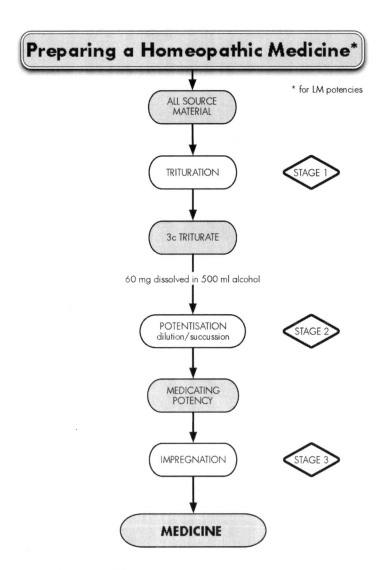

Figure 10.5 Preparing LM potencies.

material and lactose from that stage of the trituration process may be directly compressed into trituration tablets or administered as a powder.

When preparing LM potencies all source materials are triturated to the 3c potency, even plant or soluble materials (see Figure 10.5). In strict adherence to traditional Hahnemannian methods, a mother tincture cannot be used to prepare LM potencies, but availability of raw materials may make this difficult and, in some cases, may necessitate preparation from a tincture.

Stage 2

Once the mother tincture has been obtained from the source material, the process of potentisation is used to create the homeopathic medicine. This comprises a dilution stage and a succussion stage to prepare the potency scales discussed above.

An overview of the Hahnemannian method of potentisation is shown in Figure 10.6 for centesimal and Figure 10.7 for decimal potencies and the equipment employed is shown in Figure 10.8. One part of the mother tincture is first added to 99 parts of ethanol (or as specified in the pharmacopoeia: see above). Traditionally this stage would be

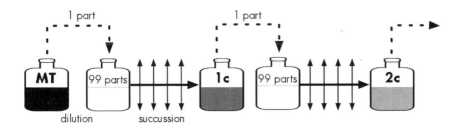

Figure 10.6 The Hahnemannian potentisation process for centesimal potencies.

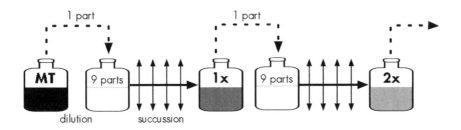

Figure 10.7 The Hahnemannian potentisation process for decimal potencies.

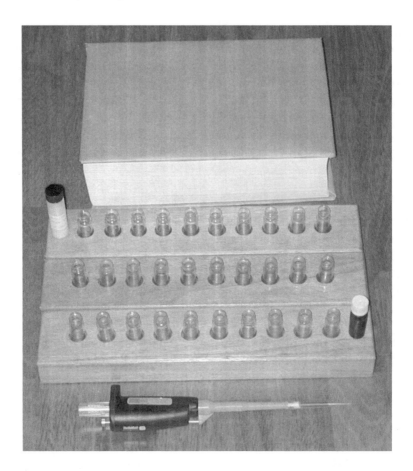

Figure 10.8 Potentisation equipment.

performed by careful manipulation of a cork-stoppered vial but in modern times a micropipette is usually employed to measure a precise pharmaceutical drop, defined as equal to 0.05 ml.[12] This mixture is then succussed to obtain the 1c potency and the process repeated with one drop transferred to a new vial containing 99 parts of ethanol to obtain the 2c potency and so on to the required potency, e.g. 6c, 12c, 30c, 200c. The decimal scale, attributed to Constantine Hering, is similar except that one part of tincture is added to nine parts of ethanol and the process proceeds as before to produce 1x (D1), 2x (D2), 6x (D6) and so on. It is often said that decimal potencies are equivalent to the centesimal potency of half the number, i.e. a 6x and a 3c are the same. Although this is certainly true mathematically – both correspond to a dilution level of 10^{-6} – a 6x potency has been succussed twice as many times as the 3c. Thus, they are certainly not the same: the decimal potency is considered to be therapeutically more potent.

Succussion is probably the most important process of all in the preparation of homeopathic medicines. Certainly we know from clinical observations that the process of striking each vial on a 'hard but elastic body', as described in the *Organon*[13], is absolutely vital for the clinical efficacy of the medicine. In Hahnemann's day, succussion was typically performed using a large leather-bound book, often a family Bible. Nowadays, books may still be used, as evidenced by Figure 6.8 although more often medicinal shakers carry out the process. With respect to our publishers, the *Martindale Extra Pharmacopoeia* makes a perfect succussion block! Some pharmacists prefer to strike the vial on the heel of the hand instead, which appears to be equally as effective, but is not always practical for higher potencies. It is important to note here that succussion should be a combination of vigorous agitation with impact: simple mixing, for example, with a vortex machine may not produce an efficacious homeopathic medicine. Many patients and practitioners have concerns about the shaking that occurs during transport of medicines. Pharmacists are often asked how liquid medicines may be protected from increasing in potency during transit. Many manufacturers overfill liquid bottles to reduce the amount of movement possible by the contents, but potentisation cannot occur without *both* dilution *and* succussion, so the risk of homeopathic potentisation in transit of a sealed liquid medicine is negligible in real terms.

The number of succussions required at each stage of potentisation is another of those great homeopathic discussion points! Hahnemann appeared unsure as to the optimum number of succussion, suggesting variously 20, 40 or 50 in the notes to the fourth edition of the *Organon*[14], only two in the fifth edition[15] and 100 in the sixth edition.[13] Although the HPUS and HAB only state that succussion should be 'thorough', the FHP, in its eighth edition of 1965,[16] also gives 100 succussions as the optimum and this is the number that is used by many manufacturers, although some pharmacists prefer a different number or a timed measurement instead.

Many small-scale manufacturers continue to prepare homeopathic medicines by hand in the traditional Hahnemannian fashion, even up to as high as 200c. This is a very labour-intensive and expensive exercise, as by definition the multi-vial method requires a new clean glass vial and fresh ethanol for each stage of the potentisation process. For these reasons, the majority of potencies higher than 200c are now prepared by the Korsakovian method shown in Figure 10.9.

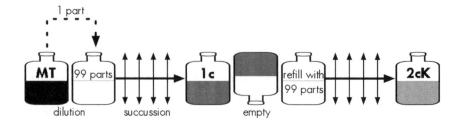

Figure 10.9 The Korsakovian potentisation process.

General Simeon von Korsakoff prepared homeopathic medicines for Tsar Nicholas I and was known as a vociferous proponent of high-potency homeopathy. He is best remembered for his alternative method of potentisation proposed in 1832 which utilises a single vial as opposed to the multiple vials employed by the Hahnemannian method.[17] The first potency is prepared as before but instead of a drop being transferred to a new vial after succussion, the vial is emptied by suction or inversion, in theory leaving a uniform amount of material adhering to the side of the vial. New ethanol is then added and the process repeated until the third potency, when the ethanol is replaced by water which is then used for the remainder of the medicine preparation, all of which is completed in a single vial. Not only is this far less expensive but it also lends itself to automation: a number of machines are available to perform very high-potency preparations, such as 1000K (MK), 10 000K (10MK or XMK), 50 000 (50MK or LMK) or higher. With such potencies the K is often omitted as it is assumed that no manufacturer makes these potencies by Hahnemannian methods.

The rather different method for preparing LM (Q) potencies is also shown in Figure 10.10. As mentioned above, the starting material

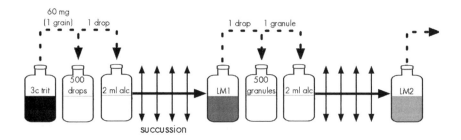

Figure 10.10 The potentisation process for LM potencies.

should be a 3c trituration, rather than a mother tincture or liquid potency.

Whichever potentisation method is used, the required potency is obtained as a 'medicating potency' or 'stock potency', usually stored in 95% ethanol and used to impregnate the appropriate dosage form for the final dispensed medication. In practice, the modern homeopathic pharmacy will often also retain some slightly lower intermediate potencies to allow the medicating potencies to be prepared quickly if supplies run low, without having to repeat the entire process. It is therefore not uncommon for a pharmacy to hold stock of unusual potency levels such as 10c, 28c, 198c or 998c, which are often known as 'prepotencies' or 'back potencies'.

Stage 3

This stage involves the impregnation of the final dosage with the medicating potency obtained in stage 2. If thousands of medicines in theoretically limitless potencies were not enough, there are also many different dosage forms available for any given homeopathic medicine (Table 10.3 and Figure 10.11).

Table 10.3 Solid oral dosage forms for homeopathic medicines

Figure 10.11	Name	Composition	Appearance
A	Tablets (hard tablets)	Lactose/sucrose	Flat, biconvex
B	Pillules (pills, globules)	Sucrose	Spherical 3–4 mm
C	Granules (poppy seeds)	Sucrose*	Spherical < 1 mm
D	Soft tablets	Lactose	Loose, cylindrical
E	Crystals	Sucrose	Sugar strands
F	Powder (sachets)†	Lactose	Loose powder
Not shown	Liquid potency (drops)	20–30% ethanol	Clear liquid
Not shown	Mother tincture	Varies by tincture	Varies by tincture

*Granules from some manufacturers may be prepared from a lactose/sucrose mix. If this is important, the practitioner or patient should check with the supplier.
†Sachets may also be prepared containing granules or crystals.

Each is impregnated with the medicating potency, using different methods depending on the dosage form and scale of preparation. Small-scale 'specials' manufacturers who are making individual medicines using traditional methods might impregnate the dosage form by hand using a process of surface inoculation. On a larger scale, a large-volume

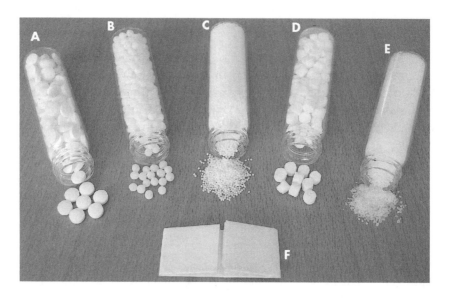

Figure 10.11 Solid oral dosage forms for homeopathic medicines.

vessel may be employed, with impregnation conducted by means of spraying the medicating potency on to the dosage forms as the vessel is mechanically rotated.

Although tablets (A in Figure 10.11) are often the preferred dosage form for the majority of patients in the UK, the choice of dosage form may be governed by a number of factors. With very high-potency treatments, usually only to be taken for a single or very small number of doses, sachets (F) containing lactose powder, crystals or granules may be preferred as individual doses may be dispensed. In other, longer-term treatments, the age and/or preference of the patient should be taken into consideration (see Case 10.1).

Homeopathic medicines are often easier to administer to babies and young children (and animals) as granules (C) or soft tablets (D) which melt in the mouth. Patients who are lactose-intolerant may prefer sucrose pillules (B) or crystals (E). Similarly for vegetarians and those patients who may have religious issues with lactose, which is usually from milk – and therefore animal – origin. Although the HAB has size standards for pills and granules, it should be noted that no composition guidance or size standards for other forms are given and therefore dosage forms may vary between manufacturers. For this reason, some offer a 7-g vial containing 50–55 tablets, whereas others offer up to 70 tablets in the same size of vial as their tablets are slightly smaller – the

CASE STUDY

Case 10.1   Selection of dosage form

Recently, a worried father (Mr A) brought his new baby into the pharmacy and asked to see me. His general practitioner had advised him to come in to discuss the severe colic that the baby was experiencing – a previous prescription for simeticone had little effect and the doctor thought I might be able to prescribe a homeopathic medicine if appropriate.

Mr A was keen to try homeopathy as his wife had taken homeopathic medicines during her pregnancy for various ailments with great success and had been recommended to take Arnica before and during labour by her midwife. However he was concerned that it might not be safe for a baby of only 9 weeks old.

During our consultation, I established that the baby was being breastfed but the mother was having a 'difficult time' of it as colic symptoms were starting mid-feed. The health visitor had discussed various techniques with Mrs A but changing position, time and length of feeding had made no difference. Likewise, expressing milk did not help, even when lactase enzyme drops were added at the suggestion of another local pharmacist – the couple's 2-year-old son was recently confirmed as lactose-intolerant.

I continued the consultation with an examination of symptoms and modalities. Using the three-legged stool approach (see below and Case 10.2), I identified that:

1. The baby was not teething (in cases of colic-like symptoms while teething, the medicine Chamomilla is often the first choice).
2. The baby drew her knees up to her chest during an attack.
3. The symptoms seemed to improve with tight swaddling (warmth/pressure).

On the basis of these indications, I decided to prescribe the medicine Colocynth 30c.

Mr A mentioned that he thought homeopathic medicines were available in drop form, which might be easier to give to a baby. However, I explained that I did not feel this would be appropriate as 'drops', i.e. a 'liquid potency', are prepared using 30% alcohol. For this reason, I rarely prescribe liquid potencies to children and certainly not in this case as I was aware that the family were practising Muslims. I also explained that a tiny amount of alcohol would be used to prepare the medicine, but this would evaporate on the surface of the solid dosage form.

In selecting the dosage form, I discounted powders or tablets/soft tablets due to the lactose content – the animal source of lactose and family history of

(continued overleaf)

CASE STUDY (continued)

intolerance rendered these inappropriate in this case. Of the sucrose dosage forms, pills are too large for use in small babies: although they can be dissolved in water, it is easier simply to use granules or crystals. Both dosage forms used by my pharmacy are 100% sucrose and therefore acceptable under Islamic dietary laws, but as granules are equally effective and less expensive compared with crystals, this was the dosage selected for this medicine.

After 2 days of administering Colocynth 30c 15 minutes before each feed six times a day, Mr A reported that the symptoms were definitely improved – mother and baby (and therefore father too!) were much happier.

physical size of the carrier does not have any impact on the homeopathic efficacy. Similarly, most UK manufacturers use granules composed solely of sucrose but there are some who use a sucrose/lactose blend, so careful consideration is required if this is an issue for the patient. Homeopathic medicines may also be administered as liquid potencies which are typically 20–30% ethanol, again depending on the manufacturer, although some LM potencies for direct oral administration may be dispensed in only 10% ethanol.

The provision of advice

In the UK pharmacists will often be the first contact for a healthcare professional inquiring as to the legal implications of prescribing specialist medicines. They are also expected by patients to advise on availability, efficacy and cost and to prescribe where appropriate. Demand for holistic and integrated models of care has risen sharply over recent years and likewise the interest in complementary medicines, particularly herbalism and homeopathy, and it is interesting to note that each recent attack on homeopathy launched by the vociferous and high-profile sceptics seems to serve to remind patients of the existence of this system of healthcare and actually *increase* this demand. Increasingly, pharmacists in the UK are finding that they cannot deny the existence of homeopathy as a rational system of medicine and, at the same time, respond to the needs and inquiries of their patients and professional colleagues.

Supply of homeopathic medicines

Important as the role of the pharmacist in the production of homeopathic medicines may be, the far more publicly *visible* role is in the supply of homeopathy. It is important to consider that 'supply' refers not only to the physical act of handing the medicines over, but also to the dissemination of advice and guidance to patients and colleagues. Pharmacists are the link between the other health professions and the patient (or, in the case of animals, the owner) and will often be the first healthcare contact. Regular opportunities to promote the benefits and possibilities of homeopathy as a system of medicine, while also advising on the availability, legal implications, limitations and administration methods, are all roles of the pharmacist.

Homeopathic medicines may be available from a UK pharmacy by sale, by pharmacist's prescription or on a prescription received from other healthcare professionals with the appropriate prescribing rights.

Dispensing

Once the correct medicine has been obtained and the prescription is ready to dispense, some thoughts should be given to labelling. As with all medicines, homeopathic preparations will have a batch number and an expiry date on the dispensed label. These details should be reproduced on the final pharmacy label that is generated from the pharmacy labelling system and appears on the medicine when it is given to the patient. This is important because if there are any quality issues with the medicine at a later date, the batch number can be used by the original manufacturer to refer to original documentation and analytical data. Placing the batch number in the patient medication record and on the label will ensure that this is readily accessible.

Counselling for the administration of homeopathic medicines is very important, particularly if the patient has not taken them before, as there are a number of points to remember. Many pharmacies that dispense homeopathy will have these instructions printed on patient information leaflets to be included with the medicines, such as shown in Figure 10.12, and may also have a brief description of homeopathy on the reverse. Similar leaflets or cards may also be available on request from the pharmacy's homeopathic suppliers.

Another supply scenario for homeopathic medicines in the pharmacy would be in dispensing prescriptions from other practitioners. It may be that the prescription is for a licensed product and that this is

---

A guide to the storage and administration of homeopathic medicines

1.   Store medicines only in the container in which they are supplied.

2.   Keep medicines out of direct sunlight and high temperatures and away from strong-smelling substances, e.g. camphor, perfumes, paint, disinfectants and household chemicals. Do not refrigerate or freeze.

3.   Medicines should not be taken within 30 minutes of anything with a strong flavour or smell, e.g. food, drink, tobacco, toothpaste, sweets.

4.   Medicines should not be handled. Tablets, pills and granules may be dispensed into the cap of the container and tipped into the mouth. Liquids and powders may be placed directly on the tongue from the bottle or sachet. Unless otherwise indicated, a dose is usually one or two tablets or pills, one powder, about 15–20 granules or one or two drops.

5.   If any medicines are spilled, they must not be placed back into the container and should be discarded immediately.

6.   Medicines are absorbed from the mouth. Therefore, tablets and pills should be sucked and not swallowed with water. Liquid medicines should be held in the mouth for 15–20 seconds before swallowing. If taking more than one remedy, allow approximately 5 minutes between each.

7.   Medicines are required to have an expiry date printed on the label or container. Unless advised otherwise by the prescriber, they should not normally be used beyond this date.

8.   You must not stop any orthodox medication that has been prescribed for you, unless specifically instructed to do so by the prescriber of that medication. Homeopathic medicines should not interact, but if you are in any doubt, seek the advice of our pharmacist.

Pharmacy contact details

Figure 10.12 Example of a patient information leaflet for homeopathic medicines. © Freeman's Homeopathic Pharmacy, Glasgow, Scotland: reproduced with kind permission.

already available in the pharmacy. In other cases, the pharmacist may be able to prepare the medicine, but this is relatively unusual in the UK due to physical limitations (thousands of medicines, lack of appropriate qualifications) or more practical limitations (lack of time, shortage of resources, no desire to take responsibility for quality control). Usually the items required will be ordered from a supplier holding a licence from the Medicines and Healthcare products Regulatory Agency (MHRA) for the manufacture of homeopathic medicines.

Other supply channels

Often a patient will purchase a homeopathic medicine from another source but then ask a pharmacist for advice after the fact. It is therefore important to consider briefly the availability of homeopathy outside the controlled pharmacy environment.

Practitioners may dispense medicines directly to the patient at the consultation or in semiprofessional environments such as a health food shop. In such cases it is good practice for them to copy the batch number and expiry date from the original bulk supply to the patient's label along with the full name of the medicine. However, this rarely happens in practice and so the pharmacist's role is limited to generic advice on the storage and administration of homeopathic medicines. The patient will have to be referred back to the practitioner for any more specific questions about the treatment.

Homeopathic medicines are also available on the internet. A variety of outlets will offer General Sales List (GSL) medicines, but some sites will also offer individually prepared 'specials'. These latter sites tend to fall into two distinct categories – straight supply and directed supply catering to different target groups. The MHRA-licensed homeopathic manufacturers have websites from which a pharmacist, practitioner or knowledgeable patient may request specific homeopathic 'specials' which can then be prepared and despatched by the pharmacy in response.

Regulatory affairs associated with the supply of homeopathic medicines

Medicines for human use

Homeopathy in the UK is subject to European Union (EU) regulations. Directive 92/73/EC of the European Parliament is the primary legislation governing homeopathic medicines as outlined in Chapter 9. The 11 articles of this directive set out the scope, manufacturing, quality control (of medicines and manufacturers) and licensing (registration) procedures. A detailed examination of the legislative position of homeopathic medicines in Europe is not within the scope of this chapter; however, a full consideration may be found in the textbook *Homeopathic Pharmacy* and in Chapter 9.[18]

Pharmacists are most likely to become involved with the procedures required to register a medicine on the basis of safety and quality alone – no evidence of efficacy is required. This is known as the Simplified Registration Scheme and a homeopathic medicine registered under this will have no brand name or give any indication of use. Similarly, 'fantasy' names that imply an indication are also disallowed and the medicine must simply be labelled with the approved name. Additionally the specific phrase 'Homeopathic medicinal product without approved therapeutic indications' is required, in stark contrast to countries such as the USA where indication of use *must* appear. A full marketing authorisation which will allow claims of efficacy is possible but it has been found to be very difficult for homeopathic manufacturers to produce the required rigorous clinical data required.[19]

Presently, in the UK, homeopathic medicines for human use are either registered under this scheme or have a Product Licence of Right (PLR) awarded to products already on the market when the first legislation was issued in 1971. These PLRs were allowed to retain their fantasy names and indications whereas newly registered products were denied both – although this situation has persisted for over 30 years, it is clearly confusing to practitioners, pharmacists and consumers.

In 2001, article 16 of the European Parliament Directive 2001/83/EC[20] recognised this situation and the difficulty of applying allopathic parameters of clinical data such as the randomised controlled clinical trial to homeopathic medicines. It permits EU member states to implement national rules for the clinical data required for a full marketing authorisation. In the UK, this was enabled by the Medicines for Human Use Rules 2006[21] and is administered by the MHRA. As these rules do not require controlled trials, indications are limited to minor, acute, self-limiting conditions. This significantly increases the accessibility of homeopathy to the general public and will benefit the prescribing of OTC homeopathic medicines. There is also provision for licensing some medicines (e.g. injections) that are not covered by the simplified European scheme.

As for allopathy, all registered homeopathic medicines available in the UK have a legal classification. Homeopathic medicines designated GSL may be sold to the public without controls and such medicines may be purchased from a number of non-medical outlets such as convenience stores, supermarkets and internet suppliers as well as pharmacies, health food shops and practitioners. Specialised formulations such as some eye drops, injections, and homeopathic medicines prepared from prescription-controlled allopathic drugs and poisons are designated Prescription-Only Medicines (POM). In between, some registered products are designated as Pharmacy-only (P) and can only be purchased by request in a pharmacy under the direct supervision of a pharmacist.

Uniquely in Europe the MHRA can issue a special manufacturing licence to small-scale manufacturers (often registered pharmacies) allowing them to prepare homeopathic medicines in response to a specific request from a healthcare professional, pharmacy, hospital or the public. Technically these are unlicensed under the articles of the EU directive and cannot be placed for retail sale – by convention these are sometimes considered to be P-category products as similar restrictions of supply apply, but, as they are unlicensed, this is not strictly true. Holders of such licences can prepare homeopathic 'specials' on a 'one-off' basis only – they cannot prepare large batches of medicines. However they are required to maintain detailed manufacturing and quality assurance records and are regularly inspected by the MHRA.

In the USA homeopathic medicines are subject to the Food, Drug, and Cosmetic Act of 1938 and regulations issued by Food and Drug Administration (see Chapter 11).

Medicines for veterinary use

European Parliament Directive 2001/82/EC raised the need for a system of registration for veterinary homeopathic medicines along similar lines to the simplified registration scheme for human medicines.[22] In the UK, this was enabled by the Veterinary Medicines Regulations 2005[23] and administered by the Veterinary Medicines Directorate (VMD) after considerable consultations with stakeholders. The first homeopathic veterinary medicine registration under the Veterinary Medicines Regulations was granted to a manufacturer for a range of Arnica potencies in 2006; five more registrations followed thereafter from the same manufacturer.[24] The medicine was classified Authorised Veterinary Medicine – General Sales List (AVM-GSL). In 2007 the VMD granted grandfather rights to a number of manufacturers who could show their human homeopathic medicines were on the market prior to 1996. This exemption did not include nosodes. Details of all registered homeopathic veterinary medicines and those eligible for grandfather rights may be found on the VMD website (www.vmd.gov.uk/ProductInfo/homeopathic.htm).

Veterinary surgeons in the UK may utilise a prescribing 'cascade' when treating animals. Once they have decided on the diagnosis and the treatment to be used they are obliged to use a veterinary medicine for use in the appropriate species first. Only if no such medicine exists can they use a licensed medicine for another species, then a human licensed medicine and finally a medicine prepared extemporaneously by themselves or a pharmacist. These arrangements apply equally to allopathic and homeopathic medicines.

The pharmacist's clinical role

The medicines licensed for retail sale may be openly displayed and made available for patient self-selection and purchase – in such cases the pharmacist's role will predominantly be in advising the patient and supervising the sale as for any medicine. Has the patient chosen to use homeopathy inappropriately? Do the symptoms suggest that an allopathic medicine or medical referral might be a better course of action? Is the patient taking other medication? Has the patient chosen the correct medicine for the symptoms? Does the patient know how to take the medicine correctly?

Depending on the answers received to the above, the transaction may be transformed from a straight sale to a pharmacist's prescription – whether by referral, counter-prescribing and subsequent sale of the correct medicine or possibly even on a National Health Service prescription under the Minor Ailments Service depending on the pharmacist's knowledge, qualifications and local formularies.

If homeopathy is a holistic therapy and the medicines are prescribed on an individual basis depending on a range of physical, mental, general and local symptoms, how can the busy pharmacist possibly hope to prescribe effectively? Although difficult, it is not by any means impossible – a more direct approach is required to assess the symptoms quickly, obtain the necessary information and select an appropriate treatment.

Initially, a pharmacist presented with a request to prescribe a homeopathic medicine for a presenting ailment may undertake a thought process such as that shown in Figure 10.13. If the decision is made to proceed with homeopathic treatment for an acute self-limiting condition appropriate to the pharmacy environment, then personal knowledge and experience, reference books or other prescribing aids such as the charts shown in Figures 10.14 (relatively simple conditions) and 10.15 (more complex conditions) might be used.[25]

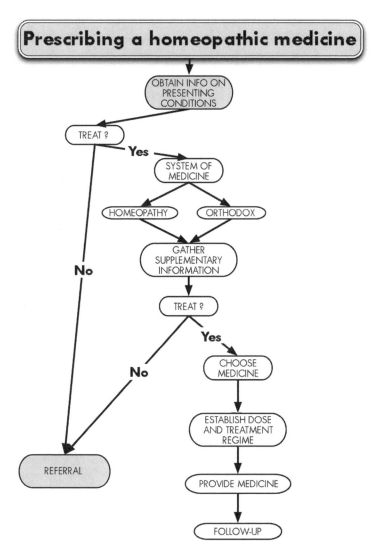

Figure 10.13 Decision process for homeopathic prescribing.

Some experienced pharmacists have likened this prescribing approach to a 'three-legged stool' (see Case 10.2). If in treating acute conditions there are three very strong indicators of symptoms, modalities or physical attributes (the 'legs of the stool') that lead to a specific homeopathic medicine, that is sufficient for the first prescription to be made (the platform or 'seat of the stool'). Indeed this approach is often

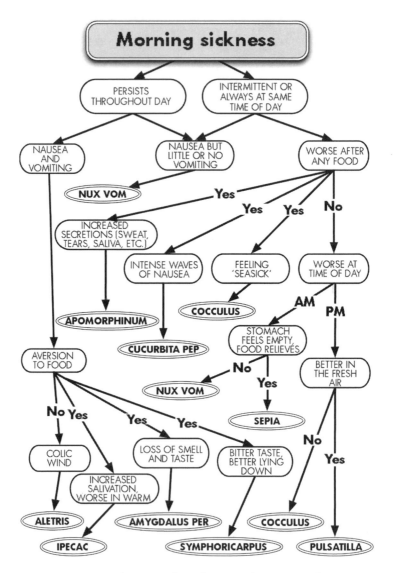

Figure 10.14 Homeopathic prescribing for a simple acute condition.

also used by other healthcare professions experiencing the same time constraints in their practice (see Chapter 3).

The alternative model employed by websites such as that of abchomeopathy[26] uses an online diagnosis tool to ask a series of questions intended to lead patients to the correct medicine to treat their condition. When the medicine has been selected the order is transmitted to a manufacturer and supplied direct to the patient. Many health

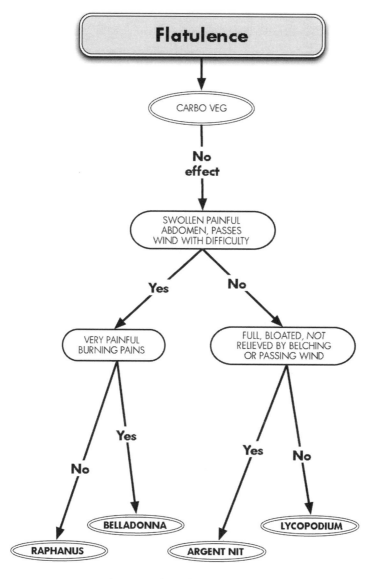

Figure 10.15   Homeopathic prescribing for a more complex acute condition.

professionals would reject this method of homeopathic 'prescribing' as valid and indeed some may argue that it actually puts the patient at risk because of the lack of professional contact. The likelihood of a misdiagnosis and the risk of masking a potentially serious disease by using homeopathy inappropriately are thought to be much higher with this system.

 **CASE STUDY**

Case 10.2 The 'three-legged stool' approach to prescribing

A middle-aged woman called into the pharmacy complaining of catarrh that had not responded to two different decongestants. She had received a course of oral antibiotics and a steroid nasal spray from her general practitioner and felt some improvement but the symptoms had worsened again since the course ended.

She mentioned that the catarrh came and went and was usually quite severe but could almost completely disappear at other times. Symptoms seemed to worsen at night, disturbing her sleep and necessitating opening a window as the fresh cool air seemed to help.

As she spoke, I considered her physical appearance – fair hair, fine features, round face, looked younger than she was, blushed and laughed nervously as she told me her symptoms. In an attempt to confirm the suspected constitutional type, I asked if taking a drink helped. She responded that cold drinks seemed to help as well as chocolate (I suspected that just made her feel better). She also revealed that the symptoms seemed to worsen after she ate Indian food, but this was not a regular occurrence as she did not really like spicy food.

I arranged the information that I had gained in our brief consultation into three categories:

1. Symptoms: catarrh – comes and goes, fluctuates in severity
2. Constitutionals: fair, blushes, laughs easily, likes sweets and cold drinks, not spicy foods
3. Modalities: worse at night, better fresh air

After some consideration, the medicine selected was Pulsatilla.

Some may argue that the 'three-legged stool' approach is too superficial to be called homeopathy. I would agree that this is not 'classical' homeopathy but, in the hands of an experienced practitioner, this technique is very well suited for the busy primary care setting. In the pharmacy, like the general practice surgery, in most cases we have only a few minutes to respond to a patient's enquiry and this makes it impossible to obtain a full history and devise a true holistic treatment.

However, the types of condition treated with homeopathy in the pharmacy are only those that are appropriate to the over-the-counter environment. Acute conditions that do not require a referral are the same ones we might treat with an over-the-counter branded product on the basis of a simple system of prescribing that very quickly 'drills down' to the major symptoms and suggests obvious first treatments. Where homeopathy is requested by the patient and deemed appropriate by the pharmacist, the three-legged stool approach is no different.

It could be argued that the three symptom indications alone would actually have been enough for the three-legged stool approach as they point clearly enough to Pulsatilla, even in the absence of any other information. This may be true, but it is important to gather as much information as possible to confirm the medicine choice. I find that considering the 'three legs' to be *symptoms*, *constitutionals* and *modalities* and not limiting how much information is placed in each category gives a much clearer picture.

Homeopathic training in the pharmacy profession

For postgraduate training, a number of options are available, as detailed in Table 10.4. The Faculty of Homeopathy accredits three levels of training, from a basic 5-day multidisciplinary basic course to specialist courses taught by experienced homeopathic pharmacists focusing on advanced homeopharmaceutic and clinical homeotherapeutic topics.

Table 10.4 Postgraduate training opportunities for pharmacists in the UK*

Qualification	Type	Course provider	Contact
LFHom(Pharm)	Basic multidisciplinary	Faculty of Homeopathy	www.trusthomeopathy.org 0870 444 3950
DFHom(Pharm)	Intermediate pharmacy	Faculty of Homeopathy	www.trusthomeopathy.org 0870 444 3950
MFHom(Pharm)	Advanced clinical	Faculty of Homeopathy	www.trusthomeopathy.org 0870 444 3950
DHPh	Intermediate pharmacy	British Institute of Homeopathy	www.britinsthom.com 01784 473800
RSHom	Advanced clinical	Society of Homeopaths	www.homeopathy-soh.org 0845 450 6611
None	Basic general	Manufacturers or employers	Various

*These courses may also be available for pharmacists resident outside the UK. Contact the course provider for further information.

Each level of training leads to a formal qualification and affiliation to the Faculty (see Chapter 8).

Pharmacists are also eligible to undertake courses offered by the British Institute of Homeopathy (Diploma in Homeopathic Pharmacy) and the Society of Homeopaths (see Chapter 13), the latter being an extensive course in clinical homeopathy not tailored specifically for pharmacists. In addition, homeopathic manufacturers and large employers may offer their own bespoke courses for pharmacists. These are often basic in nature but may feed into the more advanced courses discussed above.

Pharmacists also have an important role in educating fellow health professionals. Homeopathy is a very complex system of medicine but the pragmatic approach necessitated by application of the therapy's principles to the busy pharmacy environment can be very valuable alongside more indepth teaching of theory and practice.

Conclusion

UK pharmacists have expertise in many aspects of homeopathic medicine from source materials and production to preparation, dispensing and counselling. As a member of the multidisciplinary healthcare team, the pharmacist is responsible for quality control, dispensing, supply and the provision of advice to colleagues and patients.

Acknowledgement

The author wishes to thank Herbamed of Buhler, Switzerland for allowing him to take photographs at their premises.

References

1. *EC Homoeopathics Directive*. Strasbourg: European Parliament, 1992.
2. *The Medicines (Homoeopathic Medicinal Products for Human Use) Regulations 1994*. London: HMSO, 1994.
3. *European Pharmacopoeia*, 5th edition. Strasbourg: EDQM, 2005.
4. *Pharmacopée Française* (French Homeopathic Pharmacopoeia). Paris: L'Adrapharm, 1989.
5. *German Homoeopathic Pharmacopoeia*. Stuttgart: Medpharm Scientific Publishers, 2005.
6. *Homeopathic Pharmacopoeia of the United States*. Accessed online at www.hpus.com, 2006.
7. *British Homeopathic Pharmacopoeia*. Rutland: British Association of Homoeopathic Manufacturers, 1999.

8. Bharatan V, Humphries C J, Barnett J R. *Plant Names in Homeopathy*. Bury St Edmonds: Natural History Museum, 2002.

9. Vermeulen F. *Concordant Materia Medica*. Haarlem: Emryss bv, 2000.

10. van Zandwoort R. *The Complete Repertory*. Accessed within ReferenceWorks Pro Software. San Rafael: Kent Homeopathic Associates, 2004.

11. Adler U, Adler M. Hahnemann's experiments with 50 millesimal potencies: a further review of his casebooks. *Homeopathy* 2006; 95: 171–181.

12. Rowlett R. *A Dictionary of Units of Measurement*. www.unc.edu/~rowlett/units/dictD.html (accessed 10.11.06).

13. Hahnemann S. *Organon of the Art of Healing*, 6th edn. Philadelphia: Boericke & Tafel, 1917.

14. Hahnemann S. *Organon of the Art of Healing*, 4th edn. New York: Wm Radde, 1869.

15. Hahnemann S. *Organon of the Art of Healing*, 5th edn. Philadelphia: Boericke & Tafel, 1876.

16. *Pharmacopée Française* (French Homeopathic Pharmacopoeia), 8th edn. Paris: L'Adrapharm, 1965

17. Leary B. Cholera 1854: update. *Br Hom J* 1994; 90: 5.

18. Kayne S. *Homeopathic Pharmacy*, 2nd edn. Edinburgh: Elsevier Churchill Livingstone, 2006.

19. Keller K. Homeopathic medicinal products in Germany and Europe: legal requirements for registration and marketing authorization. *Drug Inf J* 1998; 32: 803–811.

20. *Community Code Relating to Medicinal Products for Human Use*. 2001/83/EC. Strasbourg: European Commission, 2001.

21. *Medicines for Human Use (National Rules for Homeopathic Products) Regulations*. SI 2006 No 1952. London: HMSO, 2006.

22. *Community Code Relating to Veterinary Medicinal Products*. 2001/82/EC. Strasbourg: European Commission, 2004.

23. *The Veterinary Medicine Regulations 2005*. UK Statutory Instrument 2005 no. 2745. HMSO: London, 2005.

24. Registered Homeopathic Veterinary Products. www.vmd.gov.uk/productinfo/registered.htm (accessed 01.12.06).

25. Kayne S, Kayne L. *Homeopathic Prescribing Pocket Companion*. London: Pharmaceutical Press, 2007.

26. Online Remedy Finder. www.abchomeopathy.com (accessed 10.11.06).

11

Integrating homeopathy into the US consumer market

John P Borneman

Introduction

Over the previous 15 years, homeopathic over-the-counter medicines have slowly become integrated into the consumer market in the USA. This chapter examines the structural drivers for this transition, including access to care, regulation and distribution as well as the consumer and sociodemographic factors that have been responsible for the market shift.

Drivers of the US consumer drug market

There are numerous drivers to the consumer drug market in the USA. Among them are:

- structural drivers: those that influence access to healthcare (access to providers and reimbursement issues), drug regulation and distribution channels
- consumer drivers: factors that motivate consumer behaviour.

Structural drivers

Access to healthcare

Access to providers
Unlike most of the rest of the developed world, the USA does not have an integrated system for the delivery of healthcare.[1] One of the results of the fragmented system is more than 47 million people without health insurance[2] and an increased reliance on self-medication.

There are a number of systems for reimbursement of healthcare in the USA. Consumers can be a member of a managed care organisation

(MCO) which is paid for by their employer and offers a restricted list of providers, including a 'gatekeeper' primary care provider (PCP). At the other extreme, a consumer may be a member of a preferred provider organisation (PPO), which offers generally unrestricted access that is reimbursed by the PPO. The costs are borne by employer premiums and the individual co-pays. In the middle are a number of hybrid health maintenance organisations (HMOs) offering a variety of different access-to-cost ratios. Since these programmes are generally associated with employer-provided benefits, lack of employment means alternatives are necessary. For consumers over 65, a federal tax support programme, Medicare, is available. For the poor, there is a limited-access programme provided in a state/federal partnership Medicaid, but Medicaid is generally limited to children, their parents and the disabled. For consumers who do not fall into these groups – employed and dependants of employed, over 65, poor with children, poor children or disabled – the only option is to self-pay for care. The net result is a system that leaves about 15% of the population uncovered with many, including those who are insured, looking for self-medication solutions.

Reimbursement

What is covered by medical insurance is as important as who has insurance and who pays for the insurance. Generally, if a consumer has medical insurance, provider visits are paid for whole or in part. However, payments for medications are subject to highly complicated reimbursement schemes, including negotiations between the insurance providers and pharmacy benefits managers (PBMs), who decide what medications will be covered and at what rate. Standard practice is that over-the-counter (OTC) medications, regardless of whether they are prescribed by a physician, are ineligible for reimbursement.

The combination of a fragmented system with some restrictions in access to care and a complex drug reimbursement system form a primary driver for self-medication.

Regulation

A second driver for drug delivery in the USA is the manner in which drugs are regulated. Although the topic is complex, the basic elements are specific drug regulations at both the state and federal level, as well as intellectual property statutes (patents and trademarks). The regulation of homeopathic drugs is very similar to their allopathic counterparts, with the exception of the premarket approval process.[3]

The Homeopathic Pharmacopoeia Convention of the United States (HPCUS), responsible for the publication of the *Homoeopathic Pharmacopoeia of the United States* (*HPUS*), assures that homeopathic medications are safe, accessible and legal in the USA.

Homeopathic medications have been classified as 'drugs' since their inclusion in the federal Food Drug and Cosmetic Act[4] in 1938 by the bill's primary author, New York Senator Royal Copeland, MD. Copeland, who studied homeopathy at Michigan and was later dean at the New York Homeopathic Medical College and Health Commissioner for the City of New York, was not clear on the rationale for their inclusion. Some speculate that it was to provide increased regulation,[5] whereas others suggest it was a way to 'protect' homeopathy.[6] Whatever the reason for their inclusion, Copeland's work established the definition of an official homeopathic drug as one that was monographed in *HPUS*, and firmly placed the regulation of the manufacturing, marketing and sales of homeopathic medications within the purview of the Food and Drug Agency (FDA).[3]

Although homeopathic medications were within the FDA's regulatory scope, the agency did not promulgate regulations for nearly 50 years. For the period of 1938 to 1988, the FDA essentially regulated homeopathic pharmaceuticals through 'institutional understandings' between the FDA and the industry. Since such 'understandings' were not formal, they were subject to sudden and unpleasant change. For example, the Kefauver amendments in 1962 would have made all homeopathic drugs subject to re-review (and potentially make them all prescription), but the Agency opted to exclude homeopathic drugs on the basis of their long history of safety.[5] Subsequently, in 1978, Congress included a provision in the 1979 Drug Reform Act that would have removed recognition of the *HPUS* in the Food, Drug and Cosmetic Act as part of a larger reform package, but the bill was not enacted. Elimination of the *HPUS* could have allowed the agency to reconsider subjecting homeopathic drugs to the efficacy provision of the law.[5] The 1978 developments prompted the HPCUS, under the leadership of Wyrth P Baker, MD, to produce the *Compendium of Homeotherapeutics* (*Compendium*),[7] which comprised a listing of all of the known homeopathic drugs at the time with their references in the literature.

At that time, the *HPUS* was produced by the publication committee of the American Institute of Homeopathy (AIH). In 1980, the AIH spun off the *HPUS* to the newly incorporated HPCUS, with W P Baker as the founding President. The HPCUS undertook a complete development of a monograph review process for inclusion of new monographs as well as a complete review of the contents of the *Compendium*. The review took nearly 20 years and formed the basis of the modern *HPUS*.

In 1983, a dialogue developed between the Compliance Office at the FDA and members of the American Association of Homeopathic Pharmacists (AAHP) to develop a more formal FDA regulatory policy for homeopathic drug products (HDPs). An *ad hoc* committee from the stakeholders in the homeopathic community, including physicians and consumers, met with the FDA regularly for nearly 5 years, resulting in the FDA *Compliance Policy Guide 400.400, Conditions Under Which Homeopathic Medicines may be Marketed*, in 1988.[8] The *Compliance Policy Guide* (CPG) was implemented in 1990 after a period of public comment.[3]

The *CPG* plays an important role in the regulation of homeopathic medications. For example, it specifically requires indications for use on labelling, and draws a distinction between prescription and non-prescription (OTC) homeopathic drugs. In general, a drug is considered OTC if:

- it is claimed for a self-limiting condition
- it is claimed for a condition that does not require diagnosis or monitoring by a licensed healthcare provider
- it is non-toxic in the delivered dosage form.

These criteria as presented have been simplified for this discussion, thus there are numerous exceptions to these general rules. However, they were applied by HPCUS in the establishment of the guidelines for prescription-only and OTC potencies that appear in the *HPUS*. As an example, Arnica montana 2X given orally is considered prescription-only due to toxicity, whereas potencies 3X and higher are considered OTC. Homeopathic medicines that are highly toxic or are labelled for prescription indications are considered to be prescription drugs.

This regulatory history is a primary reason why homeopathic medicines are freely available in the USA.

Distribution channels

American consumers are able to find homeopathic products in drug stores, grocery stores, natural foods stores and directly from catalogue and the internet. These channels will be explored later in this chapter.

Consumer drivers

Sociodemographics

Cross-sectional surveys of the general population in the USA tend to indicate that complementary and alternative medicine (CAM) use has become common, both in self-care and in seeking the assistance of a provider.[9-13] The first national survey of CAM use by the American public conducted by Eisenberg and colleagues estimated that, in 1991, 34% of adults in the USA had used at least one CAM modality during the previous 12 months; of those who had used at least one modality, one-third had seen a CAM provider.[9] A follow-on survey by the same team using similar methods in 1997 found that the proportion seeking out a practitioner had changed from 36.3% to 46.3%.[10] Of the 18 CAM modalities listed in 1991, one-quarter of respondents used exercise and prayer, while 1–3% used herbal products, diet or homeopathy.[9] Use of these modalities increased across the board by 1997, with approximately one-half having statistically significant increases.[10] By 2002, usage had increased further. The National Health Information Survey (2002) reported that 74.6% of those surveyed had used a CAM modality at least once, and that 62.1% had used at least one CAM modality in the previous year.[12] Users of CAM, including homeopathy, tend to be female, upper-income and educated.

Additionally, age plays a factor, with current data tending to indicate that the primary consumer is middle-aged[14] – a driver for increasing use as the large numbers of post Second World War babies age.

Psychosocial and health behaviour characteristics

Recent analyses of data from large MCOs have tended to indicate that psychosocial and health behaviour characteristics may play a role in the selection of CAM modalities, including homeopathy. People who were more likely to choose CAM tended to be former smokers who, although they may have rated their health highly, were dissatisfied with their health and with the health advice that they were currently receiving.[15] More interestingly, one of the strongest psychosocial predictor variable associations for CAM use was found for the 'emotional belief' variable. It was found that respondents who scored high in 'emotional belief', those who strongly felt that stress and emotional troubles (such as depression and anxiety) affect health, were much more likely to use CAM generally and homeopathy particularly.[15]

Types of homeopathic drug products and their use by consumers

There are over 1200 officially recognised single-entity homeopathic drugs ('single remedies') in the *HPUS*.[16] Subject to specific guidelines, homeopathic pharmacies and manufacturers are able to produce proprietary combinations of these single entities for specific indications for use.[16] Thus, while a knowledgeable consumer or physician may choose Belladonna for fever, or Chamomilla for irritability in a teething infant, a consumer with no knowledge of homeopathy may purchase a product labelled 'teething tablets' which contains a combination of these single medicines. Consequently, the delivery of OTC homeopathic medications is subject not only to channel, but to the level of knowledge a consumer has of homeopathic principles.

The consumer behaviour model

The way OTC HDPs are used, and consequently the types of demand for HDPs, falls along a continuum. At one extreme is constitutional prescribing. The constitutional approach features complex analyses of a large number of symptoms at the physical, psychological and socio-emotional levels with the objective of the prescription of a single, well-selected homeopathic medicine that is expressly matched to the patient. This type of prescribing requires significant education in both medicine and homeopathy and is most likely limited to licensed healthcare providers.

A modification of this approach is termed keynoting. Keynote prescribing reduces the number of drugs under consideration to those with well-known symptom profiles. These HDPs are called polychrests (see Chapters 1 and 10). While there are 1200 drugs available in the USA, the number of polychrest single remedies stocked at the average full-line retailer is typically 30–40. These are the well-known medicines for use by consumers with a working knowledge of homeopathy.

The simplest approach to homeopathic medicines is the use of proprietary combinations. This system requires little more than careful observation of symptoms and then selection of a product from a reputable manufacturer. Combination medicines represent the largest segment of homeopathic consumer healthcare in both size of market and growth rate (industry sources, 2006).

The direct association of consumer knowledge of homeopathic principles to type of product demanded has developed into a consumer behaviour model (CBM) that is used by marketers to structure their product line and merchandising strategies. In addition, the CBM influences the channels that manufacturers choose to deliver their products.

The great majority of homeopathic marketers in the USA specialise only in specialty products and combinations because these types of medications enjoy the largest demand. Other manufacturers offer a limited line of single-entity medicines to complement their combination offerings. Only a few full-line homeopathic pharmacies exist in the USA which carry a broad array of single remedies that are compounded to order. Thus along the continuum of the CBM, most manufacturers and marketers cluster at the proprietary product pole. Manufacturers continually work to optimise their range of products to balance access (according to their operating philosophy) and profit.

Selling environments

The selling environments for HDPs fall along a continuum that is similar to the CBM, since each environment is driven by the optimum mix of range of products carried and the amount of information about homeopathy that is provided in retailing experience. Generally, there are two options for obtaining homeopathic medications: 'bricks and mortar' operations and internet re-sellers. Consumers seeking a broad array of single-entity homeopathic medicines (single remedies) can access boutique internet sites that specialise in both a broad range of homeopathic medicines as well as large amounts of information. Some sites are associated with major manufacturers; others are independent and carry more than one brand. Some have prescribing software to assist the proper selection of the medication, and often carry background information and white papers. Consumers can also contact manufacturers directly for a wide selection. In addition, many full-service pharmacies carry a broad array of single remedies and some (Hahnemann in Berkeley, CA; TxOptions in King of Prussia, PA) can compound to a physician prescription. In many pharmacies, a pharmacist trained in homeopathy can counsel the patient, although the number of these pharmacies is small.

More common are independent pharmacies and natural food stores with a fairly large multibrand array of homeopathic medications (as many as 500 products), but that cannot compound to a doctor's order. These retail establishments may have staff who are trained in homeopathy, but counselling by a non-pharmacist is generally against regulations. These outlets rely on large amounts of written material that may help the consumer choose the appropriate single remedy. In addition, many of these retailers carry many proprietary combinations that have full indications for use on the label. While these 'full-service' natural food stores and pharmacies are convenient to the consumer, there are fewer than 7000 of these retailers in the USA. Some large natural foods retailers (Whole Foods and Wild Oats) provide this value-added consumer service.

By far, the greatest amount of homeopathic medicine sold in the USA is though large chain pharmacies (Walgreen, CVS, RiteAid, Eckerd), chain grocery (Safeway, Kroger, Albertson's) and mass merchandisers (WalMart, Kmart). These retailers carry only proprietary homeopathic products merchandised with homeopathic and allopathic products integrated into clinically designated sections (cough–cold, first aid, baby, women's health). It is rare for any staff in these retailers to be familiar with homeopathic principles, and rarely are any books or literature available for reference. The internet counterpart of these 'bricks and mortar' retailers are large 'category killers', for example Amazon.com, Drugstore.com, MotherNature.com, and CVS.com.

Where the consumer ultimately purchases homeopathic medication is a function of the standard value proposition model. Consumers motivated by personal attention, counselling or a wide product array requirement will choose the compounding pharmacy, independent pharmacy or boutique website (e.g. 1800homeopathy.com). These consumers view prices as a secondary attribute, if at all. On the other hand, consumers with specific narrow product requirements or those who are motivated by price will seek out the chain retailers or 'category killers'. More importantly, consumers purchase many homeopathic products with no knowledge of homeopathy whatsoever. These consumers are motivated solely by the product's label claim. One survey of satisfied users of a popular homeopathic product showed that fewer than 7% of respondents could identify the accurate definition of homeopathy.[17]

Marketing strategy

How do producers of homeopathic medicines reach their target customer? The CBM offers a guide. On the one extreme is a well-educated, information-intensive consumer (or physician), whose value proposition is built around product array, speed of service and knowledge availability of the retailer. These customers are 'high-touch' and principally reached through network approaches. These include word of mouth and information-rich advertising at specific touch points: journals, newsletters and conferences. This market is quite small on a relative basis and is approached by only a few manufacturers and retailers who consider themselves 'full-line' or 'full-service' sources.

The great bulk of marketing strategy is aimed at a completely different target. These consumers are motivated by a value proposition that is centred on clinical utility, ease of use and price. By this measure, these consumers are typical of those identified by most other consumer package goods companies.

We have seen previously in this chapter that the sociodemographic variables associated with CAM use generally, and indeed with the use of homeopathic medicine, are female gender, college education, upper income and Caucasian race.[15] Middle age has also been found to be a predictor.[14, 15] In addition, research has found that high self-report of health coupled with low satisfaction with health and health advice may also be associated with CAM use.[15] A related factor in predicting CAM use is the belief by the consumer that stress and health practices affect health outcomes,[15] an attribute explained by Honda and Jacobson as being associated with 'openness'.[18] Complicating this consumer profile is the large array of clinical conditions for which homeopathic medicines are offered. So, while research has confirmed the attributes of the CAM user generally, finer details of the profile will be associated with label indication. What can be said generally is that whether she is the consumer, the influencer or the purchaser, more likely than not, an educated upper-income female is involved in the purchase process.

Having established the profile of the typical consumer, the marketer is faced with the choice of the message and the medium for its conveyance. Homeopathic products are not marketed in a vacuum, as compared with other consumer packaged good products. This means that marketers are moving beyond simple features and benefits to establish a value proposition centring on health solutions and the establishment of community. This approach results in media choices that go beyond traditional print (magazines and newspapers) and broadcast (television and radio) to interactive 'experiences' which inform a potential customer in a fun and content-rich environment. For example, www.idreamofsleep.com urges visitors to share their dreams for free dream interpretation while being educated about a homeopathic sleep aid. At the end of a contest period, a visitor will be awarded a new suite of bedroom furniture. Visitors to www.bashtherash.com learn about prevention and treatment of poison ivy/oak while sharing their 'poison ivy rash experiences' to win a prize. These experiential approaches connect with the consumer at a much deeper level and attempt to build communities of loyal customers who become long-term repeat consumers. Other non-traditional approaches include weblogs (blogs) that introduce homeopathy content into web forums on specific topics (arthritis, fibrositis, lupus, childcare) and the establishment of viral networks of passionate product ambassadors (überinfluencers) who promote products in their community purely out of a passionate belief and not for compensation.

These techniques are constantly being revised and amended. But the underlying demographics and psychographics of the likely homeopathic customer match exquisitely with the characteristics of the susceptible consumer of non-traditional marketing.

Challenges

Along with the successes of the introduction of homeopathic medicines into the mainstream marketing culture in the USA have come a number of challenges.

Regulation

Although the regulatory environment for homeopathic medicines is largely stable at present, there is no guarantee that the current regulatory schema is permanent. Since homeopathic medications are regulated within the context of drugs, regulatory changes meant for allopathic drugs may have an impact on homeopathic medicines. As emphasis shifts from accelerated drug approval in the 1990s to drug safety after the Vioxx and ephedra scandals, the FDA may engage in a general tightening of drug regulation. This is a possible exogenous threat to consumer availability of homeopathic medications.

Consumer misperception

There has been long-term consumer confusion about homeopathy in the USA, particularly related to misidentification with herbal products. A comparison of allopathic, homeopathic and dietary supplement (herbal) regulations appears in Table 11.1.

Table 11.1 Regulatory issues

Medicine type	Enabling legislation	Pre-market approval	Good manufacturing practices (GMPs)	Labelling guidelines	Indication for use
Allopathic Treating disease by with agents that produce opposite effects to disease being treated	FDCA	New drug application (NDA) or monograph	21 CFR	21 CFR	Required
Homeopathic Treating disease by with minute dosages of agents that produce same effects to disease being treated	FDCA	HPCUS Monograph process	21 CFR	21 CFR	Required
Dietary supplements	DSHEA	None	Pending	DSHEA	Drug claims impermissible, 'Structure-function' claims only

21 CFR, Title 21 of the Code of Federal Regulations; DSHEA, Dietary Supplement Health and Education Act; FTC, US Federal Trade Commissions; HPCUS, Homeopathic Pharmacopoeia Convention of the United States.

Since herbal products are more loosely regulated than homeopathic medications, this misperception has the effect of creating a consumer perception that HDPs are 'unregulated'. This misperception extends to some healthcare providers and pharmacists as well. The result is a lessening of the value proposition for homeopathic medications by some consumers and professionals and the resultant impetus for government to increase regulation.

Industry behaviour

The combination of unenforced regulation and a *laissez-faire* selling environment on the internet has encouraged some unscrupulous marketers to flout or largely ignore government regulations. The result is an increase in the number of products making inappropriate or impossible claims that cannot possibly benefit the user; and that are, in some cases, potentially dangerous. These behaviours represent a long-term challenge to industry and consumer alike and act to the detriment of all. Recently, regulatory action has been taken by state regulators against some of these products – a generally new phenomenon since drugs are principally regulated by federal law.

Development of clinical data

Since homeopathic medicines are by and large 'generic' drugs, with only a small handful having patent protection, the generation of clinical data published in the literature comes into the public domain for use by all. Thus there is little economic incentive for either novel homeopathic research or research conducted to inform the literature. This paucity of data fuels critics who charge that homeopathic medicines do not, or simply cannot, work. New approaches to intellectual property protection of novel homeopathic drugs may act to resolve this matter, but a lack of a robust homeopathic literature remains.

The way forward

To the extent that it can be predicted, the future for customer access to homeopathic medications should remain robust. Consider that penetration of homeopathy into American medicine is approximately 3%[12] and that the market has an organic growth rate in excess of 15%.[17] A sustainable increase in penetration could be possible for many years ahead. It is likely that the great preponderance of these gains will be made among consumers with little knowledge of, or interest in, homeopathy *per se*, but rather who are solely motivated by the clinical utility of the homeopathic medication. If such consumers are active in supporting these products in their respective communities, the likelihood of sustained growth is arguably very high indeed.

References

1. Or Z. Determinants of health outcomes in industrialised countries: a pooled, cross-country, time-series analysis. Organization for Economic Cooperation and Development. Accessed online at: http://www.oecd.org/LongAbstract/ 0,3425,en_2649_34587_2732304_119666_1_1_1,00.html.
2. *The Uninsured: A Primer*. Washington, DC: Kaiser Family Foundation, 2006.
3. Borneman J, Field R. The regulation of homeopathic drug products. *Am J Health Sys Pharm* 2006; 63: 86–91.
4. Food, Drug and Cosmetic Act of 1938, 52 Stat. 1041, as amended, and codified in 21 USC §321(g)(1). 1938.
5. Junod S. An alternative perspective: homeopathic drugs, Royal Copeland, and federal drug regulation. *Food Drug Law J* 2000; 55: 161–184.
6. Robins N. *Copeland's Cure*. New York: Knopf; 2005.
7. Baker W P (ed.) *Compendium of Homeotherapeutics*. Falls Church, Virginia: American Institute of Homeopathy, 1974.
8. United States Food and Drug Administration Office of Regulatory Affairs. Sec. 400.400 Conditions Under Which Homeopathic Drugs May be Marketed (CPG 7132.15). Issued 5/31/88, revised 3.95. Accessed online at: http://www.fda.gov/ora/compliance_ref/cpg/cpgdrg/cpg400-400.html.
9. Eisenberg D M, Kessler R C, Foster C, *et al.* Unconventional medicine in the United States. *N Engl J Med* 1993; 328: 246–252.
10. Eisenberg D M, Davis R B, Ettner S L, *et al.* Trends in alternative medicine use in the United States, 1990–1997: results of a follow-up national survey. *JAMA* 1998; 280: 1569–1575.
11. Green L A, Fryer G E, Yawn B P. The ecology of medical care revisited. *N Engl J Med* 2001; 344: 2021–2025.
12. Barnes P M, Powell-Griner E, McFann K, *et al.* Complementary and alternative medicine use among adults: United States, 2002. *Adv Data* 2004; 343: 1–19.
13. Astin J A. Why patients use alternative medicine: results of a national study. *JAMA* 1998; 279: 1548–1553.
14. Grzywacz J G, Lang W, Suerkin C, *et al.* Age, race, and ethnicity in the use of complementary and alternative medicine for health self-management. *J Aging Health* 2005; 17: 547–572.
15. Borneman J, Cohen A, Gordon N. Prevalence and predictors of complementary and alternative medicine (CAM) by populations with specific needs: patients with breast cancer, other cancers, prostate conditions and asthma in a large northern California managed care organization (MCO). Poster, American Public Health Association Annual Meeting, November 6, 2006, Boston, Massachusetts.

16. Baker C, Borneman J, Abecassis J, *et al.*, eds. *The Homoeopathic Pharmacopoeia of the United States*. 2002. Accessed online at: www.hpcus.com.
17. Hyland. Consumer survey. 2005. Unpublished data.
18. Honda K, Jacobson J. Use of complementary and alternative medicine among United States adults: the influences of personality, coping strategies, and social support. *Prevent Med* 2005; 40: 46–53.

12

The application of homeopathy in nursing and midwifery

Elaine Hamilton and Kathleen Tomlinson

Introduction

In this chapter the use of homeopathy in nursing and midwifery practice is discussed.

Experience would suggest that many patients are looking for an alternative to the biomedical model and desire a professional who is both empathetic and caring. The nursing profession may be considered as being 'a combination of art and science' and provides the ideal situation for supporting the essential components of holism.[1] This is shown clearly by the draft *Code of Conduct* published by the UK Nursing and Midwifery Council in 2006[2] that states that nurses, midwives and specialist community public health nurses must:

- treat people as individuals
- promote the interests of those in their care to meet their physical, psychological, emotional, spiritual, social and developmental needs
- listen to the people in their care and respond to their concerns and preferences
- support them in caring for themselves to improve and maintain their health
- recognise and respect the contributions that people make to their own care and well-being.

There is thus a fundamental resonance between nursing and midwifery practice and the principles and approaches of homeopathy.

Benefits of integrating homeopathy to nursing and midwifery services

- Patient choice and control are increased: for example, where there is concern about side-effects or interactions of conventional medicine/treatment or the clinical situation makes conventional treatment unfavourable or contraindicated, e.g. during pregnancy or breastfeeding.

- Homeopathy integrates well with conventional medicine.
- The provision of additional skills in case-taking promotes improved patient–practitioner relationship, leading to better understanding of patients' conditions and disclosure of relevant symptoms which may indicate more serious underlying condition or a need for further investigation, support or treatment.
- Homeopathy respects and supports the patient's own responsibility, ability and effort to cope, adjust and achieve good health, therefore promoting empowerment and greater satisfaction for patients.
- It is considered safe, non-toxic and non-addictive. A review of the safety of homeopathy, conducted by doctors associated with the Royal London Homoeopathic Hospital, looked at papers published between 1970 and 1995 for reports of adverse effects of homeopathy. Adverse effects reported in clinical trials were temporary aggravations of symptoms or other mild and transient effects.[3]
- Patients' improved mental and emotional states lead to a reduction in the risk of depression and anxiety disorders and therefore the need for long-term medication, e.g. antidepressants.
- The use of homeopathy may lead to a reduction in the need for conventional medication, e.g. analgesia, antiemetics.
- Patients may experience a reduction in discomfort, distress and disappointment.
- There is a reduction in costs. Homeopathic medicines are relatively inexpensive and evidence suggests that homeopathy has the potential to generate savings through reduced conventional prescribing and demand for other services.[4, 5]
- Research has shown that whole-person approaches to healing have been proved to increase job satisfaction in medical professionals.[6]

Nursing

Case-taking

The main objective of homeopathy is to restore balance and facilitate the body's own healing response. In homeopathic case-taking the following criteria are necessary[7]:

- time to assess the person as an individual
- listening to the patient's narrative
- being compassionate and trustworthy
- treating the patient with respect and as an equal
- involving the patient in shared decision-making.

These skills are fundamental to good nursing and combine well with this therapeutic medicine, providing an additional tool that is advantageous in many areas of practice.

During the initial part of the homeopathic history-taking patients recall their story, revealing why they are seeking homeopathic care. In many cases the aetiology is established in the first few minutes, for example, 'I have never been well since my pregnancy with my second daughter'. This important information shows that perhaps this patient condition is related to an event during that period or a remedy that is associated with pregnancy. The practitioner then analyses the case using a hierarchy of symptoms to find the most suitable prescription. Language used, dress code, build, behaviour, mental, emotional and physical symptoms are observations essential to the case analysis. Past medical history, family history and present medical history can alert the practitioner to patterns of disease. Information pertaining to social history and family relationships can disclose traumatic events that are often revealed for the first time.

Communication and the development of a working partnership at the first consultation are paramount to the outcome. This is difficult to measure in clinic terms but must be included in the placebo response.[8]

Applications of homeopathy in nursing

Specialist homeopathic nursing practitioners in the UK can treat a wide range of conditions, examples of which are given below.

Cancer care

The number of patients diagnosed with cancer is increasing[9] and there is a trend for such patients to choose complementary and alternative medicine (CAM) for reasons which are complex. Physicians' attitudes to CAM are changing and patients are more readily able to discuss available therapies which can be integrated into their healthcare plan.[10] In nurse education complementary therapies are included in courses in cancer and palliative care but having an oncology specialist nurse with an additional qualification in homeopathy would benefit the patient from the onset of the treatment plan. This is an area of nursing where teamwork is paramount to the benefit of patient and carers. Patients' mental and emotional state could be supported more readily if a holistic approach was adopted from the onset. Psychological stimuli are known to affect endocrine and immune functions and through these influences the course of cancer can be mediated.[11] Information can often be revealed in homeopathic case-taking that may have contributed to the patient's disease state.

Patients are often in shock and denial initially and have to cope with taxing regimes of chemotherapy and radiotherapy. How they respond to the side-effects of treatment regimes depends on the individual or agent used. Specific remedy constitutions, for example, Pulsatilla or Phosphorus, can be more sensitive than others. Patients' immune response can alter during their life and during the history-taking process it is important to note allergies and reactions to conventional medicines. Homeopathic remedies such as Radium bromatum and X-ray can be administered during radiotherapy to minimise side-effects and also postradiotherapy to help with side-effects.[12] Chemotherapy medicines can be administered as a tautode, preferably in conjunction with the conventional drug to minimise iatrogenic effects, but this requires an integrative team approach. Frequently the patient presents following chemotherapy with symptoms. Further research is required in this area of oncology and the use of tautodes (see Chapter 10).

Carcinosin is commonly prescribed as an adjunct remedy in a patient with a history of cancer and is usually prescribed in high potency, although potencies vary according to the individual. A constitutional remedy can be useful in higher potency in conjunction with carcinosin.[13] Homeopathy can also be useful in the terminal stages of cancer and is often administered in LM potency[14] (see Chapter 10). Arsenicum alb can ease the anxiety, distress and restlessness which many patients experience when they are close to death.

In a study in Canada[10] two-thirds of the women in Ontario diagnosed with breast cancer were currently using CAM and the most common reasons for choosing CAM were to: boost their immune system; increase quality of life; prevent recurrence of cancer; provide a feeling of control over life; aid conventional treatment; treat breast cancer; treat side-effects of conventional treatments; attempt to stabilise their current condition; and to compensate for failed medical treatments. In breast cancer lymphoedema as a result of a mastectomy with axillary clearance can be problematic and specific remedies may be helpful for local symptomatic relief. Homeopathy can also be helpful in women who are experiencing the side-effects of oestrogen withdrawal, adjuvant hormone therapy and chemotherapy.[15] Health professionals working in this field have an important role to play in providing information to allow patients to make informed choices about various CAM options.

Hormone-related conditions

Hormone-related conditions are very common and can present at any time in a patient's reproductive life. From a holistic point of view the neuroendocrine system is very sensitive and finely attuned to other body systems.[2] The science of psychoneuroimmunology associates psychological processes and the immune system, confirmed as patients frequently present with symptoms related to hormonal imbalance. The prescribing strategy employed depends on the hierarchy of symptoms found on case analysis, i.e. resolving underlying stress often auto-regulates the system, correcting the hormonal imbalance. Today there is an increasing number of referrals in young female patients with polycystic ovarian syndrome. These patients often present with the following symptoms of hormonal imbalance: hirsutism; obesity; period irregularities and mental/emotional symptoms. Remedies commonly prescribed for hormonal imbalance are: Pulsatilla, Sepia, Carcinosin, Lachesis, Thuja, Lillium tigra and Natrum mur. Constitutional types associated with these remedies often report intolerance to conventional hormone-based treatments, as demonstrated in Case study 12.1.

 CASE STUDY

Case 12.1   Hormone-related condition

Background
Margaret is a 53-year-old woman referred by her general practitioner with menopausal flushes and has found that, since commencing hormone replacement therapy (HRT), she has put on 19 kg (3 stones) in weight, which is now affecting her joints, although HRT alleviates her symptoms. Margaret requests homeopathic referral as a friend has successfully received homeopathic treatment for menopausal flushes. She plans to continue using the HRT patches until she attends the clinic, as she could not cope with the symptoms without them.

Past history
Recurrent bronchitis in early childhood. Tooth abscess at 15 years and suffered a severe anaphylactic reaction following an injection of penicillin.

(continued overleaf)

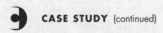 **CASE STUDY** (continued)

Dilatation and curettage (D&C) @ 22 years.
Cone biopsy @ 35 years for cervical intraepithelial neoplasia (CIN) III.
Total hysterectomy and conservation of ovaries @ 35 years.
Benign breast lumps left-sided @ 38 years.
Depression diagnosed @ 44 years: reasonably stable at the moment.

Current medication
Paroxetine 20 mg daily: a serotonin reuptake inhibitor used to treat depression.
Oestradiol (Evorel) 50 μg patches (smaller doses did not control flushes).
Allergic to penicillin, erythromycin, oxytetracycline.

Appearance
This woman appeared very tall, broad-shouldered, slim-hipped, casually dressed with long thin fair hair and a pinkish complexion. Pigmented brown spots were observed on hands and over cheekbones. Margaret's manner was very open, direct and extremely chatty. There was a feeling of high energy projecting from this person and during the interview information flowed very freely but in a disorganised manner.

Present complaint
Never well since 15 years old: periods irregular every 18–21 days with severe dysmenorrhoea and metrorrhagia; tired, worn out and felt well for only 7 days during mid-cycle. Problem intensified and subsequently had a D&C when 22 years old which did not alleviate the problem. Was then prescribed the oral contraceptive pill, which she took until her mid-30s, which helped symptoms but caused massive fluid retention. Cone biopsy for CIN III aged 35 years. At this period also suffered: weight loss; irregular periods; severe mood swings with symptom-free phase lasting only 7 days which was usually mid-cycle. Gynaecologist suggested hysterectomy with conservation of ovaries, which she underwent at 35 years. Much better following hysterectomy but at 44 years commenced menopausal symptoms of lethargy, sleeplessness, hot flushes with severe mood swings. Attended psychologist then due to 'hyped personality' who blamed Premarin HRT patches: symptoms consequently improved on stopping HRT. Commenced taking paroxetine, which helped symptoms, and now only takes paroxetine 20 mg 1–2 times weekly as she is trying to stop altogether. Also takes Evorel 50 μg, which suppresses menopausal symptoms of periods of dripping with sweat which soaks back, face and neck and is worse day and nighttime, and hot flushing of face. Feels better outside in cool air. Feels sickly with sweating: worse in morning.

→

CASE STUDY (continued)

Lethargy; joint and muscle pains in knees, shoulders and back: worse in damp weather; better for movement but worse on prolonged exertion. Mental symptoms of confusion, suicidal feelings, tiredness and insomnia are usually worse in morning. Describes her suicidal thoughts as being momentary, unpredictable and associated with feelings of despair concerning her present state but can also feel 'hyper' during the day.

Family history
Father was an alcoholic and extremely volatile with mood swings in Margaret's early childhood.

Social history
Lives alone. Adores animals and has two cats and two horses. Previous occupation was in the fashion business and she loved the glamorous lifestyle. Enjoyed travelling.

Generals
Warm-blooded and cannot tolerate anything tight around neck; likes spicy food; aversion to raw oysters and snails but can tolerate them cooked; sweet tooth. Symptom aggravation in cold damp weather; worse in winter; enjoys the sun. Sleeps on left side but very restless.

Mentals/emotionals
Margaret describes herself as being psychic, artistic, enjoying classical music with a vivid imagination. Can display a violent temper when aroused. Unhappy childhood as father was a volatile man but kind to other people; she also had a very structured upbringing.

Prescribing indications
On taking this case the author had difficulty in obtaining an exact picture of Margaret's presenting menopausal symptoms. This was partly due to the HRT therapy which suppressed the complete symptoms plus the long history of other suppressive treatment since 15 years of age which included a hysterectomy, danazol (Danol) and the oral contraceptive pill. The other problem was the extreme loquacity of the patient plus the constant jumping around from one subject to another. Margaret was also presently taking Prozac, which suppressed the true picture of the mental symptoms. The centre of gravity presenting in this case was in the mental/emotional plane with accompanying general symptoms. The symptoms expressed were lacking in sensation, aetiology, location and modality. The rubrics chosen for repertorisation were based on those that covered the description given by the patient (Box 12.1).

(continued overleaf)

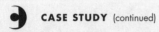 **CASE STUDY** (continued)

Box 12.1 Rubrics chosen for repertorisation[16]

Mind
Loquacity: changing from one subject to another: **Lach**., Tub.
Mania: alternating with depression: **Lach**., Tub.
Suicidal: disposition thoughts: *Lach.*
Menopause: aggravates: **Lach**., Sep
Stomach
Nausea: menopause during: Lach.
Nausea: perspiration during: *Sep.*
Female
Suppressed menses: **Lach**., *Sep.*, Tub.
External throat
Clothing aggravates: **Lach**., **Sep**., Tub.
Face
Heat: flushes: menopause during: **Lach**.
Perspiration: profuse day and night without relief: **Hep**., *Merc., Samb.*
General
Perspiration: after aggravates: **Sep**.
Convalescence: ailments during: menopause after: Graph., Lach., Puls., Sepia

Bold type indicates rubrics of greater significance, *italics* those of less significance.

On achieving an outcome based on the totality approach, the materia medica was consulted to ascertain if the outcome matched this information. On repertorisation, using the above rubrics, the three remedies that were well represented in order of importance were Lachesis, Sepia and Tub. bov. However the author prescribed Lachesis as a result of repertorising the case plus the presenting features that were confirmed in the materia medica: strength of emotions, extraordinary loquacity, projection of high energy, alternating moods, past disappointed love, inclination to mockery, satire and breaking out in laughter, unable to laugh with those who laugh, aversion to clothing around neck, menopausal symptoms described plus the history of ovarian suppression.[17] Suppression of sexual behaviour can also aggravate the condition, which encourages loquacity. The appearance of a pink mottlish colour to the circulation is indicative of Lachesis and also sepia but in sepia the face usually has a worn sagging appearance and can also have a brown saddle across the nose. Other similarities are: Lachesis and Sepia both feature in

→

●)   CASE STUDY (continued)

suppressed menses, with Sepia also in 'never been well since' the pill: both are left-sided remedies and possess menopausal symptoms with flushes upwards: both have also an intuitive perception.[18] Major differences in Lachesis and Sepia are: Lachesis is a high-energy projection whereas Sepia has mental/emotional and physical stasis with accompanying symptoms: Lachesis is warm-blooded and Sepia is usually very chilly: Lachesis has a high sex drive and Sepia is worse for sex with aversion: Lachesis has venous congestion and is better for discharge whereas in Sepia there is great sagging of the organs and tissues.

The sycotic miasm is associated with hormonal suppression and treatment and Lachesis and Sepia are both included within this miasm. Margaret's history of cervical cancer could also be linked with the proliferative symptoms of the sycotic miasm. In view of this woman's mental and physical symptoms and past sensitivity to conventional medication and current treatment, an LM1 potency was prescribed. LM1 is approximately equivalent to 5c potency.[19] LM potencies have the following advantages: they can potentially avoid homeopathic aggravations; they are able to be regulated more easily; they are useful in cases with a history of drug suppressions; and they are also effective in combination with conventional prescriptions.[14] Although Margaret was desperate to reduce or stop her HRT this action was avoided after discussion, due to the present mental symptoms of depression with suicidal thoughts and the need to discuss this matter with her general practitioner.

A patient information leaflet was given after discussion on how to take the homeopathic LM1 potency and if there were any problems the patient was informed to contact her own general practitioner. A follow-up appointment was given for 6 weeks' time. A letter was also sent to the patient's general practitioner regarding the outcome of the consultation.

Follow-up consultation 6 weeks later
Margaret was greeted in the waiting room and immediately a change in appearance was noted. She looked more confident and had taken time with her overall appearance. She described experiencing a nauseated feeling 2–3 days after taking the remedy, with an 'ice-cold' sensation all over her body lasting a couple of days. On consulting Allen's materia medica, the author noted this was a sensation identically described by a prover.[20] Margaret also spontaneously volunteered her own subjective evaluation of feeling not so tired, 'better in the head' and had consequently stopped taking her paroxetine. The suicidal thoughts related to despair regarding her lot have now disappeared. She had also booked a hair appointment for a complete new change of image. The symptoms of waking up with nighttime sweats soaking the back of her head and hot flushes are now only once or twice a week. Mentally she

(continued overleaf)

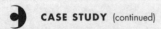 **CASE STUDY** (continued)

feels calmer, more in control and her energy levels have increased as she has been out gardening. It was noted that Margaret frequently commented either sarcastically or mockingly towards her mother in a rather silly manner.

Rubric
Mind: mocking: sarcasm: satire: desire for: *Lach.*[16] At the evaluation of the first prescription the degree to which the vitality of the organism has been stimulated is assessed.[21] The outcome of this assessment is related to patients' energy, mental, emotional state and their main complaint. In this case the author was satisfied with the outcome following the first prescription but was aware of the possibility of the case changing or relapsing in the future and therefore a different remedy might be necessary.

Plan
As Margaret had only taken the remedy for 6 weeks and was continuing to improve and after consultation with the patient's homeopathic practitioner, it was decided to continue with Lachesis LM1 3 drops daily until next visit. A return appointment was given for 5 weeks' time.

Return visit
This appointment was 12 weeks after commencing initial treatment. Margaret was initially viewed at the reception desk looking transformed and acknowledged me energetically. Her appearance was totally transformed and dynamic. Her hair had been cut short in a trendy style and coloured. She was wearing tight jeans, low-necked t-shirt, high-heeled sandals and modern designer glasses. I could quite easily visualise how Margaret had been involved in the fashion industry. On close questioning regarding her previous symptoms Margaret remarked that she had run out of the remedy 5 days ago and noticed an increase in symptoms. She feels more nauseated and less energetic. Oestradiol (Evorel) 50 µg stops the wringing sweats on face and neck but she wishes to try reducing this to Evorel 25 µg: she was advised to see her general practitioner about this. She also reports that since commencing Lachesis the hot flushes all over have increased but this seems to be tolerable. She reports to having lost 6 kg (1 stone) in weight and is finding she is craving less sweet foods now. On questioning regarding new symptoms appearing, Margaret comments on a salty taste in her mouth, which she has had for a few weeks now. This could be indicative of a proving symptom but all other issues in the consultation point to continuing with the remedy meantime. After consultation with Margaret's homeopathic practitioner Lachesis LM2 was prescribed and instructions were given to take 3–5 drops daily until continuing improvement is noted. An appointment was given for 12 weeks' time.

Gynaecological problems of dysmenorrhoea and menorrhagia readily respond to homeopathy and this is where it is advantageous for female patients to be able to access a general practitioner or specialist nurse qualified in homeopathy for treatment initially. It has been observed that women who have taken hormone replacement therapy for a considerable period of time usually take longer to achieve results with homeopathy than women who have not taken any conventional treatment. Menstrual irregularities and hormone-related symptoms also frequently present with other medical conditions and often resolve when the patient is treated from a totality point of view. Ideally menopause should not be troublesome if a patient is functioning in a balanced mode. Following a hysterectomy and bilateral salpingo-oophorectomy women can suffer acute physiological and psychological changes, resulting in a surgical menopause.[22] There is a high incidence of referral rates for homeopathy in these cases.

It has been noted that there is a high rate of disclosure of childhood sexual abuse at the homeopathic clinic.[23] This may be due to the holistic overview of the consultation. A leading question contributing to this outcome is connected to childhood and relationships in conjunction with past and present medical history and existing mental/emotional state. In association with a previous history of sexual abuse are certain diseases and pathology: endometriosis; cystitis; hormone irregularities; infertility; irritable-bowel syndrome; depression; obsessive-compulsive behaviour and self-harm. Incidence is greater in females attending than males and referrals for homeopathy are usually unrelated to the sexual abuse. Remedies frequently prescribed at the outset are Staphysagria; Lac caninum, Opium, Cannabis indica. The patient may not disclose on first consultation and sensitivity and caution are required by the practitioner in the management of this case. Occasionally it may prove too painful for the patient and additional support such as counselling, psychiatric referral and cognitive behavioural therapy may be required in an integrative team approach. Many patients have blocked out the event as a coping mechanism and remedies such as Cannibis indica, Lac caninum, Opium and Nux moschata are good for this sycotic type of behaviour.

Respiratory disease

One of the most difficult conditions to treat is often respiratory. Patients may have been treated with steroid nasal inhalers and antihistamines for many years and in many cases there are few symptoms. Prescribing approaches include nosodes to treat allergies and miasmatic nosodes, with Tuberculinum frequently being prescribed in a history of atopy.

Treating asthma is very rewarding as patients often end up having fewer frequent respiratory infections, an improvement in asthma control and therefore eventually manage to reduce inhaler use. This can have such a positive effect on sleep, cognitive function, well-being, energy levels and absence from school or employment.

It is advantageous to treat children with asthma from an early age in an integrative approach, as characterised in Case study 12.2.

 CASE STUDY

Case 12.2   Asthma

Background
Cameron is an 8-year-old boy referred for homeopathic consultation with severe asthma. After an acute attack he usually requires high doses of Flixotide 250 μg for a substantial period of time. Cameron's daily dose of fluticazone (Flixotide) 250 μg b.d. continues with Salmetarol (Serevent) 25 μg 1 puff b.d. and montelukast 5 mg nocte and the general practitioner is keen to see if homeopathy can reduce his conventional treatment needs. A housedust mite allergy is queried, as Cameron is asymptomatic when on holiday in Majorca.

Appearance
Cameron appeared robust, slightly overweight, with brown hair and eyes with a slightly large head, forehead, a small upturned nose and dry cracked lips. On first meeting Cameron confidently shook hands and smiled directly at me. This hand shake indicated warm-bloodedness. Cameron proceeded to sit in the main consulting chair whilst his mother looked on, adding to the conversation during the consultation when necessary.

Present history
Asthma commenced shortly after birth, is worse in winter and is triggered by respiratory infections. By 4 months of age, Cameron had received 2–3 doses of antibiotics for chest infections, was hospitalised with bronchitis at 13 months old and had also suffered frequent colds with green-coloured nasal discharge. At 3 years old he was commenced on salbutamol (Ventolin) and fluticazone (Flixotide) inhalers for asthma. His asthma disappeared on holiday in a seaside resort in Majorca, possibly as a result of stone floors and no

→

 **CASE STUDY** (continued)

carpets, indicative of a possible housedust mite allergy. Symptoms of seasonal rhinitis from May to September, which are: pains above eyes, clear nasal discharge; worse morning. Present cough symptoms are worse in the morning and at night, whilst lying down; better sitting propped up: cough is loose, with sticky   clear phlegm, which can be difficult to expectorate. Expiratory peak flow was 270 l/min this morning (best ever: 300 l/min). On examination chest clear: no rhonchi. Height: 133 cm (expected peak flow for age and height = 250–290 l/min). Peak flow drops rapidly in exacerbations and inhalers are increased according to general practitioner's instructions.

Drug history
Past history of frequent short courses of oral steroids but no hospital admissions.

Fluticazone (Flixotide) 250 µg 2 puffs morning, 1 puff nocte. (corticosteroid: fluticasone propionate).

Montelukast (Singulast or Montair) 5 mg 1 tab nocte (leukotriene receptor antagonist).

Salbutamol 100 µg 1–2 puffs 4–5 times daily (selective β_2 agonist).

Clarityn 2 × 5 ml nocte (antihistamine: loratidine).

Family history
Father has asthma and psoriasis. Family history of cancer and heart disease (paternal grandfather).

Generals
Sleeps on left side: sweats profusely on head: warm-blooded; throws covers off in bed at night. Food desires are: thirsty for cold milk and cold water: likes savoury foods, especially cheese and butter. Possible housedust mite allergy; has no pets and no other known allergies.

Social history
Lives with his mum and dad and a younger sister aged 2 years. Performs well in all subjects at school; enjoys the computer, history, Lego, football, playing armies, basketball and riding his bike. Is well coordinated mentally and physically and is very sociable with lots of friends.

Mental/emotional symptoms
Cameron describes himself as being both funny and confident: likes snakes and insects and has a fear of jellyfish. He is a very sensitive child who likes affection and is inquisitive and comfortable in adult company, asking lots of questions regarding various subjects.

(continued overleaf)

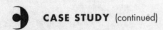

CASE STUDY (continued)

Prescribing indications

- warm-blooded
- likes savoury foods
- asthma worse in winter; worse from respiratory infection; worse becoming overheated: better in open air; better sitting up
- sweats excessively
- seasonal rhinitis
- large appetite
- great thirst for ice-cold drinks
- history of suppression with drug treatment.[24]

A constitutional prescription was issued based on Cameron's symptoms plus temperament, character, appearance and build. As Cameron's asthma was relatively stable this was a good time to commence treatment, which would hopefully stimulate a healing response in order to boost his general well-being. Sulphur 30c was prescribed on the following constitutional indications: robust, extroverted, mature outlook, sociable with an inquisitive mind; history of drug suppression; warm-blooded, likes savoury food; asthma worse in winter; worse for respiratory infection; worse being overheated; worse lying down; better in open air; thirst for ice-cold drinks.

Pulsatilla can be indicated in allergic asthma and acute infections but expectoration tends to be a yellow, green discharge from chest or nose: worse at night with heat and lying: better for sitting propped up in bed. Child is usually shy, clingy to mother, constantly craving attention and affection. Medorrhinum is one of the most frequent remedies for childhood asthma, which is better at the seaside and in open air: mucus discharges are usually thick green and present from birth. The following remedies are also indicated in asthma presenting in childhood: Tuberculinum, often with a family history of respiratory illness and an allergy to cats and milk; Calcarea carbonica in plump children with a history of many infections who are strong-willed but yet often anxious regarding security with many fears and anxieties, reflected in disturbed sleep and nightmares. In Calcarea carbonica metabolism can also be slow or defective with a weakness from exertion, poor stamina, inability to keep up with peers and craves eggs and sweets.

Management of the case
Instructions regarding Cameron's prescription were given to his mother along with an information leaflet on how to take the remedy. A warning was also indicated regarding the possibility of an aggravation of Cameron's asthma

$\rightarrow$

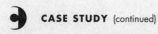 **CASE STUDY** (continued)

symptoms after taking the remedy and the need to follow the asthma treatment plan issued by the general practitioner. Cameron's mum will monitor the peak flow plus asthma symptoms and is confident of adhering to an asthma action plan. In the case of a rapid deterioration in Cameron's chest condition, the general practitioner has issued a supply of oral steroids to take according to instructions. In order to monitor outcomes, a diary with symptoms and twice-daily peak flow measurements will be maintained. Anti-housedust mite measures and the possibility of prescribing a housedust mite nosode in the future were also discussed. A follow-up appointment was given for 7 weeks' time. Instructions to contact the general practitioner or the Homeopathic Clinic were given should any problems arise.

Follow-up appointment 7 weeks' time
Cameron has had no respiratory infection since his previous visit but as this was the summer months it was his stable period. The plan was to treat constitutionally during the summer and then possibly prescribe housedust mite nosode next visit if still stable. Tuberculinum bovinum and Medorrhinum are remedies that could be prescribed at a later date, possibly in the winter months, in conjunction with his constitutional remedy Sulphur. Cameron continued on his maintenance asthma therapy.

Skin conditions

Although a skin condition presents on the surface of the body it can be very difficult to treat homeopathically as a result of years of previous treatments such as topical steroids. In homeopathic terms this means that suppression of symptoms enhances the possibility of an aggravation of symptoms, which can be distressing for the patient. Managing the case cautiously at the beginning with potency selection and re-petition frequency is essential in order to minimise potential reactions. It is advantageous if the patient presents with a relatively short history of symptoms. Parents of babies with eczema who are concerned about the side-effects of topical steroids request early referral for homeopathy. Medorrhinum and Tuberculinum are nosodes frequently prescribed in addition to local and constitituional prescribing (see Case study 12.3).

CASE STUDY

Case 12.3 Eczema

Background
Calvin is a 3-year-old boy referred for homeopathic opinion as a result of eczema. He has suffered eczema since an infant and present treatment consists of emollients with 0.5% hydrocortisone cream for acute exacerbations. Mum has withdrawn dairy products and is giving Calvin goat's milk and also prefers to use natural emollients and aloe vera on his skin. Calvin has been seen by a paediatrician as a result of his poor weight gain and has been diagnosed with lactose intolerance. He has now been discharged from the paediatric clinic following investigation of his small stature.

Appearance
Very fair-skinned with blond hair and blue eyes. Small in stature with a large head for his fine delicate frame.

Present history
Calvin has had eczema since birth. The eczema is dry, pinkish and scaly with patches mainly on back, trunk, forehead and upper arms. It is not present on skin folds. It appears to be worse since November although there is no apparent reason for this. It does not appear to be too itchy but Calvin scratches in bed at night.

Drug history
Diprobase: an emollient-based cream containing liquid paraffin 6%, white soft paraffin 15%, cetomacrogol 2.25% and cetostearyl alcohol 7.2%
  Epiderm: yellow soft paraffin 30%, emulsifying wax 30% ointment.
  Eumovate: moderately potent steroid cream containing clobetasone butyrate 0.05%; cream and ointment.
  Infaderm: bath emollient containing almond oil 30%, liquid paraffin 69.6% liquid. Also using aloe vera gel, bee propolis soap and sun cream.

Family history
Father was a heroin addict at the time of Calvin's conception. Mother's brother has eczema.

Social history
Parents separated when Calvin was 2 years old: only child.

Past medical history
Mum had a healthy pregnancy; Calvin was born by caesarean section as a

→

result of failure to progress in labour: breastfed for 3 days: received all the normal vaccinations with no problems; cow's milk was introduced at 8 months old: frequent colds since birth with a green nasal discharge with occasional ear infections; prone to flatulence; constipation when a baby.

Generals
Warm-blooded: thirsty for cold drinks and cups of tea: sleeps well; does not perspire. Has a sweet tooth; likes chocolate and crisps and is a very fussy eater.

Mentals/emotionals
Very independent child and Mum reports he has an 'answer for everything'; vocabulary good; confident and curious within his environment; prone to temper tantrums when he can strike his mother but likes affection.

Prescribing indications
The prescribing strategy employed in this case was a constitutional approach with attention also being applied to a possible underlying miasmatic influence. The simillimum was chosen on the following indications presenting during the consultation: eczema since birth; stunted growth with a large head and emaciated body. The materia medica was consulted in order to confirm the author's theory.[24]

Medorrhinum 30c was prescribed on the following indications: family history of drug abuse revealing a possible sycotic miasmatic influence; eczema and colds with a green nasal discharge from birth; severe itching of skin, worse at night. It was noted that despite severe itching the skin did not resemble the fiery red of a Sulphur case. Other indications were: history of nappy rash; temper tantrums and tendency to strike mother with the opposite diathesis of being nice at times; appearance of child undernourished with a slightly larger head for body.

Shore[21] states that when you observe an ailment from birth then you can think of a nosode, e.g. Medorrhinum. Its symptomatology is in skin eruptions with rhinitis, discharges from the eyes, ears and nose with a failure to thrive. The undernourished child is weak, white-skinned with a possible history of sycosis in the parents. Also nappy rash present from birth, which is bright red with a clear demarcation similar to a ringworm eruption, is also indicative. Such children usually sleep in the knee–chest position and when they become older express themselves more in the evening when their energy comes up and are therefore late in going to bed and rising in the morning.

Calvin's mum was given an information leaflet with instructions on how to take the remedy plus discussion on monitoring for the possibility of a

(continued overleaf)

CASE STUDY (continued)

temporary aggravation in skin condition due to the healing response of the homeopathic remedy. A follow-up appointment for 8 weeks was also given.

Second consultation: 6 weeks later
Calvin's mum reports that the skin condition improved dramatically in all areas after taking the remedy but 4 weeks later skin condition deteriorated again in upper back, shoulders, upper arms and head. Symptoms worse at night and Calvin scratches until all the areas bleed. On examination: upper arms and shoulders pink and dry with scratch marks. Overall skin looks less dry, especially hands. Calvin was previously bothered with constipation and his stools are much softer now. Slight change in behaviour noted; Calvin is less aggressive to his mum. Appetite still fussy and mum is trying to introduce other foods into diet. Calvin's mum was advised to administer Medorrhinum 30c × 1 dose.

Third consultation: 6 weeks later
Skin had continued to improve on upper arms and shoulders. Behaviour continues to improve with only one slight aggressive episode. Appetite improving and Calvin has gained 3 kg. Advised to monitor symptoms and administer Medorrhinum if symptoms relapse. Review 12 weeks.

Wound infections

The research evidence for homeopathy in this area of nursing is sadly lacking. Wound management is an area of nursing where homeopathy could prove to be very useful. Prescribing approaches include obtaining a swab of the exudate which is then sent to the homeopathic pharmacy to produce an autonosode; the offending organism can also be identified in a bacteriology swab and then administered in homeopathic potency, i.e. *Staphylococcus aureus* nosode. Other prescribing strategies include local, totality and constitutional remedies. Prescription is dependent on the stage of the infection and many remedies follow in a sequence, i.e. Belladonna in early stages of inflammation before pus is localised, Hepar sulph when the discharge is collecting with generalised sensitivity and then Silicea to promote discharge and exudate. Hyper/calendula mother tincture diluted 1/20 is very helpful for cleansing the wound to promote healthy granulomatous tissue. In the present-day situation with antibiotic resistance, wound management presents difficulties as patients seek alternative to antibiotics.[25]

Chronic fatigue syndrome

This condition can be very interesting to treat as patients present with similar symptoms but wide ranging aetiology which can include the following: never well since; sexual abuse, grief, gastroenteritis; hepatitis, vaccinations; glandular fever and tick bites. Patients are often aware of the limitations of conventional medicine and therefore request homeopathic referral. On taking the case it can often feel as if one is embarking on a mystery tour as the patient's narrative can take various twists and turns. Choice of potency is dependent on the vitality of the patient and therefore LM potencies operate well in this condition. Discussion on lifestyle changes are an important complement to the management of the case. Patients with chronic fatigue can often be very driven people who find it very frustrating to come to terms with their condition. Past and current patterns of behaviour and illness are therefore important issues to address in the patient's healing journey. It is important to communicate to the patient at the beginning that the healing time varies individually and that with any chronic condition there may be peaks and troughs. Concentrating on assessing well-being, energy, mental and emotional and physical symptoms helps the patient focus more subjectively. This is also a condition where patients often ingest many over-the-counter medicines, nutritional supplements, herbal medicines and other complementary therapies. Homeopathy has proven to be clinically significant in a randomised, controlled, triple-blind trial in patients with chronic fatigue syndrome.[26]

Musculoskeletal conditions

Patients referred with musculoskeletal problems frequently state that they are concerned about the long-term effects of conventional medication for their condition, which is usually chronic. Fibromyalgia, osteoarthritis, polyarthritis, rheumatoid arthritis and systemic lupus erythematosus are commonly referred chronic conditions for homeopathy, usually as a complement to their conventional medicine. Auditing outcomes of homeopathic treatment involves assessing well-being, energy levels, activities of daily living, mental and emotional symptoms, physical symptoms and the use of conventional medication. In these conditions any marginal improvement is positive for both practitioner and patient. In case-taking, location of symptoms with specific modalities and deformities is very important as there are many remedies suited to these conditions. Again LM potencies are prescribed as a result of the chronicity and the incidence of polypharmacy involved.

Gastrointestinal

Irritable-bowel syndrome is a very common diagnosis and often presents in multiple disease pathology. By approaching the consultation holistically it is often observed that the mental and emotional state is an underlying trigger to the condition. As stated above, irritable bowel syndrome can present in patients with a history of sexual abuse. It is also more prevalent in the following constitutional types: Lycopodium, Nux vomica, Pulsatilla, Argen nit, Phosphorus, Arsenicum alb, where fear and anxiety are commonly experienced.

Lifestyle approaches involving dietary advice, relaxation, cognitive behavioural therapy and exercise are very useful tools. Other conditions frequently referred for homeopathy are chronic constipation, ulcerative colitis and Crohn's disease.

Neurological

This can cover a wide range of conditions ranging from headaches and posttraumatic head injury disorder to a palliative approach in multiple sclerosis. In multiple sclerosis homeopathy can provide support in symptoms relating to spasms, sensory and motor disturbances, ataxia and incoordination, visual disturbances and mental and emotional symptoms. The objective of palliative care is to improve quality of life for patients and carers and remedies such as Causticum can be very useful in a patient suffering from multiple sclerosis with right-sided paresis and paralysis of the bladder with involuntary urination.

Aetiology which relates to head injury can often be resolved with remedies such as Arnica helleborus and Natrum sulph. The earlier the patient receives homeopathy following head injury the more positive the outcome.

Headaches in female patients can often be hormone-related and require good case-taking skills for the extraction of detailed information in order to reach the simillimum as there are many headache-related remedies. A complete symptom includes sensation, location, aetiology, modalities and any concomitants such as hormone changes following a hysterectomy. In chronic headaches improvement usually means that the patient reports a gradual reduction in frequency and intensity of symptoms. Natrum mur is one of the most frequently prescribed remedies in headaches and other hormone-related remedies – Lachesis, Pulsatilla and Sepia – are also predominant.[27]

Midwifery

Midwives assist, monitor and provide care for women and their babies throughout a continually changing physical, emotional, psychological and social process. They offer advice on natural lifestyle adaptations to maintain or establish health for both mother and baby preconceptionally, throughout pregnancy, labour and delivery and thereafter in the postnatal period. Midwives encourage women to tune into their own natural instincts and listen to what their body is trying to tell them. This is of particular value in labour when the body is responding and adapting continuously. Woman will naturally get into positions, go into water, drink variable amounts at different stages of labour and be overcome by the desire to push.

In 1992–1993, the *Winterton Report*[28] and *Changing Childbirth*[29] advocated 'choice, control and continuity' for women in the UK, encouraging the development of new organisations of care in order to allow midwives to care for the whole woman and her family, encouraging midwives to evaluate their care and to supplement the limited systems of treatment with more 'natural' forms of healing and help. Professionals have been encouraged to recognise the profound effect of care around pregnancy, birth and the early weeks of life on human health, physically, emotionally, psychologically and socially.

Figure 12.1 is a wonderful example of the holistic and extended effect of childbirth. This completely natural picture was taken long before this book was conceived! It shows the integration of conventional medical model of care (through Rebecca and baby Alex being inpatients) with a hospital medicine glass on her locker, with the integration of homeopathy, noted by a box of homeopathic remedies that is lying next to it. The presence of Eilidh, an elder sibling, demonstrates that the birth of a new child affects the whole family.

Applications of homeopathy in midwifery

Acute conditions

Homeopathy can be useful in relieving many disorders of pregnancy, labour and the puerperium and in the neonate and can also be used to treat more complex complications, either alone or in conjunction with conventional treatments.

Pregnancy and childbirth are self-limiting acute states and for this period of time the woman can find herself acting, feeling and reacting in

Figure 12.1 Rebecca with Eilidh and newly born Alex.

a completely different way. As a midwife taking a homeopathic consultation it is important to understand the nature of the symptom:

- Is it related only to this pregnancy?
- Is it a long-term symptom being aggravated by pregnancy?
- Is it an underlying disorder that was possibly previously undiagnosed being brought to light or accelerated by pregnancy?

Deciding whether to treat with homeopathy
If a woman has a pre-existing medical condition this is not usually the appropriate time to introduce any new treatments unless in consultation with the healthcare provider treating her condition. If conventional treatment is in place and satisfactorily controlling these conditions then this would not be the optimum time to treat these conditions homeopathically unless conventional treatment was contraindicated or

ineffective and the patient was under close supervision from the relevant care provider.

There are many minor disorders in pregnancy or whilst breast-feeding for which there are no satisfactory conventional medical treatment or for which the conventional medical treatment is contra-indicated. Some symptoms and conditions are minor and do not require any treatment with conventional or homeopathic medicine. They can be alleviated with appropriate dietary and lifestyle changes. However some symptoms can become distressing and show that the individual is struggling to cope and sending signals for adaptation or a need for help.

When the use of homeopathy is being considered there is also the possibility of an aggravation of symptoms, the temporary re-emergence of old symptoms lying dormant (Hering's law) or the possibility of an accidental proving (see Chapter 1). This all leads us to the place where we should be cautious about advising the use of any self-prescribed homeopathic medicine in pregnancy and childbirth and the neonate and encourage women who wish to use homeopathy to do so with the guidance of a suitably qualified homeopath.

It could be an emotional, physical, psychological or indeed a social problem. There are a number of questions to be considered:

- Is it appropriate to suggest the use of homeopathy?
- Are we going to affect both mother and baby or their relationship?
- Is there an 'obstacle to cure' which could be removed or adjusted without the use of any medicine? Perhaps there needs to be some lifestyle change to be in place for the healing process to be successful.
- Are we dealing with a temporary acute situation or a more chronic long-term struggle?

Deciding how to treat
Questions to be considered:

- How do we treat the totality of the individual?
- How do we recognise the pattern of that individual's symptoms?
- How do we understand the level at which the patient has the capacity for healing at this time?
- How do we recognise and select a simillimum that matches that pattern and energy of the individual's state?

In contrast with the comprehensive approach illustrated in Case studies 12.1–12.3 above, when dealing with acute states in midwifery practice the need for, and appropriateness of, a full homeopathic consultation must be assessed. If possible, during the active stage of labour a woman should not be disturbed by questioning.

The midwife is skilled in the ability to build a rapport with the patient quickly. In many cases a midwife will have spent time with the woman through her pregnancy, in labour or in the postnatal period. Usually the midwife will have access to her medical notes and possibly, if appropriate and with the woman's permission, be able to ask her partner some questions. Also with a good knowledge of materia medica (see Chapter 5) and the commonly needed remedies for certain states, there could be very little need for direct questioning. Box 12.2 gives examples of the drug pictures of two medicines used for labour.

Box 12.2 Examples of the drug pictures of two medicines used for labour

Caulophyllum
This is reputed as a powerful labour enhancer and regulator. Useful to coordinate and strengthen contractions in women who are weak and exhausted. Her contractions are painful but have little effect on the cervix.

The woman is sensitive to cold. Feeling chilly, shivery and with internal trembling *but* desires fresh air. She tends to be soft, sweet, delicate and tearful. She does not want to talk though she wants others around her.

Cimicifuga (Actaea)
Useful as pain relief and coordinating contractions. Allays fears and anxiety.

The woman feels trapped with no way out, which makes her hysterical and dissatisfied with whatever you do for her.

Everything seems wrong and she grows suspicious and very restless. Her behaviour is changeable. She is loquacious, continually talking and jumping from one subject to another then alternatively becoming very gloomy, sad, depressed and sighing.

She finds the contractions intolerable and the labour is very disjointed, incoordinate and irregular.

This woman is afraid of the birth and feels something terrible is going to happen. Feels unable to endure labour and says things like 'I can't do it' or 'I can't take it anymore'.

It helps the woman to trust the birth process and to open up.

Therefore it is not always necessary or appropriate to take a full homeopathic consultation. Rather we as midwives should gather together essential information about medical, surgical, psychiatric and social history as accurately but non-intrusively as possible and use our senses and skills to be able to ask ourselves whether we as midwives can safely treat this patient using homeopathy at this time. Then if it is appropriate try and ascertain the main symptoms with which the patient is struggling, how it is making her feel, physically and emotionally. How is she reacting? How is her behaviour changing? What is she doing to try and cope? Is there anything associated with the symptoms? Does anything make it better or worse?

Examples of conditions that may be treated

- haemorrhoids, varicose veins, vulval varicosities
- constipation
- insomnia, weakness, exhaustion, anaemia
- heartburn, nausea and vomiting
- thrush
- ligament pain, backache, sciatica
- symphysis pubis dysfunction, sciatica, carpal tunnel syndrome
- urinary symptoms, urinary tract infection, renal colic
- malposition of the baby
- failure to progress in labour, slow drawn-out labour, intolerable pain
- retained placenta, afterpains
- sore traumatised perineum
- painful wound areas following caesarean section
- haematomas, wound infections
- cracked nipples, mastitis, insufficient or excessive milk supply
- emotional problems: fear, anxiety, depression, weepy, disappointed, resentful, shocked, mourning, angry
- unsettled crying babies, bruised and sore from traumatic births, colicky, teething, sticky eyes.

In general it is recommended that pregnant women receive advice from an appropriately trained healthcare provider rather than treat themselves and, like conventional physicians, homeopaths will advise not to use any medicines in pregnancy if everything seems normal and healthy. Homeopathy should be used along with our normal tools of assessment, monitoring and evaluation and where appropriate include investigations of reasons for the condition and of the need for a change in lifestyle or need for any other treatment.

Chronic symptoms

In comparison to acute symptoms, these refer to recurrent, unsuccessful efforts of the organism to re-establish health. Such symptoms may persist because the person is constitutionally weakened from genetics, lifestyle or environmental factors or because the person is continually stressed or frequently reinfected. Chronic disease pathologies develop when a person has been repeatedly bombarded or overwhelmingly weakened to the point where destruction of cells and ability to function adequately are reached and the body has to adjust to protect itself.

Sometimes what seems to be an acute symptom is actually the result of an underlying chronic condition.

Examples of conditions that arise in or are aggravated by pregnancy and that may be treated using homeopathy (in agreement and in consultation with relevant medical practitioners) include:

- migraines, headaches
- urinary system problems, e.g. recurrent urinary tract infection, pylonephritis, renal calculi, retention of urine, urinary incontinence
- hypertension, pre-eclampsia
- psychiatric illness, e.g. depression, obsessive-compulsive disorder, bipolar disorder
- asthma, epilepsy
- rheumatoid arthritis
- skin problems
- gastrointestinal disorders.

There follows a selection of short cases (Case studies 12.4–12.8) to demonstrate how homeopathy is used in midwifery practice. Remedies were given in 30c potency.

 CASE STUDIES

Case 12.4 Nausea
A woman at 18 weeks' gestation presented with nausea, vomiting, weakness and exhaustion. Had been off work for 6 weeks. Took Ferrum phos. 3 doses. The patient felt wonderful, better than she had with either of her two previous pregnancies and was able to return to work immediately following treatment.

Case 12.5 Hypertension
A woman with hypertension and anxiety disorder which arose following a previous late miscarriage. She had required antihypertensive drugs with her previous 2 pregnancies. Took Calc carb. 3 doses then as required. She was amazed when her blood pressure normalised and stayed this way throughout this pregnancy.

→

 **CASE STUDIES** (continued)

Case 12.6   Emotional problems

A woman with emotional problems following the recent separation from her husband. She was suffering from shock, grief, low self-esteem and resentment. Took Aconite followed by Staphysagria. Eternally grateful and says she tells everyone how 'I saved her' at a time when she was extremely distressed.

Case 12.7   Haemorrhoids

A woman at 34 weeks' gestation debilitated with hugely swollen, painful, haemorrhoids. Had tried a variety of creams and was admitted to ward by general practitioner for surgical assessment. Took Pulsatilla 3 doses. Unbelievable difference. Haemorrhoids almost completely gone even after delivery.

Case 12.8   Stress incontinence

Parous lady at 7 days postnatal with stress incontinence and irritability with her loved ones. Sepia 3 doses. Incontinence stopped and generally felt much better.

In addition to the potential general nursing benefits to be gained by the integration of homeopathy the following apply to midwifery practice:

- reduction in the lower-uterine-segment caesarean section rate, e.g. for failure to progress, malposition and malpresentation
- reduction in the need for medical intervention, e.g. manual removal of placenta
- reduction in the need for women to be admitted as inpatients, e.g. with hyperemesis.

Homeopathic training for the nursing and midwifery professions

The Faculty of Homeopathy in conjunction with specific universities in the UK is offering postgraduate courses in homeopathy for registered nurses and midwives to LFHom and MFHom (Nurse/Midwife) levels (see Chapter 8). The resultant qualification allows for a more advanced role in homeopathy where a nurse can operate a nurse-led clinic.

Registered nurses and midwives in the UK practising homeopathy within the NHS require the following:

- permission from health board or primary care trust in order to practise homeopathy
- independent nurse prescribing qualification for the prescribing of homeopathic medicines at the level of competence gained
- clinical management plan *in situ*, which has been approved by healthcare manager
- vicarious liability by employer
- indemnity insurance
- operate within professional boundaries as defined in Nursing and Midwifery Council *Code of Professional Conduct*[30] and document *Standards of Proficiency for Nurse and Midwife Prescribing*[31]
- maintain continuous professional development according to professional requirements.

Conclusion

The provision of safer and effective therapeutic treatments in response to patient needs and demands will change healthcare delivery in the future. When integrated into many areas of nursing and midwifery, homeopathy provides an additional therapeutic tool. The assessment of patients holistically enhances good nursing practice with outcomes that promote greater patient and practitioner relationships.

In the future recruitment and retention of nurses and midwives will be dependent on the promotion of a career in nursing and midwifery as a positive, exciting rewarding option. The holistic approach displays the qualities that are inherent to the nursing profession and enhances its identity, which is quoted as gradually being eroded.[32] Nurse education requires innovation to meet with this opportunity.

References

1. Langley P, Fonseca J, Iphofen R. Psychoneuroimmunology and health from a nursing perspective. *Br J Nursing* 2006; 15: 1126–1129.
2. *Code of Conduct*. London: Nursing and Midwifery Council, 2006.
3. Dantas F, Rampes H. Do homeopathic medicines provoke adverse effects? A systematic review. *Br Hom J* 2000; 89 (Suppl. 1): S35–S38.
4. Wiesenauer M, Groh P, Häußler S. Naturheilkunde als Beitrag zur Kostendämpfung - Versuch einer Kostenanalyse. *Fortschr Med* 1992; 17: 311–314.
5. Unio Homoeopathica Belgica Enquette Unio – INAMI premiere semestre 1997 – *Profil de Prescriptions de Médicaments Conventionnels par les Médecins Généralistes Homéopathes*. Brussels: Maison de l'Homeopathie, 1999.

6. Reilly D. The evidence for homeopathy. Foreword to version 8.2 (update of March 02 Harvard Medical School Course version and Reilly D). *Altern Ther Med Health* 2005; 2: 28–31.

7. Mercer S W, Reilly D. A qualitative study of patient's views on the consultation at the Glasgow Homoeopath Hospital, an NHS integrative complementary and orthodox medical care unit. *Patient Educ Couns* 2004; 53: 13–18.

8. Donnelly G F. The placebo effect and holistic interventions. *Holistic Nurs Pract* 2004; Sept/Oct: 238–241.

9. Cancer Research UK. Cancer worldwide – the global picture. info.cancer researchuk.org/cancerstats/geographic/world/ (accessed April 2007).

10. Boon H, Stewart M, Kennard M A, *et al*. Use of complementary/alternative medicine by breast cancer survivors in Ontario: prevalence and perceptions. *J Clin Oncol* 2000; 18: 2515–2521.

11. Greer S. Cancer and the mind. *Br J Psychiatry* 1983; 143: 535–543.

12. Thompson E, Kassab S. Homeopathy in cancer care. *Homeopathy* 2000; 89: 61–62.

13. Ramakrishnan A U. Carcinosin in the treatment of cancer. *N Engl J Hom* 1996; 5: 17–18.

14. De Schepper L. LM potencies: one of the hidden treasures of the sixth edition of the *Organon*. *Br Hom J* 1999; 88: 128–134.

15. Thomson E A, Reilly D. The homeopathic approach to the treatment of symptoms of oestrogen withdrawal in breast cancer patients. A prospective observational study. *Homeopathy* 2003; 92: 131–134.

16. Schroyens F. *Repertorium Homeopathicum Syntheticum*. London: Homeopathic Book Publishers, 1998.

17. Boger CM. Boenninghausen's characteristics. In: *Encyclopaedia Homeopatica* 2001. Available online at: www.radar-uk.co.uk/encyclopaedia/index.php.

18. Vermeulen F. *Prisma. The Arcana of Materia Medica Illuminated. Similars and Parallels Between Substance and Remedy*. The Netherlands: Emryss by, 2002.

19. Vithoulkas G. *The Science of Homeopathy*. New York: Thorsons, 1986.

20. Allen T F. *Encyclopaedia of Pure Materia Medica*. B. New Delhi: Jain, 2005. www.bjainbooks.com (accessed April 2007).

21. Shore J. Seminar. Scotland. In: *Encyclopaedia Homeopathica 2001*. Belgium: Archibel Medical Software.

22. Chung-Park M. Anxiety attacks following surgical menopause. *Holistic Nurs Pract* 2005; Sept/Oct: 236–240.

23. Coll L. Homeopathy in survivors of childhood sexual abuse. *Homeopathy* 2002; 91: 3–9.

24. Morrison R. *Desktop Guide to Keynotes and Confirmatory Symptoms*. Nevado City: Hahnemann Clinic, 1993.

25. Viksveen P. Antibiotic and the development of resistant microorganisms. Can homeopathy be an alternative? *Homeopathy* 2003; 92: 99–107.

26. Weatherley-Jones E, Nicholl J, Thomas K, *et al*. A randomized, controlled, triple-blind trial of the efficacy of homeopathic treatment for chronic fatigue syndrome. *J Psychosom Res* 2004; 56: 189–197.

27. Muscari Tomaioli G, Allegri F, Miali E, *et al*. (2001) Observational study of quality of life in patients with headache, receiving homeopathic treatment. *Br Hom J* 2001; 90: 189–197.

28. *Winterton Report. House of Commons Health Select Committee Second Report on the Maternity Services.* London: HMSO, 1992.

29. *Changing Childbirth.* Department of Health Report of the Expert Maternity Group. London: HMSO, 1993.

30. Nursing and Midwifery Council. *Code of Professional Conduct.* London: Nursing and Midwifery Council, 2002.

31. *Standards of Proficiency for Nurse and Midwife Prescribing.* London: Nursing and Midwifery Council, 2006. Available online at: http://www.nmc-uk.org (accessed April 2007).

32. Shields L, Watson R. The demise of nursing in the United Kingdom: a warning for medicine. *J R Soc Med* 2007; 100: 70–74.

Further reading

Geraghty B (1997) *Homeopathy for Midwives.* Edinburgh: Churchill Livingstone.

Guidelines for Nurses (2006) Luton: Faculty of Homeopathy.

Idarius B (1999) *The Homeopathic Childbirth Manual.* Talmage: Idarius Press.

Integrated Homeopathic Medicine: A Guide for the NHS (2006) Luton: Faculty of Homeopathy.

Moskowitz R (1993) *Homeopathic Medicines for Pregnancy and Childbirth.* Berkeley, CA: North Atlantic Books.

Perko S (1997) *Homeopathy for the Modern Pregnant Woman and her Infant.* San Antonio: Benchmark Homeopathic.

Webb P (1999) *Homoeopathy for Midwives and All Pregnant Women.* Glasgow: BHA Book Service.

13

The professional homeopath

Felicity Lee

Introduction

In this chapter a broad picture will be painted of the rich and colourful development of professional homeopathy and examples given of how it is practised in the UK and further afield for the benefit of a wide range of patients. The full scope of the term 'professional homeopath' will unfold as the chapter proceeds.

Definition

A 'professional homeopath' is a practitioner who has qualified from a recognised college of homeopathy, and practises in such a way that all the criteria for registration requested by the professional body continue to be fulfilled.

History

Samuel Hahnemann's second wife Melanie was the first professional homeopath. She worked very closely with him in an intense apprenticeship and so had a thorough grounding in its healing applications. In Paris in 1847 she also became the first homeopath to be prosecuted for practising medicine without a licence! Another early pioneer was Carl von Boenninghausen, the Director of the Munster Botanic Garden. There seemed to be something about homeopathy that attracted enthusiastic devotees who had sufficient time and funds to give to studying homeopathy but who did not train as doctors. They became known as lay homeopaths, with the implication that they were self-taught amateurs. Chambers *Dictionary* defines 'lay' as not in holy orders, unprofessional. Having made strenuous efforts to become professional,

professional homeopaths find the term 'non-medically qualified practitioner' unsatisfactory. It emphasises a lack rather than focusing positively on the nature of our qualifications and training. Later in this chapter details will be given of the marked improvements in education over the last 30 years. Within the National Health Service (NHS) the roles of many professionals are being redefined, and professional homeopaths may be considered in the same light as prescribing pharmacists, specialist nurse consultants and clinical psychologists. The number of registered homeopaths in the UK has grown steadily over recent years and has now reached 2500 practitioners.

Professional homeopathy in practice

At the heart of homeopathy is the consultation with the patient. From informal observation and discussion with colleagues and patients, the approach taken by homeopaths depends more on their personality and the influences in their homeopathic training and practice rather than whether they have had medical training or not. There is very little published research in this area, but Caroline Eyles is currently halfway through a PhD investigating this area at the University of Southampton, UK. The 20 homeopaths she has interviewed so far were all concerned with the same thing: letting individual patients tell their story and trying to find a remedy to help them. 'Medical and non-medical homeopaths talk about healing being about clarity, or a shift in consciousness. They both talk about an energetic connection with their patients which is intense'.

The following two cases show how different approaches to homeopathic treatment may be applied. Case 13.1 is based on Dr J Scholten's teachings.[1]

Quoting from the introduction in Scholten's book[1]:

> The group analysis method cannot be applied from bits and pieces of superficial information, hence we are forced to go on questioning until we have found the most deeply disturbed level in our patient. Anybody who starts to use this book will soon discover that it will add an extra dimension to his diagnostic techniques: a well known picture gets a well known remedy, a peculiar picture gets a peculiar remedy and a picture that is not fully understood will unfortunately but inevitably get the wrong remedy.

One of the benefits of working in private practice is being able to offer patients longer consultations – a 90-minute first appointment and 45-minute follow-up are common. Long and comprehensive

CASE STUDY

Case 13.1   Based on Dr Scholten's approach to mineral remedies

This gracious woman with a delightful sense of humour looked in her early 60s. A small growth on her collarbone had been removed a year ago and chronic lymphocytic leukaemia was diagnosed. Radiotherapy was an option if other enlarged lymph nodes continued to grow, or possibly chemotherapy, and she was having blood tests every 6 weeks. She had been a county councillor for years and was on a government advisory committee until she had to finish at the age of 70. Now 83, she continues to chair a local health committee. Her energy level is low and she is too breathless to take her dog for a proper walk. She had not been told what stage she had reached in the disease, but it was presumably at least 1B since she had lymphocytosis with lymphadenopathy, but no anaemia or obvious hepatic or splenic enlargement.

From her general approach to life I felt she might need a mineral remedy and so considered which of Jan Scholten's description of series in the periodic table of the elements best fitted her.[1] The gold series seemed most appropriate as it covers the key words responsible, distinguished, maturity and blindness (she had lost the sight in one eye from temporal arteritis). The next step was to decide the stage my patient had reached. Stage 2 seemed to fit best – covering the central aspects preserving, holding on and protecting. This combination of series and stage comes to the remedy Aurum. In his book, Scholten comments that, although George Vithoulkas described Aurum as full of black despair and suicidal impulses, and Sankaran accentuated the responsible and serious side, he himself felt the most characteristic aspect is guarding their flock. Such characters cannot let down the person who has been entrusted into their care. This woman seemed softer than other Aurums I have treated, suggesting the remedy was a salt I hadn't met before. She had been a very responsible mother, tending a baby born in 1939 with an imperforate anus while her surgeon husband was away in the Royal Airforce. The child died age 10, and she was widowed in 1964 and brought up her other two children alone. This and many other aspects led me to Aurum muriaticum. Repertorisation of the main characteristics of her case, together with the rubric of red circumscribed cheeks and her dreams and fears of being late, confirmed this as a possibility.

The patient was given a single dose of Aurum muriaticum 30c, which was repeated monthly, and eventually went up to 200c, repeated as necessary. Apart from one dip when she fell and broke her wrist, the lumps gradually got smaller, she had more energy and her blood count was falling. It was decided to stop active treatment after 2 years, as her condition was stable. A chance meeting at a concert 2 years later revealed that she was feeling very well.

consultations are emphasised during training. Again, this can become a matter of personal preference or dictated by the approach taken.

It seems that longer times and persistence in questioning may be required to reach the current emphasis on uncovering the patient's vital sensation advocated by Dr Rajan Sankaran and the Bombay School.[2] In Case 13.2 this method was adapted to suit the needs of a child.

For some patients, if the homeopath says as little as possible during the consultation the patient will soon be encouraged to reveal the centre of the case, whereas for others silence is deeply disturbing and uncomfortable. Dr Brian Kaplan's comprehensive book *The Homeopathic Conversation* draws in strands from related disciplines such as psychotherapy, art therapy and making the best use of dreams, further illuminating the point that versatility and a whole spectrum of approaches are needed.[3]

 CASE STUDY

Case 13.2   Using Dr Rajan Sankaran's miasms

A 7-year-old boy was brought to see a homeopath colleague Sue Trotter suffering from sleeplessness and nightmares following the unexpected death of both grandparents. He was unable to sleep unless his dad was by his side. The homeopath discovered that the boy has an imaginary friend he believes is trying to kill him by stabbing him in his sleep. This imaginary friend has already stabbed another of his imaginary friends. The boy does not know the name of his friend but says: 'I just call him the little one, and all I know about him is he was hanged'. The details of the case point to the Solanaceae plant family and repertorise to Stramonium. At the centre of the case are themes of isolation, being an outcast and cruelty, suggesting the miasm is leprosy by Sankaran's recent definitions. Hence the remedy Mandragora could be indicated. Looking further into the materia medica, the therapist discovered that the German word for the mandrake plant translates as 'little man of the gallows'.

This resulted in the prescription of a single dose of Mandragora 1M.

Following an aggravation, the boy sleeps better and is less violent and disruptive at school. Following the sale of his grandparents' house several months later, he starts to hear voices again, this time telling him to kill his parents and his dog and set fire to the house. He tells the homeopath that the voices say it is her fault for sending 'the little one' away. Calm is restored once more by a 10M dose of Mandragora.

The depth of action of remedies

Homeopathic remedies are effective at many different levels. Parents can readily learn to use homeopathy for minor trauma and self-limiting childhood illnesses. Remedies are also used by practitioners such as physiotherapists, naturopaths and osteopaths in an adjunctive way rather than the deeper holistic methods described in this chapter. This difference has not always been made clear to other practitioners and the public. Case 13.3 illustrates this point and demonstrates how questioning more deeply leads to accurate and effective prescribing.

 CASE STUDY

Case 13.3 Questioning more deeply

One of the chiropractors at a clinic returned from a break to find wasps had built a nest in the corner of her bedroom. Two wasps flew at her and stung her on her right thumb and left elbow. She felt a hot stinging pain and noticed immediate swelling. She was shocked and wobbly, so she put on cold compresses and selected Apis 30 from her first-aid kit. As this was no help in 20 minutes, she phoned for advice. Questioning a little more revealed scant response to the cold compress even though that was what she felt she wanted to put on it. She said her bedroom had been invaded, and her own personal space spoilt. After a single dose of Staphisagria 30 she was soon feeling better and had less pain; the swelling resolved overnight.

Homeopathic remedies can be remarkably effective, even if the patient is also taking prescribed drugs. In Case 13.4, a prescription of the indicated remedy was effective even though the patient was taking an anticonvulsant.

Current working situations for professional homeopaths

As there is no career structure and little security of employment, professional homeopaths need to be both resourceful and resilient. To keep up their incomes some practitioners need to carry on parttime with their previous careers after qualifying; others may return to their careers if their practice is slow to build, breaking continuity for their patients. In the UK at present, 85% of registered homeopaths are women, some of whom

 **CASE STUDY**

Case 13.4 Combining homeopathy and conventional medicine

A 66-year-old woman presented in 2002 with 'funny turns' that she'd been having regularly for the last 18 months. They started in the pit of her stomach and then spread up through her, leaving strange sensations in her head. Waves of nausea came over her until she was eventually violently sick, and then felt better. The whole episode lasted about 24 hours. She felt she'd had a good life until 10 years ago, when she lost her mother and two brothers in 5 months. The joy of her daughter's pregnancy disappeared when the baby developed severe epilepsy. 'I had so much responsibility. I had no chance to stand back and collapse'. She had seen various consultants, and had a computed tomography scan and an electroencephalogram, but the diagnosis was unclear and she was on no medication.

After a single dose of Calcarea carbonica 200, the frequency of 'funny turns' dropped from every 15 days to 6 weeks, but gradually shortened despite repeating the remedy. She was feeling much better in herself. A neurologist then diagnosed temporal lobe epilepsy, which he said was extremely difficult to treat. She was told to stop driving and commented: 'my little car is my escape and I drive every night in my dreams, telling myself I shouldn't be doing it'. She was prescribed increasing doses of Epilim, and once she reached a steady level she came back for more homeopathy as she was still having attacks every few weeks. The last episode had been particularly bad and she was very down and disappointed for 2 days afterwards; then she was back to her usual bright and active self, always doing something.

Delving more deeply into the materia medica, Indigo tinctoria seemed well indicated. After a single dose of the 30c potency she had a very mild attack 3 weeks later, but then no more. As she has now been free of fits for over a year, the consultant has said she can reapply for her driving licence. If she is still well in another year he will consider reducing the medication.

choose to work parttime to suit childcare arrangements. The majority of professional homeopaths work in private practice, either alone or in clinic settings. As more homeopaths are trained, various types of group practice are beginning to emerge. One such example is given below.

The Homeopathy for People (HOPE) project

HOPE was formed by a group of seven professional homeopaths with the aim of offering homeopathic treatment to people in the English county of Herefordshire who are disadvantaged by either low income or severe health or social problems. Treatment was made available to clients of five local groups free of charge throughout the 6-month pilot project. The homeopaths gave their time free of charge and project costs were paid for by the Homeopathy Action Trust and Herefordshire Voluntary Action. One of the case histories is given below (Case 13.5).

 CASE STUDY

Case 13.5 Patient with asthma and a history of alcohol and drug abuse

Trevor, age 37, presented with asthma and was using Ventolin and Becotide inhalers on a daily basis. He has an 18-year history of drug abuse and alcoholism but has been off alcohol for a year. He still smokes and takes occasional amphetamines. He started misusing drugs at the age of 19 when his father 'ascended to the spirit world'. He has suffered black depression for 5 years and feels threatened, judged and too fearful even to go out to supermarkets. He has had delusions of demons and goddesses – 'I have travelled the universe in my mind'. First prescription: Hydrogen 30c.

At the first follow-up his dreams were less dark and paranoid. The asthma was improving and he had forgotten to use his inhalers. His speech was still rambling and he had many ungrounded ideas. Second prescription: LSD 30c.

At the next follow-up he had been exercising and eating better but had some alcohol 2 weeks ago. He was more aware of his feelings: he feels powerless, a victim, and knew he had a chip on his shoulder. He was generally more grounded. Third prescription: Hydrogen 30c.

When he came back a month later he is breathing with long laboured inspirations – he tried to give up smoking and failed. He has been thinking about his teens when he was terrorised for 3 years by a bunch of skinheads. He lost his innocence and softness then and has harboured the anger and pain for years. He has routines now and is teaching a friend to swim. 'I've been everybody's madman for too long.' Fourth prescription: Hydrogen 30c.

At his last follow-up he said: 'The despair has gone and I feel more in my body. It's as if a window is opening up'. He went for hypnotherapy and has given up smoking. He finds people are more friendly and he has started seeing a counsellor. Fifth prescription: Hydrogen 30c.

Over the 6 months of treatment, together with support from the community service, he has moved away from his drug-using acquaintances and is undertaking a variety of activities rather than staying in bed all day. His asthma is greatly improved; he is forging better family relationships and has continued to see a counsellor.

Quoting from the conclusion of the report to the funding bodies:

Despite the extreme nature of these clients' problems we have been pleased to have established that homeopathy has a role to play in improving their overall health. We have observed many instances of profound changes in people's sense of well being and in their ability to cope with their life circumstances. We have seen improvements in physical health and a better level of adaptation to emotional and psychological challenges as well as a reduction in the number of GP [general practitioner] visits.[4]

Homeopathy Action Trust is a charity that brings together the public, practitioners and students. Over the last 2 years it has received and awarded over £35 000 (€51 500) to projects that aim to make homeopathy more available to the public. The projects have varied from small local low-cost clinics to more ambitious undertakings such as the HOPE project described above.

Specialising

UK homeopath Diane Seymour, from Hebden Bridge, Yorkshire, looked closely at the child's experience of coming to see a homeopath and calls her practice Homeopathy for Children. She now runs workshops focused on problems such as children getting bored during the consultation and how to get discussion going on tricky areas such as bereavement, fears, difficult family dynamics, behavioural problems and humiliating symptoms. She has produced illustrated leaflets for both children and parents to read before the first appointment. She also visits aptly named Calderdale Baby Café, which provides professional support and a support group for breastfeeding mothers.

Several professional homeopaths work in the field of terminal care. Hospice care is provided through charitable funding rather than the NHS. Serena Scrine has been working at St Luke's Hospice in Plymouth for the last 6 years.[5] Having originally considered trying small remedies that would be palliative and partial, she soon discovered that patients responded more fully when she selected remedies based on the totality of their symptoms. In her general practice, she prescribed single doses, separated in time, but, building on the experience of Robin Murphy and Dr Ramakrishnan, she has been using daily doses for patients with life-threatening disease. Case 13.6 is an example of such a case.

A wide range of cases is published regularly in the journals *The Homeopath* and *Homeopathic Links*.

CASE STUDY

Case 13.6   Constitutional case taken in August 2004
This woman of 32 had grown up in India and then moved to England. At 15, she developed a painful lump in her neck and she gradually became breathless on exertion. Thyroid cancer was diagnosed and at first she responded well to both homeopathic medicine and to radioiodine treatments, but by 2003 she had a secondary lung tumour, with a cough and chest pain. Her husband was now ill and other stressful factors were making her feel weak and unwell, and she developed headaches.

She spoke freely in the session, but the referral mentioned she normally kept her feelings to herself, although clearly stressed. She felt the cold a lot, especially on the chest and neck. This area of her chest would also sweat if uncovered, so she always wore high-necked clothes. She had always been very religious and was an obedient child. She was afraid of the dark and reacted strongly to a horror film once, not sleeping for nights afterwards. When upset her throat chokes up but she cannot cry. She took responsibility for herself from a very young age and was sent away to school. 'Maybe I'm too independent for my own good ... I was always responsible for others. When I worked I divided my salary to send home ... It was sudden when I found I was away from my father, and that was the hardest thing. I am always on the phone to my family and we pray for each other.'

I prescribed Thuja 200c once daily. I saw her several times, and repeated the remedy. By September she was coughing less and her chest was the best it had been for a long time. She was due to have repeat radioiodine treatment, and in preparation her normal thyroxine had been stopped. This would usually make her feel bad, but this time she felt fine. Her headaches were also less frequent. By January 2005 she said that a computed tomography scan after the radiation treatment showed everything was clear in the thyroid.

Working within the NHS

Since 1991, it has been possible for GPs to delegate their work to other suitably qualified practitioners. In his report describing the homeopathic treatment of 500 consecutive patients at Bounds Green Group Practice in London, Francis Treuherz included the protocol shown in Box 13.1. This was distributed to all members of the primary healthcare team to aid appropriate referral.[6]

Box 13.1 Objectives for clinical work and criteria for referral at Bounds Green Group Practice

---

- To reduce the need for long-term palliative medication
- To reduce the demands made by some patients on their medical practitioner
- To prevent the need for non-urgent surgery
- To reduce costs through the provision of homeopathy
- To assist patients where there is no known diagnosis, where tests disclose nothing abnormal, but the patient is suffering
- To assist patients with chronic diseases where there may be a poor prognosis without an alternative approach
- To assist in cases where drug treatments are contraindicated, for example in pregnancy
- To prevent the need for referral to expensive specialists
- To provide an environment where the relationship between a patient's physical and emotional or somatic problems may be discussed without any label of mental illness
- To provide information and guidance on safe homeopathic self-care for minor ailments and so prevent the need for medical intervention

---

Alistair Dempster made a similar evaluation of homeopathic treatment of common mental health problems at a GP surgery in West Yorkshire. This showed a significant saving of GP time with a group of patients who tend to incur large service costs in terms of repeat visits and medication.[7] Discovering the context of their problems through homeopathy increased patient awareness of how to deal with, or avoid, triggers.

Unfortunately, circumstances changed when fund-holding practices disappeared with a change in government and the attitude to homeopathy hardened. Possibly only one such direct service remains, given by Andrew Ward at St Margaret's Surgery in Wiltshire, and this continues to be cost-effective.[8] In the current climate, NHS contracts can be short-lived. Despite winning both an NHS Alliance Award and an award from the Prince of Wales' Foundation for Integrated Healthcare and carrying out research that demonstrated effectiveness, the homeopathy arm of the West End Complementary Therapy Project in Newcastle has been cut back due to a lack of funding.

By investigating other forms of government funding, several homeopaths have established clinics under the Sure Start initiative. This aims to give young children in deprived areas the best possible start in life. Preschool education, childcare, health and family support are brought together under one umbrella. Alison Fixsen, who is a senior lecturer at Westminster University, has been involved in Sure Start since 2002 in Swindon. She makes the following comments:

> One of the major goals of Sure Start is to bring families closer together and to encourage parents to take a more active role in improving their children's health and development as well as their own. Treating patients for free has enabled me to see several members of a family concurrently, and it has been interesting to observe family healing taking place. Among the common problems are poor housing, domestic violence and multiple or absent fathers.

A researcher from Bath University carried out an evaluation. She concluded that the homeopathic approach was empowering and parents said that they had learnt more about themselves and their children.[9]

The development of professional homeopathy in the UK

The first UK homeopaths were all close colleagues of Hahnemann in Paris, returning to London to set up practices in the 1830s. Two of these men were not medically trained, but had apprenticed with Hahnemann – so William Leaf, a silk merchant, and the Reverend Everest appear to have been the first British professional homeopaths. Peter Morrell has documented in detail the rather variable growth of professional homeopathy in the UK.[10, 11] The first association seems to have been formed briefly in 1970, in response to the introduction of the Medicines Act. Homeopathic remedies were defined as medicines, leading to unfounded concerns that their availability might be restricted to doctors. Thomas Maughan and John Damonte became important teachers in London for some years, and following their deaths in 1975 and 1976 their students felt the need to meet together in a more formal grouping. By 26 July 1978, a critical mass had formed with enough energy to set up the first college and the Society of Homeopaths.

The development of the Society of Homeopaths

Refinements that followed included a public register, a journal and professional indemnity insurance. The Society soon became known for its innovative approach to continuing professional development (CPD) through conferences and seminars with international teachers such as

Rajan Sankaran and George Vithoulkas. Mindful of the need for patient safety, the *Code of Ethics and Practice* has been continuously updated.[12] The majority of complaints from the public can be resolved through mediation by the professional conduct officer, but there have been a few matters that warranted an adjudication hearing. Penalties range from a first warning to a suspension and the panel may require that the homeopath undergoes counselling, supervision or further training. Three registered members have been struck off the register, but one of the current disadvantages of common law is that the Society has no sanction to stop such people practising.

One important part of being a practitioner is being able to recognise when you are out of your depth. Quoting from the most recent *Code of Ethics and Practice*[12]:

> A competent homeopath identifies those occasions when a patient's condition is:
>
> - beyond the present limits of their clinical competence and expertise
> - likely to receive more immediate, effective benefit from another form of treatment.
> - showing signs and symptoms suggestive of an underlying condition which requires referral for investigation and other medical diagnosis.

This last point amplifies the fact that homeopaths are trained to be highly observant and question patients carefully, not only to aid in the prescription of the remedy but also because they do not have direct access to diagnostic tests.

Education and registration

The Society of Homeopaths has been working intensively with colleges since 1994 to raise standards for education, and maintains a list of recognised courses. At the time of writing there are 18 such courses and two colleges have recently celebrated their silver jubilees. Course providers must show that they have appropriate facilities and staffing. Courses must fulfil the criteria in the Society's *Clinical Education Guidelines*[13] and have a minimum duration of 4 years parttime or 3 years full-time. The process of college recognition has evolved into peer and self-evaluation together with reviews by the Society's education advisers. Currently, three of the courses lead to degrees at the universities of Central Lancashire, Middlesex and Westminster.

All courses emphasise medical sciences, homeopathic philosophy and the study of materia medica. There has been some criticism of the content of these courses (see Chapter 1).

Watching live video cases, sitting in with homeopaths and working under supervision in student clinics bring the theory alive. Individual prescribing styles emerge and are generally based on single remedy at any one time, based on the widest totality of symptoms. Each course has its own distinct ethos, yet all are based around the National Occupational Standards in Homeopathy[14] and the Society's core criteria.[15] Other organisations for professional homeopaths have become established over the years, each with its own character,[16] but none has evolved such a comprehensive scheme of college recognition as the Society.

As the education of professional homeopaths has evolved, so has registration. It is now a process involving participation in a specific 3-year programme. Under the direction of a mentor, each homeopath attends regular meetings and prepares a reflective CPD portfolio for assessment. Registration is also open to students who have not undergone training at a recognised college or who have qualifications from outside the UK through an accreditation of prior learning scheme. The Society arranges regional CPD seminars and there are many informal case discussion meetings throughout the country. All practitioners are encouraged to continue with supervision throughout their years of practice.[16]

The public's viewpoint

Under common law in the UK, anybody may set up as any type of practitioner, whether trained or not. One of the biggest disadvantages of the present situation for the public is the lack of a single register of trained homeopaths. It is not easy to check the validity of qualifications or whether a practitioner is insured or not. This difficulty is being addressed through the Council of Organisations Registering Homeopaths (CORH), which was established in 1999. At present, CORH represents some 2500 registered members on 10 separate registers; individual registers vary in size from just 10 members in the Scottish Association of Professional Homeopaths to 1600 in the Society of Homeopaths. A complete list of the organisations can be found at www.corh.org.uk/members.html. By the time this book is published, the same initials may well stand for Council of Registered Homeopaths with a single register and a new regulatory body to support voluntary self-regulation for the whole profession.

Research

This is another area that has seen healthy growth in the last few years, despite difficulties obtaining any kind of funding. The National Service Evaluation is a pilot project funded by the Society of Homeopaths, involving individual members collecting data from their patients. The Society's research group selected the outcome measure Measure Yourself Medical Outcome Profile (MYMOP) because it has already been validated and widely accepted in the medical world. The first evaluation is about to be published and will give basic information on the types of conditions and symptoms for which patients are currently seeking homeopathic treatment, and how helpful it has been.

The Department of Health is currently funding several training fellowships in homeopathy. Elaine Weatherley-Jones' initial work on homeopathic treatment of chronic fatigue syndrome[17] has led to her joining forces with Dr Thompson and Dr Thomas. They published a paper questioning the validity of conducting placebo-controlled trials in homeopathy.[18] The authors conclude: 'For clinical trials of homeopathy to be accurate representations of practice, we need modified designs that take into account the complexity of the homeopathic intervention. Only with such trials will the results be generalisable to homeopathic practice in the real world.' They propose that comparative trials of untested treatments be compared with those where there is evidence of effectiveness. Clare Relton has been specialising in using homeopathy for symptoms of the menopause. She has already completed an audit of clinical outcomes using MYMOP and is now working on a pilot study.[19] Both Clare and Elaine are based at the University of Sheffield. Further details of these and other research projects can be found on the Society of Homeopaths website (www.homeopathy-soh.org).

Having completed a PhD looking at all past trials of homeopathy,[20] Michael Dean is establishing a database of homeopathic research and developing agreed standards of homeopathic trial reporting at York University.

Research from the outside

In 2003, one of the first papers that specifically studied professional homeopaths was published in the mainstream medical journal *Thorax*. It caused great controversy, as it appeared to show that adjunctive homeopathy offered no improvement in childhood asthma compared to placebo.[21] One major criticism of this paper has been that symptoms of the asthmatic children were already so well controlled that there was no room for improvement. A flurry of letters to the editor ensued. The Director of Research at the Royal London Homoeopathic Hospital jointly signed one of these with the Research Development Adviser at the Faculty of Homeopathy and the Director of Research at the Society of Homeopaths.[22] They pointed out that the paper's conclusions do not adequately reflect the shortcomings of the trial and were concerned that their bias in interpretation will carry through to future meta-analyses and reviews.

Provings

A new era of provings in the UK began in the 1990s when Jeremy Sherr introduced a proving to each intake of his Dynamis postgraduate course, and he has continued this in other countries where he runs the course, including USA and Germany. At the same time, he published a systematic protocol.[23] Hydrogen, Chocolate and Germanium are amongst the 24 newly proven remedies. The school's website includes a comprehensive catalogue of worldwide provings.[24] The School of Homeopathy has also been busy in this area, and its published provings include the acquired immunodeficiency syndrome (AIDS) nosode and Falco peregrinus.[24]

Practising in other countries

The European situation

The legal and educational requirements differ from country to country and are discussed in detail in Chapter 9. In France only medically trained doctors may practise homeopathy, whether or not they have had specialist training in homeopathy, whereas in Ireland the situation is broadly similar to the UK.

In Germany, homeopathy can be practised either by doctors or by licensed practitioners known as Heilpraktikers (see Chapter 9). They may not officially call themselves a homeopath, although they can indicate on their practice sign or appointment cards that they practise homeopathy. Verband Klassischer Homöopathen Deutschlands (VKHD), together with the Stiftung Homöopathie Zertifikat (SHZ) have jointly defined the educational requirements in homeopathy; since 2003, the SHZ has been registering homeopaths, teachers, supervisors and colleges.

The European Council for Classical Homeopathy (ECCH) is an international council consisting of representatives from associations of professional homeopaths within individual countries (see Chapter 9). Established in 1990, the council currently has 24 members from 20 countries, listed in Box 13.2. Membership is only open to associations that maintain a public register, set stringent educational and training standards and maintain a code of ethics and practice to which their members are accountable.

Box 13.2 Countries with professional association membership of the European Council for Classical Homeopathy

Armenia
Belgium
Bosnia and Herzegovina
Bulgaria
Croatia
Czech Republic
Denmark
Finland
Germany
Greece
Ireland
Israel
Italy
Netherlands
Norway
Portugal
Serbia and Montenegro
Sweden
Switzerland
UK

Over the years, the council has published policy documents on education and public health and acts as an advisory body to national and international governmental institutions. ECCH has a comprehensive website that includes contact addresses for all its member organisations. Professional associations of homeopaths outside Europe, including North America and Australia, are also listed.

South Africa

Since the change of government in 1994, regulations concerning the practice of homeopathy have also undergone changes. To practise legally, it is necessary to register with the Allied Health Professions Council (AHPC). Graduates in homeopathy from the Durban Institute of Technology are automatically registered with the AHPC, but at present it is not possible for professional homeopaths from other countries to gain registration. Colleagues have said that the working situation is different from the UK, with more emphasis on prescribing combinations of remedies and nutritional supplements. There is no national health scheme, and few people have the funds for private medical insurance. The patterns of disease are different too, with the western Cape having the highest rate of tuberculosis in the world together with a very high rate of human immunodeficiency virus (HIV) infection. (For more details, see Chapter 15.)

North America

Canada

At present the situation in Canada parallels that in the UK and there is no law against practising as a homeopath. A group of homeopaths in Ontario is in the process of applying for official recognition at the provincial level.

USA

The right to practise under common law does not exist in the USA. Instead, each state creates its own legislation, and in most cases, any form of healing – even massage or healing touch – is confined to licensed practitioners. A growing national health freedom movement has created a wind of change. Health freedom laws have now been passed in California, Idaho, Louisiana, Minnesota, Oklahoma and Rhode Island and allow even uncertified practitioners to operate under certain constraints. Despite the legal difficulties, perhaps the largest growing group of practitioner in the USA is the professional homeopath.[25] In April 2006, history was made when the first annual Joint American Homeopathic conference was held in California. Licensed doctor homeopaths and naturopaths and unlicensed professional homeopaths all came together. During the conference, the National Center for Homeopathy presented its annual service award to Richard Pitt, a professional homeopath originally from Bristol, for his work in developing homeopathy in North America.

Australia

Professional homeopaths are self-regulated under government guidelines that require a national register and curricula that deliver competencies defined by the profession and endorsed by the government. There are about a dozen registered colleges delivering homeopathy courses in Australia. Homeopaths in clinical practice are obliged to adhere to the legal requirements of their state legislature, and this can vary from state to state.

Overseas projects

Last but not least are the homeopaths who are prepared to go to war-torn and disaster-stricken parts of the world. Matthias Strelow, chair of Homöopathen ohne Grenzen in Germany and a former psychologist, has experience in treating posttraumatic stress disorder. His organisation has established projects in Togo, Honduras, Kenya and most recently in Sri Lanka following the 2005 tsunami. Similar organisations exist elsewhere in the world to bring homeopathy directly to people in trouble. In the USA there is Homeopaths without Borders and in the UK Frontline Homeopathy. One of Frontline's most recent projects was hosting a homeopathic first-aid workshop for a mixed group of Iraqi doctors and lay people during their visit to Scotland. They hope it will sow the seeds of a course in Iraq once the security situation improves.

Individual homeopaths have also established many other charitable projects, such as the Maun Homeopathy Project in Botswana. As a town, Maun has one of the highest rates of HIV and AIDS in the world. Teams of two homeopaths working together with translators run clinics for people who have these diseases or women who have been traumatised by rape. Practitioners who have worked on the project have noticed the extent to which homeopathy and antiretroviral drugs can complement each other.

Conclusion

Below are just three of the spontaneous comments made by patients when they were asked: What is the single most important thing to you about homeopathy?

- 'I like what it's doing for my self-esteem – yet I came for a physical complaint.'
- 'The optimism it gives me – that my symptoms make sense and out of that something can help'.
- 'It's been effective where conventional treatment wasn't'.

Homeopathy is a particularly energy- and resource-efficient form of medicine and, as such, the worldwide need for it is great, and likely to rise as global warming increases. As many competent practitioners as possible are needed, both medically and professionally trained, so that all patients can find the homeopath best suited to their needs.

> The physician's highest and *only* calling is to make the sick healthy, to cure, as it is called (Samuel Hahnemann[26]).

Acknowledgements

With thanks to all my colleagues who provided discussion and inspiration and to those who supplied examples of their practice, and to Mary Clarke, Kate Gathercole, Patricia Hatherly, Ulrike Kessler, Robin Logan, Suzanne Noble, Misha Norland, Josephine O'Gorman, Melanie Oxley, Miranda Parsons, Jeremy Sherr, Michael Thompson and Elaine Watson.

References

1. Scholten J. *Homeopathy and the Elements*. Utrecht: Stichting Alonnissos, 1996.
2. Sankaran R. *An Insight into Plants,* vols I and II. Mumbai: Homeopathic Medical Publishers, 2002.
3. Kaplan B. *The Homeopathic Conversation*. London: Natural Medicine Press, 2001.
4. *Interim Report to Funders*. Northampton: Homeopathy Action Trust, 2005.
5. Scrine S. A hospice practice. *Homeopath* 2005; 23: 22–25.
6. Treuherz F. *Homeopathy in General Practice*. Northampton: Society of Homeopaths, 1999.
7. Dempster A. *Homeopathy within the NHS*. Northampton: Society of Homeopaths, 1998.
8. Christie E, Ward A. *Report on NHS Practice-Based Homeopathy Project*. Northampton: Society of Homeopaths, 1996.
9. Fixsen A. Success of Sure Start clinic in Swindon. *Soc Homeopaths Newslett* 2006; summer: 10–11.
10. Morrell P. A brief history of British lay homoeopathy. *Homoeopath* 1995; 59: 471–475.

11. Morrell P. *British Homeopathy During Two Centuries*. PhD thesis, 2000. www.homeoint.org/morrell/british/abstract.htm.

12. *Code of Ethics and Practice*. Northampton: Society of Homeopaths, 2004.

13. Society of Homeopaths' Clinical Education Guidelines, May 2007 revision. Available online at: www.homeopathy-soh.org.

14. National Occupational Standards in Homeopathy. www.skillsforhealth.org.uk/get_competence.php?id=1126.

15. Core criteria. Appendix C. *Code of Ethics and Practice*. Northampton: Society of Homeopaths, 2004.

16. Ryan S. *Vital Practice. Stories from the Healing Arts: The Homeopathic and Supervisory Way*. Portland: Sea Change, 2004.

17. Weatherley-Jones E, Thomas K J, Nicholl J P, *et al*. A randomised controlled triple-blind trial of homeopathic treatment for chronic fatigue syndrome. *J Psychosom Res* 2004; 56: 189–197.

18. Weatherley-Jones E, Thompson E A, Thomas K J. The placebo-controlled trial as a test of complementary and alternative medicine: observations from research experience of individualised homeopathic treatment. *Homeopathy* 2004; 99: 186–189.

19. Relton C, Weatherley-Jones E. Homeopathy service in a National Health Service community menopause clinic: audit of clinical outcomes. *J Br Menopause Soc* 2005; 11: 72–73.

20. Dean M E. *The Trials of Homeopathy. Origins, Structure and Development*. PhD thesis. Essen, Germany: KVC Verlag, 2004.

21. White A, Slade P, Hunt C, *et al*. Individualised homeopathy as an adjunct in the treatment of childhood asthma: a randomised placebo controlled trial. *Thorax* 2003; 58: 317–321.

22. Fisher P, Chatfield K, Mathie R. Homeopathy in childhood asthma. Letter to the editor. *Thorax* 2003; 58: 827.

23. Sherr J. *The Dynamics and Methodology of Homoeopathic Provings,* 2nd edn. Malvern: Dynamis Books, 2002.

24. Norland M. *Signatures Miasms Aids*. Abergavenny: Yondercott Press, 2003. www.homeopathyschool.com.

25. Pitt R. *Homeopathy in the USA. An Overview of the Evolution of Homeopathy in the USA Today*. www.rpitt.home.igc.org.

26. O'Reilly W B. *Organon of the Medical Art*. Redmond, WA: Birdcage Books, 1996.

Contact details

Allied Health Professions Council of South Africa. www.ahpcsa.co.za.

Australian Homeopathic Association. www.homeopathyoz.org.

Council of Organisations Registering Homeopaths (CORH), 11 Wingle Tye Road, Burgess Hill, West Sussex RH15 9HR. Tel: 01444 239494. www.corh.org.uk.

Dynamis School for Advanced Homoeopathic Studies. www.dynamis.edu.

European Council for Classical Homeopathy (ECCH), School House, Market Place, Kenninghall, Norfolk NR16 2AH. Tel: 01953 888 163. www.homeopathy-ecch.org

Frontline Homeopathy, 3 Hanging Lees, Rochdale QL16 3SG. Tel: 01706 880209.

Homeolinks Publishers, PO Box 68, 9750 A B Haren, The Netherlands. www.homeolinks.nl.

Homeopaths without Borders. www.homeopathswithoutborders-na.org.

Homeopathy Action Trust, PO Box 5497, Northampton NN6 0ZH. www.homeopathyactiontrust.org.

Homöopathen ohne Grenzen. www.hom-og.de.

Maun Homeopathy Project. www.homeopathybotswana.com.

North American Society of Homeopaths (NASH). http://www.homeopathy.org.

Society of Homeopaths (SoH), 11 Brookfield, Duncan Close, Moulton Park, Northampton NN3 6WL. Tel: 0845 4506611. www.homeopathy-soh.org

Stiftung Homöopathie Zertifikat (SHZ). www.homoeopathie-zertifikat.de.

Verband Klassischer Homöopathen Deutschlands (VKHD). www.vkhd.de.

14

Veterinary homeopathy

Peter Gregory

Introduction

In this chapter the considerations that apply in the various areas of homeopathic veterinary practice are considered and some of the specific challenges that present themselves to the veterinary homeopath are discussed.

The practice of homeopathy in animals presents challenges in addition to those faced by practitioners in the human field. There are, for instance, no provings of homeopathic remedies in animals, and even if there were, the information gained would almost certainly be of a purely physical nature. There is of course much information on toxicology, but the depth of information necessary for the practice of homeopathy is lacking. In addition, there are major difficulties in interpreting the mental symptoms that constitute such an important part of human remedy pictures into a form that is relevant to animals. Conversely there is an uncertainty inherent in attempting to interpret an animal's behaviour in human 'mental' rubrics. Some information, such as the character of pain, is obviously impossible to collect from an animal: in fact there is very little information that emanates from a veterinary homeopathic consultation that can be relied on with absolute certainty, beyond that of a purely (and often advanced) pathological nature. For this reason alone it is of vital importance that any animal presented for homeopathic treatment be first examined by a qualified veterinary surgeon. Stories abound of animals treated with homeopathy by persons with no formal training which have subsequently been found to be suffering from a condition totally unrelated to that for which they had been receiving treatment. One example was a Golden retriever dog who was suffering from halitosis and loss of appetite. Homeopathic treatment at a distance by an unqualified practitioner had centred on liver function. An examination by the author over a week later quickly revealed a piece of stick lodged across the roof of the mouth, which was readily dislodged.

The lack of reliable symptoms with which the veterinary homeopath is faced requires that as much as possible must be done to ascertain every scrap of information from the patient. Hence an extremely detailed physical examination will be made, and it is possible that the veterinary homeopath might resort to laboratory tests more readily than a human counterpart. It has often been said that the study of homeopathy makes a veterinary surgeon better at the job generally, as it obliges him or her to be more meticulous in the examination of the patient.

When the patient cannot speak directly to the prescriber, adaptations may need to be made in how the necessary information is obtained and analysed. Extra complications may be presented by the way animals are managed, for instance as members of a multispecies household, or in a large group such as a herd of cows or flock of sheep, and this can further stretch the ingenuity of the veterinary prescriber.

The surgical situation

One of the most satisfying aspects of being a veterinarian is the fact that, in general practice at least, the patient can be under one's direct care right through from the initial consultation to the conclusion of treatment. In the case of an animal suffering from a surgical condition this means that it may well be the same veterinarian who performs all the diagnostic procedures, carries out the surgery, oversees the aftercare and prescribes the postoperative medication, and may even deliver the patient back to its owner!

Homeopathy may be appropriate at any stage of this process. The majority of the surgery performed on animals in western society involves the elective neutering of dogs and cats. Females undergo complete ovarohysterectomy and males orchiectomy. Veterinary homeopaths often discuss the appropriateness of such procedures, some considering that they remove one of the routes of expression of the sycotic miasm, thereby rendering the animal open to deeper levels of sycosis. However, in the case of females, the alternative is to keep an animal that is designed to breed at least annually in a state of continually active hormonal cycle. A similar situation exists with the male that is never allowed to mate. It is thus debateable as to which is the greater hazard. Certainly surgical neutering is to be preferred to chemical suppression of hormones, which brings with it the inevitable risk of genital problems such as pyometritis, which an understanding of homeopathy predicts. Furthermore, homeopathy can be useful in dealing with the consequences of neutering, such as alopecia (Case study 14.1) or urinary incontinence (Case study 14.2), without recourse to hazardous synthetic hormones.

CASE STUDY

Case 14.1 Alopecia
Sally was a 3-year-old tabby cat who was presented suffering from alopecia of the abdomen and thighs. The involvement of parasites such as fleas had been ruled out, and it was considered that the problem might be due to the hormonal imbalance induced by ovarohysterectomy. Oestrogen 3x twice daily proved successful. This prescription is of course only palliative and the remedy had to be repeated from time to time.

CASE STUDY

Case 14.2 Urinary incontinence in a speyed bitch
Martha was a 7-year-old Labrador cross bitch who was presented for urinary incontinence, for no apparent cause, but hormonal deficiency was suspected; this is the time of life when many speyed bitches develop this problem. Constitutionally Martha presented as Sepia and a course of Sepia 200c cleared the symptoms, this remedy being of major importance for conditions resulting from a fall in female hormone levels. Over the years the remedy has had to be repeated from time to time but now at the age of 12 occasional courses of LM potency (see Chapter 10) keep her dry.

Unavoidably, surgery in animals is performed on an unconsenting and often unwilling patient. Not surprisingly, this results in a mental and emotional state of indignation, and for this reason, many veterinary homeopaths include Staphysagria in the routine prescriptions for surgical patients. (It is in any case indicated for the relief of postoperative pain.) Failure to do so can result in psychological and physical problems postsurgically, particularly in cats, as evidenced by the following case history (Case study 14.3).

CASE STUDY

Case 14.3   Skin disease as a result of surgery

Leo (shown in Figure 14.1) was a 1-year-old male tabby and white cat presented for miliary eczema. Routine examination showed no evidence of parasites; however the consultation revealed that the problem had begun around 3 weeks after Leo had been routinely castrated. His behaviour and demeanour corresponded to the indignation that marks the mental picture of Staphysagria. A short course of this remedy in 30c potency resolved the problem.

Figure 14.1   Leo, a cat treated with Staphysagria (see Case study 14.3).

Many other remedies can, of course, be used in the surgical situation. Arnica and Hypericum help with bruising and pain, while other more specific remedies may be indicated depending on the precise procedure. Examples include Bellis perennis for surgery around the pelvic area or where surgery has involved deep muscles (for instance, where a fractured femur has been repaired) and Carbo veg to help with the resuscitation of pups born by caesarean section.

Dystocia is also part of the remit of the veterinarian and again homeopathy can be of immense value. One common problem is that of incomplete cervical dilatation (particularly prevalent in ewes where it is known colloquially as 'ringwomb').

Caulophyllum will often remedy the situation.

General practice veterinary medicine

There is a slow but steady trend in the veterinary profession towards integrating homeopathy into the practice of veterinary medicine, considering each case individually and prescribing whichever form of medicine is best suited to that individual. This may mean the patient receives homeopathy alone, conventional medicine alone, or a combination of the two. Certainly this must be in the best interests of the patient, and provided care is taken that the forms of medicine are compatible, success rates will inevitably be higher using this approach compared to using one modality alone.

The financial realities of general practice have resulted in a system in which consultations for small pet animals such as cats and dogs are rarely afforded more than 10 minutes. This limits the amount of information that can be gathered in order to make a homeopathic prescription and consequently some compromise has to be made. Fortunately acute conditions predominate so a complete understanding of the patient's constitution is rarely needed.

Despite this, it is usually possible to gain some idea of the animal's general demeanour, if only from its behaviour in the consulting room, but the prescription will invariably rest on the major presenting symptom together with those factors linked with it. Concomitant symptoms are of immense value, as are the characteristics of the symptoms. As previously mentioned, 'character of pain' is not available to the veterinary prescriber, though the characteristics of any discharges are. In the case of diarrhoea, owners will often furnish graphic descriptions of the animal's stool, and the powers of observation fostered by a career spent treating non-speaking patients are generally sufficient for the veterinarian to make an accurate assessment of any other local signs.

However it is around the modalities that most such 'local' prescriptions centre, as Case study 14.4 shows. These are factors of which owners are often well aware, and they are generally only too happy to describe them. In fact, one of the joys of homeopathic veterinary practice is that owners are given permission to talk about those very details which would be irritatingly irrelevant to a conventional professional.

 CASE STUDY

Case 14.4 Importance of modalities

Bert was presented to me in a crowded evening surgery. He was a 10-year-old neutered Jack Russell terrier who had been in a road accident 2 weeks beforehand. He had suffered only bruising at the time, and received homeopathic Arnica at the time. He was, however, still stiff and apparently in pain. The owners described very accurately the modalities of 'worse for first movement', but marked 'amelioration on continued movement'. He was also worse on cold damp days. If he lay down after a walk the pain was even worse. These modalities alone were sufficient to prescribe Rhus tox. In order to utilise the broader effect of the low potencies I used it at 6c twice daily for 10 days. There was complete resolution of the symptoms within 2 days.

This approach does require some knowledge of the materia medica; in order to ask the right questions one has to know some of the possible answers! However a logical approach to considering the symptomatology in question will ensure the modalities are found. For instance, with locomotor problems it is the movement modalities that are most important; with skin problems time modalities and those appertaining to bathing are important; with bowel problems character of the stool, time modalities and an assessment of the presence or otherwise of straining (tenesmus) will usually be sufficient.

Causality can also be a relatively quick route to finding the simillimum, and in animals, emotional upsets and vaccination probably represent the two most important issues to bear in mind in this context.

More detailed discussion of the mental and emotional aspect of veterinary prescribing will be found later in the chapter but at this juncture it is sufficient to state the author's belief that animals exhibit the same range of mental and emotional states as those of which their human guardians are capable; the challenge is to interpret their behaviour accurately enough to ascertain them.

In general, any condition arising within a month of a major incident in the history, such as the two factors already mentioned, should be viewed with suspicion, and in general the closer the event, the higher the level of suspicion. However the lag period could be as long as 3 months. See Case study 14.5 for an example of prescribing for a condition relating to grief.

 CASE STUDY

Case 14.5   Emotional prescribing – grief

Ali was a 10-year-old Border collie cross speyed bitch presented with a lick granuloma over the left carpus. She was a highly strung but affectionate dog.

Questioning of the woman owner revealed that she had recently lost her husband and had consequently returned to work as a parttime office manager for the first time for some years. Ali was therefore suffering from a double dose of grief: she had lost one of her lifetime companions and the other was deserting her every day. Based on the aetiology, rather than the pathology, Ignatia 1M produced rapid and complete resolution.

Referral practice: the chronic case

In view of the relative shortage of qualified homeopathic veterinarians, a number of them provide referral services, either as part of a general veterinary practice or from a specialist practice.

The caseload in these circumstances is inevitably comprised almost entirely of chronic disease, with skin and locomotor problems predominating.

The problem of suppression

Commonly, patients have already undergone much conventional treatment and this presents the homeopath with a considerable obstacle: the patient's original symptomatology has effectively been 'buried' under the weight of suppressive medication. This tends to be most marked in the patient with chronic skin disease, as the ubiquitous corticosteroids are particularly efficient at suppressing any vestige of the original remedy state. Courses of antibiotic extending to several weeks exacerbate the problem, and in recent years the widespread use of ciclosporins has added another level to the process.

Not only the symptoms but the patient's character may also be obscured; hence the first object is to clear the picture. In general any attempt to prescribe more specifically in the early stages of homeopathic treatment is likely to fail.

However the initial step is to obtain as complete a history as possible in order to gain some understanding of the process that has brought the patient to the present state of disease. This initial history-taking may give some idea of the disease state before it was suppressed by conventional medicine and moreover may throw light on the causality.

Once again an emotional upset may have been the initiator of the process, but in chronic disease the possible role of overvaccination should also not be overlooked. Despite there being little evidence to support the practice, it has for many years been the fashion to administer booster vaccinations to dogs and cats annually. Critical evaluation of the histories of animals suffering from chronic disease will not uncommonly suggest that the condition has been triggered or exacerbated by an unnecessary vaccination, and it is well to bear this in mind when searching for the appropriate remedy to the case.

Thuja is a prime candidate for use in this situation, but many other remedies are represented under the heading 'ailments from vaccination', Silica and Sulphur being prominent among them. Indeed, it may be that virtually any remedy state may be thus instigated.

The history will also delineate what conventional treatment has been administered. In the case of a referral from another veterinarian, the referral letter and accompanying history will provide this.

The role of tautopathy

If the history suggests that conventional medicine has contributed to the remedy state of the patient as presented, it may be necessary to use tautopathy to remove its effect sufficiently to proceed. Sometimes it is clear that the animal is experiencing a proving of the conventional drug; this is occasionally the case with corticosteroids, whose proving exhibits itchiness and erythema. In such cases the patient may receive cortisone 30c or prednisolone 30c daily, while dosage of the conventional steroid is very gradually reduced. This usually provides at least some relief of the symptoms, along with a clearer picture of the remedy state. Gradually the patient will start to exhibit its character again, and the pathological symptoms will become more precise; perhaps a time modality will reappear, or a symptom will alter to become more distinctive (see also Chapters 3 and 10).

Identifying the miasm

Next it may be prudent to look at the miasmatic nature of the case (see Chapter 3). While the miasmatic make-up of the animal patient *may* be surmised by the mental and emotional state, it is the author's experience that it is more reliable to concentrate on the pathology; thus for example an animal suffering from exostoses and benign tumours might reasonably be classified as sycotic, whereas a dog suffering from atopy with an erythematous rash that comes and goes quickly may be classified as tubercular.

If a strong miasmatic tendency can be identified, the appropriate miasmatic nosode may be administered. Sometimes this may also be the simillimum, but even if it is not, then some resolution of symptoms will occur. Even those that remain may well change slightly but significantly and this may lead to a more specific subsequent prescription.

Bowel nosodes

Even at this stage it may still not be possible to prescribe a homeopathic medicine on the similia principle. There may still be more than one remedy which appears well indicated, and in this case it may be appropriate to prescribe a bowel nosode. Usually the remedies that merit consideration will all fall within the same group, associated with a particular bowel nosode (see Case study 14.6).

Other remedies with a reputation as clearing remedies may also be useful, in particular Sulphur and Nux vomica. In the case of skin diseases, the suppression of symptoms by conventional medicines frequently induces the Sulphur state, so the initial impression of the case may suggest that Sulphur is the indicated remedy. This may be so at the time of the first consultation but it may also be found that Sulphur will only produce a superficial response and sooner or later another remedy picture will appear which necessitates a different remedy. Sulphur also provides another method which may be used for weaning a patient off

CASE STUDY

Case 14.6 Bowel nosode

King was a 5-year-old German Shepherd with a chronic skin disease. Analysis of the history provided the possibility of prescribing Thuja, Lycopodium or Sulphur. All three of these remedies fall within the associated remedies for Morgan Bach. Consequently Morgan Bach 30c was given. b.i.d. for 5 days.

One month later the skin was reported to be 25% better, but King had become rather more dominating of smaller dogs and was occasionally passing flatulent diarrhoea. Lycopodium 1M resolved all the presenting signs.

In contrast Aza was a 9-year-old German Shepherd dog who had been acquired from a rescue kennels some 3 months previously. He was nervous of other dogs but if threatened he would suddenly attack them. He was also suffering from mild conjunctivitis and otitis externa. Aza's medical history was unknown but he had been confined for many months in a garden shed. My colleague had seen him first and had prescribed Ignatia 1M on the basis of his behaviour and the apparent aetiology of grief. One month later he was happier in himself but now itching all over and becoming more difficult to handle. He was developing the habit of running away in the park and refusing to come back. Aza was a lean dog with a good appetite and was quite restless in the consulting room. On the basis of his miasmatic picture I prescribed Tuberculinum 1M as a single divided dose (1 tablet morning and night for 3 doses only). One month later his skin, eye and ears were much better, but he was tending to become more dominant. At that point I prescribed Lycopodium 1M, which set in process a gradual improvement in his temperament, but with a slight worsening of his skin condition.

Finally a 5-day course of Morgan Bach 30c effected a complete resolution.

---

corticosteroids. The author's strategy is to administer Sulphur in low potency (usually 6c or 12x) on a continual basis while concurrently reducing the steroid dosage.

Following such an approach another remedy state will gradually become apparent and a second prescription can be made which will far more closely resemble the fundamental remedy state of the patient.

There are of course some chronic cases where it is possible to prescribe on totality or constitution from the start, but even then there are hurdles to overcome which are unique to veterinary homeopathy, as detailed below.

Using the 'mentals' chapter in the Repertory

There is a problem in attempting to ascertain the mental symptoms in a species which is non-speaking, and in which there is a social hierarchy and set of behavioural norms which differ markedly from those under which the human being operates. The use of the repertory in such circumstances is problematical.

The solution to these dilemmas lies in the following:

- It is necessary to understand the normal behaviour for a member of that species, for instance the pack mentality of the domestic dog.
- It is necessary to assume that animals are capable of experiencing the same range of emotions as their human counterparts. Case study 14.7 is a good example of this.

 CASE STUDY

Case 14.7 Prescribing using mentals (1)
Eric, a 10-year-old female (!) neutered cat had recently started to spray urine around the house. Conventional hormonal treatment had been ineffective. The history revealed that the behaviour had commenced after a new tomcat had arrived in the garden and seemed intent on taking over Eric's patch. Based on the rubric 'mind – indignation' the remedy Staphysagria was selected and administered in 1M potency as a single divided dose. The new cat was subsequently allowed to dominate the garden but Eric let go of his need to mark the house and accepted his position in the hierarchy.

- One may have to be somewhat creative and imaginative in transcribing behavioural traits in an animal to a human repertory. For instance if a dog buries bones it may be appropriate to use the rubric 'fear of poverty'.
- It may be possible for the prescriber to use the psychodynamics of the consultation to intuit some of the emotions involved. For instance, Digger was an old Labrador dog who was going stiff and weak on his back legs. There were no obvious modalities, and little in the way of homeopathic mentals and generals, but as he entered the waiting room I felt immediately and intensely sympathetic towards him. Not surprisingly he responded well to Causticum (Mind – sympathetic).
- In the author's experience owners are remarkably perceptive about their animals and can be quite specific in their language (see Case 14.8).

> **CASE STUDY**
>
> ---
>
> **Case 14.8   Prescribing using mentals (2)**
> Tiger had suffered from recurrent abscesses as the result of fighting with another cat. He had responded to Hepar sulph and Silica but after the last episode was still acting fearfully and in a strange way, and not eating properly. The owner described his behaviour in this way: 'He suddenly looks across the room and then races off up the stairs – it's just like he's being chased by a ghost'. Using the rubric 'mind – delusions – spectres: is pursued by', I chose the remedy Stramonium. A short course of this remedy in 30c potency returned him to normal.

Interpretation of general symptoms

The interpretation of general symptoms in animals can also be subjective, depending on the circumstances. For instance, it is not always easy to ascertain clear heat modalities. Owners' answers will often be equivocal and they may be unclear as to whether their animal is a 'heat-seeker' or a 'cool-seeker'. Indeed, in order to obtain an accurate understanding of such a symptom it may be necessary to pose the question in more than one way, such as:

- Where does he lie in winter when it is cold?
- How long will he lie in the sun before he seeks the shade?
- What about the midday sun on a hot summer's day?
- Does he lie near to a heat source or right on top of it?

Similarly, thirst can be difficult to be accurate about: it will always be increased if dried foods are fed, compared to tinned food or a natural diet. Some species such as sheep and cats may naturally drink very little anyway. However some animals will prefer water from specific sources such as ponds or streams and this may be a pointer to certain remedies.

Measures of appetite may also be less than reliable. Many dogs appear to be greedy, as a normal state of being, and will readily consume putrefying food, yet sometimes they will fast for a day or two by choice; in contrast it is not uncommon for cats to be extremely fastidious with regard to what they will eat.

Specific food desires are rarely very significant in animals, though 'desire for indigestible things' may be a reliable rubric, so long as it is appreciated that the eating of the faeces of other species is normal canine behaviour and even the habit of eating one's own faeces is far less significant in that species than in humans. Nearly every dog likes cheese and sweet things; most cats like milk. Food aversions may, however, be more helpful; a cat that does not like fish or a dog who does not like meat is exhibiting significant symptomatology.

With both these factors a *change* of preference, especially if it is sudden, must be afforded more weight in the analysis.

In view of the foregoing, it can be seen that prescribing on totality may not always be as accurate in animals as it is in the human patient, however the success rates of experienced veterinary homeopaths attest to the fact that given patience and understanding it is possible to prescribe on this level with sufficient confidence to afford reliable results.

A veterinary repertory

In a further attempt to overcome these problems veterinarians world-wide are involved in more than one project to develop a comprehensive veterinary repertory. At present these projects consist of making additions to the existing human computer repertories. These may comprise the addition of remedies to existing rubrics, marked as being of veterinary origin, or the incorporation of new rubrics of veterinary relevance such as 'buries bones'. At the time of writing these projects are still in the relatively early stages of development but they are certain to become more relevant as they progress. All such projects are bound to suffer from the drawback that veterinary additions can only deal with objective symptoms and behaviour, whereas many successful prescriptions are made after an imaginative use of the repertory in interpreting the observations of owner or veterinarian. Consequently, while there is no doubt that such repertories represent an enormous advance in the practice of homeopathy it is unlikely that a comprehensive, purely veterinary repertory will ever be created.

Constitutional prescribing in animals

Whenever there is chronic disease, veterinary homeopath, like their medical counterparts, will usually strive to prescribe on a constitutional level. This concept is particularly valuable in this field, as it adds another dimension to the information which can be added to the analysis in a case which may otherwise be lacking in reliable symptoms. Indeed it is often easier to ascertain the characteristic mental and general states appertaining to the patient's constitution (i.e. when the patient is well) than to find any such symptoms associated specifically with the disease state. Historical information may also be useful in this context, though one should be aware that only a small number of animal patients retain the same homeopathic constitution throughout their lives.

One example of a constitutional prescription was that given in Case 14.9.

 CASE STUDY

Case 14.9 Constitutional prescribing

Sam, a 10-year-old Labrador retriever, is shown in Figure 14.2. He was presented for treatment of his arthritis. On examination his joints were swollen, there being exostoses on all the major joints. He had several lipomas, and countless warts all over his body. Sam loved to sit facing the stove, with his nose close to the oven door. He had a prodigious appetite, with no obvious food preferences, and would sometimes lick cement. He was overweight, sluggish and lazy, and had been so all his life. He was quite open and friendly, had never been in a fight but did seem to get anxious if he thought he was going to be left alone. He was not keen on exercise and was reluctant to leave the house, especially if it was raining. However he did like swimming. He loved to be cuddled by the two small children in the house. There were no strong modalities to the stiffness apart from the fact that he was a little worse when he had been lying down, and correspondingly limbered up when he had got moving. Without the characteristics which made up his constitution, it would be very difficult to pick one homeopathic remedy for Sam; however when his constitutional picture was taken into account it would be difficult to prescribe anything but Calc carb. A short course of that remedy in a 30C potency saw a marked improvement in his gait, and less reluctance to go for a walk.

Constitution and breed

All domestic animals are the product of selective breeding and this has resulted in groups of individuals conforming to a particular homeo-

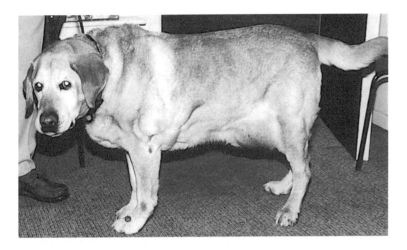

Figure 14.2 Sam, prescribed Calc carb (see Case study 14.9).

pathic constitution. Sam is a good example of this (Figure 14.2). The very attributes that mark him as Calc carb. in constitution are the same ones that are recognisable in most Labrador retrievers. One can easily understand why, if one's aim is to develop an animal whose primary function is to stay at home and be an integral part of the family, one would tend to select out those individuals who exhibit the Calc carb. constitution. Similarly if one is attempting to breed a large horse who is easy-going, steady and strong, one would select the same type of individuals to produce the Calc carb. constitution as represented by the Shire horse.

There is a danger, however, in taking this concept too far in terms of homeopathic prescribing. There are, for instance, many Labradors who do not exhibit the Calc carb. constitution; moreover, given a sufficiently strong deranging force, an animal exhibiting a Calc carb. constitution may develop a totally different remedy state, and this is always something worth remembering when considering constitutional prescriptions.

There is often debate as to how strongly one should weight an individual's characteristics when they are reflections of the breed type, rather than of the individual. The author's opinion is that these characteristics are nevertheless an essential part of the individual's make-up and hence should be given appropriate significance. More important, however, would be any characteristics that go against the breed norm.

Other considerations in veterinary homeopathy

Administration of medicines to animals

As with humans, the preferred route of administration of homeopathy in animals is by mouth, though less reliance is placed on absorption from the oral mucosa. Lactose tablets are usually well accepted by dogs, though cats may be more reluctant, and most owners are capable of developing the skill of tipping a tablet into the lid of the container, thus avoiding touching it personally, and tossing the tablet down the animal's throat. Sucrose pillules tend to stick to the tongue less readily and will roll down a cat's throat more easily. Failing this, liquid remedies may be prepared, and administered to the oral mucosa by lifting the animal's upper lip. As a last resort the tablet may be crushed and added to food or milk. While this is not ideal and there is always the risk of antidoting the remedy, it does usually seem to be effective. Occasionally injections may be used, and, in emergency care, remedies may be added to an intravenous drip. Horses may also be dosed by using tablets, either whole or crushed to a powder, if necessary hiding them in an apple or other bland foodstuff such as bread to facilitate the process.

In farm animals there are financial and logistical reasons why it may not be practicable to dose animals individually. Not only is it time-consuming, but the stress of collecting animals together may be an important factor in causing exacerbation of symptoms. This could be critical, for instance, in the case of a group of calves suffering from pneumonia. For these reasons the preferred method may be to mix a liquid remedy into the drinking water, either in individual troughs or in the header tank which supplies them. The rate of 10 ml liquid remedy per trough is a commonly used rule of thumb in these cases. Interestingly there does seem to be a dose-related effect associated with this, in that there is a limit to how large a body of water can be medicated by a single dose of the remedy. Too much dilution and the effect of the remedy appears to wane, so while little specific work has been done to shed light on this issue, it would seem inadvisable to stretch the limits too far.

This method may be used wherever there are a number of animals that all need to be treated with the same remedy, such as in a boarding kennels or in a herd of dairy cows. In such a situation, however, it is necessary to be aware of the effect of environmental conditions. Sunshine, for instance, will rapidly inactivate a medicated trough of water; if outside troughs are to be used, it may be necessary to erect some shading.

In dairy cattle an alternative route of administration is to spray the remedy into the vulva. The remedy is added to water contained in a garden hand spray bottle and a dose sprayed into the vulva as the cow waits in the milking parlour. The same apparatus may be used to spray the noses of sheep – this is often the preferred method in this species as the animals often drink little.

Posology

There seem to be differences in the way that animals respond to homeopathic remedies when compared to their human counterparts.

While single (or single divided) doses of high-potency preparations do seem to be effective in animals, lower potencies often seem to need more frequent repetition. For this reason, if for instance the 30c potency has been selected, many veterinary homeopaths will commence treatment with a course lasting 5–7 days, rather than the single dose which a medical homeopath might have chosen.

The reason for this difference has been attributed either to the higher metabolic rate of the smaller animals, or to the fact that the majority of domestic pets have been neutered. Weight is lent to the former explanation by the author's experience that birds and very small animals such as guinea pigs certainly seem to require much more frequent repetition of remedies than even dogs and cats.

Another species difference encountered is that horses appear to be far more sensitive to homeopathic remedies than any other species. Exactly why this should be so is also a matter for debate, but horses exhibit very coherent remedy pictures and this may aid the veterinarian to prescribe more accurately than in the smaller animals. By and large the horse as a species is subjected to far fewer conventional drugs than are small animals; antibiotics are used less regularly, corticosteroid therapy is relatively rare, and vaccines contain fewer and less virulent components. Added to this, equine nutrition still remains relatively more natural than in dogs and cats. It may be a combination of these factors which explain this phenomenon.

Prescribing for groups of animals

Most farm animals are kept in groups in one way or another – they may be housed or kept at pasture – and disease will usually affect more than one animal in the group. Prescribing homeopathic remedies for these groups presents its own difficulties.

Constitutional remedy for group

Occasionally selective breeding results in a herd of animals, all of which exhibit the same constitution. The health problems from which these animals suffer may be linked to the constitution, in which case all the members of the group may be treated with the same constitutional remedy. This situation may occur in a herd of dairy cows where the owner has a preference for a particular type of cow – the preference may be linked to production, so it is not uncommon for such a herd to exhibit a preponderance of heavy-boned Calc carb. constitution cows. These would be high-yielding and even-tempered, though they may not necessarily be the most efficient milk producers, having a large body mass to maintain. Another farmer may prefer Calc phos. types as these may be similar in yield but, being lean, may be more efficient at converting food to milk. They will also be quicker in and out of the parlour. However they may well be more difficult to deal with, exhibiting the Calc phos. irritability and restlessness which may make them less pleasant to milk. In such circumstances, for instance if the level of mastitis in the herd becomes unacceptable, it may be possible to help by simply administering a dose of the constitutional remedy.

This technique is appropriate to any species, as the Case study 14.10 shows.

In such a homogeneous group of animals the administration of the constitutional remedy may prove generally beneficial even if the symptoms themselves do not correspond to the constitutional remedy.

 **CASE STUDY**

Case 14.10 The use of a common constitutional remedy for a group of dogs
Mrs M had a pack of Siberian huskies which she used for sled racing. All 8 of them exhibited the same tubercular constitution. They exhibited various manifestations of the miasm and its associated remedy Tuberculinum bovinum, varying from bouts of chronic diarrhoea to upper respiratory disease and 2 cases of eosinophilic granuloma of the mouth. Each time one of these conditions arose she would give the dog involved a dose of Tub. bov. 200c. Often this was enough to treat the condition effectively; sometimes a follow-up (usually tubercular) remedy was necessary and occasionally some complementary conventional medicine was necessary to complete the cure.

In a group of more disparate individuals it is necessary to use other techniques.

Multiple prescribing

In a group of calves suffering from pneumonia, there may be a range of symptoms exhibited, corresponding to two, three or even four separate homeopathic remedies. This probably depends on the virulence of the organism, and its consequent ability to impose the pattern of the genus epidemicus on any individual. Thus our pen of pneumonic calves may contain some individuals exhibiting the remedy state of Bryonia, some of Antimonium tart., and some of Phosphorus. It will probably not be feasible to administer the indicated remedy to each individual. The compromise is to mix the three remedies together and give the resulting complex to the whole group. This form of multiple prescribing can be extremely effective, but should be distinguished from the practice of using 'off-the-shelf' commercial mixtures, which may contain a large number of remedies, not selected specifically for the group. While such commercial complexes seem to be helpful in a large number of cases, it is the experience of many veterinarians that a complex formulated specifically for a group of animals is more effective.

Totality of group

A group of animals that spend sufficient time together are capable of acting as a single individual – this is exhibited with striking clarity by colonies of ants and hives of bees – and from a homeopathic point of view the same can apply to a group of animals, particularly if they have been reared as such. In these cases it is possible to collect all the diverse symptoms exhibited by the individual members of the group and consider the group as a single patient. Use of the repertory will help in identifying a single remedy to cover all the symptoms and this may then be administered to the whole group. As the group is functioning as a single individual, even those animals whose symptoms do not fall within the materia medica of the remedy will benefit to some extent. Those who fail to resolve completely can be treated individually at follow-up.

Isopathy

The use of isopathy obviates the need to consider the symptomatology at all. For this reason the use of nosodes is a mainstay of homeopathy in farm animals. It is in any case necessary to make a specific diagnosis before any homeopathic treatment is commenced in an animal, this being standard good veterinary practice whatever form of treatment is to be considered. The identification of a specific disease makes it possible to use a nosode, either produced from disease products of the patient itself (autonosode) or of a member of the group to be treated (isonosode). These types of nosode seem to provide the best results; however the major homeopathic pharmacies (in the UK at least) stock a number of ready-prepared nosodes (general nosodes) which may also be very effective. One of the major advantages of the latter is the speed with which they may be procured; in addition a general nosode is likely to prove less costly than one prepared from an individual specimen. In addition to the general nosodes which have been developed from cases of disease, there are also a number of potentised remedies that have been developed from pure cultures. These pathodes, as they are sometimes termed, can be used in a similar way (see also Chapter 10).

Mulitlevel prescribing

With the uncertainties inherent in prescribing for a group of farm animals, veterinarians will often opt to combine these approaches. For instance, in a group of piglets suffering from diarrhoea after weaning, the regimen may include a remedy that covers the causality of grief (e.g. Phos acid), a remedy based on the clinical signs and a nosode. This is sometimes termed a 'layered' approach.

Other uses of isopathy

Strictly, isopathic medicine is a system distinct from homeopathy; however some would see it as a vital apart of the armamentarium of the homeopathic veterinarian, so to omit to mention it would be to present an incomplete picture of veterinary homeopathy. The use of nosodes as referred to above can be applied to many disease situations, as follows.

In clinical disease

Some caution should be exercised in this situation, as troublesome aggravations may be encountered. This is particularly relevant in the case of subclinical mastitis in a dairy herd. The accepted measure of level of udder health in a herd of dairy cattle is the somatic cell count. The cell count also has a bearing on the suitability of the milk for human consumption. Generally it must be below 250 000/ml to escape penalties from the milk wholesaler. The administration of a mastitis nosode to a herd of dairy cows may cause a transient rise in the cell count before the beneficial effect is observed; there may also be a transient increase in the number of clinical cases in the herd. This is significant for obvious reasons. Indeed, if this response is too dramatic, the exercise may have to be delayed while other management changes are made to improve udder health generally. Nosodes, then, do need to be used cautiously if there is active disease present. However trials in this area have certainly shown the effectiveness of the approach.[1, 2]

Prevention of disease

There seems little doubt that nosodes can be effective in reducing morbidity in an outbreak of disease. Day published an account of the use of a kennel cough nosode in a boarding kennels suffering an outbreak of this disease: when an isonosode was administered to all incoming dogs, the incidence fell dramatically.[3] Saxton demonstrated a similar effect using Distemper nosode in a welfare kennels.[4]

What is more controversial is the issue as to whether nosodes are effective in preventing enzootic disease when administered in a predetermined regime. It has become common practice among veterinary homeopaths to administer nosodes based on the same range of infectious diseases as those against which animals are routinely vaccinated. In the case of dogs, these include Distemper, Infectious Canine Hepatitis, Parvovirus and Leptospirosis. A trial performed on canine parvovirus in USA showed no protective effect but the numbers involved were small and the trial has not been repeated.[5] Conversely, rats exposed to the spirochaete which causes tularaemia in that species were afforded a 30% protection rate by pretreatment with an isopathic nosode.[6] Whatever the relative merits of these trials may be, the practice of using nosodes as a substitute for conventional vaccination is relatively widespread among veterinary homeopaths and only rarely are problems reported in the form of 'breakdowns' of protection. However this whole issue is contentious, even between homeopaths, and a great deal more research is required to make the true value of the procedure clear.

Obstacles to cure in animals

While Hahnemann exhorted the aspiring homeopath to ensure that obstacles to cure were removed, it is unlikely that even he could have foreseen what this might mean for the modern veterinary homeopath.

Diet

Living as we do in an age of convenience, it is perhaps not surprising that the owners of our animal patients have been persuaded to feed their animals on processed concoctions of animal and industrial byproducts rather than the fresh foods for which they have evolved. Sadly the veterinary profession has been seduced into colluding with the feed manufacturers, not only recommending, but actually selling these products. However a critical view of the whole concept of a dried and pelleted product being fed as an exclusive diet will expose the lack of logic in it. It seems unlikely that scientists sufficiently understand the minutiae of the nutrition of humans, never mind of animals, to formulate a diet which supplies all the nutrients necessary for optimum health; any minute deficiency in the food is compounded as time goes on and new nutritional requirements are continually being discovered. Secondly, given the decline in nutritive value inherent in the processes, it is not logical to suggest that subjecting the ingredients to cooking, extrusion under pressure and a considerable period of storage can produce anything but a suboptimal product. Thirdly, commercial dog and cat foods are often formulated from cheap, poor-quality ingredients even before the process begins.

This being so, the feeding of processed dry foods to dogs and cats may represent a major obstacle to cure and in the author's opinion every effort should be made to change the diet gradually to one made of fresh raw ingredients, such as described by Ian Billinghurst in his book *Give Your Dog a Bone.*[7]

Similar issues are represented in other species; in the case of high-yielding food-producing animals it may not be possible to effect a change in management, due to economics, but the prescriber needs at least to be aware of the problems this may represent.

Overvaccination

It has been standard practice for many years to vaccinate dogs, cats and horses annually, despite there being little scientific evidence to support the practice. Despite this lack of evidence, the recommendations of the vaccine companies, coupled with the reliance of most veterinary practices on the income thus generated, have resulted in enormous resistance from the profession as a whole to moves to effect a change in the policy. While there are as yet no figures to support the assertion, it is the opinion of many veterinary homeopaths that much of the chronic disease that is seen in our patients is caused, or at the very least exacerbated by, overvaccination. Certainly the symptoms of atopic dermatitis, colitis and epilepsy frequently appear to be aggravated by annual vaccinations. In such patients in particular the recommendation will usually be made to suspend vaccinating them; in any case this is supported by the datasheet recommendation that only healthy animals should be vaccinated.

In general terms, there are signs that the profession is steadily moving towards a more enlightened policy on the use of vaccines, in particular in the case of dogs and cats, but progress is slow and in the UK only a tiny minority of practices seem to have taken note of the recommendations of some highly authoritative figures in this field. Nevertheless, with the advent of viable alternatives such as the regular measurement of antibody titre levels, and the observation that protective levels in vaccinated animals persist for several years, there is hope that this obstacle to cure may become of less significance in the future.

Environmental factors

Other obstacles to cure can reside within the household, or with the management system imposed on the animal. Severe training regimes of performance animals or stressful situations within the pet animal's home may have to be addressed before homeopathic treatment can have its optimum effect.

Owner–animal interactions

It has long been recognised by many veterinary homeopaths that as soon as a prescription is made the owner often remarks 'that is precisely the remedy my homeopath gave me last week' or 'I often take that remedy'. This happens so often that some veterinarians, the author among them, have started to investigate whether this phenomenon may be useful, either to the veterinarian or to the owner's homeopathic practitioner. Certainly it is the author's experience that, when faced with the common dilemma of which of a number of remedies to prescribe, recourse to the owner's homeopathic history may prove useful in making the decision. It is not always appropriate for the veterinarian to delve into the owner's medical and emotional history, but where a suitable atmosphere of trust has been established additional information of significant importance may be revealed. Naturally experiences of bereavement are likely to result in both owner and patient exhibiting similar remedy states, though just how accurately one may reflect the other is often quite surprising. Suffice it to say that in a case of chronic disease, where a close relationship between animal and owner can be established, if there is no correspondence between the remedy states, and particularly the constitution, of owner and animal, the prescription may be viewed as uncertain.

Homeopathic training in the veterinary profession

Veterinary prescribing presents a number of challenges over and above those which the medical homeopath faces. The adage 'they can't talk, can they?' takes on additional significance when one is attempting to prescribe homeopathically. The individual best placed to overcome these challenges is the registered veterinary surgeon who has undergone additional training in homeopathy. In this context it is worth mentioning that it is in any case illegal for anyone except a registered veterinary surgeon to treat animals with homeopathy. It is to be hoped that the foregoing will have provided some understanding of the reason for this protection; it is only with the benefit of a thorough training in veterinary medicine that the unique difficulties encountered in veterinary homeopathy can be effectively overcome.

At present there are three teaching centres in the UK accredited by the Faculty of Homeopathy to teach veterinarians to Vet MFHom level. They are the homeopathic hospitals of Glasgow and Bristol, and the Homeopathic Professionals Teaching Group, based in Oxford. The latter also runs courses for veterinarians overseas. At the time of writing there are more than 70 Veterinary Members and Fellows of the Faculty, most of them resident in the UK, but also in Australasia, South Africa, Ireland and the USA. While the need for such qualified veterinary homeopaths continues to grow, this means that no animal in the UK should be denied the benefits of homeopathic treatment. Similar qualifications exist in other parts of the world, notably the certificate awarded by the International Association for Veterinary Homeopathy, based mainly in continental Europe, and the Diploma of the Academy of Homeopathy in USA, see also Chapter 9.

Conclusion

Veterinary homeopathy is thriving and growing apace on a global scale. Its popularity attests to its efficacy and to the success of the methods used by its practitioners. It will surely not be long before it takes its rightful place as a form of medicine practised as a first-line treatment, in an integrated approach to veterinary medicine. This will afford our animal patients the very best that veterinary care can provide.

References

1.	Day C. Clinical trials in bovine mastitis using nosodes for prevention. *Int J Vet Hom* 1986; 1: 15.
2.	Day C. *The Homoeopathic Treatment of Beef and Dairy Cattle*. Beaconsfield, UK: Beaconsfield, 1995.
3.	Day C. Isopathic prevention of kennel cough. *Int J Vet Hom* 1987; 2: 57.
4.	Saxton J. Use of distemper nosode in disease control. *Int J Vet Hom* 1991; 15: 8.
5.	Larson L, Wynn S, Schultz R D. A canine parvovirus nosode study. *Proceedings of 2nd Midwest Holistic Veterinary Conference* 1996.
6.	Jonas W B. Do homeopathic nosodes protect against infection? An experimental test. *Altern Ther Health Med* 1999; 5: 36–40.
7.	Billinghurst I. *Give Your Dog a Bone*. Bathurst, Australia: Billinghurst, 1993.

Further reading

Allport R (2000) *Heal Your Cat the Natural Way*. London: Mitchell Beazley.
Allport R (2000) *Heal Your Dog the Natural Way*. London: Mitchell Beazley.
Allport R (2001) *Natural Healthcare for Pets*. Glasgow: Harper Collins (Element).
Couzens T (2007) *Homeopathy for Horses*. Shrewsbury, UK: Kenilworth Press.
Day C (1995) *The Homeopathic Treatment of Beef and Dairy Cattle*. Beaconsfield, UK: Beaconsfield.
Day C (1998) *The Homoeopathic Treatment of Small Animals*. Saffron Walden, UK: CW Daniel.
Hunter F (2004) *Everyday Homeopathy for Animals*. Beaconsfield, UK: Beaconsfield.
Saxton J, Gregory P (2005) *Textbook of Veterinary Homeopathy*. Beaconsfield, UK: Beaconsfield.

15

Practising homeopathy in a multiethnic community – a personal view

Cleve McIntosh

Introduction

In this chapter the application of homeopathy in a rural setting in South Africa will be described.

My setting

I work in a rural part of South Africa near a village called Acornhoek, close to the Kruger National Park and the border with Mozambique (Figure 15.1). Public healthcare in South Africa is solely allopathic and there is no formal integration of homeopathy. I am employed within the government health system as a clinic doctor. Depending on patients' needs, I offer them either donated homeopathic medication or allopathic medication provided by the clinic, or both.

Each day I visit a different clinic, some as far as 50 km from the local hospital. The clinics are busy, seeing up to 5000 patients each month. The severe shortage of doctors in public healthcare, particularly in rural areas, means that clinics are staffed by nurses who assess patients and then prescribe. Only patients with complex problems and who are not responding to allopathic treatment are referred to me as the visiting doctor. As in many rural areas, everyone functions at a level higher than his or her position; nurses function as general practitioners while the doctor functions as a consultant.[1]

All the patients are black and speak Sesotho or Xitsonga; only a few are able to speak English. They live in two former *homelands* which were created by the former apartheid regime in the 1960s when black South Africans were forcibly removed from their homes and densely resettled according to their ethnic background in *homelands* where there were few employment opportunities or basic infrastructure such as electricity or clean water. They were only permitted to leave these

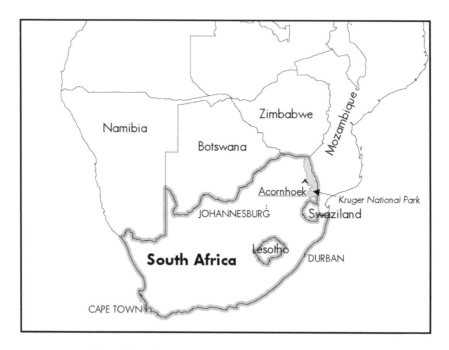

Figure 15.1 Map of Southern Africa.

areas if they had proof of employment elsewhere and were required to leave their families behind and become migrant workers.

Although apartheid ended more than 10 years ago and South Africa is now a democratic country, the social disruption and the poverty resulting from the homeland system still impact directly on the lives of many of my patients. Malnutrition, human immunodeficiency virus (HIV), acquired immunodeficiency syndrome (AIDS) and other preventable diseases are extremely common. Many have very little education and are unemployed, relying on relatives who are either employed or receive monthly government grants for disability or old age. Frequently 10 or more people are dependent on one person who receives a monthly wage or government grant of less than 1000 South African rands (less than £100 per month) (see Figure 15.2).

Integrating homeopathy

When I started working here 5 years ago, there were many challenges to providing even basic healthcare. There was an ongoing problem with the supply of allopathic medication. Patients who had chronic illnesses

Figure 15.2 Woman going to collect water.

such as hypertension or diabetes mellitus, who were finally well controlled on their allopathic treatment, would travel far only to find their
medication out of stock. Basic diagnostic tests, such as urine dipsticks
or fingerprick glucose tests, and even equipment to check blood pressure, were sometimes unavailable. Practising allopathic medicine was
extremely difficult without these basic investigations or a consistent
supply of allopathic medication.

Despite the frustrations, I realised that I could still help patients
with homeopathy. When allopathic medication or diagnostic investigations were not available at the clinics and patients could not afford the
transport to or the fees at the local hospital, I would offer them homeopathic treatment. I saw dramatic results with homeopathic treatment
which increased my confidence in homeopathy more and more. As a
result I offered homeopathy to more patients, particularly those on
long-term allopathic medication who were not improving or those at
risk of potentially severe side-effects from allopathic treatment. Case
study 15.1 provides an example.

Clinic staff and homeopathy

When I started offering homeopathic treatment to clinic patients (see
Figure 15.3) I expected the nurses to be wary of medicines with which

 **CASE STUDY**

Case 15.1 Dementia

One of the first patients I treated homeopathically was Khizose, an 83-year-old woman who was dementing. She had no idea where she was or who I was during the consultation. For the previous 2 years she had been walking around her house and shouting all night, keeping her whole family awake, and she was verbally aggressive. She was convinced that people were following her and that there were worms and mosquitoes on her body, which made her scratch herself. Her daughter pleaded for something that would allow her family to sleep at night.

Sitting in on the consultation were three final-year medical students doing their rural public health rotation. They had just completed their psychiatric rotations so I asked them what they would advise. They appropriately recommended starting her on a low-dose antipsychotic to sedate her at night. On the rare occasion that we have antipsychotics available at the clinic, it is only the typical or older-generation antipsychotics such as haloperidol. We discussed the side-effects of these antipsychotics in the elderly and the increased likelihood of these side-effects because she would probably need lifelong treatment. We all agreed that if there was an effective and safer option we should use that first, only using a long-term antipsychotic as a last resort. Khizose's behaviour was better when she had company and she had developed a marked craving for sugar since she had become ill. I gave her three powders of Phosphorus 30c to be taken over the next 3 days.

Her daughter returned the following week to say she couldn't believe the change in her mother. Khizose was now sleeping 6 hours each night, giving her family hours of much-needed rest. She still had some auditory hallucinations and would talk alone, but was very much more manageable and the auditory hallucinations seemed less frequent and less distressing. Khizose's daughter did not mention any aggressiveness, nor that Khizose was scratching herself any longer and was satisfied that the most disturbing of her mother's symptoms were now much better. Her daughter asked if she could please have more powders, so that she could continue giving them to her mother. I pointed out that, despite taking only 3 powders, Khizose had slept each night for a whole week and had improved generally. I explained that homeopathic treatment did not always need to be taken long-term as it addressed the cause of the problem. I gave her 5 more powders of Phosporus 30c to use only if Khizose deteriorated again, advising her to return if she needed more. Several years later, she has never come back and one of the clinic nurses who stays close to Khizose told me that both Khizose and her family are still sleeping well at night.

Figure 15.3 Queue of patients outside clinic.

they weren't familiar, yet the response was quite the opposite. Perhaps because they had worked with me for some time and I had treated many of them before, there was a level of trust between us and they were completely open to it. They came to consult about health problems they or their family members had which had not responded to allopathic treatment. The improvement they saw in themselves and in patients with chronic refractory problems gave them confidence in homeopathic medicine and quite soon senior nursing managers from all over the area were coming for homeopathic treatment.

Asania, an effervescent nurse who each morning preaches a sermon and gives a health talk to patients in the waiting room, consulted about urinary incontinence she'd been having since menopause. We discussed the option of hormonal therapies, as well as the associated risks. She decided first to use homeopathic treatment, and was delighted when her chronic urinary incontinence resolved completely on Lachesis. 'It was very embarrassing when my husband and I woke up and I had wet the bed. But now it's gone.'

At another clinic, Tiva, the bright and friendly cleaning woman, had suffered for several years from painful arthritis in both hands. The pain and stiffness were sometimes so severe that she could not use her hands or work at all for several days. When she could use her hands, she

Figure 15.4 Tiva cooking vuswa.

would go to great efforts to heat water as she found it intolerable to handwash linen, clothes and crockery in cold water. After 3 doses of Phosphorus 30c and one of Tuberculinum bovinum 200c, she was completely painfree. More than a year later she still shows her gratitude by cooking lunch for me each time I visit the clinic. She always prepares the local specialty she knows I love, *vuswa na miroho na timanga* (Figure 15.4). *Miroho*, the indigenous wild spinach, is boiled with locally grown peanuts, tomatoes and onions. It is eaten with the local staple, *vuswa*, which is finely ground corn cooked into a thick paste. Delicious!

Medication

A homeopathic dispensary of medicated granules of several hundred different remedies in varying potencies, mostly 30c, and a few in 200c and 1M, was donated to the clinics. I visit each clinic with a mobile dispensary containing very small bottles of medicated granules which I refill regularly. This mobile dispensary allows me to prescribe any one of several hundred remedies while visiting different clinics. I add medicated granules to unmedicated powders and give each patient an average of 3 powders. This keeps the cost of each prescription below 1 South

African rand (£0.08 or €0.11). It is essential that it remains cheap because all treatment is provided free of charge at government clinics and some patients could not afford to pay even if there was a small fee.

When visiting a doctor or a clinic, most patients expect to given at least 3 or 4 different sachets of pills. When I give them only 3 doses of homeopathic medication, they are usually very sceptical that it will help. They often ask where the rest of the treatment is. However, once they experience the results their perspectives change completely. Thereafter, even if they are given vitamins, botanicals or allopathic medication, they are not satisfied unless they get a homeopathic powder.

Some patients, for example, those with osteoarthritis, sciatica or epilepsy, seem to need repeated or daily doses to control their symptoms effectively. Yet it was not financially sustainable to provide patients with their own bottle of granules or daily powders. I then advise patients to dissolve one medicated powder in 1 litre of clean water and take one teaspoon of this solution as necessary. Initially I was not sure how well this would work but I didn't have any other affordable options for giving repeated doses. However, since using this system I have had a number of experiences which have convinced me of its efficacy (see Case study 15.2).

 **CASE STUDY**

Case 15.2 Epilepsy

Silas, a 15-year-old boy (see Figure 15.5), had been in status epilepticus for several hours many years before and ever since had been profoundly learning-disabled with spastic paraplegia. His epilepsy was still severe and poorly controlled. He had frequent seizures, sometimes as many as 10 each day, despite adequate blood levels of allopathic anticonvulsants. He never seemed to recover from one seizure before he had another. I continued the allopathic anticonvulsants he was taking but added homeopathic treatment. The opisthotonic positions he was in while fitting, together with the fact that when I first saw him, he seemed either to be fitting or in a sedated dream-like state the whole day, prompted me to start him on Cicuta virosa. The frequency of his seizures improved dramatically. Later, when his seizures seemed to be precipitated by him sensing that someone around him was angry and becoming angry himself, Nux vomica followed well. His seizures then became even less frequent but they increased in intensity, which led me to

(continued overleaf)

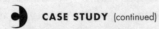

CASE STUDY (continued)

Cuprum metallicum. Over several months he became more alert, showed an interest in what was happening around him, stopped drooling, made eye contact and recognised family members. His mother said, 'If strangers come to the house now, his face looks so bright and he looks so well they would not even know his mind was not right'. The community rehabilitation worker who visited Silas regularly, giving him basic occupational therapy and physiotherapy, described his improvement as miraculous and decided to order a wheelchair for him, so that his mother could take him out of the house more often now that he was so much better.

Silas' mother is illiterate and innumerate and has no idea how many seizures he has each day. To her the numbers don't mean anything and whenever I asked about his seizure frequency she would just talk about how much better Silas was generally. Fortunately, Silas' elder sister is literate and kept a record of his seizures for me. On homeopathic treatment, his seizure frequency reduced steadily over several months from up to 10 per day down to 2 seizures per month. Each day he took one teaspoon from a litre of water into which medicated granules of Cuprum 9cH had been dissolved. Whenever the Cuprum solution was finished, he would start having 4 seizures a day, but would improve again as soon as it was restarted. When I asked his mother why she did not come back for more medication when Silas had more seizures, she explained that she could not always afford the cost of the transport to the clinic and there was sometimes no one available to watch her home while she was out as she had no locks on any of her doors.

Bewitchment

It is quite unnecessary for a doctor serving the patients I do to have malpractice insurance. The doctor is hardly ever blamed when a patient dies because most patients believe that disease and death are caused by bewitchment. Most relatives of the deceased, even when they are nurses, never even ask about the cause of death. Sometimes surviving family members appreciate an explanation when it is offered, but rarely embrace the western explanatory models of illness. Family members seem to be thinking, 'Yes, he did have a lung infection, but that isn't why he died. He only got a lung infection and died because someone bewitched him.'

Patients are often unsure who is bewitching them or why or at times may blame a family member or someone else in their community. Occasionally it is someone of whom others are jealous because of

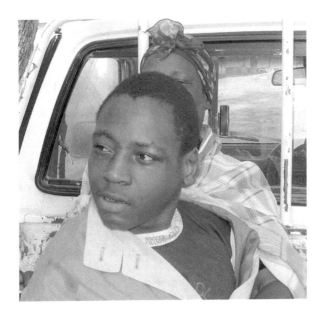

Figure 15.5 15-year-old Silas sitting in the back of the truck where we would always consult because he is unable to walk.

financial success or it may be someone who has been marginalised and is more vulnerable because of a poor social or familial support system. Grieving family or community members sometimes murder those they believe are bewitching others. As a result, in South Africa it is a criminal offence to accuse someone of witchcraft and the accuser can be arrested immediately.

The following two case histories (Case studies 15.3 and 15.4) illustrate what a profound impact this perception of health and illness has

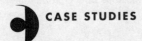 **CASE STUDIES**

Case 15.3 Bewitchment
It is difficult to know what to do when one of your patients is convinced that a family member is bewitching him. Steven, 32 years old, worked as a security guard at one of the clinics I visited. He had been having chronic headaches for which he was using analgesics frequently. He was terrified that he might

(continued overleaf)

● **CASE STUDIES** (continued)

have a brain tumour and would not be able to work, which he feared would result in desperate poverty. Throughout the first consultation, he was wiping his chest and his armpits with a facecloth. When I asked him what he was doing, he explained that he did not want any perspiration on his shirt. He seemed to be very anxious and fastidious, particularly about money and his health. His headaches resolved completely on Arsenicum album.

A year later he came to see me again. He had recently been fired after being absent from work without leave for a month. He had stayed at home because he had not been feeling well and, without consulting a doctor or informing his employer, had decided that he needed a month to recover, yet was quite surprised when he lost his job as a result. Already an anxious person, Steven now had no money to support his wife and child. His relatives were already poor themselves, so he could not rely on their help. Overwhelmed by this stress, he presented with a long list of somatic complaints. He had consulted an African traditional healer and been to the local hospital for treatment, but was not feeling better. The African traditional healer had offered him an explanation of his illness which he had fully embraced. He was now convinced that living in his abdomen was a snake which had two heads at each end of its body. Sometimes the snake would move into other parts of his body, such as his shoulders or arms, causing pain there too. He believed his illness was the result of a curse which had been put on him by an aunt, who disliked him, or so he thought. When asked why he thought his aunt felt this way towards him, he explained that she had not given him money when he asked for it. Fortunately, he had no malicious plans towards his aunt. He was given Arsenicum album, which improved a number of his symptoms briefly, but did little to shift the delusions. This was followed by Phosporus, after which there was no change at all. Unfortunately I did not have the opportunity to prescribe for him again as he did not return. However, considering the stress he was under and the influence of repeated visits to the African traditional healer, I was not surprised that there was little improvement in his symptoms or change in his delusions during treatment.

Case 15.4 Bewitchment
Lindiwe, a competent and extremely experienced 56-year-old clinic nurse, came to see me for a repeat prescription of her antihypertensives. A concerned enquiry into her emotional well-being elicited a flood of tears as she told me the story of a chain of events that had recently turned her life upside down.

It all began 12 months before when her 26-year-old son was tragically killed in a motor vehicle accident. Within a few weeks of her son's death, her

→

husband, who was a schoolteacher, developed shortness of breath and was diagnosed with cardiac failure. Althought Lindiwe stopped working to take care of him, he rapidly deteriorated and died within a few months. After his funeral, while still grieving her husband and barely finished grieving her son, her late husband's parents fingered her as the person who had bewitched their son and grandson. They turned the rest of the family against her and chased her out of her own home. For her own safety, she left her home and went to stay with friends in another village. She was never able to return to her home and had to change her mobile number because of the constant death threats. She responded very well to Ignatia but the memories of what she had endured were never forgotten.

on patients' lives. The first patient, Steven, believed that his aunt was bewitching him, whereas the second, Lindiwe, was persecuted by her relatives for having bewitched her late husband and son.

The AIDS epidemic

Most patients at the clinics would like to be seen by a doctor. However, because there are so many patients, and I only visit each clinic once a week, the patients are all assessed by the clinic nurses first. Only those patients the nurses are unsure how to treat are referred to me as the visiting doctor. Before I started using homeopathy, patients with arthritis would just be given long-term analgesics by the nursing staff. Those with particularly severe arthritis, who could afford to get to the local hospital, would often be referred on for specialist care at another hospital 3 hours' drive away. However, due to logistical and financial barriers, very few were able to make use of this service. After seeing patients with rheumatoid arthritis respond very well to homeopathic treatment (see Case study 15.5), I encouraged the clinic nurses to refer any patients they suspected may have arthritis. They were delighted to be able to do more than give chronic analgesics.

Homeopathy in the face of hopelessness

Many patients are referred from the local hospital for homeopathic treatment. They usually have severe or far-advanced problems which are

CASE STUDY

**Case 15.5 Human immunodeficiency virus (HIV)/
acquired immunodeficiency syndrome (AIDS)**

Naledi, a 30-year-old woman, was referred by a clinic nurse with a provisional diagnosis of rheumatoid arthritis (RA). Two months before, Naledi had suddenly developed pain, stiffness and swelling in her elbows, wrists, hands, fingers, knees, ankles, feet and toes. It had developed rapidly, becoming so severe that she could not continue working as a cook in a restaurant. She had returned home where her family could help her with domestic chores which she could no longer do for herself.

At an emotional level, Naledi preferred not to talk about her problems. She kept her feelings to herself and did not like to be consoled. She was the eldest child, and had always felt responsible for her siblings after her parents died prematurely. There did not seem to be any clear precipitants or stressors that were linked to her joint pains. She had enjoyed working at the restaurant where she was a cook, had not experienced any recent losses and her relationships seemed stable. She had left her boyfriend behind when she worked as a cook far from home, although she did not miss him while she was away. This unsentimental, pragmatic approach was more apparent when she mentioned that she also wanted to be tested for HIV. It is very unusual for my patients to request an HIV test. Many refuse to have a test even when it is recommended, preferring to live in denial rather than knowing that they have HIV because of the severe stigma and the poor prognosis without good nutrition or antiretroviral therapy.

On physical examination, she had generalised lymphadenopathy and was emaciated. Her joints were tender, swollen and warm. The symmetrical involvement of predominantly smaller joints was compatible with a diagnosis of RA. However, the extremely high local prevalence of HIV, her concern about being infected, together with her emaciation and generalised lymphadenopathy, all suggested that she was HIV-positive. This made HIV arthropathy a more likely diagnosis than rheumatoid arthritis.

At a rural clinic, with only symptomatic treatment available for all types of arthritis, and patients who cannot afford transport to specialist clinics, distinguishing between RA and HIV-arthropathy is only of academic value. I gave Naledi one dose of Natrum muriaticum 30c, followed on subsequent days by one dose of Natrum muriaticum 200c and one dose of Natrum muriaticum 1M, and explained where she could have an HIV test.

When she returned 3 weeks later, the pain and stiffness in her elbows, wrists, hands, knees, feet and toes had completely disappeared. She only had slight pain in both ankles after prolonged exertion and some stiffness in

$\rightarrow$

 **CASE STUDY** (continued)

her hands. She had tested positive for HIV, yet did not seem surprised or upset, or at least didn't show it. She complained of a poor appetite and felt that she was losing weight. Her weight was 44 kg and she had a very low body mass index of 16.6. At the time there were no antiretrovirals available to patients in the public health system and she could not afford to buy them privately. I repeated her Natrum muriaticum 1M, and also gave her a multivitamin and a local botanical, *Sutherlandia frutescens*, which is effective in stimulating appetite and slowing the wasting associated with AIDS and cancer.[2]

In the first 3 months of treatment she put on 12 kg and, at her most recent appointment, she weighed 64 kg, having put on 20 kg since starting treatment 2 years before. She returns whenever she runs out of *Sutherlandia*, multivitamins or Natrum muriaticum. Her joints are completely painfree, as long as she takes a weekly dose of Natrum muriaticum 1M, and she has returned to work as a cook and supports her family.

challenging and stimulating to treat. Even when the prognosis seems poor, I do my best because they have often travelled a long way and allopathic options have already been exhausted. One such patient was Lebo (see Case study 15.6).

 **CASE STUDY**

Case 15.6   Hopelessness
Several years ago, before integrating homeopathy into my practice, I was working in the 40-bed psychiatric ward at the local hospital. One of my psychiatric inpatients, 15-year-old Lebo, had been severely learning-disabled since early childhood. Quite inexplicably, 5 months before her admission, she had started jumping up and down, waving her arms, running into walls and shouting gibberish all day and night. She was incontinent of urine and stool, which she would pass anywhere. She was extremely strong and it took several strong adults to restrain her in order to wash her. She was aggressive and destructive, unexpectedly striking people, and destroying doors, windows

(continued overleaf)

and furniture in her house. She would rip up all her clothes and wander off naked. Whenever she was left alone outside the house, she roamed far away on her own and would not return unless her family went to find her.

After extensive investigations at the referral hospital it was decided that Lebo had temporal lobe epilepsy. Yet even with this diagnostic label and adjusting her medication many times in consultation with the visiting psychiatrist, there was no change. After several weeks in the ward, her mother insisted on taking her home, but brought her back to the hospital for follow-up, despite any change in her condition.

No longer working in the psychiatric ward, I had forgotten about Lebo. Then, 2 years ago, the doctor working in the psychiatric ward said to me, 'Lebo is still not better. Can I send her for homeopathic treatment?' My heart sank. Just hearing her name brought back all the feelings of helplessness I'd had years before.

When Lebo came for homeopathic treatment, she was just as unmanageable as I remembered her in the psychiatric ward several years before. Despite all the psychiatric medication she was on, her mother brought three strong adults along to restrain her when she was aggressive. She was constantly hitting, biting or scratching those close to her, talking gibberish incessantly, shouting and laughing raucously. I gave her Hyoscyamus niger 200c daily for 3 days.

Four weeks later, she was much better. She was no longer assaulting her family. She allowed her mother to bathe her and she would now sit quietly outside the house for hours, without wandering away.

I gave her another dose of Hyoscyamus niger 1M, which maintained the improvement for another 4 months, before it needed to be repeated. I gradually increased the frequency of Hyoscyamus niger 1M, finding that she was well controlled on a weekly dose, but would deteriorate again on day 8 or 9 if it was not repeated. Her family was very happy with her condition and came regularly to get more homeopathic treatment. At a follow-up visit, it emerged that she was well all month, although for a few days before her menstrual period she would deteriorate briefly. She was changed to Lachesis 1M weekly, on which she improved further. She even started using the toilet, which made an enormous difference to her family who before had resigned themselves to cleaning up after her.

It was costly and inconvenient for them to go to the hospital to collect psychiatric medication and she no longer seemed to need it. For several months before stopping it completely, the only psychiatric medication they were giving her was a weekly dose of sodium valproate! Whenever they gave it to her, she would just sleep all day. Now, 18 months after starting homeopathic treatment, the family have long since stopped all her psychiatric medication and she is very well on Lachesis 1M weekly.

Translating language and culture

South Africa is a country characterised by diversity. It has a population of over 40 million people, the majority of whom are black, although there are also significant minorities of white, mixed-race and Indian people. There are 11 official languages, including English, Afrikaans, Xhosa, Zulu, Sesotho, Setswana and Xitsonga. I can greet, establish rapport and take a basic medical history in a few local languages, but because so few patients speak English, I need an interpreter to take a detailed homeopathic history.

Working with an interpreter introduces a whole new dynamic into a consultation and can be extremely frustrating. To minimise this, I usually carefully explain my expectations to the interpreter beforehand. Despite this, the biomedical emphasis of nurse training means that most interpreters do not understand the relevance of the patient's emotions or social context. They often close open-ended questions or translate only those parts of a patient's answer they think are relevant – leaving out the precious strange, rare and peculiar symptoms! Added to this, if the interpreter looks bored or lacks empathy, it is virtually impossible for patients to talk about their emotions.

An additional challenge is that nurse interpreters are accustomed to treating patients themselves, so they tend to take over the consultation. I sometimes find myself a spectator at a consultation between the nurse interpreter and the patient. To pre-empt this, I arrange the seating in a way that keeps the patient and me in the centre and the nurse interpreter next to me, but further from the patient than I am.

Despite the challenges of using an interpreter, I have discovered a number of compensations. I have learned to avoid jargon or complex questions or explanations.

With an interpreter, the interview is more paced. While patients speak, I don't have to concentrate on what they are saying, but can closely observe their body language while I reflect on what they have previously said. A homeopathic medicine may come to mind and I will have a chance to think about a new line of enquiry to confirm or exclude it. Having to pause to give the interpreter a chance to translate what they have said, patients have the opportunity to reflect on what is most important to them before they speak again. Although one gets less history, there are usually a sufficient number of clear and unusual rubrics indicating a homeopathic medicine and I rarely feel overwhelmed by too much information, which can make analysis more difficult (see Case study 15.7).

> **CASE STUDY**

Case 15.7 Working with an interpreter

One time I had five professional nurses who were preparing for their post-graduate diplomas in primary health care sitting in with me. A young mother brought in her 5-year-old son Tsakani, who had juvenile chronic arthritis. She cradled him in her arms like a little baby. His arthritis was so severe that he had never walked in his life and could not stand; he would just fall over if his mother tried to prop him up to stand. Every joint in his body, including each interphalangeal joint in his toes, was inflamed. He could not even turn his head or nod because of the stiffness and pain in his cervical spine. He had been taking methotrexate and prednisolone for several years, and was so stunted that he looked like an 18-month-old even though he was 5 years old.

With five nurses sitting in, I was not able to get even a complete allopathic history, let alone the amount of detail I would have liked for an accurate homeopathic prescription. I spent most of the consultation teaching the nurses around the subject of arthritis, which would be essential to them when they returned to their clinics and had to manage patients without supervision. Tsakani's mother mentioned that putting her son in a bath of ice-cold water gave him tremendous relief. He wanted to be held all the time and would cry if his mother lay him down. I gave him a daily dose of Pulsatilla 30c for 3 days and advised his mother to return 3 weeks later.

At his follow-up visit 3 weeks later Tsakani walked into the consulting room. I checked my notes to make sure I was not confusing him with someone else. I wasn't! One week after taking the Pulsatilla he had surprised his whole family by taking his first steps and over the subsequent 2 weeks had walked further and further each day. He lives close to the clinic and has never returned for further treatment.

Disability grants

In most African countries, those who are physically disabled receive no financial support from the government. In South Africa, there is no social welfare system for the unemployed, but those who are medically unable to work receive a monthly government grant known as a disability grant. Most of the people living near the clinics I visit are poorly educated, unemployed and very poor. As a result, patients frequently present at the clinic with a health problem but their real agenda is getting the doctor to write a letter so that they can receive a disability grant. Patients who want a disability grant will usually have a long list of exaggerated and inconsistent symptoms, and regularly mention how difficult it is for them to function or work because of their illness. As expected, they are very unlikely to respond to treatment and are even less likely to report any improvement in their symptoms, making it very difficult and frustrating to treat them. This is why I try to establish as early as possibly what each patient's agenda is before trying my utmost to solve a problem they don't want solved (see Case study 15.8).

CASE STUDY

Case 15.8   The hidden agenda

Mr Ngobeni, a 64-year-old man, was referred from the local hospital where he had consulted regularly each month for several years about the same problem. He had constant excruciating burning pains on the left side of his body, affecting his left arm, his left trunk and his left leg. There was nothing abnormal on examination and special investigations had not revealed anything. He had been seen by an occupational therapist and a physiotherapist, which had also not helped. Mr Ngobeni repeated over and over again how severe his pain was and how it made it impossible for him to do anything, including work. He previously worked as a lumberjack, but had resigned because of the illness. There was no physiological, anatomical or pathological explanation for his symptoms, so I assumed he must be malingering in order to get a disability grant.

Yet the strange thing was that Mr Ngobeni was already receiving a disability grant, and had been for several years. Which then begged the question, why was he spending the little money he got from the government going back to the hospital each month and going from doctor to doctor in search of a cure for his pain? It was quite clear that his symptoms were very real to him and were causing him great distress. I asked him more about his problem and discovered that his symptoms had started after his wife had died several years before. It was obvious that he loved his late wife very much, and although he had remarried, still missed her dearly. He was engaging and talkative, all his symptoms were strongly left-sided and he strongly disliked bread. I gave him Phosphorus 30c daily for 3 days and asked him to come back 4 weeks later. When he returned, he was beaming and said, 'For the first time my pains are

(continued overleaf)

CASE STUDY (continued)

gone, completely gone.' That's wonderful, I replied, also smiling. He then became more serious and lowered his voice. 'Does that mean I'm going to lose my disability grant now?'

I knew Mr Ngobeni had really been helped. Firstly, he came to see me with a problem even though he was already receiving a disability grant, and then, congruent with a Phosphorus constitution, he was so delighted to be well he even risked losing his disability grant by coming to tell me he was better!

Grief

If I was asked by a group of medical doctors to name one of the conditions for which homeopathy works particularly well, I would avoid mentioning any particular diagnosis. However, I would say any diagnosis where the start of the illness can be linked by the patient or the practitioner to some kind of loss does particularly well with homeopathy. In my experience, irrespective of the diagnosis, where there is a clear aetiology of grief there is often a dramatic response to homeopathic treatment. South Africa has the highest number of HIV/AIDS patients in the world – around 6 million people are infected with HIV. Almost every South African has lost a family member or someone they know well to AIDS. There is a lot of grief around: thank goodness I have homeopathy to treat those who desperately need it (see Case study 15.9).

CASE STUDY

Case 15.9 Grief
Sipho is a severely learning-disabled 19-year-old man. He was developing normally until the age of 5, when he started having frequent generalised tonic-clonic seizures. Despite assessment by neurologists, and a barrage of

$\rightarrow$

◗ **CASE STUDY** (continued)

investigations, including computed tomography scans and optimal allopathic treatment, he had such frequent seizures he became learning-disabled. His baseline level of function is that of a 3-year-old, the age group he most enjoys playing with. He recognises familiar people and can greet and use simple sentences. He is helpful and obedient, fetching things his mother asks him to. However, he needs supervision for activities of daily living, such as dressing himself or washing. Over the years he has been on a wide variety of anti-convulsants in varying doses but was finally controlled on the maximum dose of carbamazepine. His mother is happy with his control, explaining that he usually only has between one and two seizures a month, which she says are 'short and very mild'.

All of a sudden, 3 weeks before coming to see me, there was a dramatic deterioration in his condition. He started having three long and severe gen-eralised seizures each night. He was so exhausted by the frequent seizures that he started drooling, slept all day and stopped speaking. He would just stare at his food, too tired even to feed himself. During the consultation he drooled profusely, could not sit up straight and kept falling asleep.

Until I drew his family genogram, there was nothing to explain the sudden deterioration in his condition. Sipho's mother mentioned in passing that 3 weeks before his uncle had been buried. Sipho's uncle had worked as a migrant labourer in Johannesburg, but had returned home several months before, when he became ill, most likely with acquired immunodeficiency syn-drome (AIDS). Sipho had become very close to his uncle and the day after the funeral he started fitting three times each night. I gave him Ignatia 30c on the first day, followed on subsequent days by one dose of Ignatia 200c and one dose of Ignatia 1M.

When he returned 4 weeks later, he looked entirely different. He sat up straight, made eye contact, smiled brightly and did not drool. His mother said it was the 'greatest improvement I have ever seen'. From the moment he got the first dose of Ignatia, he didn't have another seizure. He was eating well again, following instructions and playing with other children. With English not being her first language, his mother struggled to find the words to explain just how much better he was, and said, 'He was like an animal before; now he's a human being. He really listens to you now.' She was so inspired by the improvement in her son, even above his usual baseline, that she wanted to start teaching him to do more things for himself, something she had never considered doing before.

I did not repeat Ignatia, but arranged to see him again 6 weeks later. During that time, he had had only one mild seizure, and his mother did not see the need for further homeopathic treatment.

Conclusion

Practising homeopathy in a multiethnic setting like rural South Africa is exciting and stimulating. On a daily basis I meet fascinating patients who have minimal formal schooling, little contact with western allopathic doctors and an intuitive approach to life. As a result, they routinely volunteer unusual symptoms: 'When it's full moon my son has more frequent seizures' or 'There's a snake inside my abdomen, and it's moving around my body'. They don't interpret, censor or analyse before describing their symptoms. They seem to be more in touch with their bodies and volunteer nuggets of prescribing gold which more than make up for the challenges created by language barriers and cultural differences.

The importance of trying to learn the local language cannot be underestimated. Wherever I am working, I try to learn the local language. The clinic staff deeply appreciate even the clumsiest efforts to speak their language, and reciprocate by being friendly and helpful. When the doctor makes an effort to understand and learn the patient's language, the consultation is less formal and the power dynamic between the doctor and patient becomes more equal.[3] The patients respond to this interest in themselves and their language by speaking more openly about their problems.

Homeopathy is system of medicine that truly transcends culture. It is the medicine of all human beings who have suffered, who have known the joy of falling in love and the pain of having lost someone dear. Homeopathy does not rely on expensive and inaccessible investigations, it is affordable and often does not need to be taken long-term. It is effective in rural and urban settings, amongst rich and poor, and in all cultures. Having seen the efficacy and accessibility of homeopathy in diverse ethnic settings, I am overwhelmed by a sense of the immense global relevance of this elegant system of medicine.

Patient's names have been changed and permission obtained to quote cases and reproduce photographs.

References

1.   Mash B (ed.) *Handbook of Family Medicine*. Cape Town: Oxford University Press, 1999.
2.   Van Wyk B, Van Oudshoorn B, Gericke N. *Medicinal Plants of South Africa*, 2nd edn. Pretoria: Briza, 2000.
3.   Ellis C. *Learning Language and Culture in the Medical Consultation*. Parktown North: Sue McGuiness, 1999.

16

Incorporating homeopathy into Japanese practice – a personal view

Ryoichi Obitsu

Introduction

In this chapter I explore the basis of the holistic approach to medicinal practice and what I understand as integrative medicine. I describe how and why I use homeopathy in the management of cancer patients and give some examples of the medicines that I use.

Adopting a holistic approach to practice

The challenges

To explain why I decided to incorporate homeopathy into my practice I must first reflect on the history of Obitsu Sankei Hospital (OSH), which I founded. The hospital (see Figure 16.1) was launched in November 1982 under the slogan of 'combining Chinese and western medicine'. Dealing with cancer from day to day, I was faced with a structural limitation of western medicine that focused largely on the parts and leaned too heavily on reductionism. In an attempt to overcome this limitation, I reached the conclusion that combining Chinese medicine, which emphasises the importance of connection between individual parts, into my practice was crucial.

At this stage, practising western medicine in conjunction with Chinese medicine was foremost in my mind and I had not yet considered the idea of holistic medicine. Rooms to prepare traditional Chinese medicines, to facilitate the treatment of acupuncture and moxibustion, and for qigong were set up in the hospital. Chinese medicinal porridge was also included in the hospital diet. The hospital was established with great enthusiasm and high spirit but the time was not yet ripe and its launch gained very little public attention.

Figure 16.1 Obitsu Sankei Hospital, Tokyo.

Lack of interest

I was fully prepared to be mocked at by my fellow medical colleagues but I was somewhat taken aback when our potential patients failed to show interest too! People's reaction (or in this case lack of reaction!) was not enough to deter me completely for I was aware that I had just stepped into previously uncharted territory and, therefore, some initial difficulties were likely to be unavoidable.

As time went on, some colleagues became aware of my attempt at combining Chinese and western medicine in cancer treatment and I was asked to give a lecture to the Holistic Medicine Study Group, a group organised by medical students at Tokyo Medical University. The group, inspired by Dr Andrew Weil's *Health and Healing*,[1] subsequently became the Japan Holistic Medical Society. I took part in the establishment of the Society in 1987.

An energy-based view of life

The establishment of the Japan Holistic Medical Society coincided with my awakening to the holistic concept. At this early stage, in order to convince my colleagues in western medicine of the significance of holistic medicine, I used an analogy based on the following concept of energy and entropy.

In order to sustain life, numerous reactions and responses take place inside a human body day and night. Energy that promotes responses comes from the sun, which provides energy to our body through a process of photosynthesis. Once the energy from the sun enters the body, it is then converted to various energies based on different responses. Whenever energy is converted, it gives rise to entropy.

Entropy, a concept in thermodynamics, is described as $S = k\log W$, where k represents for Boltzmann's constant and W represents a number of possible states. In short, a higher value of entropy signifies a higher number of states, which in turn results in acceleration of disorder. In other words, as more and more entropy is generated in our body, further disorder takes place inside the body and our health is compromised.

Yet despite these actions, we are able to wake up each morning fresh and with energy. The current accepted theory, which explains this phenomenon, is offered in a work of entropy by Erwin Schrödinger (1887–1961). Schrödinger made important contributions to the development of quantum mechanics and received a Nobel Prize in 1933.[2] The theory states that:

> increase of entropy generated within human body is prevented by attaching entropy to heat and other substances and discard them from the body as waste heat and waste material.

Waste heat and waste material are expressed in the human body as aspirated air, perspiration, urine and faeces that are eliminated and this mechanism sets a stage for Chinese medicine, which is also known as 'medicine of elimination'. In this way, a larger system of medicine is formed by a combination of western medicine, which focuses on the energetic aspect of the life process, and Chinese medicine, which focuses on entropy.

The importance of considering the mind

Around the same time that I began to be aware of the holistic idea of connecting to the parts and integrating the aspects of energy and entropy, I also began to notice the importance of our mind. In my practice as a surgeon and operating on my patients from day to day, I scarcely paid any attention to their feelings and emotions. Despite the fact that psycho-oncology was assuming greater importance in the medical field, I was set in my belief that it was surgery that cured cancer and not our mind.

However, in Chinese medical practice, the patient's face is examined in great detail. In this system of medicine, there are four bases of diagnostic methods:

1.   inspection
2.   auscultation
3.   interrogation
4.   palpation.

The most important form of diagnosis is inspection, which involves looking at the patient's face. As I lead my patients in a daily morning qigong practice at my hospital (Figure 16.2), I am in a better position to observe their faces and notice, little by little, what lies beyond. In this way, I begin to understand that there is a close connection between our state of mind and the transition of diseases.

Figure 16.2   Ryoichi Obitsu leading patients in a daily morning Qigong practice.

Based on the realisation that a patient cannot be seen as a whole unless the mind is also being treated, I set up a team comprising one doctor specialising in psychosomatic medicine and two psychotherapists, each a founding member of Japan Holistic Medical Society. Since we had little experience of the mental care of our patients, we first incorporated the mental imagery method, developed by Dr O Carl Simonton, a pioneer in this field.[3]

Unfortunately our satisfaction at having accomplished a true holistic medicine, by adding mental care to western and Chinese medicine, was short-lived. Soon a sense that something was amiss began to be apparent. I started to feel that it was probably not enough simply to incorporate a treatment method that targets different areas and that a brand new methodology was required to see and capture a whole person in his or her entirety.

The meaning of 'whole person' – the life field

I began my search by analysing the meaning of a whole person. It is said that we are comprised of body, mind and spirit. Because of its visibility, we have no problem in understanding our body. Difficulty arises in attempting to understand the mind and the spirit. In my course of research, I reached the conclusion that the mind and the spirit are the energy of what I call 'life field'.

We human beings exist in various 'fields', including electromagnetic field and gravitational field. In physics, when some physical quantity is distributed in continuum within a limited space, it is called a 'field'. For instance, the electromagnetic field involves electric and magnetic fields that are distributed in continuum. Both fields exist within our body as a matter of course. Although its presence is yet to be discovered, it is not difficult to imagine a presence of physical quantity which has a direct bearing on our life and spirit and creating a corresponding field. In this respect, I have decided to call different fields in our body collectively 'life field'.

This internal energy of the life field is what we call our life. It is my understanding that when this energy is diminished, for any reason, an attempt at recovery can be made through three different pathways. These are:

1. natural healing power – capacity that is inherent in the field
2. healing – influenced by external sources
3. yojo – an idea of achieving and maintaining health and longevity by personal effort in eastern culture.

Furthermore, if the mind can be seen as a product of the ever-changing state of the life field expressed to the external world through brain cells, the main body of the mind must also be energy of the life field. Hence, if one is to understand a whole person as a unification of the flesh and the life field, it must also mean that our body is a particular feature of the life field. Therefore it is no exaggeration to say that a whole person is the life field itself.

The inner life field is connected to the environmental field. Or rather, it could be said that part of the environmental field dwells within our body to form the life field. In this respect, the life field cannot be discussed without considering the environmental field.

This is what one means by taking a person as a whole and it is this thinking that forms the basis for equating holistic medicine with medicine of the 'field'.

A system of holistic medicine based on body, mind and spirit

Just because one has not yet grasped the methodology of the holistic medicine, one cannot stand by and be idle, especially when faced with patients. Consequently, in an effort to approximate holistic medicine as closely as possible, a system that was closer to integrative medicine was devised. This combines western medicine, which works on the body; various forms of psychotherapy, which works on the mind; and complementary therapies, which work on the spirit.

There are countless disciplines of complementary medicine existing in the world today. With time, new discipline was gradually added to cater to the needs of patients at the OSH. At that time, however, homeopathy was merely one of numerous complementary medicines that were available to me and I did not give it much thought. Even when I paid a visit to the Royal London Homoeopathic Hospital, I was more interested in finding out about an audit, a system to assess outcomes of treatment that they were just starting to practice, than in homeopathy.

Homeopathy and the life field

On my return to Japan, an opportunity arose to attend a lecture on homeopathy during which I was exposed to two opposing views. One came from western medicine, which stated that the idea that water which carries no single molecule is effective can only be due to a placebo effect. On the other hand, the homeopathic argument stated that a spirit resides in the medicine after the active substance has been diluted out. I realised that if the illness can be cured as a result of introducing a medicine then that medicine must raise the field energy of the life field. I became convinced that for those of us who aspire to practise holistic medicine, homeopathy is a necessary path one must take.

The evidence base for complementary medicine

Western medicine is supported by evidence whereas most of complementary medicine deals with the energy field and is largely unsupported by evidence. It is good to strive and seek evidence but one must not chase it too far. Instead of evidence, complementary medicine is equipped with intuition. Perhaps intuition is born as a result of resonance between energy fields or through a collision of overflowing energies. In *L'Intuition Philosophique* the French philosopher Henri Bergson (1859–1941) stated that *élan vital* manifests at the moment when intuition is born and subsequently we are filled with a deep sense of joy.[4] This development comes as no surprise if we are to regard *élan vital* as small explosions of the life field.

At the same time, we are deeply indebted to science, that is to say, evidence, for enabling us to lead a comfortable life. Yet here Bergson poses an important question. In the course of living our life, which is more significant, comfort or joy? It goes without saying that it is the latter and therefore, Bergson concludes, *intuition must come before evidence.*

Evidence-based medicine (EBM) is a hotly debated issue and we must recognise that it is one of the necessary pathways in medicine today. Nevertheless, people, by nature, are extremely individual beings that cannot be defined by EBM alone. And this is where narrative-based medicine (NBM) can make a significant contribution.

'Narrative' is not merely a story but an internal manifestation of the life field. Because NBM includes the body, mind and spirit of the narrator, a listener can grasp an overall picture of the narrator just by listening to his/her story. As with homeopathy, it all begins from paying attention and actively listening to the story that is being told and it is this feature that makes homeopathy a most holistic medicine among the various medical systems existing today.

Components of integrative medicine

Integrative medicine is not merely a *sum* of western and complementary medicine but an *integration* of the two. This means dismantling both sides and reassembling the parts again so that a totally new system of medicine can be constructed. Needless to say, it is not an easy task. As it calls for considerable will and determination on both sides, more time is required.

Moreover, we cannot be idle and wait for integration to take place since there are many parts that require our immediate attention and need integration. For example:

- integration of cure and healing
- integration of the body and the energy field
- integration of reductionism and holism
- integration of evidence and intuition
- integration of EBM and NBM
- integration of doctors and patients
- integration of pathogenesis and salutogenesis.

Pathogenesis, a concept of seeking origin of illness within one's body, has reigned supreme as a fundamental concept of western medicine. This idea will continue to exist, particularly in matters related to the human body. Salutogenesis is an alternative-medicine concept that focuses on factors that support human health and well-being rather than on factors that cause disease. The term was first used by the American–Israeli medical sociologist Aaron Antonovsky (1923–1994), who studied the influence of a variety of sources of stress on health and was able to show that relatively unstressed people had much more resistance to illness than more stressed people.[5]

Whereas cure refers to the idea of repairing the damage caused in the body as if trying to fix failure in machinery, healing is restoring and improving the energy of the body and the spirit.

It is said that human beings comprise body, mind and spirit. Body is exactly what we see. Spirit concerns itself with energy of our internal life field. If we regard the mind as an ever-changing and moving life field that is outwardly expressed through brain cells, it can be said that the essence of the mind is also the life field energy and, therefore, a human being is comprised of energy field (in this case, the life field) and the body, instead of the three elements mentioned earlier.

Although reductionism, which forms a basis of science, is important from the outset, a concept of holism, which states that a whole has a higher level of significance than a sum of its parts, is just as valid. However, when viewed from a perspective of salutogenesis and the energy field, we are seen as beings that continuously strive to elevate the life field energy and, therefore, factors that contribute to heightening the energy can be found in this process.

The consultation

The final area that requires integration is that of doctor and patient, without which integrative medicine cannot fully be practised (Figure 16.3). This state of integration is described as 'non-separation between the primary and the subordinate' by my respected senior colleague, Hiri Shimizu, Professor Emeritus of Pharmacy at Tokyo University.[6]

Figure 16.3 State of integration between doctor and patient.

In western medicine, attention is paid to the body and the patient is seen as a broken machine that is in need of repair. In this context, the doctor's job, as a professional, is to offer knowledge and skill to the patient, an amateur, who lacks such knowledge and skill. In other words, because there is a separation between the primary and the subordinate and the interaction is one-sided, the doctor is not at all affected by the patient that he/she is seeing. This situation changes drastically when that other person is regarded as an energy field. Through a collision of energy fields between doctor and patient, their respective energy of the field heightens. The process is akin to a combative sport. But it is by no means the kind that shatters one's opponent. It is a kind of interaction that is gentle on the body and the mind and helps to raise one another up to a higher ground, a ground where there is no separation between the two.

Practice of integrative medicine at the Obitsu Sankei Hospital

Dealing with the whole person

Despite individual differences, both complementary and integrative medicines deal with various stages of illness. The difference between the two is merely a matter of methodology and this is where homeopathy takes on a different aspect. Since it deals with a whole person, homeopathy does not stop at a stage of illness but, rather, engages itself with life, ageing, disease and death and thereby encompasses much larger concepts and subject matter.

Although clinical practice for cancer at the OSH strives for holistic medicine, it is not suitably equipped to 'capture' a whole-person. Instead we see a person from the perspective of body, mind and spirit and address each person individually. So in a sense, the medicine we practise is closer to integrative medicine.

A strategic order

But there are no manuals that we can refer to. Individual strategy is devised based mainly on each patient's wishes and each strategy is built on a certain order.

You are invited to picture a house made of building blocks (Figure 16.4). The foundation of the house represents the core aspect, the mind. It is the most individual yet most universal aspect within us.

The basic unit for our daily effort can be found in a cycle through which our mind travels. The cycle begins from the sorrow that comes from being alive. We feel sorrow, because we are all travellers whose journey begins from an empty space. If sorrow is the nature of being human, it sets a firm and solid foundation for us all, a foundation from which a large tree of hope is born and nurtured. One can never have too many hopes and our heart is elevated each time one hope is fulfilled.

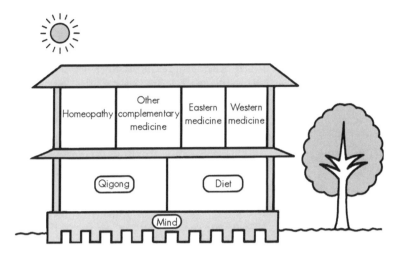

Figure 16.4 Graphic representation of house conquering illness.

It is this sense of elevation that is described as *élan vital* by Henri Bergson. The occurrence of *élan vital* is like a small explosion that takes place in the life field and as we experience this feeling of elevation time and time again we become more cheerful and positive. Because this attitude originates from sorrow in the first place, it is not as fragile and fleeting as commonplace cheerfulness and positive attitude. What is more, instead of stopping our journey when we reach a state of rapture, we always inevitably come back to sorrow. In this way, a cycle of sorrow, hope, elevation, cheerful and positive attitude and sorrow is completed.

The first floor represents Diet and Qigong.

Diet

Although there is no single recipe that suits all tastes, the basis of the traditional Japanese diet is plain and simple fare. This consists of (in the order in which it is taken) vegetable, seafood and meat. While it is important to pay attention to ingredients, we must also not forget that food is a source of joy. We must also not forget to treat ourselves to delicacies once in a while in order to keep our hearts uplifted.

Qigong

A traditional Chinese way of health maintenance, qigong is also a method of heightening the energy of the life field through regulation of body, breath and mind. Out of numerous forms of qigong, we have decided to offer about 15 programmes and it is up to our patients to choose which ones to take part in.

Now that the foundation and the ground floor of the house are completed, let us move on to the *first floor*. The first room is western medicine where options including surgery, chemotherapy and radiation therapy are carefully investigated. Next to be considered are various methods of complementary medicine, including Chinese herbal medicine, acupuncture and moxibustion, mental imagery, relaxation, music therapy, aromatherapy and health supplements. Needless to say homeopathy plays a part in sustaining the first floor. It is like a newcomer, a latest resident to join this household.

Homeopathic practice at OSH

Homeopathic practice began rather timidly at the OSH in July 2000. It eventually spread like wildfire and has now become indispensable to holistic cancer treatment.

Compared to western countries, homeopathy has not yet gained full recognition in Japan. However, those who are admitted to my hospital are aware of, and are interested in, homeopathy. They can advance their knowledge through research or through conversations with their fellow patients who have been admitted to the hospital for some time. This helps me greatly since, by the time they come to their strategy meeting, held one week after their admittance, there is hardly any need to explain homeopathy in detail.

After a brief interview at the strategy meeting, a questionnaire regarding their constitution is given to the patient to complete. Our homeopathy treatment begins from the moment the questionnaire is completed and returned to us. In my hospital roughly 70–80% of patients, out of a total of 99 beds, are cancer patients. Although there are some exceptions, most request homeopathic treatment during and after their stay at the hospital. In cases of cancer, patients do not leave the hospital because they are completely cured, but, rather, because they are in remission, or a strategy for their treatment has been established. In cases such as these, most patients end up choosing to continue their homeopathic treatment. Whatever the reason or circumstance, there is no doubt that its incomparable gentleness towards body and mind, as well as a certain response it creates, contributes to the popularity of homeopathy.

A remedy is prescribed weekly to inpatients. Firstly, a constitutional remedy is prescribed and then a further remedy is decided based on information obtained through weekly rounds on Tuesdays. After patients leave the hospital, a remedy is sent to them by post. Patients are asked to report any changes that they experience both physically and mentally in the form of a questionnaire every fortnight. A suitable remedy can then be chosen. Patients are asked to return to the hospital every 1–3 months so that I can capture an overall picture of their health.

In hindsight, I feel that letting homeopathy occupy a room on the first floor helped to strengthen the house made of building blocks. I imagine that the presence of homeopathy responds to the heart of the foundation and together they heighten the energy that is present in the entire house and its field. I recall a time, soon after homeopathy was introduced to the hospital, when one of the doctors fondly reminisced and said: 'Don't you think the atmosphere of the hospital ward has become much brighter? It must be due to homeopathy'.

In order to make use of homeopathy, doctors get into the habit of paying close attention to the patient's delicate state of mind and attempt to deal with symptoms no matter how minor they are. This helps to increase patients' trust in doctors and creates a good placebo effect. In other words, it allows us to go back to the basic premise of medicine.

Homeopathy and the management of cancer

As I began to practise homeopathy, I learned for the first time that cancer patients are often stricken with a variety of different symptoms on a daily basis. When I reflect back to my earlier practice, I wonder if I had been, perhaps, ignoring many delicate symptoms on the pretext of treating primary diseases.

When various symptoms, no matter how minor, are overlapped and prolonged, they contribute to a reduction in quality of life, and this in turn compromises immunocompetence. Given this factor, it becomes necessary to pay close attention to symptoms that are not directly related to primary diseases. Homeopathy can play a major role in this respect.

Below is the list of some symptoms that I frequently encounter among cancer patients and some of the remedies that are used to treat them.

Symptoms related to primary diseases

- cervical lymph node metastasis: Conium, Hydrastis, Phytolacca
- superior vena cava syndrome: Apis, Graphites, Lycopodium

- cough, sputum: Arsenicum album, Bryonia, Drosera, Phosphorus, Spongia tosta
- haemosputum: Arsenicum album, Phosphorus, Hamamelis
- pleural effusion, pericardial effusion: Aconite, Apis, Bryonia, Graphites, Lycopodium
- chest pain, back pain: Bryonia, Calcarea carbonica, Kali carbonicum
- nausea, vomiting: Ipecacuanha, Nux vomica
- flatulence: Argentum nitricum, Carbo vegetabilis, Lycopodium
- ascites: Apis, Arsenicum album, Conium, Lycopodium
- diarrhoea: Arsenicum album, China, Lycopodium, Podophyllum
- constipation: Alumina, Baryta carbonica, Calcarea carbonica, Sepia, Sulphur
- abdominal pain: Arsenicum album, Carbo vegetabilis, Colocynthis, Lachesis, Lycopodium, Thuja
- oedema: Apis, Graphites, Lycopodium.

Mental symptoms

Due to the nature of the disease, cancer patients display a variety of mental symptoms. Reducing and alleviating these symptoms will help to increase patients' vigour and immunocompetence.

- anxiety: ranges from a vague and indefinable anxiety to anxiety concerning a possible relapse. It is no exaggeration to say that there is no single patient who does not feel some form of anxiety at one point: Aconite, Argentum nitricum, Calcarea carbonia, Carcinosin, Nitricum acidum, Phosphorus, Sulphur
- Irritation: Alumina, Arsenicum album, Calcarea carbonica, Graphites, Natrum muriaticum, Nux vomica, Sepia
- Restlessness: Anacardium, Arsenicum album, Carcinosin, Mecurius, Pulsatilla
- Anger: Aconite, Bryonia, Lycopodium, Nux vomica, Staphysagria
- Grief: Causticum, Ignatia, Natrum muriaticum, Phosphoricum acidum
- Depression: Aconite, Arsenicum album, Aurum, Calcarea carbonicum, Carcinosin, Graphites, Natrum muriaticum, Rhus toxicodendron, Sepia, Suphur, Thuja, Zincum.

Although cancer is deeply related to the mind and the spirit, and not just an illness of the body, not enough attention is being paid to these two aspects in the process of treating this illness. If and when cancer is to be conquered in future, that will be the day when full attention will be paid to the mind. I believe that the fastest path to reach this goal is through the promotion and diffusion of homeopathy.

Symptoms associated with adverse drug reactions

For reducing the side-effects of the so-called 'three major therapies', operation, radiation therapy and chemotherapy:

- postoperative anxiety: Argentum nitricum, Gelsemium, Lycopodium, Silica
- postoperative physical pain and mental anguish: Bellis perennis, Staphysagria
- compromised immune system: Cadmium sulphuratum, Sepia
- anaemia and leukopenia: Arsenicum album, Calcarea carbonica, Ferrum, Phosphorus
- alopecia: Baryta carbonica, Calcarea carbonica, Florium acidum, Phosphoricum acidum, Sepia, Sulphur
- gingivostomatitis and dysgeusia: Arsenicum album, Borax, Mercurius, Natrum muriaticum, Nux vomica, Sulphur
- arthralgia: Bryonia, Dulcamara, Ferrum, Pulsatilla, Rhus toxicodendron, Ruta
- numbness in hands and fingers: Agaricus muscarius, Arsenicum album, Conium, Graphites, Nux vomica, Phosphorus.

Case 16.1 details the role of homeopathy in an integrative cancer treatment.

 CASE STUDY

Case study 16.1   Intestinal cancer
For *definitions of abbreviations, see glossary below*
SY 57-year-old female. Cancer of transverse colon and ileus. Operated on for cancer of the uterus.

Background
10.11.1996: Operation for endometrial cancer at a prefectural cancer centre.
   Operation: Simple total hysterectomy, salpingo-oophorectomy, lymph node dissection in pelvis. Tissue type: adenoacanthoma.
   09.02.2001: Computed tomography (CT) detected lung metastasis, para-aortic lymph node metastasis.
   Chemotherapy: Due to complication of intestinal pneumonia after therapy utilising cyclophosamide (Endoxana), epirubicin and cisplatin, chemotherapy

(continued overleaf)

> **CASE STUDY** (continued)

was terminated after the third course. However, the metastasis mentioned above has disappeared.

13.08.2004 CT detected suspected hypertrophy in the wall of transverse colon and peritonitis carcinomatosa.

23.08.2004 Hospitalised for ileus. Remission gained from conservative treatment. Discharged from the hospital but similar symptoms recurred. Treated with chemotherapy and paclitexel (Taxol) and carboplatin based on the diagnosis of peritonitis carcinomatosa. Although abdominal pain was temporarily relieved, it exacerbated and the therapies were terminated after the third course. The patient underwent chemotherapy afterward.

Frustrated family member, exasperated from continuing abdominal pain, decided to consult OSH.

Initial consultation at OSH
Thin and pale. Abdominal distension and resistance in epigastrium. Elevation of left diaphragm detected in chest X-ray. Patient could not take in much food. Bowel movement once every 2 days accompanied by diarrhoea stool.

Chinese medicine features
Pulse: sinking and thin. Tongue moss. Stagnation of blood.

Remedy: Chinese herbal medicine prescribed at a nearby hospital, Durotep (fentanyl) 25 mg, MS Contin (morphine sulfate) 10 mg as needed.

Blood test results (figures in parentheses refer to normal values): W: 2700 (3300–9000), Hb: 8.5 (11.5–15.0), PLT 35.0 (14.0–34.0), TP: 5.9 (6.7–8.3), GOT: 20 (10–40), GPT: 18 (5–45), LDH: 207 (120–240), CA125: 21 (<35), CA19-9: 235 (<37).

Homeopathic features
Mind: Ill-tempered, anxious, restless, changeable mood, not tidy, likes to be consoled.

General: Chilliness of the body, thirst, difficulty falling asleep, likes sweets, eggs, fatty food. Anaemia.

Local: Tinnitus, ageusia, allergic conjunctivitis, rhinitis, stiff shoulders, cough, nausea, epigastralgia, abdominal distension, diarrhoea, stiffness in hands and feet in the morning.

Remedy: Arsenicum album 30c. A dose for 3 successive days and 4 days of no treatment and repeat the same on the following week

11.03.2005: Completed chemotherapy yesterday. Nausea, appetite loss, malaise. Patient expressed her wish not to continue with anticancer drug. Took 3 g of arabinoxylan, a health food supplement.

$\rightarrow$

CASE STUDY (continued)

Remedy: Sepia 30c.

01.04.2005: Patient visited . Abdominal pain and vomiting. Based on the diagnosis of peritonitis carcinomatosa and ileus, patient is hospitalised.

02.04.2005: Results of the blood test: W: 3600, Hb: 9.4, PLT: 49.8, TP: 6.3, GOT: 15, GPT: 7, CA125: 37.4, CA19-9: 419. Dehydration is observed.

06.04.2005: CT detects colon cancer and patient immediately underwent barium enema. Apple core was detected near hepatic flexure of transverse colon and diagnosed as colon cancer. Plan is made for surgical operation. W: 3100, Lymph: 7.5%.

Remedy: Carbo V 30c for 3 days to decrease bloating.

1.04.2005: Operation of rs hemicolectomy. Tumor, 45×30 mm, type 3. Lymph node metastasis no. 222–223 2/3 ss. Ly 1. V2.

Remedy: Staphysagria 30c was prescribed on 11–14 April.

16.04.2005: Elevated to GOT: 567 and GPT: 250.

18.04.2005: GOT: 195, GPT: 359.

20.04.2005: GOT: 976, GPT: 883.

Remedy: In consideration of the effect of operation and anesthesia, Staphysagria 30c was prescribed on 20–22 April.

22.04.2005: GOT: 152, GPT: 448.

27.04.2005: GOT: 16, GPT: 77, ALP: 311, W: 4800, Lymph: 11.0%, Hb: 9.2. Diarrhoea continued.

Remedy: Arsenicum album 30c was prescribed on 27–29 April, targeting anaemia, low lymphocyte rate and diarrhoea.

03.05.2005: Diarrhoea stopped and kidney function improved. W: 3300, Hb: 9.6, GOT: 17, GPT: 24.

Remedy: Arsenicum album 30c was prescribed (3 days).

10.05.2005: Down to CA19-9: 20.2, W: 2800, Lymph: 14.5%.

Upon reflection, patient felt anger towards her former doctor.

Remedy: Staphysagria 30c was prescribed (3 days).

Patient began to practise mental imagery therapy and Qigong.

Remedy: Staphysagria 30c was prescribed (3 days).

25.05.2005: Tinnitus. W: 3000, Lymph: 21.0%.

Remedy: Hydrastis 30c was prescribed (2 days) for malignancy.

Patient was discharged on 28 June, later than previously expected due to prolonged recovery of nutritional status and white blood cell count. During the period of hospitalisation, she also took Gelsemium 30c and Carcinosin. Patient suffered from insomnia, fatigue, bleary eye and knee pain after she was discharged. As Arsenicum, Rhododendron, Rhus toxicodendron, Calcarea carbonica and Carc. were prescribed according to her symptoms, her condition gradually improved.

(continued overleaf)

CASE STUDY (continued)

02.11.2005: W: 4600, Hb: 12.0, Lymph: 18.4, CEA: 1.5, CA19-9: 7.8, GOT: 21, GOT: 22.
    07.12.2005: Difficulty falling asleep and irritated.
    Remedy: Sulphur 30c was prescribed for 3 days.
    14.12.2005: No sign of relapse detected in ultrasound diagnosis.
    28.12.2005: Patient caught a cold.
    Remedy: Ars. 30c was prescribed (3 days).
    13.01.2006: Patient began taking Super-Orimax and extract of Shi Quan Da Bu Tang.
    02.08.2006 W: 5000, Hb: 13.5, Lymph: 22.4%, CEA: 1.6, CA19-9: 12.3.
    Almost complete recovery. CT indicated no sign of relapse.
    23.03.2006: Allium cepa 30c prescribed for hayfever, with intermittent use of Carc. 30c.

Glossary of abbreviations used in blood test data
CA, cancer antigen; CEA, carcinoembryonic antigen; GOT, glutamic-oxaloacetic transaminase; GPT, glutamic pyruvic transaminase; Hb, haemoglobin in blood – a measure of the severity of anemia; LDH, lactate dehydrogenase; Lymph, lymph content in blood; PLT, platelet count; TP, total protein; W, white blood cell count.

Comment on case study 16.1

*   A preconceived notion about peritonitis carcinomatosa as well as a belief that diagnosis posed no problem since it was made at a prefectural cancer centre caused a delay in the diagnosis and treatment of transverse colon cancer. With every patient, one must always go back to basics and keep an open mind. It was not surprising that homeopathy was not effective in treating subileus caused from colon cancer since operation is the only method of bringing relief.

•   Staphysagria had a beneficial effect on relieving postoperative pain and in the prompt treatment of postoperative hepatitis.

•   Arsenicum album had a beneficial effect on anaemia, low lymphocyte rate and diarrhoea caused by long-term subileus state and chemotherapy.

•   Staph and Ars. alb. had a part to play in the major contribution made by homeopathic remedies in enhancing postoperative recovery.

•   Staphysagria was effective in dealing with the patient's feeling of indignation towards her former doctor for not discovering cancer of the transverse colon. This kind of situation is not uncommon in the course of

$\rightarrow$

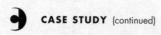

CASE STUDY (continued)

treating intractable diseases and homeopathy can offer an excellent countermeasure.
- In addition, patients who struggle with intractable disease for a prolonged period of time can suffer from numerous mental strains, including anxiety, depression and irritation. We can draw fully upon the strength of homeopathy to improve the situation.

Case study 16.2 demonstrates the effect of homeopathy, which enabled a patient to complete an entire cycle of the chemotherapeutic drug gemcitabine (Gemzar), often a difficult treatment to complete due to the side-effects, and make good progress.

CASE STUDY

Case 16.2 Carcinoma of the pancreatic tail
KT: 74-year-old male. Carcinoma of the pancreatic tail.

Background
01.04.2005: Operated at a cancer hospital. Developed complications of intra-abdominal abscess after distal pancreatectomy, splenectomy and resection of the transverse colon.

Initial consultation at Obitsu Sankei Hospital
25.05.2005: The drain remained inserted. Remedy: Staphysagria 30c.
    15.06.2005: Inflammation and pus are detected on the opening of fistula after the drain has been removed. Remedy: Silica 30c.
    29.06.2005: Remedy: Silica 30c.
    13.07.2005: Treatment of fistula.
    15.07.2005: Discharged from the hospital.

Homeopathic features
Cheerful and optimistic. Likes to travel. Wakes up in the middle of the night.

(continued overleaf)

CASE STUDY (continued)

Chilly. Thirst. Likes sweet food, salt and eggs. Tendency to constipation. Remedy: Carcinosin 30c.

24.08.2005: Chemotherapy – gemcitabine (Gemzar) administered for 3 weeks followed by a 1-week rest-period. Remedy: Cadmium sulphuratum 30c.

07.09.2005: No particular change. Remedy: Cadmium sulphuratum 30c.

21.09.2005: Leukopenia. Remedy: Calcarea carbonica 30c.

05.10.2005: Signs of improvement. Remedy: Calcarea carbonica 200c.

20.10.2005: Patient underwent cataract operation after recovering from leukopenia. Remedy: Staphysagria 30c.

16.11.2005: Resumed chemotherapy. Remedy: Cadmium Sulphuratum 30c.

01.12.2005: Recurrence of leukopenia. Remedy: Calcarea Carbonica 30c. Showed signs of recovery.

29.12.2005: Remedy: Calc carb 200c. Brisk recovery.

26.01.2006: Began chemotherapy. Remedy: Cadmium sulphuratum 200c. Higher potency was chosen to prevent leukopenia. As a result leukopenia did not occur.

09.02.2006: Chemotherapy is completed as planned.

22.9.2006: Elevated blood sugar level. Strong hunger. Remedy: Anacardium 30c.

08.03.2006: Remedy: Anacardium 30c.

23.03.2006: Remedy: Anacardium 30c.

Each remedy was administered consecutively for 3 days followed by a 4-day rest period.

01.04.2006: Good condition over a year after the operation and is actively practising Qigong.

Factors such as ovarian deficiency syndrome resulting from operation and after-effects of postoperative chemotherapy are all troublesome features that can lead to a significant reduction in quality of life. In Case study 16.3 these symptoms were alleviated through homeopathy and the patient was able to regain her quality of life within a year of beginning taking homeopathy.

More often that not, symptoms experienced by this type of patient are seen as not directly life-threatening and disregarded in the course of cancer treatment. However since a reduction in quality of life can lead

 **CASE STUDY**

Case 16.3   Ovarian cancer
UT: 48-year-old female. Ovarian cancer.

Background
22.09.2004: Operation at a Cancer Centre Hospital.

Initial consultation at Obitsu Sankei Hospital
06.04.2005: Complained of insomnia, hot flush and numbness in plantae.

Homeopathic features
Likes someone to be nearby and likes to be consoled. Likes fresh air. Not too chilly. Dislikes heavy and rich food. Remedy: Pulsatilla 30c.
   20.04.2005: Able to sleep more easily but developed facial rash. Remedy: Sulphur 30c.
   05.05.2005: Hot flush continued. Remedy: Sulphur 200c.
   19.05.2005: Numbness increased in left planta. Remedy: Rhus tox 30c.
   08.06.2005: Caught a cold. Remedy: Gelsemium 30c.
   22.06.2005: Symptoms alleviated. Good condition. Remedy: Carcinosin 30c.
   29.06.2005: Difficulty falling asleep again. Remedy: Pulsatilla 30c.
   25.07.2005: Felt dull. Hypotension. Remedy: Carbo veg 30c.
   10.08.2005: Stiffness in both feet upon waking. Remedy: Apis 30c.
   25.08.2005: Stiffness improved slightly. Remedy: Apis 200c.
   14.09.2005: Insomnia. Remedy: Arsenicum album 30c.
   20.10.2005: Insomnia improved but hot flush increased. Remedy: Pulsatilla 30c.
   07.12.2005: Returned to work.
   21.12.2005: Alopecia. Remedy: Graphites 30c.
   19.01.2006: Began to recover from alopecia. Remedy: Graphites 30c.
   09.03.2006: Able to fall asleep more easily but wakes up at night. Remedy: Sulphur 30c.
Each remedy was administered consecutively for 3 days followed by a 4-day rest period.

05.04.2006: Patient's comments: There is a slight pain and numbness when she gets tired or walks too much but numbness in her toes is not bad enough to disrupt her everyday life. Hair started to grow back so alopecia does not bother her. She is able to fall asleep more easily but sometimes wakes up once or twice at night. She hopes to get 6 hours of uninterrupted sleep. This year, hayfever did not bother her at all. This may be due to homeopathy. Hot flush still comes back once in a while.

to compromised immunocompetence, we must always deal with these symptoms with the utmost care.

It is my sincere wish that the benefit that homeopathy brings to this field will gain wider recognition in the future.

The antitumour effects of homeopathy and complementary medicine are shown in Case study 16.4.

 CASE STUDY

Case 16.4 Malignant lymphoma
HK: 41-year-old female. Malignant lymphoma (B-cell).

Background
22.05.1999: Developed tumour of the left cervical lymph node and abdominal tumour. Based on biopsy result, diagnosed as malignant lymphoma (B-cell). Went into remission with chemotherapy and rituximab (Rituxan) but relapsed in the summer of 2005. Tumour of the left cervical lymph node was 30 mm diameter in size. Abdominal computed tomography (CT) showed tumour, which surrounded aorta. Chemotherapy was recommended, but patient requested, and gained, permission from her attending physician to try complementary therapies full-time.

Initial consultation at Obitsu Sankei Hospital
12.09.2005: At the time of admittance to Obitsu Sankei Hospital, patient's white blood cell count is 1200 and soluble interleukin-2 receptor (SIL-2R) level was 1390 (<466). Felt relatively well, good appetite and bowel movement and slept well. Patient made a plan to stay at the hospital for 1 month and eagerly attempted diet regimen.

Chinese herbal medicine features
Arabinoxylan, aromatherapy and homeopathy.

Homeopathic features
Optimistic by nature but feels slightly depressed upon admittance to the hospital. Chilliness troubles her. Loves alcoholic beverages. Dislikes tightness around her neck and abdomen. No perspiration.

17.09.2005: Remedy: Nux vomica 30c followed by Nux vomica 200c was prescribed to target depression and chilliness.

→

🎯 **CASE STUDY** (continued)

The patient carried out all of her regimen with enthusiasm and without any problem and was discharged on 9 October 2005. At this stage, chilliness had disappeared and depression had improved. Her demeanour was much brighter and beyond comparison from the time she was first admitted. SIL-2R level decreased slightly to 1270. White blood cell count remained at 1200.

Cervical and abdominal CTs were performed by the former doctor. Size of the tumours remained unchanged. Since SIL-2R level was decreased, decision was made to take a wait-and-see approach rather than begin chemotherapy immediately.

18.10.2005: Remedy: Nux vomica 200c prescribed to maintain the good condition.

02.11.2005: Became increasingly positive. Remedy: Carcinosin 30c. After a while, Carcinosin 200c was prescribed.

17.01.2006: No change detected in the size of shadow shown on CT. Complained of itch on her left ear. Remedy: Carbo veg 30c.

22.02.2006: SIL-2R level decreased significantly to 676. Remedy Carcinosin 200c.

Decision was made to continue with various complementary therapies, including homeopathy.

Remedies associated with Carcinosin 200c were prescribed.

Each remedy was administered consecutively for 3 days followed by a 4-day rest period.

Since homeopathy is an established system of medicine, it is only natural that it has an antitumour effect, as this case demonstrates. But at the same time, it is first and foremost an energy medicine and therefore a completely different methodology from that of repairing a mechanical failure is required. In homeopathy one does not attempt to fix at once but, rather, move forward step by step. Patience is asked for. And those around the patient must also be patient. In this respect, this particular patient was fortunate to be treated by her former doctor who displayed patience and understanding.

Conclusion

Healing, the energy field, holism, salutogenesis, intuition and NBM – they are all attributes of complementary therapy. Homeopathy not only includes these elements but also excels in terms of quality and quantity. From this respect, it is not an overstatement to say that integrative medicine cannot be discussed without taking homeopathy into account. Looking back on the paths that I have taken, I feel that it is my unequalled good fortune that I became acquainted with homeopathy in the process of attempting to surpass integrative medicine and move towards holistic medicine, although there is an undeniable sense that the encounter came a little late in my life. Homeopathy is the forerunner for the era that is to come, the era of integrative medicine.

References

1. Weil A. *Health and Healing: Understanding Conventional and Alternative Medicine*, Boston: Houghton Mifflin, 1983.
2. Schrödinger E. *What is Life?* (Chapter 6 Order, disorder and entropy.) Cambridge: CUP, 1992.
3. Simonton O C, Mathews-Simonton S. Congress papers: cancer and stress: counselling the cancer patient. *Med J Aust* 1981; 1: 679–683.
4. Bergson H, Vibert, P E. *L'Intuition Philosophique: communication faite au Congress philosophique de Bologne le X avril M.CM.XI.* Paris: Editions d'art Edouard Pelletan, 1927.
5. Antonovsky A. *Unraveling the Mystery of Health: How People Manage Stress and Stay Well.* San Francisco: Jossey-Bass, 1987.
6. Shimizu H . *Ba no shiso* (*Philosophy of the Field*), Tokyo: University of Tokyo Press, 2003.

Index